Baker, Liva
Felix Frankfurter. New York, Coward-McCann [1969]
376 p. illus., ports. 24cm.

Bibliography: p. [335]-339.

1. Frankfurter, Felix, 1882-1965.

FELIX FRANKFURTER

Coward-McCann, Inc.
New York

FELIX FRANKFURTER

by Liva Baker

Library of Congress Catalog Card Number: 69-11057

PRINTED IN THE UNITED STATES OF AMERICA

For Len

Acknowledgments

I WISH to express appreciation to all those whose names are listed in "A Note on Sources," pp. 335–339, for sharing memories of Felix Frankfurter. Appreciation is also due to Bishop William Scarlett, who kindly lent his unpublished manuscript "A Parson's Tale," and to those who lent photographs from their private collections: Miss Helen Denman, David M. Dorsen, Malcolm A. Hoffman, Wilmarth S. Lewis.

I am obligated to the staffs of the various libraries listed in "A Note on Sources" for facilitating research, especially to the staff in the Manuscripts Division of the Library of Congress, Washington, D.C. I would like to thank especially Miss Elizabeth B. Mason, assistant director of the Oral History Research Office, Columbia University, New York City, and Miss Elizabeth B. Drewry and her staff at the Franklin D. Roosevelt Library, Hyde Park, New York.

I am indebted also to Miss Julie Grenier, formerly associate editor of the *Harvard Law School Bulletin;* Mrs. Patricia A. Moore, editor of the *Harvard Law School Bulletin;* Irving E. Levine, director of the Office of Public Relations, the City College of the City University of New York; Renee R. Roth, administrative assistant of the Alumni Association of the City College of New York.

Special thanks are due Miss Helen Denman for her indispensable help, her fortitude in wading through an early draft of the manuscript, and her frank criticism of it. My appreciation also goes to Ellis Amburn, senior editor at Coward-McCann, for skillful editorial midwifery.

Special thanks are due also to Robert C. Toth, who conducted interviews in London with Oliver Gates, Sylvester G. Gates, and Mrs. Venetia Kershaw; to William E. Leavitt; and to Sheila R. Sullivan for her hospitality.

Contents

PART I

Beginnings

[1]

IN January, 1906, President Theodore Roosevelt hired Henry L. Stimson, a New York corporation lawyer, to houseclean the office of the United States Attorney for the Southern District of New York.

Although this was the principal law-enforcement office of the federal government in the most densely populated and important district in the nation, it had been a sinecure for hacks, politicians, and fortune hunters. It reflected the laissez-faire era of President William McKinley, the "good old days" when government rarely interfered with private affairs and watched nonchalantly while wealth begat wealth, when there was little for a federal law-enforcement officer to do because laws to break were relatively few. The staff of the United States Attorney's office was made up, not of full-time attorneys, but of lawyers in private practice who supplemented their incomes, sometimes grandly, by winning legal cases for the government and receiving in return part of the government's "take." Stimson's predecessor, Henry L. "Lightning-Eyes" Burnett, a friend of McKinley's, collected in the neighborhood of $100,000 a year in this fashion, most of it from small customs cases. When the rare big case arose, Burnett referred it to outside counsel.

However, Theodore Roosevelt intended to alter these conditions. He had a sometimes self-righteous concern for the inequities of American life which had developed alongside the new industrialism following the Civil War. He also had a national perspective—part theory, part instinct—which he translated into Presidential authority to use the national government in behalf of the national welfare. He had acceded to the Presidency in 1901, when an assassin ended McKinley's second term, and, after a lackluster beginning, had inaugurated a program of social and economic reform. In 1904 he was elected President in his own right, and self-confident that his election signified public enthusiasm for these reforms, he spent his energies—which in Roosevelt were considerable—on more reform. A by-product of his actions was an attempt to shovel out the trash—the incompetents and the grossly political appointments—from government offices, including the office of the United States Attorney for the Southern District of New York, and to hire loyal but able office-holders.

As the new United States Attorney, Henry Stimson was ordered to try cases himself instead of referring them to outside counsel. The old contingency fee system which had grossed his predecessors a fortune was abolished; Stimson was paid a salary of $10,000, plus an allowance of $22,000 for eight assistants. Stimson, who at thirty-nine had a reputation for integrity, exacted a condition of acceptance: He made it clear to Roosevelt and the Attorney General that although he was a loyal Republican, he would not play politics with the office and would not consider political sensitivities a factor in any litigation with which his office became involved.

Roosevelt's enforcement of old laws and success in persuading Congress to pass new ones created a surge in government legal business. Stimson's first task was to recruit a first-rate, full-time staff of assistants to handle the increase in litigation.

Stimson went first not to established lawyers in downtown law offices—which his budget could not afford—but instead to the deans of the law schools, from whom he solicited the names of promising recent graduates. These young men, Stimson realized, were working for low salaries as clerks in the large law firms. If he could not raise their incomes, he could perhaps lure them with a promise of more interesting opportunities than their clerkships offered. If they were short on experience, the freshness and enthusiasm of their youth would compensate. In addition, they were not so long out of their classrooms that they had unlearned their lessons.

Stimson recruited a remarkable group of young men. Among them were Goldthwaite H. Dorr, a future State Department official and leader of the New York bar; Thomas Thacher, a future New York State Supreme Court justice and U.S. Solicitor General; Emory Buckner, one day to be an Assistant Attorney General and prominent trial lawyer; Winfred T. Dennison, later an administrator of the Philippines; Henry A. Wise, Stimson's successor as United States

Attorney for the Southern District of New York and future distinguished lawyer.

He also enlisted Felix Frankfurter. Of all the men on Stimson's team, including Stimson himself, Frankfurter was to have the greatest significance in American history. Within twenty years he would be one of the most controversial men in America. Within thirty years he would be one of the most influential men in America. Within forty years he would sit, controversial and influential, on the Supreme Court of the United States.

Dean James Barr Ames of Harvard Law School, from which Stimson had been graduated in 1890, submitted Frankfurter's name to Stimson. Frankfurter had begun his career at Harvard Law School with little confidence. He had frankly admitted, on encountering the urbanity of his classmates, many of them from what were later to be called Ivy League colleges, that he was "scared stiff." [1] But he went on to cut an intellectual swath through the school, led his class for all three years, edited the *Harvard Law Review,* and was graduated in June, 1906. After a brief period of assisting a professor, John Chipman Gray, write a book, he joined the prestigious New York law firm of Hornblower, Byrne, Miller and Potter at a salary of $1,000 a year. He was the first Jew to be hired by that firm and one of the few young Jews hired in that time by any of the big New York law firms.

In the late summer of 1906 Stimson summoned Frankfurter to his office in the old Post Office Building in Park Row and offered him a job as Assistant United States Attorney. He explained to Frankfurter that he was trying to put new life into the office. Stimson said he intended to turn it into a genuine law-enforcement arm of the United States government and run it with the integrity it deserved.

Stimson apologized that he could not pay much—$750 a year was his offer, a cut in salary for Frankfurter. But Stimson hoped the experience an eager young attorney aches for would compensate for the low salary.

Frankfurter did not give Stimson an answer that day, although even with the cut in salary the offer was enticing. It was an opportunity to practice law, an exciting kind of law, without the requirement, always distasteful to Frankfurter, of courting clients. But the offer also raised problems in Frankfurter's mind, and he told Stimson he would require time to consider it.

His work at the downtown law office had only just begun. He felt guilty about leaving. Frankfurter talked over his dilemma with fellow clerks and with partners in the firm; he wrote Dean Ames at the law school for advice. Ames, unhelpfully, advised Frankfurter to follow his instincts. The partners at Hornblower said Frankfurter was crazy to leave the firm with its promise of future munificence and prestige which must be alluring to any young lawyer. What's more, to leave it for the precarious position and drab work of a public servant, with the added indignity of a pay cut, was fantastic.

Up to this time Frankfurter had not decided what phase of the law he wanted to enter. Nobody is more plastic than the law student. Often he attends law school because it allows him extra time to decide on a career and at the same time affords him the greatest flexibility of choice. At Harvard Law School, Frankfurter had immersed himself in learning the law, to his endless delight, but had neglected to decide how he would utilize that learning after he left the academic womb.

Frankfurter was fond of characterizing himself as a man with "a kind of healthy, live-in-the-moment disposition." [2] He looked neither forward nor back and had a tendency to "float with the tide." [3] At the same time he seldom suffered regrets.

He did not remember a time when he didn't want to be a lawyer. His brother, Paul, once told a family joke that "Felix was born in November, 1882, and the family tradition is that by the following January he had decided he wanted to be a lawyer." [4] Felix always said he had an "inner compulsion" [5] to study law. To Frankfurter the law meant civilization: order as opposed to the arbitrariness of the nineteenth-century Viennese society into which he had been born. "I do take law very seriously, deeply seriously," he once explained, "because fragile as reason is and limited as law is as the expression of the institutionalized medium of reason, that's all we have standing between us and the tyranny of mere will and the cruelty of unbridled, undisciplined feeling." [6]

But his instinct for law provided only a general direction and had not at all been narrowed down at Harvard Law School. The school prided itself on turning out disciplined minds but gave little thought to teaching a trade. One could learn the business of being an attorney later as an apprentice, or clerk, in a practicing attorney's office.

While Frankfurter was still a law student, two events dramatized for him a conflict in his own mind between careers in private practice and public service.

One was a Sunday afternoon call by a group of students on the philosopher William James. As the boys left, James turned to Frankfurter, intellectual leader of his class, and said, "And what are you planning to do?" Frankfurter answered that he was going to New York to practice law. James thundered: "Yes, I see you are like all the rest, you are going to New York to make money! That is always the way," [7] and he swept Frankfurter unceremoniously out the door.

The second incident was a talk by Louis Dembitz Brandeis to the Harvard Ethical Society. The already eminent "people's lawyer," as Brandeis was known, deplored the tendency of the most capable lawyers to gravitate to the profitable defense of established wealth.

"The next generation must witness a continuing and ever-increasing contest between those who have and those who have not," Brandeis said. "The industrial world is in a state of ferment. The ferment is in the main peaceful and, to a considerable extent, silent; but there is felt today very widely the inconsistency in this condition of political democracy and industrial absolutism. . . ." [8] There was no stopping the labor movement at this point, Brandeis warned, and it would fall within the province of the lawyers of the future to guide it along lines of evolution if it were not to become revolution.

The opportunities for a young lawyer at that time were severely limited compared to later years. There was practically no situation where the job sought the law school graduates, nor, beyond a dean's letter of recommendation, was there much organized effort to assist graduates to find jobs. Clerkships with judges were few; government positions were not numerous. A law student relied for placement on his own or family connections with established lawyers.

The Frankfurters had no such connections; as an added fillip, they were Jewish at a time when it was less than fashionable to be Jewish. Frankfurter, fortified by an excellent record at law school and an enthusiastic letter from Dean Ames, in an extraordinary exercise of will and determination, made the rounds of the New York offices during his last semester's spring vacation. After several rejections, he was hired by Hornblower, Byrne, Miller and Potter; he began work shortly after graduation. Then came the offer from Henry Stimson.

He considered it carefully. It was characteristic of Frankfurter all his life that he seldom acted impulsively; he would write himself long memos and call on his friends for advice at every important juncture.

He finally decided the United States Attorney's office was where he wanted to be. He accepted the job and went to work for Stimson. As it happened, neither the job nor the pay cut were as significant as the lifelong influence of Stimson on Frankfurter and the introduction of Frankfurter to public service.

The two men should have been antipathetical: Stimson of the tall, lean, athletic body suggesting aristocratic pleasures of hunting and riding fine horses, of the wry wit that suggested a perceptive intellect, of the austere countenance that suggested proportionate austerity of character; Frankfurter, short, rather slight, with dark, searching eyes that suggested a rare intelligence but belied the offsetting gaiety and exuberant spirits.

Stimson was a New York Brahmin; if America had an aristocracy, he would have been a baron. His ancestors had fought in the French and Indian War, the Revolution, and the Civil War. His father, Lewis Atterbury Stimson, was a prominent New York City surgeon. The Stimsons had lived abroad—in Berlin, Zurich, and Paris—while Lewis perfected his surgical skills, at one time studying with Louis Pasteur.

Frankfurter, nearing his twenty-fourth birthday in the late summer of 1906, had lived abroad, too. He had been born in Vienna, where the only law was the emperor's and the ghetto served not only as a prison but a fortress against the intermittent anti-Semitism that had plagued the city's Jews since they had arrived about the tenth century. With his family, Frankfurter had come to the United States in 1894 aboard a typical immigration tub called the *Marsala,* having traveled, like most immigrants of the time, steerage from Europe. He quickly developed a disingenuous and outspoken patriotism, which later in life could, if provoked, become aggressive and arrogant.

The Stimsons were socially prominent Presbyterians. The Frankfurters were unsocially prominent Jews. They did not keep a strictly kosher house, as many Jews of German cultural background did not; Leopold Frankfurter, Felix's father, was fond of singing Jewish ritual to opera tunes on the gayer holidays. But Felix Frankfurter was proud of his heritage. He abandoned formal Judaism as a very young man, afterward calling himself a "believing unbeliever" or a "reverent agnostic" [9] and once referred to "Your God and My Equivalent" [10] in a letter to a clergyman. But he remained to the end of his life strongly identified with Jews as a people. In college a professor made a discriminating remark about his name. Frankfurter replied: "Some day you will be proud to have known the owner of that name." [11] When a partner at the Hornblower firm suggested he change his name, he indignantly refused, and he remained contemptuous of any Jew who did. To a New Englander who had been tracing her family genealogy at the Library of Congress, Frankfurter once remarked with quiet pride: "My ancestors go back to David." [12]

The Stimsons were well-to-do. The Frankfurters had intellectual distinction: Felix's father came from a long line of rabbis and had himself been schooled for the rabbinate but had not finished. Felix's uncle later became a learned and much-honored librarian in Vienna. But the Frankfurters were materially poor. Because they were German, they settled first in a German neighborhood on the Lower East Side of Manhattan. In time they accumulated enough money to move uptown to Park Avenue, which was a somewhat better neighborhood but was not yet the fashionable section it later became. Frankfurter's father sold linens from a shop in his home and summers peddled door to door among estates outside the city. But he was not much of a businessman and was remembered as a man of "frail health, a dreamy, charitable soul who enjoyed giving baskets of food to poorer neighbors." [13] Frankfurter later claimed his inheritance from his father as "a strong tendency of indifference to external measurements —a sense that things that matter are not proved by office or bank account or what is called 'sucess.' . . ." [14]

While Henry Stimson's family—lawyers, doctors, clergymen—drank tea in their drawing rooms and, secure in their tight universe, discussed what course the family Stimson should take—carefully avoiding mention of John Stimson, who had followed his maverick instincts into the world of art—Frankfurter, in rare moments of leisure, sat in coffeehouses where ghetto dwellers read newspapers from a rack, as they had in the old country, sipped tea, and discussed the Socialists, Shakespeare, and the promises of a ward heeler named Al Smith.

Henry Stimson had an aristocrat's education: at Phillips Academy at Andover; Yale College, not intellectually exciting in those days but respectable; and Harvard Law School. Following graduation from Harvard, he became law clerk to a Yale graduate and friend of his fiancée's family; a year later, through family connections, he transferred to the law office of Elihu Root.

In contrast, Felix Frankfurter grew up in the New York City public schools. In one of his rare intellectual failures, he lost a scholarship to Horace Mann, a private school in the Bronx, which would probably have led him to Columbia College. His formal education was at P.S. 25 and the City College of New York, where an immigrant's son could get a first-rate education without paying tuition.

His real education came from the public libraries and that downtown institution to which many an immigrant owed his education: Cooper Union. Frankfurter had a terrible compulsion to learn, as the children of most immigrants of the time had. Learning, in the minds of the ghetto dwellers, was synonymous with "arriving," and they pushed and prodded their children. Harry Golden's story puts it succinctly and touchingly. When the immigrant mother was asked, " 'How old are your children?' she would reply with confidence and dignity, 'The doctor is four and the lawyer is two and a half.' " [15]

Frankfurter later boasted that as a boy he had as a matter of course read every newspaper in the New York Public Library; he was fond of telling of the time when he could identify almost any newspaper in the country by examining a few lines of type. He read indiscriminately and voraciously, mixing Dickens with John Morley, spending at least four afternoons a week in the main hall of Cooper Union. He kept track of new books coming into the library as closely as he later kept track of Supreme Court opinions, and he read them as avidly. Here is where the future lawyer, law teacher, scholar, judge, and judicial philosopher was born. Here began the mental discipline, aided by an unusually retentive memory and a facile brilliance which gave Frankfurter the depth and breadth of learning he eventually achieved.

Frankfurter was a serious youth, ambitious, intent on making a solid future. He had no time for athletics, as Stimson did at Yale. Nor had he the time, as Stimson did in the social service traditions of his class, to work in a mission in the poor quarter of town. At City College, Frankfurter's extracurricular activities were intellectually oriented. While maintaining high marks in his class, he was vice-president of the senior class, an assistant editor of a college publication called *Quips and Cranks,* and a member of the Chess Club. His major activity was debating, and his arguments in behalf of a debating organization called the Clionian Society fifty years later were remembered by classmates as incisive and convincing.

The only consideration for Henry Stimson in choosing a career was what he wanted to do: He wavered between the ministry, medicine, and law. When he finally chose law, he had only to take himself to Harvard; the question of money did not even enter his mind. In contrast, the only important consideration in Frankfurter's mind was money, and determined to study law, he tutored and worked in the Tenement House Department of New York City for a year after graduation from City College in 1902 in order to pay for law school. He experimented with night courses at the New York Law School and New York University Law School; the caliber of both disappointed him. He intended to enroll at Columbia. Then a doctor advised him, after a bout with flu, to seek out a less urban environment. That, plus a chance meeting with a Harvard law student who persuaded Frankfurter he didn't have to be rich to go to Harvard, induced Frankfurter to enroll at Harvard Law School.

In mental habits, as well as in background, Frankfurter and Stimson were opposites. Stimson had a plodding, patient, persistent intellect; Frankfurter, a flashy, facile brilliance. And yet, looking back, Goldthwaite Dorr commented: "I think Felix contributed more to Henry L. Stimson than any of us, just because he fitted into his mind and approach. Felix had a remarkable facility, both in ideas and in finding roots for them in the law. Stimson did not have these gifts, but he had a determination to fully understand any question, no matter how seemingly pedestrian and painful that process might seem, both to himself and to those who worked with him. But he had, also, with that a gift of what may be called a sudden flash of genius which often put the rest of us in our place. Felix, in his close association and give and take with Stimson, and a realization of his magnificent qualities, naturally came to idolize him." [16]

Stimson's task as the new United States Attorney was to declare war on the corporate giants—the industrial trusts, railroads, bankers—who were using subterfuge to avoid Roosevelt's regulatory legislation. President Roosevelt, with his program of the Square Deal, was a leader of what came to be known as the progressive movement: the movement of government into private affairs in an effort to regulate business, finance, industry, and transportation, make them more responsive to the masses, and ameliorate the poverty created by these corporations as they relentlessly accumulated dollar upon dollar. Progressivism, as articulated by Theodore Roosevelt, was essentially a conservative movement—a self-defensive attempt to conserve the institutions on which American life depended under rapidly changing conditions. It was at least partially motivated by fear of more radical schemes, becoming increasingly popular, which planned the destruction of these institutions. The United States Attorney's office was an enforcement arm of the movement, translating Roosevelt's program into jail sentences for corporate criminals.

The United States Attorney's office was Frankfurter's first practical application of progressivism. As a boy living in the ghetto, where poverty bred poverty as rapidly as corporations accumulated wealth, Frankfurter's hero had been William Jennings Bryan, whom he saw as an enemy of capitalist exploitation and spokesman for the underdog, however unsophisticated his theories and politics were. Frankfurter had played hooky from school to hear Bryan speak and had campaigned from the back of a horse cart for Bryan's election in 1896. As a young man Frankfurter discovered his spokesman for the underdog in Theodore Roosevelt, politically and philosophically more astute than Bryan—and dedicated to preserving fundamental American institutions to which Frankfurter had become zealously attached, as only an immigrant can. It would be Theodore Roosevelt's progressivism as a way of ordering government that would underlie his later arguments for minimum wage legislation, his engineering of New Deal legislation, and his opinions for the Supreme Court of the United States.

Declare war, Stimson did. In addition to routine smuggling, fraud, and immigration cases, Stimson and his staff—his youthful aides working days and evenings in the office and weekends at his Long Island estate—collected evidence and prosecuted spectacular cases involving millions of dollars in railroad rebates, sugar frauds, and illegal financial manipulations. Over the three years of his tenure as United States Attorney, from 1906 until 1909, Stimson collected almost $500,000 in fines, recovered about $2,500,000 out of which the government had been defrauded, and sent the heads of guilty companies to jail.

"More important," wrote Stimson's biographer, "in his prosecutions he obtained rulings on disputed points of the laws regulating corporations which were sustained in higher courts and thus made the continuation of the effort to regulate corporations easier in the future. Most important, by his successful prosecutions he informed the public. His cases increased the growing confidence of the citizens that malefactors of great wealth could not only be detected in their wrong-doing, but punished." [17]

Frankfurter prosecuted only a few cases during his three years—1906–9—in the United States Attorney's office. His usual job was to compile evidence for Stimson to take into court, to do the extensive research that enabled Stimson to go into the courtroom prepared to win. Stimson's method was to rely not on cleverness or imagination, but on the patient accumulation of massive amounts of evidence, and it was Frankfurter who ferreted out the information. Henry Wise, Stimson's assistant and successor as United States Attorney, remembered Frankfurter as "a remarkable bookworm, an omnivorous reader, and the little devil used to mark up all the law books with things he considered important." [18] The disciplines Frankfurter had perfected as a young boy in the public library were put to practical use.

Stimson was out to get the perpetrators of crime—but not at an inflated price. He kept his office impeccably clean and his own reputation sharply independent. He made good his promise to keep politics out of the United States Attorney's office, and he refused to do the bidding of party leaders.

Nor was he willing to punish criminals at the price of the integrity of his men; to do so would have been not only immoral but self-defeating. He insisted his staff maintain a fastidious obedience to the Constitution and the laws of the nation. Frankfurter always said he learned his criminal law at Stimson's knee. Law officers, Stimson believed—and imposed his belief on his staff—ought to be the most consistent observers of the law. He refused to countenance wiretapping or any other prevalent shortcuts to prosecution. And Frankfurter later recalled many a shivering cold morning when he had to get up early to accompany the Secret Service men who were executing a search warrant to make sure they kept within the limits of the warrant.

What was transmitted from Stimson to Frankfurter—and the main influence Stimson was to have on the rest of Frankfurter's public career—was the older man's high moral standard. In Henry Stimson, of old American stock and the highest character, Frankfurter saw the ideal of public service and the ideal of the public servant. Frankfurter had spent his early years in Austria, where the aristocracy exhibited irresponsibility and arbitrariness, where justice was the exception rather than the rule. In the person of Henry Stimson he observed the opposite: an American patrician with the highest sense of public responsibility and a perfectionist moral attitude. It was concrete evidence to Frankfurter that the law was a means toward the perfectibility of a system of justice. Stimson's training showed up much later in Frankfurter's Supreme Court opinions.

These years in the office of the United States Attorney were Frankfurter's introduction to public service, its excitement derived from a sense of valuable achievement, its challenge, in those early years of reform, to a legal intellect, its contrast with solving the relatively insignificant problems of individual clients. He initiated a romance with public service to which he was faithful for more than half a century and which left no branch of government untouched—executive, legislative, or judicial.

Shortly after Frankfurter entered the United States Attorney's office, there occurred one of those events that has little significance at the time but takes on importance later. This was the meeting between Frankfurter and Franklin Delano Roosevelt, a distant cousin of President Theodore Roosevelt.

Like his cousin and like Henry Stimson, Franklin Roosevelt was an aristocrat of old American stock, a factor of increasing importance to Frankfurter, first-generation American, product of such conflicting forces as Harvard Law School and the ghetto on the Lower East Side of Manhattan. Frankfurter and Franklin Roosevelt had been contemporaries at Harvard but had never met—possibly because Frankfurter had been at the law school and Roosevelt in the undergraduate college; possibly also because Roosevelt played the social circuit, Frankfurter the intellectual.

In 1906 Grenville Clark, a classmate of Frankfurter's at Harvard Law School and a colleague of Franklin Roosevelt's at the law firm of Carter, Ledyard and Milburn, introduced Frankfurter and Roosevelt casually over lunch at the Harvard Club in New York. For both, it had no more meaning than two young lawyers sharing a table and pleasant conversation. They became casual acquaintances, nothing more, neither suspecting that their acquaintanceship would grow much later into intimate personal friendship and that their mutual public philosophies would one day affect the policies of the entire nation.

Henry Stimson resigned from the office of the United States Attorney on March 4, 1909—the day Theodore Roosevelt was succeeded by William Howard Taft as President. Stimson returned to his New York law office; Frankfurter joined him shortly. Frankfurter later returned for a brief period to the United States Attorney's office to help dispose of some cases which had overflowed Stimson's term.

Then, in 1910, Stimson attempted to translate his ideas into political action by running on the Republican ticket for governor of New York. Frankfurter was again at his side as private secretary, for the first time immersed in practical politics.

Whatever moral and intellectual qualities Stimson had displayed, he was not a political being. He knew it; his sponsor, former President Theodore Roosevelt, knew it; the party regulars knew it. On the other hand, his candidacy held some hope. A party man, he was loyal to and admired both Theodore Roosevelt and President Taft, whose feuds were now becoming public and were finally to culminate in their conflict in the Presidential election of 1912. Stimson was also a willing candidate, eager to use his candidacy to help preserve party harmony.

The Republican Party stood close to schism. One faction followed Theodore Roosevelt, who had announced at Osawatomie, Kansas, on August 31, 1910: "I stand for the square deal. But when I say that I am for the square deal, I mean not merely that I stand for fair play under the present rules of the game, but that I stand for having those rules changed so as to work for a more substantial equality of opportunity and of reward for equally good service. . . ." He advocated getting rid of special interests in politics and government and doing it by imposing unprecedented government supervision of all corporations doing an interstate business and government control of the big trusts—all of it "directly in the interest of the common good."

The conservative wing of the Republican Party, heirs of William McKinley and loyal to President Taft, recognized in Roosevelt's audacious progressivism a threat to laissez-faire and conditions essentially as they were. Taft, who had been Secretary of War in Theodore Roosevelt's Cabinet and, as such, was in effect an assistant President, had promised to carry forward Roosevelt's reforms when he acceded to the Presidency. But he was not temperamentally equipped to assume a Roosevelt-style leadership. Although there were some social gains during his administration, his ineptitude and willingness to listen to the more conservative elements of his party cast him in the role of reactionary.

Charles Evans Hughes, reform governor of New York, had been appointed—and, in effect, silenced—by Taft to the Supreme Court of the United States in April, 1910. This left the governor's race in 1910 wide open, an important prize for whichever of the two factions within the Republican Party could capture it.

Stimson was caught between the two. He feared potential violence if business continued to crush the masses ruthlessly as it had during a period of expansion since the Civil War. But his aristocratic person also feared genuine rule by the masses. He believed responsibility for national policy lay with the men of his own class, and so he was in favor of rehabilitation of business by its sponsor, the Republican Party. Contemplating his gubernatorial candidacy, he wrote to Theodore Roosevelt: "... it seems vitally important that the Republican Party, which contains, generally speaking, the richer and more intelligent citizens of the country, should take the lead in reform and not drift into a reactionary position. If, instead, the leadership should fall into the hands of either an independent party or a party composed, like the Democrats, largely of foreign elements and the classes which will immediately benefit by the reform, and if the solid business Republicans should drift into mere obstruction, I fear the necessary changes could hardly be accomplished without much excitement and possibly violence. . . ." [19]

The open break and formation of a third party did not come for two more years. For 1910, it was sufficient for the Roosevelt faction to control the New York State convention in September and nominate Stimson for governor. For Taft supporters, it was sufficient to cut off their backing of this flagrantly reform candidate.

Stimson scheduled a four-week campaign, with a whistle-stop tour of the entire state and speeches six or seven times a day. Frankfurter, always close at hand, was an administrative assistant. Making such far removed concerns as high-level strategy and the placement of campaign posters his own, Frankfurter was the impresario charged with keeping the campaign orchestra working smoothly. Bustling from car to car of the train, he attempted—unsuccessfully—to keep

Stimson in contact with the press and to soothe reporters who were irritated at Stimson's refusals to meet with them. Racing for telegraph offices in small upstate towns, he kept Roosevelt and Republican headquarters at the Hotel Manhattan in New York City apprised of campaign progress. He culled information on the Democratic candidate, John A. Dix, and suggested how Stimson might use it best. He helped Stimson develop issues and devised strategy.

The issues were not very complex. Stimson campaigned for a continuation of Charles Evans Hughes' reforms and against the Tammany control which he believed the election of Dix meant. Dix campaigned against Taft conservatism, against the expense of Hughes' reforms, and against Stimson as Roosevelt's man—which must have required a certain political agility.

Stimson's campaign went badly from the beginning. His style was not calculated to win elections. Politically naïve, cool in manner, intellectually sophisticated, he could not run in the American political tradition. His speeches were intellectually sound, but their weighty explanations of principles fell flat on the ears of upstate farmers, however hard he tried to convince them he was a farmer like themselves. He shied away from self-congratulation for his work in the United States Attorney's office. With the desertion of the Taft forces, he had little organization support; with his reserve and aloofness, he alienated much of what he had.

Theodore Roosevelt attempted to bolster Stimson's campaign with personal encouragement and a speaking tour of the state. But even the charisma of Roosevelt could not rescue the Republicans. He drew immense crowds; he had to silence their cheers and yells just to speak. But he could not elect Stimson.

Election day in November, 1910, dawned cold and wet—especially for Republicans. Democrats won nearly three-fifths of the seats in the national House of Representatives and both houses of the legislature in New York. Franklin Roosevelt won his first elected office by defeating the Republican candidate for a seat in the New York State Senate. Woodrow Wilson, Theodore Roosevelt's philosophic heir, won the governorship of New Jersey on a reform platform of direct primaries, public utility regulation, referendum and recall. In general, the trend throughout the nation was away from the party of Taft and toward the more progressive platforms of the Democrats. Dix collected 689,700 votes to win the governorship of New York; Stimson received 622,229; the entire Republican ticket was defeated.

Stimson's failure stopped him in his political tracks. Had his try for the New York governorship succeeded, he later admitted, even the White House doors might have opened to him. His victory also might have brought together the quarreling factions within the Republican Party to work out the issues peacefully, thus averting the break that came two years later.

It remained only to write finis on the season of politics for both Frankfurter and Stimson. Stimson wrote on November 9 to Theodore Roosevelt: ". . . my only regret is that I could not have accomplished more for you in the fight. . . ." [20] He hoped that Roosevelt's kind of Republicanism would one day lead the nation again.

Frankfurter telegraphed his chief: "THERE NEVER WAS A MORE GENUINE PEOPLE'S CAUSE THAN THAT WHICH YOU LEAD AND IT WAS NEVER LED MORE CLEANLY MORE FEARLESSLY NOR MORE UNSELFISHLY. THAT SHOULD BE A SOURCE OF PERMANENT SATISFACTION TO YOU." [21]

As for the ebullient Theodore Roosevelt, he blamed the defeat on an "alliance for evil between Tammany Hall and the powerful and crooked section of Wall Street," [22] plus a general sweep against the Republican Party, and went on undismayed to rebuild his forces into a third party for the Presidential election of 1912.

Thus had begun an enduring relationship between Frankfurter and Stimson. It spanned more than forty years, broken only by Stimson's death in 1950. Built on a solid base by the professional intimacy of the United States Attorney's office and the campaign of 1910, it was able to weather frequent and vigorous disagreement. Their differences were not over essentials—they shared public philosophies and public goals, if for different reasons—but they parted on methods, on the extent of the role government should play in private affairs. What Frankfurter termed creativity, Stimson called encroachment.

There was at least a tinge of father and son about the relationship. Stimson, childless, frequently was protector, counselor, and critic. He also admired and respected his young, brilliant, and enthusiastic protégé; if his affection was less than floridly expressed, his correspondence makes clear it was nevertheless strong. On Frankfurter's side there was a filial devotion, articulated in outspoken and lavish terms; his letters abound with gratitude for "the priceless privilege of your fostering friendship." [23] For Stimson, whose austere presence put off flowery personal expressions and who was unaccustomed to such frank appreciation, Frankfurter's continuing and open regard, sincerely felt, not only was flattering, but was a welcome antidote to the daily cares of a public servant.

In spite of the fact that Frankfurter's public position ultimately outranked Stimson's—Frankfurter was an Associate Justice of the Supreme Court when Stimson was Secretary of War for the second time—Frankfurter continued to be "Felix" to Stimson and Stimson remained "Mr. Stimson" to Frankfurter.

Frankfurter was fond of illustrating their relationship with this story. The two men stopped to chat at a Washington funeral and found themselves moving together in line inside the cathedral. Very aware of protocol, Stimson told Frankfurter, "You take your proper place" (up ahead with the Supreme Court Justices). Frankfurter hung back. "After all," Frankfurter recalled, "I had worked under him as a youngster, but Stimson was conscious of the Court's position and he said: 'You little cuss, take your proper place.' " [24]

Along with his expressions of personal affection, Frankfurter was unstinting of praise for Stimson's personal and professional character—his courage, integrity, loyalty—drawing Stimson as the man Stimson wanted to see in the mirror. He knew Stimson's limitations; he knew, for example, that Stimson shared many of the prejudices of his class during that time, that his progressivism was a mixture of snobbism, self-defense, and humanitarianism—in what degree probably Stimson himself did not know. So he wrote to Stimson in glowing phrases of the humanitarian goals of progressivism, at the same time pointing out Stimson's unique ability to further them, hoping that what he called "the right kind of sympathies, real faith like Lincoln's and Roosevelt's in the permanent sense and possibilities of the people" [25] would submerge self-interest. He would remind Stimson of his independence of mind, his probity, generosity. From some men such lavish praise could be interpreted as presumptuous, officious, the work of a sycophant. Under Frankfurter's careful tutelage and encouragement during difficult times, it was made perhaps a little easier for Stimson, of impeccable innate character, to see the man he wanted to see in the mirror.

This relationship between Frankfurter and Stimson was one of Frankfurter's early exercises in friendship by expectation, a style for which he later became well known. The most famous example, much

well enough to become later an architect of Franklin Roosevelt's New Deal, a cousin of Theodore Roosevelt's Square Deal.

In February, 1912, the inevitable break between President Taft and former President Theodore Roosevelt came. Roosevelt decided to try for the Republican Presidential nomination in June. When he lost the nomination to Taft, Roosevelt and his followers defiantly formed a third party, with Roosevelt as the Presidential candidate, to run against Taft and the nominee of the Democratic Party, Woodrow Wilson, in November.

Throughout his tenure as Secretary of War, Stimson had tried to work for Taft and maintain his friendship with Theodore Roosevelt. In spite of his sympathies with Roosevelt's progressivism, he believed Roosevelt's opposition to Taft was both self-defeating and weakening the Republican Party. He said so in a Chicago speech shortly after Roosevelt announced he would try for the Republican nomination. Stimson's sharp words angered Roosevelt, their long friendship dissolved, and they did not meet again for three years.

Frankfurter's position was emotionally complicated by his loyalty and high regard for Stimson, his boss, and his loyalty to Taft, also his boss, but for whom he had very little regard. Taft, he believed, was not utilizing the full powers of his office for social betterment, as Theodore Roosevelt had. He was, Frankfurter complained, neither liberal nor conservative, but had "no dominating impulse or passionate interest . . . and *there* is the tragedy. . . ." [3] In one of his intermittent disagreements with Stimson over means, Frankfurter wanted to leave the War Department and campaign for Roosevelt.

Politically, Frankfurter was an eclectic. ". . . Neither party has a congenital genius for excellence in government, nor congenital incapacity," he wrote to Stimson later. "Either party will find ample ability at its disposal if its leader is guided by matured purposes and determined to translate them into actuality." [4] He realized the importance of party solidarity, but he found the spectrum of ideas within a party too broad and thus the men who could embrace a party faith far too varied. He found himself "politically homeless" and "a tenant at will." [5]

His votes were for men who cared about the goals he cared about, the men whose general directions—not necessarily their stands on specific issues—seemed to Frankfurter imaginative, promising, and courageous. During his lifetime he voted—and worked—for Democrats, Republicans, and the candidates of third parties.

Frankfurter had reservations about Theodore Roosevelt, as he would later have about Franklin Roosevelt. He believed Theodore Roosevelt was intellectually undisciplined, sometimes groping and inarticulate. But he admired enormously Theodore Roosevelt's ability to use his office to cope with social and economic problems. He admired his courage in challenging entrenched wealth. He admired his genius for devising schemes to control this wealth and redistribute it without destroying business itself. In June, 1912, Frankfurter wrote to a friend that Theodore Roosevelt represented to him, as twenty years later Franklin Roosevelt was to represent, a leader "genuinely stirred to the new social function of government" and a cognizance that "it's the business of statesmanship 'to effect by policy what revolution effects by force.' " [6]

Following the convention of Bull Moose progressives and their nomination of Theodore Roosevelt as the Progressive candidate for President in August, 1912, Frankfurter wrote to Stimson that "the call for active work in the Progressive Party is all too insistent" [7] and that he must leave the War Department to campaign. Not only did he believe in Roosevelt's candidacy, but he thought the formation of the third party would sweep in progressives from both the Republican and the Democratic parties, that the memberships of both parties would realign and readjust, resulting in time in more creative government.

Stimson, who believed "reform should go in the way of a regeneration of the Republican Party and not by the formation of a new party," [8] soberly replied that Frankfurter, equally soberly, ought to reconsider. Frankfurter, Stimson warned, was caught up in the "thrill" of the campaign, "alluring to the fighting blood of any man." But, continued Stimson, he ought to stay at his desk in the War Department, where important work remained to be done in the very causes for which Frankfurter would be campaigning. Further, Stimson wrote, "the real work to be done in the Progressive cause will come in the long months after election day when it will be necessary to bind together and re-unite the Progressive factions which are not split. . . . Do not be misled by the hurrah about you, into a misjudgment of the comparative good which you can accomplish in the two paths which lie open before you. . . ." [9]

Thus appealed to, Frankfurter did remain at his desk in the War Department of Stimson and Taft. He did refrain from active public campaigning for the Progressives. But he "freely expressed [his] alignment with the Third Party, in conversation and correspondence with friends, as well as to all other persons . . . who mistakenly assume my political support of the President because of my continuance in office here." [10]

Woodrow Wilson, the Democratic governor of New Jersey, won the election of 1912. (Theodore Roosevelt ran second; Taft ran a very poor third.)

Stimson left the War Department a few days after Wilson's inauguration in 1913. A new administration entered the executive offices. However, Frankfurter, instead of returning to practice law with Stimson in New York, stayed on in the War Department under Lindley M. Garrison, successor to Stimson as Secretary of War. The problem of the Philippines and American attitude toward the islands, as well as the new problem of the use—and misuse—of waterpower, still interested Frankfurter; he hoped to continue working on solutions, guiding the issues in progressive directions. In addition, he was favorably impressed with his new chief. Although he later described Garrison as a man of limited imagination, at first glance Frankfurter thought Wilson's first Secretary of War came "to his office with a single-minded desire to do his job and leave things a little better than he found them. He is a hard worker, has a sense of proportion, initiative and ample ability. . . ." [11]

Explaining to a friend why he did not go to New York with Stimson, Frankfurter wrote: "I am afraid I am spoiled more and more for the allurements of the profession. Somehow or other my heart does not quite respond to it. One trouble is that the things I should like to do in the profession have not very much relation to the bulk of clientele work." [12]

Garrison had mixed feelings about Frankfurter. He described him this way: "Every time Mac [James C. McReynolds, Attorney General; later Associate Justice of the Supreme Court] or I ask this fellow a question of law that is relevant to some aspect of our problem of the government of dependencies, instead of getting an answer of what the law is, we usually get about sixty-five pages of what the law ought to be." [13]

Not the least of Washington's attractions for Frankfurter were his living arrangements. After stopping briefly in an apartment for bachelors, he and a group of men had pooled their resources and their public philosophies and rented a high brick row house at 1727 Nineteenth Street, in the northwest section of Washington.

They were young men, well educated—some at Harvard Law School—and intellectually inclined. Most were in government service and at the thresholds of varied and distinguished careers. They had common tastes in public philosophies, and they shared a concern for the conflicts looming in American life. Because in long and vigorous conversations which characterized their parties they always seemed to be searching for some unknown truth, someone had whimsically named the place the House of Truth.

Their names were not well known in those early days, at least not outside Washington. There were, besides Frankfurter, Eustace Percy, aide to the British ambassador; Loring C. Christie, Canadian graduate of Harvard Law School, who held a post in the United States Attorney General's office—he later returned to Canada and became Canadian Minister to the United States; Robert G. Valentine, commissioner of Indian Affairs, who owned the house and had leased it to the men while his wife and ailing daughter visited a healthier climate; Winfred Dennison, Assistant Attorney General, who had worked with Frankfurter in the United States Attorney's office in New York. These formed the nucleus; others came and went. Some stayed for long periods; others stayed only overnight. Together they formed an intellectual coterie, rather elite, that must have been satisfying to Frankfurter who had not been a member, at Harvard Law School, of the "Gold Coast Set," the school's social elite.

They attracted philosophically sympathetic people from all over the city and from out of town to their frequent parties. Friends of friends brought letters of introduction to the men who lived there. A clique gathered there at the feet of Justice Oliver Wendell Holmes, Jr., who often came to dinner. Boston lawyer Louis Brandeis, on trips to Washington, stopped there. Sculptor Gutzon Borglum outlined his plans for the Presidential heads on Mount Rushmore on the dining-room table at the House of Truth. The young men shook cocktails and carved roast beef for Supreme Court Justices, writers, Cabinet officials.

The talk went on into the morning: talk about people and events and materialism and social reforms and labor and the bright dreams of young men. Some of the talk was trivial; most of it was provocative; all of it was free.

Winfred Dennison wrote to Frankfurter's mother in New York: "Felix is getting on here with his usual speed as you must see from the number of his friends here and their faith in him. . . . We enjoy living together in this nice house very much and Felix keeps us alive most of the time. The only trouble with him is that he wants to sit up all night and sleep all day. And he's terribly slow about getting dressed and washed and down to breakfast. Why in the world did you fail to teach him that black air means night and time to sleep and white air means day and time to be awake? Otherwise than that you've brought him up tip top. . . ." [14]

When Frankfurter had left for Washington in 1911, he carried with him a letter of introduction to Justice Oliver Wendell Holmes, Jr., written by his former Harvard professor John Chipman Gray. In a very real sense Holmes took up Frankfurter where Stimson had left off. Stimson had guided Frankfurter to an understanding of one part of himself—the self that searched for standards, moral and ethical. In the War Department he had helped Frankfurter see how government could function creatively. It remained for Holmes to guide Frankfurter's practical experience into legal philosophy.

Pre-World War I Washington saw the pair frequently tramping the broad, nearly autoless streets: a tall man with a thatch of snowy hair, matching mustaches, and a long stride, accompanied by a short man half running to keep up and breathlessly talking. Frankfurter remembered quiet evenings by the fire in Holmes' living room or his study, quiet conversation exciting in its quality—philosophy, law, life—very exhilarating for a young man.

Like Stimson, Holmes was a Brahmin. Most of Frankfurter's close friends were Brahmins—Holmes, Stimson, Franklin Roosevelt, Dean G. Acheson. All of them came from a stock long and deeply rooted in American soil. All were public servants of the highest integrity. No doubt they represented to Frankfurter, coming from a people who had been abused on the Continent, all that was noble, just, dignified, and liberal in America—the civilization for which he unceasingly strove.

Holmes was the son of Oliver Wendell Holmes, physician, man of letters, "Autocrat of the Breakfast Table," and Amelia Lee Jackson, daughter of Charles Jackson, associate justice of the Massachusetts Supreme Judicial Court. He frequently referred to his Puritan ancestry and its traditions, saying of it, "I love every brick and shingle of the old Massachusetts towns where once they worked and prayed." [15] Although he lived his later years in Washington, he returned periodically to Boston and the North Shore where his Puritan roots were deep planted.

A patrician by birth, he had patrician tastes. "He did not prefer, he said, a world with a hundred million bores in it to one with ten. The fewer the people who do not contribute to beauty or thought, the better," [16] wrote Francis Biddle, a secretary and biographer of Holmes and Attorney General of the United States.

Holmes was also an intellectual aristocrat. An 1866 graduate of Harvard Law School, he was a former member of its faculty and a former chief justice of the Massachusetts Supreme Judicial Court. When, in 1911, Frankfurter offered his letter of introduction, Holmes had been sitting on the Supreme Court of the United States for nine years. He had also written a legal classic, called *The Common Law,* which, in its careful search for the roots of law in human behavior, in a new way "gave the most powerful direction to legal science. The way in which Holmes conceived law," Frankfurter later wrote, "and its judicial development was out of the current of the period. He reoriented legal inquiry. The book is a classic in the sense that its stock of ideas has become absorbed and become part of common juristic thought." [17] Holmes was not primarily a lawyer; he was first a philosopher, and he injected a philosophic perspective into his law.

Holmes transmitted to Frankfurter his approach, his traditions, his philosophy, and gave his philosophic heir direction. Holmes made Frankfurter see, as he saw, the Constitution as a way of maintaining a living, continuing government and not as a dead document. He made Frankfurter see, as he saw, the law as an instrument of society, as a way of ordering life, and not as a cold abstraction or an end in itself.

"The life of the law," Holmes wrote on the first pages of *The Common Law,* "has not been logic; it has been experience. The felt necessities of the time, the prevalent moral and political theories, intuitions of public policy, avowed or unconscious, even the prejudices which judges share with their fellow-men, have had a good deal more to do than the syllogism in determining the rules by which men should be governed. The law embodies the story of a nation's development through many centuries, and it cannot be dealt with as if it contained only the axioms and corollaries of a book of mathematics. In order to know what it is, we must know what it has been, and what it tends to become. We must alternately consult history and existing theories of legislation. But the most difficult labor will be to understand the combination of the two into new products at every stage. . . ." [18]

Where this approach led these two fundamentally different men, however, was along divergent paths. As a patrician and a conservative from Back Bay Boston, Holmes had little sympathy with some of the social, economic, and political reforms that were devised in the early twentieth century; he still identified with an economically Darwinian society with its catchphrase "survival of the fittest" in an atmosphere of unrestrained competition.

If some of his dissents written on the Supreme Court of the United States concerning social legislation became classics in American liberalism, it was because Holmes conceived the Court's function as one of utmost restraint: The Court could not intrude unless the Constitution specifically allowed it. If "Brandeis, Holmes and Stone dissenting" became a familiar announcement on opinion day in the 1920's, when the activist—and conservative—Taft Court reached a historic peak in declaring social and economic legislation unconstitutional, it was because Holmes refused to read his private predilections into what he believed the Constitution said. Whether or not he believed in the efficacy of minimum wage laws, he did believe the Constitution did not deny legislatures the power to pass such laws.

Frankfurter agreed, but where Holmes' approach to social legislation was negative—if the Constitution did not forbid such statutes, *he* certainly could not forbid them—Frankfurter's approach was positive—the legislatures had both the right and the *duty* to pass social legislation as long as it was constitutionally sound. This was the very essence of democracy: experimentation in social and economic legislation until an approach suitable, useful, and equitable to all was found.

Frankfurter's father had been a struggling merchant; Frankfurter had watched as a boy the cruelties imposed on the ghetto dwellers by unchecked economic competition and neglect of social needs. He wanted to alter the system that had brought about a lopsided distribution of the nation's wealth. He had seen avenues of approach in the United States Attorney's office and in his work in the War Department. He turned progressive and reformer, recognizing that the law could be used positively as a major weapon of reform.

Much later, when Frankfurter sat on the Supreme Court, he earned heavy criticism for his judicial restraint—his insistence on permitting the legislative branch of government to establish laws which, though they might be repugnant, he believed were constitutionally above reproach.

In spite of their differences, Frankfurter and Holmes had a close relationship. Frankfurter guarded it jealously—and closely. He advertised the fact of it, but he published very few of its details. He admired Holmes' intellect and his opinions enormously. He usually referred to Holmes as the Master and never tired of quoting him. He often said his feeling for Holmes bordered on reverence.

Frankfurter became the foremost interpreter of the Holmesian judicial philosophy, so much so that Holmes believed that should there be a demand for his legal biography, Frankfurter should write it.

Frankfurter brooked no criticism of his hero. The late Arthur M. Schlesinger, Sr., a teacher of history at Harvard at the time Frankfurter taught at Harvard Law School and a close friend of Frankfurter's, told how once he casually and innocently mentioned having heard a friend say that Holmes had a streak of vanity. "Felix erupted like a skyrocket," [19] Schlesinger later wrote. Frankfurter spent the remainder of the evening berating the man who had made the remark and Schlesinger for repeating it. A few days later Frankfurter wrote an explanation for his effusion to Schlesinger in which he berated all Boston for its provincialism and dullness, adding: "But of course it was a foolish thing for me to have exploded the way I did, instead of availing myself of the opportunity of telling you with great particularity what manner of man this Holmes is. . . ." [20]

If Frankfurter's admiration sometimes seemed excessive, still the friendship was far from one-sided. Holmes found in Frankfurter "a very vivid, articulate, brilliant youngster," [21] said one who knew them both. "I have suspected that it may be part of Jewish bringing up to emphasize the cheerful view of things," Holmes wrote in 1920 to Harold J. Laski, whom Frankfurter had introduced to Holmes, "at all events Felix always is comforting and he sees the powers that be at so much shorter range than I do that I value his intimations." [22]

In the spring of 1913, Frankfurter met the woman who was to become his wife.[23] Her name was Marion A. Denman. She was both beautiful and bright. She had rich chestnut hair and green eyes. Oliver Wendell Holmes likened her to a portrait by Luini and came to call her affectionately "Luina." [24]

She had been graduated the previous year from Smith College, where she had been junior class president, head of student government, and Phi Beta Kappa. After graduation she had taken a position as secretary to the associate head of the Spence School, a fashionable preparatory school for girls in New York City. It was a position she detested, entailing as it did little more call on her energies and intellect than answering telephones and taking the girls for walks down Fifth Avenue.

She was not Jewish. She was the daughter of a Christian clergyman, Mark A. Denman, whose family had been in the United States since pre-Revolutionary days. Her attitude toward religion was somewhat negative. It was the rather disillusioned attitude of the minister's daughter suffering from a very heavy dose of churchgoing as a child which was combined with her absorption of her father's feeling later in his life that the church was sometimes not a very Christian institution. (Mr. Denman left the ministry in 1921, having observed too many cases where he believed Christian action and Christian ethics did not square.) Later she no doubt also absorbed some of Frankfurter's agnosticism.

She came from a very bookish family that had managed to acquire a large collection of books on an average minister's salary and spent a good deal of its leisure time reading around the library table. Miss Denman herself was literarily oriented.

In the spring of 1913 she was spending Easter recess from the Spence School in Washington visiting a former college classmate, who introduced her to Frankfurter. In the old-fashioned way, he wooed her over teacups and poetry during the brief visit.

When she returned to New York, later transferring to a private girls' school in New Jersey—which proved as unsatisfactory as the position at Spence—he continued to court her with long letters, all packed with the events that were crowding his life.

[3]

At thirty-one, Frankfurter had examined the law from several angles. He had seen it from the philosophical heights of Holmes and from the practical, day-to-day viewpoint of government prosecutor. He had seen it from the angle of the corporation lawyer, and he had helped Henry Stimson put it to public use in the War Department. None of these appealed to him as a permanent occupation, and he had become vaguely restless.

On June 12, 1913, Winfred Dennison, Frankfurter's longtime friend and housemate in Washington, wrote to his friend Edward H. Warren, of the Harvard Law School faculty: "Dear Ned: If you see any reasonable opening in your faculty for Frankfurter I wish you would let me know about it. The administration here appears willing and anxious to have him stay and he is content to do so but . . . I think it might be a good thing for him to settle down permanently in your faculty. . . . He has made a tremendous impression with the Supreme Court. The Chief Justice and two of the other Justices have spoken to me with great enthusiasm of his work and I understand their views are shared by the other members of the Court. . . ." Dennison added Frankfurter did not know he was writing and that he was not sure Frankfurter would accept an offer from Harvard, but he thought he "would sound the land." [1]

Warren replied that "to a man" [2] the faculty wanted Frankfurter. There was no existing vacancy, but Warren and his colleagues believed an endowment could be raised for a new professorship for Frankfurter. The salary, he said, would probably be $4,000, perhaps $5,000, with an eventual increase to $7,500.

At first, Frankfurter, recalling the legal giants on the Harvard Law School faculty during his student days, shrank back. Brandeis, asked for his advice, told Frankfurter he ought to let the people who invited him worry about his qualifications.

Brandeis, in fact, was the only man among the friends Frankfurter asked for counsel on this crucial decision who argued *for* Frankfurter's joining the law school faculty. And over the years it would always be Brandeis urging Frankfurter to stay at Harvard Law School when other opportunities were offered: a seat on the Massachusetts Supreme Judicial Court, Solicitor General of the United States. Frankfurter's influence, Brandeis believed, would be far more profoundly and widely felt in the life of the nation if he remained a law school professor, multiplying himself in the hundreds of young lawyers and potential leaders of the bar, than if he sat on a high state court or became the advocate for the United States government.

The other men to whom Frankfurter applied for advice told him to decline. Stimson believed Frankfurter could more effectively use his talent in government where ability was in short supply. Herbert Croly, editor of the *New Republic,* thought Boston would be stultifying after New York and Washington. Theodore Roosevelt warned Frankfurter of the parsimony of a professor's life.

It was Holmes, however, who grasped the essential conflict in Frankfurter's mind. As Assistant United States Attorney and then as counsel in the War Department, Frankfurter had become accustomed to legal activism; life in an ivory tower could prove confining for a man with Frankfurter's interest in public affairs. Holmes advised Frankfurter not to go to Harvard, writing: "Academic life is but half life—it is withdrawal from the fight in order to utter smart things that cost you nothing except the thinking them from a cloister. . . ." [3]

Against all the objections, however, Frankfurter decided to teach, on a five-year trial basis, then to reassess his situation. For one thing, the alternatives did not excite him. There was an invitation to try industrial relations, but that did not appeal to him because it meant narrowing his field of interest. He did not want to stay in Washington because he had lost faith in Wilson's ability to accomplish much reform. And he still cringed at courting clients in a private law firm.

But his decision was not all negative. He also believed that in the immediate future, strong and far-reaching social forces which reflected the technological and scientific strides of the last half of the nineteenth century and which were turning a nation of farmers into a nation of industrialists and city dwellers—from a nation of individuals into a nation of interdependent people—would be set in motion. These forces would require guidance if they were to evolutionize, not revolutionize. They would demand coordination, mediation, and interpretation. Lawyers, Frankfurter believed, were the proper medium of leadership: for framing legislation, for arbitrating disputes, for interpreting the law, for helping men in public office translate goals into action, for assisting the nation to adjust to its changes of life. If the bar was to face its tasks adequately prepared, the law schools—and Harvard Law School was the leader among them—had to assume the responsibility of preparing it. In that case the academic life, Frankfurter concluded, need not be a cloistered one; in fact, it could conceivably offer the widest range of all for public work. And so he accepted an invitation to teach at Harvard Law School.

Stimson, who had advised Frankfurter against accepting the offer and had even suggested to the dean of Harvard Law School that there were plenty of other able lawyers on whom he could call for pedagogical talent, wrote encouragingly to Frankfurter: ". . . the transition from administrative work in Washington to the seclusion of scholarly research and teaching at Cambridge will be even greater and more sharp than it was to me to come here to New York from Washington a year ago, but I think it will be good for you and I have no doubt whatever that you will be good for it. . . ." [4]

Frankfurter's appointment became effective on September 1, 1914. He was scheduled to teach criminal law and public service companies (which he renamed public utilities and taught for the remainder of his academic career). The course dealt with legal problems arising under the Interstate Commerce Act of 1887, amendments to it, and all the legal problems of regulatory systems in general. He also taught a graduate course in penal legislation and administration.

He left Washington in the summer of 1914 and spent the hot months commuting from his room in Sharon, Massachusetts, to the law school library stacks, catching up with judicial decisions handed down since his graduation eight years before.

Frankfurter answered Stimson's note: ". . . You are right in thinking that the change in life for me is rather sharp, but there is certainly no let-down to stimuli. I am sure the job should call forth all the stuff there is in me. . . ." [5]

To Emory Buckner, friend from the United States Attorney's office, he wrote: "It's full and quiet and books without end here. I shall like it beyond my most optimistic imaginings. . . ." [6] To Buckner's wife he also wrote: ". . . I'm not *enough* of a scholar but I do love to get into the library. What is it all but the deposit of past experiences, past problems. Those boys [730 of them that term]—I'm thrilled and awed and humbled when I think of the job ahead of me. I wish I had time—oh loads of time—the amount of preparation is so enormous. . . ." [7]

The school whose faculty Frankfurter joined was a 97-year-old leader among legal institutions, the oldest American law school in continuous existence. Its alumni lists even then resembled a *Who's Who* of the legal world. It was a proud school. It derived dignity from its venerability. Its faculty was recognized as authoritative in the legal world. An above-average number of its students became preeminent in that world. It could develop justifiably a self-confident sense of its own mission.

The legal papers and pedagogy of its faculty frequently pointed the direction of American legal development. The man who was dean during Frankfurter's student days, James Barr Ames, as a professor working with his predecessor, Dean Christopher Columbus Langdell, had remodeled the school by introducing the so-called case method of legal instruction.

It was a time when there was an explosion of discovery in the natural sciences. Langdell and his disciple Ames believed the law could be scientized nearly as efficiently as chemistry or biology. If one could isolate gases, observe their properties, and draw conclusions from which scientific principles could be developed, why could one not study legal precedents, reach back into time for the earliest of applicable cases and trace their growth, observe the properties of each, and from them develop certain constant legal principles?

It was a new, pragmatic approach. For years most of the colleagues of Langdell and Ames opposed the case system. Then gradually it became more widely accepted and used until it was standard fare when Frankfurter was a student.

Ames had died in 1910, four years before Frankfurter returned to the law school as a professor, but the case system was thriving. Frankfurter believed the method far superior to the old-fashioned textbook system, by which law was approached via philosophic principle. ". . . Precedents, not underlying philosophic principles, form our legal habit of thought," Frankfurter had written in 1912. "It is the case system, which is the empiric, scientific method, that gave us the necessary data and method, first, for a historic, and then for a sociological basis of the law. . . ." [8]

Before the innovations of Langdell and Ames, professors imparted abstract doctrine to students who listened passively. A corollary of the case system was obligatory student participation. The student was expected to ferret out the abstract doctrine that applied to a case under consideration, then justify his findings in open debate with professor and fellow students—debates which frequently turned Frankfurter's classes into free-for-alls, with the development of mental agility an important by-product.

The faculty which Frankfurter joined in 1914 consisted of the dean, Ezra Ripley Thayer, nine other professors, and three lecturers. The titan among the titans then was Roscoe Pound, whom Frankfurter and Emory Buckner had urged the law school to hire in 1910. The Frankfurter-Buckner influence on the school's decision to invite Pound is probably negligible; nevertheless, he was appointed Story Professor of Law on May 9, 1910. A familiar sight in a green eyeshade, Pound was a genius frequently intolerant of opposing points of view, but he was also a leader in legal scholarship, translating the results of his scholarship into concrete and practical terms. A botanist by education, he had never taken a law degree, having left Harvard Law School after one year of study without his LLB. Nevertheless, he had begun practicing law in his native Nebraska following his departure from Cambridge. At the same time he undertook a distinguished career of legal scholarship, becoming dean of the University of Nebraska College of Law. When he returned to Harvard as a professor in 1910, he brought with him a new approach to law called sociological jurisprudence. Its essence was that law was not an isolated discipline but was related to all the other social sciences, that to study law, one must incorporate sociology, economics, history, government, geography, psychology. Law, Pound believed, must be put into the context of the human condition.

This approach became a major route by which Frankfurter led his students toward their LLB's. In fact, there were those who wondered, as he ranged over the entire history of the Populist movement in the United States, when—or if—he would get around to treating law at all.

Frankfurter refined Pound's philosophy to the point where Frankfurter's students joked about his unorthodox method of teaching.

His lectures often had little to do with the case in point, and a stranger wandering in could, on occasion, mistake the class in law for a class in history or literature. His public utilities course was later nicknamed the Case-of-the-Month course because it proceeded at about that pace. One class wit put the Frankfurter style to verse:

> You learn no law in Public U
> That is its fascination.
> But Felix gives a point of view
> And pleasant conversation.[9]

And so it seemed "pleasant conversation" as students absorbed Frankfurter's entertaining tidbits about judges, Senators, Presidents, philosophers, economists, complete with the warts on their noses, where these men originated their ideas, and sometimes their personal idiosyncrasies. Unhurriedly—but thoroughly—they studied case records and discussed legislative and judicial backgrounds, the lawyers who argued a case, the geography of the area in which a case originated—preferably reported by a native. The classroom talk ranged over the whole gamut of human experience until, wrote a student, "slowly—innocents that we were—came some measure of awareness . . . of what was happening to us and of the excitement that awareness brought with it. We were gaining some measure of understanding of law that both reflected and shaped a nation's growth—some understanding of its method and some appreciation of its content. We were witnessing the infinitely varied and subtle interplay of ideas, assumptions, desires, and aspirations that contributed to the irregular and patternless, yet organic growth of law. We were coming to understand a little how the diffusion of authority made the patternless pattern the more unpredictable but—perhaps—gave the greater promise that the vital and persistent force would find its outlet for development. Above all, we gained a sense of function and responsibility in the profession we had chosen. . . . We gained some awareness that the institution in which we would have some part was not, and could never for long be, either brake or whip, but would ceaselessly demand of us a critical appraisal of all we would be called on to do, an appraisal that must be kept afresh in its critical standards by all the learning and understanding that a fallible intelligence could bring to bear. . . ." [10]

This was precisely what Frankfurter intended. As a high priest in the legal temple that was Harvard Law School, it was his passion to unveil in all its manifestations the god of law to its worshipers, then to send them like holy men out into the world to live in the memory of their vision and try to build a heaven on earth. It was the rule of law that buttressed American democracy, that separated Washington from Vienna. It was law that would ameliorate conditions of the tenement factories of New York, not violence or revolution. It was law that protected or punished on the merits, not on the spelling of a man's name or the contents of his purse. And it was law that would build the society of tomorrow: a "civilization," he later wrote, "at once kindly, self-respecting, beautiful and alive." [11] It was of course not a statement of fact but of Frankfurtian anticipation—anticipation which perhaps might never be realized, as Frankfurter himself was acutely aware on the many occasions when he watched the law subjected to perversion and abuse. Nevertheless, it was a mystical vision worth guarding and worth passing on to the young, the future keepers of the faith.

In 1915 Frankfurter told the American Bar Association his standards for lawyers, the men who came from his classes:

> . . . It is not enough that young men should come from our schools equipped to become skillful practitioners, armed with precedent and ready in argument. We fail in our important office if they do not feel that society has breathed into law the breath of life and made it a living, serving soul. We must show them the law as an instrument and not an end of organized humanity. We make of them clever pleaders but not lawyers if they fail to catch the glorious vision of the law, not as a harsh Procrustean bed into which all persons and all societies must inexorably be fitted, but as a vital agency for human betterment. . . .[12]

He claimed to disdain teaching methods; nevertheless, his own seeming lack of method—his "pleasant conversation"—was in itself a method. It was his way of turning the law from abstraction into concrete reality, fitting it into the human situation.

The law, he believed, could not be taught as an abstraction because it is not an abstraction. It *is* judges, Senators, philosophers, economists, and lawyers; it *is* criminals, prosecutors, soldiers, businessmen, laundry workers and bakers, pioneers and social workers and dam builders. It embodies the past of a nation and points the way to the future.

And to fill the hours of "pleasant conversation," Frankfurter contributed his own experiences in government, in court, in politics. During all the years he taught at Harvard Law School, he worked in the community—state and national—drafting legislation, arguing court cases, advising governors and Presidents, placing young lawyers in positions of public service, working behind political scenes, investigating the actual modes of criminal justice because these were the realities from which the legal abstractions derived. His best casebook was compiled from his own experiences.

What was considered formal education Frankfurter believed was secondary to development of intellectual independence. "Talk about 'courses' and methods of teaching seems to me tosh—an emphasis on minor matters instead of major," [13] he once told a lawyer. One developed clarity and mental ability by cultivating one's mind—by reading, as he had. His conception of prelegal education was a broad understanding of the English language, of literature, poetry, art, music, history.

Recalling the thousands of Harvard Law School students he had taught, Frankfurter was fond of citing as his single major triumph Adrian S. Fisher. Fisher had gone to the law school with the legalistically unimpressive background of a major in mathematics and a minor in football and the announced intention of returning to Memphis, his hometown, to "make as much money as I could." [14] Under Frankfurter's program for broadening young minds, Fisher worked industriously during his three years at the law school, returned to study for a doctorate, and was recommended for a clerkship with Justice Brandeis—Frankfurter's highest accolade to a student. Fisher did not return to Memphis to make money. Instead, he entered government service, eventually becoming deputy director of the United States Arms Control and Disarmament Agency and assuming a prominent role in United States-Russian disarmament negotiations under President Lyndon B. Johnson.

Those students who gathered for Frankfurter's classes saw a smallish man with sardonic gray eyes. Sometimes he perched on the back of his chair, other times he darted back and forth on the dais, and sometimes he sat in the back of the room among the students, the better to promote stimulating discussion. He disliked formal lectures and avoided them when possible. He preferred small groups and vigorous discussion—the method implicit in the case system of instruction. Roscoe Pound compared his seminars to the "thinking shop" of Socrates in which professor and students cooperated to elicit legal principles from the mass of facts of a given case. In fact, Frankfurter thought of himself as Plato's midwife of the mind who fertilized the intellect of incipient lawyers and brought out whatever lay dormant in them.

Frankfurter found his forte in teaching. Except for the interruption of World War I, he remained at Harvard Law School until 1939. His teaching was not confined to the classroom in Cambridge, as Holmes had feared it would be. It radiated into articles, books, legislation writing, court arguments, politics. Where he was gathering data for his casebooks, he was also imparting legal philosophy. He continued this practice on the Supreme Court bench and, to the dismay of his colleagues, in the Supreme Court conferences. For all the apparent diffusion of his energies over fifty years of public life, these energies were in fact concentrated. He was a professor of law from the moment in September, 1914, when he stepped into his first class at Harvard until he died in Washington in February, 1965.

Marion Denman, whom Frankfurter had met and wooed in Washington in the spring of 1913, had abandoned any idea of finding her niche in the unchallenging office work of girls' schools and had decided to explore the only other career open at that time to women graduates of liberal arts schools: social work. She had enrolled in the New York School of Social Work.

However, climbing tenement stairs and the pace of the work took too large a toll of her energies, and she went to Saranac, in upstate New York, to recover her health. Frankfurter had been writing her regularly; when she went to Saranac, he visited her.

He returned from one of these visits by way of Springfield, Massachusetts, where the Denman family was then living, to report to her mother on her convalescence.

Mrs. Denman had gone limp at the suggestion that he stop to see her. She realized he was beginning to be serious. She turned preparations for dinner over to another daughter.

It was a typical first meeting between a girl's family and her suitor—except that in this case the girl was not there to help smooth the way. There was a younger brother, who refused to dress for his sister's beau but sat sulky and dirty from a tennis game at the table; there was a mother a little bit quivery; a special dinner which no one remembered eating; and the young man tense, his voice—never a low-pitched one—higher-pitched with excitement.

And after he left, there was Mrs. Denman remarking, "You know, I think he wants to marry Marion." [15]

One of the first events to disprove Holmes' prediction that the ivory tower at Harvard would be "but half life" was Frankfurter's collaboration with Louis Brandeis, a leader of the Boston bar and fighter for social causes.

With Stimson and Holmes, Brandeis became the third in the triumvirate that shaped the thought and life of Felix Frankfurter, still young and embryonic. Adding practicality to Stimson's moral standards and Holmes' philosophy, Brandeis showed Frankfurter how to use the law, how to put his philosophy to work, how to take the abstractions and bend them into tools to mitigate the tragic conditions of the industrial world.

In the late nineteenth and early twentieth centuries the nation was split into two factions. There were the individualistic conservatives who shouted the shibboleths "liberty of contract" and "property rights" and worked toward a world of yesterdays. They interpreted the Fourteenth Amendment to the Constitution, which forbids the states to "deprive any person of life, liberty, or property, without due process of law" as an absolute guarantee of their liberty to make any sort of business contract that was advantageous.

What they meant was that industry—or business or finance—was free to use labor in any way the owners saw fit or profitable. It was a buyer's market, with industrial units—which had grown to gigantic size and amassed proportionate power—the buyers of labor and in a position to dictate terms.

The practical result of this trend was that most men were forced to work sixty-hour and seventy-hour weeks and count themselves lucky if their weekly pay envelopes held $10. There were no paid vacations—only unpaid layoffs when work was slack. If workers were killed or incapacitated, there was no insurance or workmen's compensation for their dependents. Wives worked; children worked—some 2,000,000 of them under sixteen was the official estimate, although no one knew the exact figure. Safety standards were poor, more often nonexistent; substandard lighting and sanitation took a large toll of the healthy; fires in factories not properly equipped with exits took lives. Businessmen argued that any attempt to revise such a system, as some states were attempting to do via hour and wage standard statutes, infringed on their property rights.

Opposing this view was that of the reformers. They believed the rising tide of immigration and the flight of workers to the cities, with the resulting rapid urbanization, had turned society into a cooperative venture. In the first decade of the twentieth century, they evangelized through political parties and the press. Their object was social and economic legislation to protect humanity from the ravages of the machine—and its owners.

Theodore Roosevelt's progressivism had given the movement force with regulation of business. Safety standards were being imposed on mines and factories. Meat-packing houses were being compelled to adopt sanitation standards. Encouraged by progress, some states were passing laws to establish minimum wages and maximum hours. Some reformers were even trying to limit an employer's prerogative to hire whom he chose—they were trying to abolish child labor.

The lower courts were upholding some of the reform legislation. The Supreme Court of the United States, however, was striking much of it down.

At the time the Supreme Court had begun its rise to the top of the ladder to judicial supremacy, from which it was not to be toppled until 1937. Nearly a century before, John Marshall, in the classic decision of *Marbury v. Madison,* had established the Court's duty to decide the constitutionality of all laws of the American system—the duty of judicial review. Chief Justice Marshall had conceived his own edict with a sense of restraint. By the early years of the twentieth century, however, the Justices of the Supreme Court had thrown off restraint and conceived their role as passing not on the constitutionality of laws but on the desirability of them. It was only a natural outgrowth that the Justices who had spent their formative years in the heyday of unrestrained laissez-faire would write Herbert Spencer's economic and social views into their decisions on the high bench. The Supreme Court had become the protector of "liberty of contract."

Into this conflict between the possessors and the dispossessed came Louis Brandeis to fight on the side of the reformers. He was the son of Bohemian Jewish immigrants to the United States who had settled in Louisville, Kentucky, and built a grain-brokerage business. Louis, born in 1856, had been educated in Germany and at Harvard Law School, from which he was graduated in 1877 with the most distinguished record the school had ever experienced. After a year of graduate study at Harvard and a brief period practicing law in St. Louis, he returned to Boston in 1879 and opened a law firm with a Harvard classmate, Samuel D. Warren. The firm prospered at once and continued to prosper. For thirty-seven years Brandeis practiced law in this firm and in its successor, which he founded.

Many of the Brandeis-Warren firm's clients were businessmen and manufacturers. A thorough man, Brandeis refused to give legal advice until he understood his client's business as well as, if not better than, the client himself. Through these investigations he become well grounded in the ways in which business operated.

At the same time he became increasingly interested in the reform movement. Socially conscious friends introduced him to the squalid conditions in poorhouses, factories, and prisons; he talked with Henry Demarest Lloyd who had exposed the Standard Oil trust in all its unsocial aspects for the *Atlantic Monthly* and became keenly aware of the unsocial results of the concentration of wealth—which he was later to call "the curse of bigness."

Brandeis had dealt with individual labor problems in the course of advising clients, but he did not really become aware of the enormousness of the labor problem until 1892. That summer United States Steel, at its plant in Homestead, Pennsylvania, solved its labor difficulties by shooting it out with the union men who had resisted a wage reduction. The incident brought Brandeis up short, and he began a thorough study of industrial relations, to which he brought a synthesis of legal, social, and economic knowledge and experience. From this study and his dealings with industrial and business clients, he drew the conclusion—obvious now, but not so obvious at the time—that the way to solve labor problems was for manufacturers to try to understand labor's grievances, Labor, he also held, ought to attempt to understand management's problems. With cooperation between both factions—a partnership of power—most labor trouble could be avoided. He so counseled the manufacturers who came to his office and kept several of them out of court.

Increasingly during his years of private practice, Brandeis was drawn into public causes. He helped save historic Boston Common from a railroad company which wanted to cross it with tracks. He helped wrest control of the Boston transit system from private companies, which had been arrogantly picking the public's pocket, to place the system in control of the city. He reorganized the Boston gas system to the benefit of the consumers and exposed financial scandals in the life insurance industry.

When Frankfurter was a student at Harvard, Brandeis had already established a reputation as "the people's lawyer." In 1914, when Frankfurter returned to Cambridge, Brandeis was one of the city's most controversial figures. He had, besides becoming a phenomenal success, pricked the complacency of the city's wealthy and begun to chip away at laissez-faire.

As a War Department lawyer Frankfurter had seen how the federal government, in a creative mood, could move a few steps toward economic democracy. Where Holmes had theorized about the application of law to human experience, Brandeis actually applied law to human experience in what came to be known as the Brandeis brief. This affected not only methods of presenting cases to the courts, but also the attitude and rulings of those courts and the viewpoint of the general public.

Brandeis believed the new social legislation required new techniques for argument when it came before the courts. The judges, spokesmen for the preceding generation as judges frequently are, had to be educated to the social changes taking place. He believed the principles of the law ought to be expounded in his briefs, but he also believed that all the relevant facts that described a situation should be presented to support the legal arguments of a case. This was a significant departure from the traditional style of brief writing. Sometimes the legal sections of his briefs were but a few pages long; the expository sections might run hundreds of pages.

Brandeis first put this method to use in 1908 in the Supreme Court of the United States. A laundry owner, Curt Muller, had been arrested the year before in Portland, Oregon, for violation of a state law limiting women to ten-hour workdays in factories and laundries. The state courts had upheld the law. Muller took his case to the

Supreme Court. He believed the Constitution guaranteed him the right to keep his employees at work as long as he chose.

Three years earlier, the Supreme Court had declared unconstitutional a similar New York State law limiting bakers to a ten-hour day. Justice Rufus W. Peckham had written for the Court: "... The statute necessarily interferes with the right of contract between the employer and employees.... The general right to make a contract in relation to his business is part of the liberty of the individual protected by the Fourteenth Amendment of the Federal Constitution...." Peckham admitted that the state had certain police powers to legislate certain conditions of employment—the state might pass health laws, for example. However, Peckham said, concerning the ten-hour day, "We think the limit of the police power has been reached and passed in this case." [16]

Despite the Court's decision, the reformers continued their fight. In New York the National Consumers' League, which had been organized in 1899 to crusade for labor reforms, took up the cause of the ten-hour law for women in Oregon. The league persuaded Brandeis to argue, as unpaid counsel, the case of Oregon in the Supreme Court. Brandeis dictated his requirements to Consumers' League researchers: Compile material for the brief along new lines; gather facts, all the facts available, concerning the effect of fatigue on women, their family life, their children born and unborn, from anyone whose credibility was dependable, such as factory inspectors, physicians, trade unionists, economists, social workers.

"From the whole sordid, miserable record of exploited workers under unregulated hours," wrote Josephine Goldmark, secretary to the Consumers' League and Brandeis' sister-in-law, "there stood out—the regeneration that followed a decent limitation of hours. But could this be shown in a legal document? It could, said Mr. Brandeis, because this part of the brief need not be legal at all." [17]

Brandeis argued the case of laundryman Curt Muller versus the State of Oregon on January 15, 1908. On the legal side, he told the Supreme Court that the right to purchase or sell labor guaranteed by the Fourteenth Amendment to the Constitution is subject to restraints the state may impose in the exercise of the police power for the protection of health, safety, morals, and general welfare; that the Oregon ten-hour law was enacted for the purpose of protecting these very things; and that the law should be upheld. In addition to the legal argument, he submitted a voluminous collection of facts citing the dangerous aspects of overlong hours and the benefits to both women and industry of regulated hours for women.

On February 24, 1908, the Supreme Court handed down a unanimous decision holding the Oregon ten-hour law for women constitutional. Without overruling their previous decision on the New York ten-hour law for bakeries, the Justices said that "woman's physical structure and the performance of maternal functions place her at a disadvantage in the struggle for subsistence. . . . The limitations which this statute places upon her contractual powers, upon her right to agree with her employer as to the time she shall labor, are not imposed solely for her benefit, but also largely for the benefit of all. . . ." [18]

Brandeis had won. The Brandeis brief had been accepted as a way of argument. Human decency became a regular advocate in the courtroom.

The decision encouraged other states to pass similar laws and other reform labor legislation. Brandeis spent the following seven years defending the constitutionality of these new laws. Then, on January 28, 1916, he was named by Woodrow Wilson to the Supreme Court of the United States. After several months of controversy, during which all the financial forces he had fought against rose in opposition to his appointment, Brandeis took his seat on the Court on June 5, 1916.

He passed the torch of reform to his willing pupil, Frankfurter. Once again, Frankfurter was the knight-errant, jousting with big business as he had in a lesser capacity in the United States Attorney's office and in the War Department.

Brandeis had been working on briefs to defend an Oregon ten-hour law for men (*Bunting v. Oregon*) and on an Oregon minimum wage law (*Stettler v. O'Hara* and *Simpson v. O'Hara*). He had already argued them once; they were scheduled for reargument in January, 1917. After Brandeis was appointed to the Supreme Court, reargument fell to Frankfurter, who succeeded Brandeis as unpaid counsel for the National Consumers' League.

It was not Frankfurter's first appearance in the old Senate Chamber in the Capitol, which served as the Supreme Court from 1860 until the new marble building was completed in 1935. As law officer for the Bureau of Insular Affairs he had argued appeals from the supreme courts of Puerto Rico and the Philippines, and he was at ease in the courtroom.

Wages and hours laws, however, on which feeling was running high in the United States, were issues far removed from appeals from island courts so remote from the immediate scene. "It was regular trench warfare. I had to fight step by step," [19] Frankfurter reported to George M. Brown, Oregon attorney general, shortly after his day in court.

There were two days of argument. The minimum wage case was argued first, the ten-hour law last. In the Brandeis style, Frankfurter presented the detrimental effects of low wages on laborers and the conditions which had led to the passage of the legislation in Oregon and other states. He cited foreign legislation which had successfully corrected such conditions. He outlined alternatives that had confronted Oregon and the reasons the legislators chose the path they had.

Justice James C. McReynolds, whom Frankfurter as a War Department lawyer had irritated when McReynolds was United States Attorney General, gave him a particularly difficult time.

"You are talking facts," McReynolds admonished. "I should like to hear about law."

"You cannot dissociate facts from law in these cases," Frankfurter replied. "You cannot apply the Constitution *in vacuo*. An understanding of the facts is essential before you can say whether or not the State transcended its proper boundary." [20]

Frankfurter did get around to law, however, offering his interpretation of the Fourteenth Amendment to the Constitution and declaring that the state should be allowed to have full scope in dealing with its local conditions so long as its conduct was neither arbitrary nor spoliative. Much later, as a Supreme Court Justice, Frankfurter was to advocate the rights of the states to legislate for themselves and to discourage the invalidation by judicial fiat of what he considered constitutionally sound laws.

Frankfurter concluded the argument for the minimum wage with the contention that in the light of the evils that Oregon had to deal with and the experience of the world upon which the remedy was based, any disinterested tribunal had to decide that Oregon had honestly and sensibly sought to correct real evils.

In his argument for the ten-hour law, Frankfurter followed the same procedure, describing the latest statistics culled on the result of fatigue on human life and factory efficiency. The issue turned, he said, not on whether the state can regulate hours of labor in industry, but on what evils are manifest; what tendencies are disclosed that present a reasonable field for legislative repression; what remedies are available that present a reasonable field for legislative encouragement. And again Justice McReynolds turned on him.

"Ten hours! Ten! Why not four?" McReynolds asked.

"Your honor," answered Frankfurter, "if by chance I may make such a hypothesis, if your physician should find that you're eating too much meat, it isn't necessary for him to urge you to become a vegetarian."

Holmes added, "Good for you." [21]

Frankfurter was justifiably fearful of the outcome of the minimum wage case. "There is no doubt about it that the court is afraid of what is implied by the Minimum Wage legislation," [22] he reported to Brown in Oregon. He was confident, however, that he had won the ten-hour case.

Nearly three months later the Supreme Court handed down its decisions. The Oregon ten-hour law, as Frankfurter had predicted, was upheld unanimously; the long fight to establish the right of the state to regulate hours of work was won.

However, Frankfurter's fears about the outcome of the minimum wage cases were valid. The Court divided evenly (Brandeis did not participate because he had been counsel in the cases before his appointment to the Supreme Court). In effect this upheld the lower court judgment and allowed the Oregon minimum wage law to stand. Frankfurter had won a skirmish. He had not won the war, however, because the divided Court did not uphold the constitutionality of minimum wage laws. It was two decades and much litigation later before the Supreme Court did rule conclusively on the constitutionality of minimum wage laws.

Brandeis had opened for Frankfurter a new approach to translating ideals into life and had himself tutored his protégé in its use. The lesson was not lost. Before Frankfurter again took labor's cause to court, World War I intervened. But far from being an interruption, his position during that war was in the front line of the domestic labor conflict. From this experience he gained new insights that were to be invaluable to articulating the premise that democracy, a partnership of power, must come to industrial relations.

[4]

Hardly anyone in the United States was prepared for the holocaust into which Europe plunged in the summer of 1914. The prevailing attitude in the United States was shock, which rapidly turned to horror, accompanied by resolution to keep out of the foreign conflict at all cost. President Wilson announced that the United States would remain neutral.

Wilson maintained his own neutrality overlong, but the country he led soon began to take sides. The middle class, Anglophiles and Francophiles in the South, East, and West, pointed to Germany as the aggressor and supported the Allied cause. Labor supported neither cause: Either the labor leaders or their parents had left Europe precisely to avoid such catastrophes; they were not going to make the munitions makers of either side wealthy at the cost of their lives, nor would they enlist to bolster some petty prince's ambitions. And they feared that the trend toward social and economic justice, just beginning to gain momentum, could not weather interruption and subsequent setback through war.

The nation remained divided, the interventionists privately organizing support for the Allies, those opposed to intervention propagandizing against America's entering the conflict, and Wilson unsuccessfully attempting to mediate and stop the war while German U-boats brazenly stalked American merchant ships.

Finally, on January 31, 1917, the German ambassador in Washington announced that his country's submarines would be instructed to begin sinking the next day any ship, American or otherwise, that entered a war zone surrounding the British Isles or the Mediterranean, and a few days later diplomatic relations between the United States and Germany were broken. The vacillation was nearly over. German submarines made good the promise of the ambassador and strengthened the Allied cause in the American mind. In the first week of April, 1917, the United States declared war on Germany.

Although the country had had nearly two and a half years to prepare for war, it was not prepared either militarily or industrially. Wilson had hoped, almost until the end, that he could find some way to stop the destruction or at least to avoid United States involvement. His advocacy of preparedness waxed hot and cold. Congress, like the people it represented, was divided, and preparedness measures were often watered down by the noninterventionists in the Capitol. Nor had there developed any plan for setting the war machine in motion. It was reported that "Washington is occupied much more in attending dinner parties and dinner dances than it is in preparing for war. . . ." [1]

The fleet and the Army were undersized and underequipped. Both had to be instantaneously taken out of mothballs, refitted, and enlarged. There was disunity of command in the government, with overlapping jurisdictions and consequent confusion.

The rapidly growing Army needed guns, clothing, and food immediately. In the industrial area, although some manufacturers had already geared up to sell supplies privately to the Allies, factories had to be enlarged and whipped to bigger production schedules. Labor was restless, fearing that newly won improvements in working conditions might be dissipated in the name of national emergency. Although the success of the war effort depended on a healthy partnership between management and labor, each was jealous of its right; neither volunteered to surrender its autonomy even temporarily.

The man to whom the bulk of the labor problems fell, because of their relationship to equipping the Army, was the Secretary of War, Newton D. Baker. A former mayor of Cleveland and a well-known pacifist, Baker had been appointed in March, 1916. He succeeded Lindley Garrison, who had resigned the month before in protest against Wilson's procrastination in preparing for war. After Baker became Secretary of War, however, he overcame his pacifist inclinations to become an advocate of military preparedness.

In the early days of the war, most labor problems filtered naturally through the War Department into the Department of Labor, and the War Department was not much more than a referral service. The system broke down, however, because the manufacturers did not think of the Labor Department as authoritative. They thought of it as a peacetime mediation service, whose recommendations they could accept or reject as it suited them. The War Department, on the other hand, could not so handily be ignored when it brought official pressure to bear in an emergency. Nor could the War Department, as the supplier of the armies, waste valuable time while the Labor Department attempted to adjust labor disputes. So the War Department began to develop administrative machinery for dealing directly and officially with all labor problems which affected production and procurement of military supplies.

At Harvard Law School, Frankfurter had been advising Washington since 1914, when he had been commissioned a major in the Army Reserve under the Judge Advocate General's office. Secretary of War Baker, who had known Frankfurter when the former was president of the National Consumers' League and Frankfurter was its counsel, had asked Frankfurter for legal solutions to labor problems that had come up in the War Department. While war was being declared in the Congress of the United States during Holy Week, 1917, Frankfurter and Baker were conferring by telegram on impending labor questions. Frankfurter offered to confer in person in Washington during the law school's Easter recess; Baker accepted, and Frankfurter packed for a short trip. He returned to Cambridge no less than two years later. Baker made him his assistant, and Frankfurter fought World War I on the labor front in Washington.

Frankfurter was well prepared for the jobs to be done. His collaboration with Louis Brandeis and his work with the National Consumers' League had familiarized him with the background to the complexities of the problems that arose during the Great War. He also had a natural ability to cut through irrelevant smog and to get to the bottom of things. John Lord O'Brian, then head of the Department of Justice's War Emergency Division, said: "It was remarkable the way in which he kept himself informed of what was going on in Washington.... His perspicacity in foreseeing trends ... was quite an unusual quality. He steadily built up over those years a larger and larger group of men who believed in him, who were sympathizing with him...." [2]

Twice during the war, Frankfurter went abroad. The first time, in the summer of 1917, he accompanied Ambassador Henry Morgenthau on an abortive mission to Gibraltar to try to detach Turkey from the Central Powers; on the return trip he stopped in Paris to report on the early arrivals of American troops in France. The second trip, in February, 1918, took him to England, where he surveyed the English labor situation.

Except for these interruptions, Frankfurter concentrated on problems similar to those he had worked on at his desk in his Cambridge study when he was counsel to the National Consumers' League: questions of hours and wages, employment of women and children, safety conditions in the burgeoning factories, and labor organizations.

Almost overnight the United States had become the largest employer in the world. Because of the emergency, the vast and sudden demands on the country had an unprecedented immediacy about them. Supplies had to be produced—yesterday at the latest. It became the duty of the War Department to see that the armies were adequately equipped, to keep the guns, food, and clothing flowing into the camps and overseas. There was little time for bickering of management and labor. The principal problem became: Should hard-won labor standards be relaxed—can women work at night? can the eight-hour day be expanded? can safety standards be overlooked?—for the duration in order to ensure quick and efficient output? England had tried relaxing such standards in the early days of the war but had had to reinstate them to keep her industrial army at its machines. Soon after America's entry into the war, the Council of National Defense enunciated the policy that it was desirable that none of the standards established "by law, mutual agreement or by custom" [3] in the separate states should be modified except in the most extreme emergency. Although the statement was inadequate in its specifics, it served as a guidepost until the specifics could be worked out, clause by clause, and encouraged common cooperative support of the government in the war emergency.

It was a lofty statement. The reality was something different. Relations between labor, fighting for recognition and rights, and management, clinging to its right to profits, were bitter. Management feared both the government, which might be inclined to intervene on labor's side, and labor itself—plus, of course, the dwindling of its profits. Labor feared federal intervention in behalf of management because of the abnormal conditions. It also feared repressive measures by management and the loss of its improved

their differences was a major hurdle for the President's commission. What the men sought, through strikes, slowdowns and violence, was the opportunity to articulate their grievances through established channels.

The commission's first stop on the trip West was Arizona, where the copper mines had been shut down for some months. The state produced 28 percent of the country's copper; reopening of the mines was vital. But here, as elsewhere, industry was sick with hate.

Specifically, in the spring of 1917, when the country went to war, the copper miners of the state had asked that before they accepted the extra burdens the war need for copper would necessarily impose, some machinery be established for conciliation when disputes arose between the companies and the miners. They refused to be exploited in the name of patriotism, should the war continue over a long period of time.

The State Council of Defense had considered this a reasonable request, and a subcommittee was appointed to establish some body to hear both sides in any controversy. A date was set for the subcommittee, composed of representatives of labor and management, to meet in Phoenix. But management, unwilling to meet with labor, boycotted the session, and three of the labor delegates had not been able to come because they could not afford the trip. When the managers were finally persuaded to enter the same room with those labor representatives who had come, they were able to outnumber and outvote the workingmen. The plan for setting up mediation machinery failed; the copper miners went out on a statewide strike.

The President's commission had for its mission getting the mines producing copper again. The commission traveled from desert hamlet to desert hamlet for three months, often sleeping and eating in railway cars, writing reports after hearings ended late at night. Day after day the members of the commission listened to laborers and owners parade their grievances with all the bitterness that had built up. An observer compared a hearing in Globe, Arizona, to "the breaking of great waves of human indignation against the mind of the Commission." [6] Frankfurter was so discouraged by the situation in Globe that he wired lawyers in the Departments of War and Justice in Washington to explore "with utmost discretion" [7] the possibilities of the government's commandeering the copper mines.

(The reply was that authority to commandeer copper mines was doubtful under existing law, and so Frankfurter could not use it even as a threat.)

The specific quarrels varied from mine to mine. In some the issues were wages and hours; in others they were hospital conditions or safety devices; in still others two unions fought for the loyalty of the men. On management's side there was anger at the infiltration of "foreign" and therefore unpatriotic labor and fury at agitators who were stirring up the laborers to strikes. Maintaining the prevalent attitude of industry at the time, the owners said that the mines were their private property, and they had every right to operate them like fiefs.

Frankfurter brought two important assets to the Arizona labor strife. He was able to cut through peripheral issues, discover the essential problem, and articulate it, as, for example, when he asked a union official in Clifton, Arizona: "Is the fundamental trouble here the question of wages, or is the fundamental difficulty . . . a long series of differences between the men and the companies and involving the basic relations between them, the treatment the company has given them as human beings?" [8] Wages were only a symptom of the disease that gripped Clifton; its cause was that the men who worked the mines had no voice—management refused to give them one.

Frankfurter's second contribution was his ability to establish a rapport with embittered men—owners and laborers both—and to persuade them to talk with him when they would not talk with each other. Wherever the commission went, Frankfurter quickly sought out the men in whom the local power resided. He was informal and impartial and was able to win confidence from both sides that his was a mission of disinterested digging out of the facts. There were daily formal hearings; there were also private dinners with mine officials and midnight conferences, after the hearings had adjourned, with laborers and prominent citizens. A tough union leader in Clifton named McClusky was soon "Mac" [9] to Frankfurter. Later in San Francisco, where the commission had difficulty getting union leaders of the Pacific Telephone and Telegraph Company to meet with it, the men arrived late one evening at Frankfurter's hotel room with this sullen greeting: "We're ready to go to Alcatraz." [10] Frankfurter countered by offering them a drink, and before the evening's talks ended, sparring had turned to discussion. Frankfurter once told a colleague at Harvard Law School many years later that he had spent most of his life bypassing bureaucracy in order to get things done.[11]

The commission settled the industrial disputes in Arizona by setting up machinery for airing the grievances of both miners and their bosses—which was what the men had originally requested—for the duration of the war. As a substitute for the strike, a federal mediator was assigned to the district to arbitrate any dispute, however petty, which arose. The right of men to organize in unions was protected. Satisfied that they had secured a voice in the common industrial effort, the miners returned to work. It was a long way from the sophisticated machinery of industrial relations which they won much later. But it was a beginning of industrial democracy.

In the midst of the commission's settlement of the copper strikes, what became internationally notorious as the Bisbee Deportations came to the commission's attention.

Lying in the heart of one of the largest copper-producing areas of the country, the town of Bisbee, Arizona, had been called the capital of the copper country in the Southwest. Although management was in some respects enlightened, unions were not recognized. Like copper towns across the state, Bisbee's mines had no orderly channels through which controversies between employers and employees could be peacefully settled. When the statewide strike was called, feeling ran particularly high because the workers in Bisbee were engaged in an interunion conflict between the IWW and the AFL. Rumors of violence, although apparently unfounded, demoralized the town, and shortly after the strike was called, the county sheriff asked for federal troops. An Army officer twice surveyed the community, found it peaceful, and the request was denied. When troops were not forthcoming, vigilantes went into action. Early on the morning of July 12, 1917, the sheriff and a large armed force, backed by officials of the local mines, rounded up 1,186 strikers. The laborers were deported to the desert, where they were without food and shelter for two days. When the deportation was brought to the attention of the War Department, the men were moved to a nearby town, where they were maintained by the government until mid-September. The deportations affected the attitudes of laborers throughout the country and embarrassed the United States in the eyes of its allies.

An Arizona clergyman talking with Frankfurter aboard the President's Mediation Commission train late one night in Phoenix, asked him what the commission planned to do about the Bisbee Deportations.[12] Frankfurter replied that the Secretary of Labor felt it was too hot a potato to handle. The clergyman argued that if this was to be the answer of the commission, there was little chance for industrial peace in the state and one could hardly blame the men for anything they subsequently did. Frankfurter realized this was so, but Secretary of Labor Wilson was the obstacle. However, Frankfurter agreed to try once more to persuade Wilson to go to Bisbee. He was successful, and the commission shortly departed for the embattled town.

In its investigation the commission found that the deportations were "wholly illegal and without authority in law, either State or Federal.... Immediately after the first deportations, and until late in August, the function of the local judiciary was usurped by a body which to all intents and purposes was a vigilance committee, having no authority whatever in law...." [13] The commission sent President Wilson a scathing report, which resulted later in trials of the principals. The report was signed by all the members of the commission, but it was written mainly by Frankfurter.

The problem in Bisbee was, said the commission report, much the same as it was in all the other Arizona towns torn by labor strife: There was no democracy in labor relations—"no machinery for the adjustment of difficulties between the companies and the men which provided for the determination of alleged grievances by some authoritative disinterested tribunal in which both the companies and the men had confidence and before which they had an equal opportunity of urging their respective claims...."

The report recommended legal steps which the federal government and the state government of Arizona could take to cope with the immediate problem of the deportations. But most significant, the commission worked out a plan, as it had in other mining districts, "establishing such machinery whereby in the future, at least during the war, grievance will be settled by an orderly, impartial process, and the resort to strike or lockout will be wholly without foundation...." [14]

The final consequence of the commission's work in Bisbee was summarized by Frankfurter some years later in a letter: "... It did not put anybody in jail—partly because of the existing state of law, and partly because of the incompetence of those who administered what law there was. It did not take any vengeance on the perpetrators of the deed. . . ." [15] But something of importance did happen. The commission was able, through its work and report, to instill a sense of shame for the deportations. By setting forth a truthful and fair-minded analysis of the occurrences, the commission was helpful in "stirring up a different state of mind and generating different feelings" from those that had prevailed previously in Arizona.

From Arizona the President's Mediation Commission went on to the California oilfields, the lumber mills of the Northwest, the telephone strike on the Pacific Coast, the meat-packers' strike in Chicago. Early in the mission, Secretary of Labor Wilson took charge of the proceedings. As the work became heavier, Wilson, not well and in bed a large part of the time, turned over more and more duties to Frankfurter; gradually the work of the commission revolved around Frankfurter.

Using the same methods it had in Arizona, the President's Mediation Commission had varying degrees of success throughout the rest of the mission. In providing redress of specific wage and hour grievances, plus company agreement not to discriminate against union men, the commission headed off a threatened strike in the California oilfields. The telephone strike was ended. In the lumber camps the most the commission could achieve was public hearings. In the stockyard disputes in Chicago the commission was able to establish a principle of negotiation and arbitration as a substitute for strike and lockout for the duration of the war.

In the early fall of 1917, when President Wilson gave his Mediation Commission its instructions, he had said: "There is one final matter for this Commission to look into, which is a very disturbing matter. That is the Mooney case." Then he turned to Felix Frankfurter and added: "Mr. Frankfurter, as the lawyer of the Commission, it will be your special task to charge yourself with inquiring into that case."

Frankfurter answered: "Very well, sir." [16] But having been abroad during the summer of 1917 when the Mooney case was covered in the press, he had not the remotest notion what the Mooney case was; indeed, he had to ask whether it was spelled M-O-O-N-E-Y or M-U-N-I.

Had Frankfurter been in this country, he could hardly have avoided the hysteria that accompanied the trial of Tom Mooney, a San Francisco labor agitator, and his lieutenant, Warren Billings.

The summer before the United States entered the European war, pro-Ally businessmen had organized a Preparedness Day parade to march up Market Street in San Francisco. Antiwar elements, about half the community, had opposed the parade, however, and union labor had boycotted it. Letters threatening violence had been sent to leading citizens. It was a tense and anxious city that watched as the martial music of the parade began on July 22, 1916.

The spectators had not long to wait for the violence they feared. A bomb exploded into the crowd, killing nineteen people and injuring forty others, some of whom subsequently died.

Within four days the police arrested Thomas J. Mooney, a well-known labor radical and advocate of direct action in labor's battle with management. He seemed a prime suspect. Shortly before the Preparedness Day Parade he had been arrested and charged in the dynamiting of a San Francisco utility—the Pacific Gas and Electric Company. Although he had been acquitted in that case, suspicion of his involvement lingered.

Police also arrested his wife, Rena Mooney; his friend Warren K. Billings, who had been previously convicted of carrying explosives illegally; and Israel Weinberg and Edward D. Nolan, both acquaintances of Mooney. In an atmosphere of public frenzy, trials were held and convictions were obtained. Mooney was sentenced to death; Billings got life imprisonment. Mrs. Mooney and Weinberg were tried and acquitted; Nolan was not tried.

The investigation of the case had been undertaken by a private detective for San Francisco utilities which suspected Mooney of past dynamitings. The controlling evidence at the trial was given by a cattle rancher from Oregon, a man named Oxman. He claimed to have seen Mooney, accompanied by Billings, plant the bomb which killed the spectators at the Preparedness Day Parade.

After Mooney was sentenced and the case had gone to the Supreme Court of California for review, it was authoritatively established that Oxman's damning testimony had been perjured. It was because of this discovery that Mrs. Mooney and Israel Weinberg were acquitted.

The Mooney case soon became significant far beyond San Francisco. Organized labor rallied to it as a symbol, regardless of Mooney's personal merits. Laborers in Russia held protest meetings. In time the liberal sentiment of the entire nation was aroused because it felt Mooney had been railroaded for his labor agitation.

It was while the case was before the California Supreme Court that the President's Mediation Commission arrived in San Francisco. Lawyers for Mooney had been trying to get a new trial on the ground that Oxman, chief witness against Mooney, had been found to be a perjurer. The judge who presided at Mooney's trial believed he was jurisdictionally without power to grant it. In an extraordinary letter to the state attorney general, however, the judge requested that officials take the necessary steps to return the case to the local court for retrial. The attorney general, in turn, asked the Supreme Court of California to return the case.

Before Frankfurter left Washington for the West in September, 1917, he had found out the basic facts of the Mooney case. He also wired several lawyers in San Francisco to have the trial records, other pertinent documents, and a description of the situation ready for him when he arrived in San Francisco. Lawyer after lawyer refused; it was too hot an issue. Frankfurter finally persuaded an attorney to do the job, and preoccupied with affairs en route, he pushed the Mooney case to the back of his mind.

When Frankfurter got to San Francisco, he found a city embroiled in a controversy as emotional as any he had found in Arizona. He followed the same methods he had used effectively in the disputes he had helped settle all along the route. He studied the formal records and listened to anyone who had anything to say: attorneys for the defense, attorneys for the prosecution, independent members of the bar, prominent citizens. He lunched with a leading member of the California Supreme Court and dined with an influential Catholic prelate who was knowledgeable about both California industrial problems and Tom Mooney. He talked with the attorney general and the other members of the State Supreme Court. He visited Mooney in San Quentin, where he was awaiting the decision of the state's highest tribunal.

The upshot was a report, supervised by Secretary of Labor Wilson but written by Frankfurter and submitted to President Wilson on

January 16, 1918. The report condemned the atmosphere in which Mooney was convicted ("an impregnating atmosphere of guilt" [17]), it condemned the community for accusing a man for a crime on the basis of his political views, and it condemned the newspapers for playing on the passions aroused by the case. The report recommended that should the State Supreme Court not return the case to San Francisco for retrial, the President use his executive powers to urge the governor of California to intervene for a new trial. The commission did not attempt to decide the guilt or innocence of Mooney. It only attempted to determine whether "a solid basis exists for a feeling that an injustice was done or may have been done in the convictions that were obtained, and that an irreparable injustice would be committed to allow such conviction to proceed to execution. . . ."

Because the Mooney case affected situations beyond San Francisco and California, "the feeling of disquietude aroused by the case must be heeded," the report declared. ". . . If unchecked, it impairs the faith that our democracy protects the lowliest and even the unworthy against false accusations. . . ." [18] If America were to fight abroad for moral purposes, morality ought to begin at home.

The State Supreme Court did find its hands tied jurisdictionally and sustained Mooney's conviction. President Wilson acted on the commission's recommendation that he urge Governor William D. Stephens of California to grant a new trial. The governor acted, but only to commute Mooney's sentence to life imprisonment. Although Mooney was saved from the electric chair, he spent the next twenty-two years in prison. His case was argued in the Supreme Court of the United States. The Court ruled that only if the prosecutor had known Oxman was perjuring himself had Mooney been deprived of life and liberty without due process of law. The case was returned to California, where after long hearings it was found that the prosecutor did not know Oxman had lied. Again Mooney lost.

Finally, early in January, 1939, ironically two days after Frankfurter's appointment to the Supreme Court was announced and the day a subcommittee of the Senate Judiciary Committee began consideration of his appointment, Tom Mooney was pardoned, by the governor of California, Culbert L. Olson.

Frankfurter became nationally known for his reports on both the Bisbee Deportations and the Mooney case as the advocate of radicals.

Whenever his name was mentioned, he was remembered for what was thought to be a defense of Mooney. His patriotism and even his integrity were questioned. The district attorney, Charles M. Fickert, who had prosecuted Mooney, went so far as to accuse Frankfurter of believing Mooney guilty but defending him in order to placate labor both in the United States and abroad.

Frankfurter replied to the charge in this manner: "I never, directly or indirectly, by implication or suggestion, expressed an opinion in regard to Mooney's guilt or innocence. On innumerable occasions I said that I neither had an opinion nor was entitled to have an opinion on the merits as to Mooney's guilt or innocence. . . ." [19]

James M. Beck, Solicitor General of the United States, attacked Frankfurter on his home ground—by writing a letter in 1921 to the *New Republic,* of which Frankfurter was a trustee. In it he said Frankfurter was presumptuous to "sit in judgment on a result in which twelve jurymen, a trial judge, a Supreme Court, and a Governor of a state alike concurred." [20] An editor of the *New Republic* took the letter to Frankfurter and asked him to answer it. Frankfurter used the opportunity to defend publicly the commission's report for the first time. He reiterated the facts of the Mooney case as he had set them down in the report, which, he charged, Beck had not read, although it would have taken him only ten minutes to do so.

There was no such concurrence among the jury, judge, Supreme Court, and governor, Frankfurter reminded Beck. It was *after* Mooney's conviction that the damaging testimony against the man was discredited. He then reminded Beck that such irreproachable men as the trial judge and the attorney general of California had in fact petitioned the Supreme Court to return the case for retrial and that the governor had in fact commuted Mooney's sentence to life imprisonment precisely because he had doubts about the original verdict—"although, with amazing illogic," Frankfurter added, "he saw nothing strange in incarcerating a man for a lifetime despite these doubts.

"What makes the Mooney case important," Frankfurter continued, "is not merely that the verdict in a capital case was discredited by the discrediting of the chief witness, but that the chief figure in the case symbolized 'labor' both to the bitter opponents of organized labor as well as in the minds of the workers and their sympathizers. It was this aspect which stirred deep feelings about the case at a time when we were fighting for the vindication of 'the moral claims of unstained processes of law.'..."

As long as Mooney was not afforded a new trial in which to establish his guilt or innocence fairly, "so long will the Mooney case continue not merely an ordinary criminal case, involving 'disputed issues of fact,' but an incident in a long and bitter industrial conflict," Frankfurter said. "Surely the Solicitor General of the United States, when seeking the causes of contemporary lawlessness, should find it incumbent to add his voice of protest against the failure to vindicate the adequacy of Anglo-American law from the distrust which is being sown by a case which, more than any other, symbolizes to millions the perversion of legal machinery as a partisan in the industrial conflict. . . ." [21]

The most famous of all the charges was made by Theodore Roosevelt, former President of the United States for whom Frankfurter had wanted to leave the War Department and campaign in 1912. Shortly after the commission returned from the West, Roosevelt wrote to Frankfurter: ". . . you are engaged in excusing men precisely like the Bolsheviki in Russia, who are murderers and encouragers of murder, who are traitors to their allies, to democracy and to civilization, as well as to the United States, and whose acts are nevertheless apologized for. . . . In times of danger nothing is more common and nothing more dangerous to the republic, than for men, often ordinarily well meaning men, to avoid condemning the criminals who are really public enemies by making their entire assault on the shortcomings of the good citizens who have been the victims or opponents of the criminals. . . ." [22]

Roosevelt called the commission's report of the Bisbee Deportations "misleading." "No human being in his senses doubts that the men deported from Bisbee were bent on destruction and murder. . . . When no efficient means are employed to guard honest, upright and well-behaved citizens from the brutal kind of lawlessness, it is inevitable that these citizens shall try to protect themselves. . . ."

To which Frankfurter replied that if Roosevelt had looked into the facts of the cases with disinterest and dispassion, he would have found that "I pursued the inquiry in a thorough-going judicial, and sensible way. . . ."

On the industry-labor situation in general, he added: ". . . I should like to go over with you in detail the whole industrial situation in Arizona and to make you realize the clash of economic forces that are at stake, make you realize the long, persistent and organized opposition to 'social justice,' to the establishment of machinery for the attainment of such justice, which culminated in strikes in the Arizona copper districts last year. It is easy to disregard economic abuses, to insist on the exercise of autocratic power by raising the false cry of 'disloyalty.' It is too easy. If you had traveled through the Southwest and the Northwest as I have the last few months and come into intimate contact with what is going on beneath the surfaces, studied the forces that are gathering in the industrial world of the United States, I am sure you would feel . . . that but for an almost negligible percent all labor is patriotic, is devoted to the purposes of the war and its prosecution, but that there are industrial conditions which demand remedy and quick remedy, that the masses insist upon an increasing share in determining the conditions of their lives. If we do not bestir ourselves to rectify grave and accumulating evils we shall find the disintegrating forces in our country gaining ground." [23]

The President's Mediation Commission's final report, a joint project with a distinct Frankfurterian tone, said much the same thing: that labor must be recognized as a first-class citizen of the industrial community. ". . . Only by a proper balance of adequate power on each side can just equilibrium in industry be attained. . . ." Under existing conditions—essentially nonrecognition of labor unions—such a balance could not be struck and would continue as the basic cause of American labor troubles.

In addition, "too many labor disturbances are due to the absence of disinterested processes to which resort may be had for peaceful settlement. Force becomes too ready an outlet." For the adjustment of labor conflicts, there was needed continuous administrative machinery by which inevitable disputes could be settled before they reached the proportions they had reached in the West.

Continued repression would breed continued trouble, "turn radical labor leaders into martyrs and increase their following."

The report recommended the elimination of profiteering and the establishment of collective bargaining, means for arbitration of disputes, and the eight-hour day. It urged a unified direction of the labor administration in the government, the surrender by labor of "all practices which tend to restrict maximum efficiency," [24] and, in conclusion, an effort on the part of both labor and management to learn and respect the needs of the other. Education, for Frankfurter, was then and continued to be the most effective means for settling controversies. He always believed there was no problem that could not be talked out by rational men.

The months he spent as counsel to the President's Mediation Commission were Frankfurter's first experience in the front lines of labor disputes, where he came into contact with the whole industrial spectrum. He had grown up among the sweatshops in New York City, had theorized about the problems, and had argued for labor in the courts. Then, in 1917, in the desert mining towns he had seen terrorism at firsthand. He had seen starvation and grief. He had talked long into the night with tough and sometimes uneducated laboring men. He had skirmished with skillful industrial lawyers and listened to the problems of well-meaning and not-so-well-meaning management. He saw cities torn by labor strife and valid issues obscured by bitterness.

And, he concluded in the report: "Not only is the country ready for 'tremendous advances' as to labor problems, but we had better take them and take them rather quickly." [25] Otherwise, the terrorism and the starvation and grief would begin to pain so much that it could climax only in violence.

When the United States entered World War I, the rapid growth of new agencies in Washington and the sudden shortage of men cried out for the help of women. The women responded. Up to that time they had been relegated largely either to social work or teaching; the war was a rare opportunity to prove themselves and contribute something vital.

With this influx came Marion Denman, and Frankfurter's courtship continued, the two devoting a large part of their leisure time to each other. In a typical Frankfurterian gesture of solicitude, he suggested she might be happier with a member of her family in town and arranged for her sister to take a job in the War Department.

Shortly Miss Denman, who was with the War Camp Activities Bureau, was assigned to go to England to survey Englishwomen's war organizations.

She was to sail from New York across a sea infested with German submarines. Frankfurter went up to see her off. The night before the boat sailed, they rode together in a hansom cab around Central Park. It was the traditional romantic setting—moonlight, the steady beating of the horses' hooves, the pleasant muffled sounds of a still-friendly city. And Frankfurter responded in the traditional way; they became engaged.

Miss Denman soon returned safely from Europe. Her sister met her at the boat, and as she hurried down the gangplank, the first thing she said was: "You know, I'm going to marry Felix." [26]

When Frankfurter returned from his trip West, he found the War Department under heavy criticism, with Secretary Baker at the center. The unprecedented wartime demands on the department, accustomed to the slow pace of peacetime work, had brought chaos. Communications had broken down within the department. The influx of personnel had overcrowded the big gray building next to the White House which still housed the Departments of War, Navy, and State.

Organization was faulty because there was too much organization, too many new subdepartments without clear guidelines, so that they either overlapped or left gaps, and disputes arose, further delaying the war effort. The result was that troops arrived in the camps and there were no uniforms. Troops drilled with broomsticks because there were not enough guns. Epidemics ran through the camps. Congestion and confusion clogged the railroads and harbors. Chaos, combined with particularly bad winter weather, threatened to destroy the war effort.

Secretary Baker, as head of the department responsible for expediting the war, became the rallying point for public and political criticism: public because men were being sent ill equipped to unsanitary camps; political because Republicans had expected prominent members of the minority party such as Theodore Roosevelt to be taken into the confidence of the government by appointment to war jobs and the expectations had not been fulfilled.

In December, 1917, Senator George Chamberlain of Oregon, chairman of the Senate Military Affairs Committee, announced that his committee would conduct a full investigation into the war effort.

Frankfurter wrote to Secretary Baker a few days before Baker was to testify at the Senate hearings: ". . . the creation of a single-headed manager to direct the industrial energies of the war is inevitable. Is not the wisest way by which such an adjustment will come to pass for you to take the lead in securing it? In addition is not the response to the need for such a step in reorganization, together with the establishment of a single-headed labor administrator, *the* constructive mode of dealing with the Senate inquiry, and at the same time the most constructive way of educating the public? . . ." In an attached memorandum he wrote that it was the system, not the administrator, that was at fault for conditions, that ". . . it became evident even long before the European war that the Secretary of War was exercising a multiplicity and diversity of functions which necessarily involve the sacrifice of one or another important field in his jurisdiction. . . . All these functions no one person could direct. . . ." [27]

Frankfurter recommended that the duties of the Secretary of War be split up and that the three big divisions under his control—Army, industry, and labor—be divided among three executives, with the Secretary of War concentrating his energies on the Army. There should also be created a ministry of munitions, along the lines of similar ministries abroad, to absorb the large number of hurriedly organized and competing committees and intradepartmental and interdepartmental agencies which had proliferated, to the war effort's detriment. He advised Baker to transfer the problems of war industry, which were consuming a great deal of Baker's time and energy, to one administrator, distinct from the Department of Labor and created for the duration of the war. The creation of such a post, he believed, would "focus dramatic attention to the special labor problems raised by the war and . . . deal with them on the war basis," [28] as well as dissociate the situation from the Labor Department, which thus far had had little influence with management.

Baker did reorganize the War Department more efficiently during the winter of 1917–18. President Wilson, who had received a similar memorandum from Justice Brandeis, did create a single-headed administrator for war industries by appointing the Secretary of Labor to the job of War Administrator, with the assignment to take charge of all government war labor policies. As a result, two major agencies were created within the Labor Department to expedite labor-industry problems: the National War Labor Board, a semijudicial body empowered to settle industrial disputes, and the War Labor Policies

Board empowered to establish the standards on which the National War Labor Board would act.

President Wilson originally considered drafting Brandeis for the chairmanship of the War Labor Policies Board; Frankfurter was among the group that recommended that appointment. Chief Justice Edward D. White, however, did not approve the transfer, believing a Supreme Court Justice should limit his work to that of the Court. In the end President Wilson appointed Frankfurter chairman.

The War Labor Policies Board was established in May, 1918, and Frankfurter wrote to a friend: "... You know the general mess of the labor situation. ... I have been asked to go to the Department of Labor as immediate assistant to Secretary Wilson to undertake the coordination of all the war-labor activities, and I am going. It is a man's—several men's—job and high time it is done. Incidentally ... it ought to furnish medium for dealing with the problems that loom beyond. ..." [29]

The War Labor Policies Board was to accomplish this enormous task of coordination by including a ranking member of any government department or agency engaged in the labor field—representatives from the War Department, Navy Department, Shipping Board, Railroad Administration, War Industries Board, War Labor Board, and Department of Agriculture.

The representative of the Navy Department was Franklin Roosevelt, Assistant Secretary, whom Frankfurter had met and known casually in New York when both men were only recently out of law school. At about that time Roosevelt had announced to his fellow apprentices at Carter, Ledyard and Milburn that he had mapped out his career (parallel to his cousin Theodore's): a seat in the New York Assembly, Assistant Secretary of the Navy; governor of New York; President of the United States. By the time Roosevelt's and Frankfurter's paths crossed for the second time, Roosevelt had fulfilled the first half of his boast. In 1910 he won a seat in the New York State Senate; in 1913 President Wilson appointed him Assistant Secretary of the Navy.

Working together on the War Labor Policies Board, Roosevelt and Frankfurter turned casual acquaintanceship into close friendship. They found they shared public philosophies. Franklin Roosevelt had always been attracted to Theodore Roosevelt's progressivism; only an accident of politics had placed him in the Democratic Party. He had first articulated his own developing philosophy of government in a speech at Troy, New York, in 1912. He had chastised the accumulators of great wealth for their arrogance and irresponsibility, then demanded government's right to intervene on behalf of society's welfare. "... Competition has been shown to be useful up to a certain point and no further," he had said. "Co-operation must begin where competition leaves off...." [30] Otherwise the system must fail.

Roosevelt's doctrine of public supremacy found conditions congenial to its growth and refinement on Frankfurter's War Labor Policies Board. Although Roosevelt seldom attended formal meetings of the board, he and Frankfurter devised an arrangement whereby they dealt with Navy Department questions directly, and they were in daily contact. The essential problem then—and later in Roosevelt's Presidency—was to persuade—and force, if necessary—the competitive factions of the community to work for the common good. On the War Labor Policies Board, it was to affect the cooperation of business and labor groups to produce for the nation during the war emergency.

"Our first step," Frankfurter told a New York *Times* reporter in May, 1918, "will be to find out what the labor needs are.... Out of this a labor budget can be made." Frankfurter hoped it would be possible to redistribute manpower to the places it was needed. He assured business that all the complexities of its problems would be considered carefully, "but the prime consideration ... is that industries essential to the production of war materials and those instruments necessary to carry it must be satisfied at all costs...." [31]

The War Labor Policies Board met every Friday morning at 11 A.M. at 1607 H Street Northwest, a private home converted to offices, across Lafayette Park from the White House and the War Department. Frankfurter presided over the meetings in a manner that was unobtrusive but firm and effectively efficient. He himself conferred and assigned other members to confer with representatives of industry and labor and with representatives of government agencies involved in industrial problems.

After four months on the job, he described his work as "spending a good part of the day in reconciling conflicting egotisms even of the people who are bent upon the same purpose ... egotism tinctured by selfishness, and the rest of the day overcoming the tenacious obstructions of ignorance and old habits. . . ." [32]

One of the supreme egos Frankfurter encountered was that of a seventy-two-year-old Illinois corporation lawyer who had amassed a steel empire: Elbert H. Gary. Gary was much more accustomed to having the government do *his* bidding than he was to listening to a thirty-six-year-old Harvard professor lay down rules for his steel mills. The steel industry continued to operate on a ten-hour day long after the government had decreed an eight-hour day for war industries, and Frankfurter insisted steel must be brought to its knees.

Just meeting with Gary, who had once been an Illinois rural judge and had kept the title, required months of maneuvering by Frankfurter, Gary, and others. Frankfurter began with polite notes in which he explained his board and its aim of the "formulation and administration of policies of industrial relations for the period of the war" to assure "maximum productive energies of the country indispensable to the successful prosecution of the war." [33] At first Gary simply ignored the notes; then he replied haughtily: "We have experienced little difficulty in our own labor matters during a good many years, and we dislike very much to see any agitation which is calculated to disturb our relations. . . ." [34]

In time Gary agreed to meet with Frankfurter and invited him to come to New York. Frankfurter, recognizing the advantage of fighting on one's home ground and the dignity of the United States government, refused, countering with proposals for Gary to come to Washington.

Eventually the pair, dissimilar in background and goals but each as facile a lawyer as the country could produce, met in Frankfurter's small office on H Street. The two fenced for hours. They came to no satisfactory agreement. Gary was as unbending as the product he manufactured. He had dealt with the government before, usually on his own terms. Presidents came and went in relatively short periods; United States Steel, which he headed, and the need for its products would remain long after Woodrow Wilson had left. After listening with some impatience to Frankfurter, Gary walked out in a huff. His industry continued to be strife-torn for many years.

The work of the War Labor Policies Board was concerned primarily with establishing in war industries the basic policies recommended in the President's Mediation Commission report which Frankfurter had authored and with implementing them by making them part of government contracts.

Most of the board's difficulties came in administering the eight-hour day. Frankfurter was committed to it. In 1917 he had argued the State of Oregon's right to legislate a ten-hour day for women. In 1916, in a letter to the Boston *Herald,* he had championed the eight-hour day not only on the basis of protection for workers from chronic health hazards, excessive fatigue, and mental stultification by the machine, but also on the basis of increased efficiency for the industry. As chairman of the War Labor Policies Board he continued to support the eight-hour day not only as "the best industrial standard, judged by the needs of production carried over an appropriately long time and dealing with industry properly managed, but that such a working day is also essential in order to give those opportunities for fruitful leisure, which alone can give us an educated and responsible democratic citizenship. . . ." [35]

But because of the complexities of the laws establishing the eight-hour day, its administration was difficult. Some industries were subject to it; others were not. Even some departments within an industry had to honor the eight-hour day while others did not. Consequently, the government was flooded with inquiries about who was subject and who was not; it was also flooded with complaints from organized labor that certain plants were not complying with the law. The War Labor Conference, established to adjudicate such matters, could come to no agreement, and as the war wore on, a number of questions concerning application of the law rose to require the government's attention. It was the task of Frankfurter and his War Labor Policies Board to deal with them.

Although in the summer of 1918 the Supreme Court had held the federal child labor law unconstitutional, the War Labor Policies Board suggested to the War Department that it insert in all procurement contracts a clause prohibiting the employment of child labor; this the War Department subsequently did.

In similar ways, the board set standards for the right of labor to organize, regular channels for arbitration, night work for women, and sanitary codes in the war factories. The board also devised a scheme for centralizing the recruitment of labor under the United States Employment Service—in a market with a shortage of labor caused by the exigencies of war, there was a great deal of raiding from plant to plant and subsequent price rises which had to be controlled.

If the board was not an unmitigated success in devising panaceas for all the labor problems which beset the nation during World War I, it did give labor problems a national scope. It also moved toward setting standards for the future and providing precedents for later progress in industrial relations. It proved that decent standards in industy did not decrease production but, on the contrary, increased it.

The War Labor Policies Board had been confronted with production problems and the pressures of war. The members had not had time for "humanitarian sentiment, idealistic theory, nor fanciful speculations," [36] Frankfurter later said. Whatever standards the government had imposed on industry had always been from the point of view of production. And the board was successful. The mobilization for war was a foundation for what Frankfurter had been arguing and was later to argue in the courts: that decent conditions for laborers ought to be provided at least selfishly by management.

A fringe benefit of the war "to make the world safe for democracy" was making the industrial world safer for industrial democracy, although it would be some years before the standards established by such bodies as the War Labor Policies Board would be accepted as necessary by domestic industry.

Frankfurter considered industrial democracy essential to the postwar nation. There must be, he believed, a partnership of power. "What American business needs," he told a Conference on Demobilization in 1918, "is a substitution of the processes of law and order for the present oscillation between anarchy and autocracy by which it is too largely governed. But not the 'law' of an imposed will, and the 'order' of the police club. Not until we realize that a copper camp is a community and that a factory makes the same demand upon its people as our political institutions, not until we constitutionalize industry shall we approach aright our industrial questions." [37]

The Armistice of November 11, 1918, put the War Labor Policies Board and agencies like it out of business. Some time after submitting its proposals for facilitating labor demobilization, Secretary of Labor Wilson directed that the board be terminated. Frankfurter announced his resignation on February 10, 1919, and Louis McHenry Howe, who would later become President Franklin Roosevelt's right hand in the White House, took over the chairmanship until the board was dissolved in May, 1919.

When Frankfurter resigned the chairmanship of the War Labor Policies Board, he sailed for France and the Peace Conference in Paris, not as a representative of the United States government, although while there he did help the American delegation with labor problems, but as a representative of the Zionist Organization of America.

On November 2, 1917, the British, in the Balfour Declaration, had promised a national home for the Jewish people in Palestine. Worldwide Jewry's hopes were high that the promise would be realized in the peace treaty that would emerge from the hubbub and hullabaloo that characterized the Paris Peace Conference of 1919. It was to help secure this promise that Frankfurter went to Paris.

He identified deeply with Jews as a people, and out of his friendship with Louis Brandeis, leader of American Zionists and a potential candidate for leader of world Zionists, grew an ardent faith in Zionism and the cause of Israel. In Zionism he found a vital cause through which he could announce and articulate his pride in his Jewishness. And through this faith in the Jewish people he could translate his faith in mankind and in the perfectability of man.

Frankfurter had been Brandeis' lieutenant in America for some years. At the Peace Conference he was Brandeis' eyes, ears, and spokesman.

The Zionists set up headquarters in the Hôtel Meurice in Paris. Since Turkey, which had ruled Palestine, had been defeated with the Central Powers, they intended to lobby for world support of the Balfour Declaration. They hoped to get Britain appointed temporary trustee over Palestine to assure Jewish development of the country and to control the indigenous Arab population, which opposed a large-scale Jewish immigration. The Zionists were one of the small voices which struggled to make themselves heard while the big powers sliced up the world like so many pieces in a pie.

Palestine was a touchy, if minor, subject at the Peace Conference.

France, one of the four great powers, had been assiduously extending its sphere of influence in the Middle East since 1815. She was not about to accommodate Great Britain, her strongest rival, as a mandatory over Palestine. Britain, which recognized the value of a Western-oriented and educated Jewish population in Palestine with Britain in control but which also had responsibilities to the Arabs, found herself, as Frankfurter reported to Brandeis, "between the millstones of Arab fears and Jewish hopes. . . ." [38] American approval had been tentatively given to Zionist goals by President Wilson, and he had included a British mandate for Palestine in his fourteen-point peace program. But at the Peace Conference he frequently wavered in promoting it as he faced the reality of the power struggles and the subsequent disillusionment that the world, after all, had not been made very safe for democracy, that the old rivalries of Europe had not been dissipated but only temporarily sublimated and were returning as strongly as ever.

Frankfurter became a frequent caller in the headquarters of Colonel Edward M. House, Wilson's top aide—occasionally to the annoyance of House, who wrote in his diary two months after Frankfurter's arrival in Paris: ". . . Frankfurter came again about his old trouble 'Palestine for the Jews. . . .' " [39] When conditions at the Peace Conference indicated Wilson was retreating, Frankfurter prodded Wilson himself: ". . . the task is to keep literally millions of Jews in check," he wrote in mid-May, 1919. "Uncertainty, indefinite delay, seeming change of policy, bring a feeling of hopelessness which only those in intimate contact with the people whose fate is at stake can fully gauge. We are bending every energy to prevent the slow attrition of the spirit of such a people." [40]

Through an interview and subsequent exchange of public letters with Prince Feisal, the responsible voice of Arab interests at the Peace Conference, Frankfurter was instrumental in obtaining, at least at the official level, Arab approval for the proposed Jewish immigration.

But the Peace Conference dragged on—and on and on—with no solution of the Middle Eastern problems. Others superseded it; the intransigence and vacillation of Wilson, near collapse and uncertain of his mandate from the United States, contributed significantly to the delay. The Peace Conference, which had begun in hope and ended in hopelessness, closed without solving the problems of the distribution of Turkish territories.

PART II

Harvard Law School

[1]

DURING the thirteen years since Frankfurter's graduation from Harvard Law School he had tasted liberally from the smorgasbord of opportunity laid before a young lawyer. He had come under the tutelage of the three most important older men in his life—Stimson, Holmes, and Brandeis—and had absorbed something useful from each.

He had enormously enlarged his circle of friends, many of whom he continued to keep in touch with, some of whom became valuable contacts in later public life. Franklin Roosevelt had captivated Frankfurter with his personal charm and way of ordering government as they worked together during World War I. Their careers diverged during the 1920's. Roosevelt unsuccessfully ran for Vice President in 1920, then was stricken with polio in 1921. Except for a brief exchange of letters and a visit during Roosevelt's illness, Frankfurter and Roosevelt had no contact until Roosevelt became governor of New York in 1929. Then Roosevelt was to find in Frankfurter both a congenial and stimulating companion and an effective instrument of policy.

For his authorship of the President's Mediation Commission reports, particularly those on the Bisbee Deportations and the Mooney case, Frankfurter had achieved national notoriety.

While he was chairman of the War Labor Policies Board, he had been wrestling with the decision of what to do after the war. He was acutely sensitive to the vast social and economic changes which had been set in motion before the war and which would, after the war, inevitably effect changes in the structure of the nation. He had assumed when he left Cambridge for Washington in 1917 that he would return. But after two years as an activist in national affairs and a lawyer-about-Washington, in a considerably more influential position than he was in Henry Stimson's War Department, the decision was difficult.

He finally decided to go back to Cambridge for two reasons: at Harvard he would have the "opportunity of influencing year by year the dominant minds in the legal profession in a country which necessarily to such a large degree is governed by the legal profession." In addition, Roscoe Pound, by this time dean of the law school, had promised him sufficient free time for extracurricular activities, and Frankfurter could anticipate "being very active in public affairs in my fields of interest. . . ." [1] In returning to Harvard, once again he was not compelled to choose between the academic and activist life; he could have both, and he did—in full measure.

Frankfurter returned to Harvard in time for the opening of the 1919 academic year, two months short of his thirty-seventh birthday. He stayed twenty years, until his appointment by Franklin Roosevelt to the Supreme Court of the United States.

Frankfurter found Harvard at the beginning of the 1919–20 term no different from other universities as returning World War I veterans scrambled to be admitted and enrollments at colleges across the nation soared. He feared the crush would lead to future enrollments of more than 1,000 students and the accompanying problems of a factory approach to education. Within five years his fears proved accurate. It was a development in legal education he never fully adapted to. He was, as he said, "a small crowd teacher." [2] Years later he still yearned for the old days when students were fewer and teaching was a more intimate relationship between student and professor. But for the immediate present he found himself getting into the stride of the law school with enthusiasm.

The early weeks Frankfurter devoted to settling back into academic work and catching up on legal developments since he had last taught law in 1917. He resumed his course in public utilities, plus two third-year courses—contracts and combinations in restraint of trade, and municipal corporations—plus also a graduate course in administrative law which covered the legal problems of all law-administering agencies outside the courts.

In November, 1919, Frankfurter bubbled to Henry Stimson: "Of course I want Mrs. Stimson and you to be of the first to know that I'm to be married during the Christmas recess. It counts as nothing to you to be told her name is Marion A. Denman; and if I add that my taste and interests in life will give you some inkling, except that the . . . guardian angel that seems to make me her special case has even now exceeded generosity you will suspect me of lover's prattle. . . ." [3]

It had been a rather long courtship. Frankfurter had met her in the spring of 1913, when he was counsel to the Bureau of Insular Affairs under the War Department.

They were married on December 20, 1919. They had a quiet ceremony performed by Benjamin N. Cardozo, a friend of Frankfurter's, a justice of the New York Court of Appeals, and the man Frankfurter would replace in 1939 on the Supreme Court of the United States.

The newlyweds quickly adjusted to the life of a university professor, briefly in a small apartment in Boston, then in the house at 192 Brattle Street, Cambridge, where they lived until 1939.

When they returned to Cambridge from their honeymoon in Southern Pines, North Carolina, Harold Laski described them as "two cooing doves. To see their anxiety for each other's protection against the snow, etc. is charming. The boy is very happy. The girl is still rather reticent and shy . . . but she makes him sing an unceasing song. . . ." [4]

Their relationship was not one of easy stereotyping; it was highly charged, emotionally and intellectually. They were completely different and completely complementary. Her reserve set off his ebullience. His indulgence was matched by her toughness. His tastes were legal; hers, literary. He used reason; she frequently used intuition, which Frankfurter proudly described: ". . . I have learned through Marion that there is evidence and evidence. Often she would give judgments of people that would surprise me, and when I asked her what her evidence was she used the formula, 'nothing that you would regard as evidence.' And almost invariably a few years later I would come like a faithful little dog bringing his offering and saying, 'Would you like to have some evidence for what you said about so-and-so?' " [5]

Frankfurter was proud of his wife; his correspondence is filled with "Marion says," "Marion believes." He took pride in her beauty, her intelligence, her wit, and her devastating tongue, even though he was frequently the victim. Friends were quite accustomed to her "Oh, Felix, there you go running off again" and "Felix, don't get so excited." She often said there were two things about his conversation that appalled her, and she never could decide which was worse: One, he interrupted every thought with a long, parenthetical excursion, and, two, he never failed to return after having closed the parenthesis.

She could cover in a very few well-chosen words what Frankfurter covered in several pages. She was a master, too, of the bon mot, each of which revealed in her a shrewd and discerning judgment reinforced by a broad range of experience and knowledge. People quoted her pithy pronouncements with delight long after they had forgotten her husband's prolix statements. All this gave her a skill with a blue pencil, and she used it effectively on Frankfurter's articles and speeches, even on some of the technical reports of crime surveys with which he later became involved. A colleague once complimented her on what she had done with his survey report: "... I think she is the unusual phenomenon of an editor with heart. The way she made my jumbled sentences acquire meaning and purpose and clearness is amazing. ..." [6] And Frankfurter was fond of telling how later as Justice Frankfurter he told Justice Jackson that his wife edited his nonjudicial writings. Jackson replied: "Why don't you extend the censorship?" [7]

She made him sing an unceasing song which he never stopped singing. He loved the company of women, especially gay, attractive women with wit. "But," a law clerk once wrote, "there was really only one woman in his life—Marion Denman Frankfurter, his wife. She has a rare, almost an unearthly sensitivity—antennae attuned to the slightest vibrations of feeling and a poet's responsiveness to beauty. Frankfurter revered these qualities in her, thinking of himself, by contrast ... as a more earthbound soul." [8]

Two months after Frankfurter returned to Cambridge, he gave both Boston and the Harvard community a strong hint of the direction his sense of professionalism would take in the public controversies of the era.

It was a period of reaction to the war just finished, a period of exhaustion when the nation wanted nothing more than to withdraw into itself and recover. Through fear of a threat to recovery, perhaps even to the "American way of life," public opinion ran strongly and emotionally against the revolutionary Russian Communist regime, and with only slight effort of transference, "Lenin," "labor," and "liberal" became synonymous. Dean Pound had told Frankfurter while Frankfurter was still abroad at the Paris Peace Conference that the Tories at Harvard—and at universities all over the country—were attempting to get rid of "everybody suspected of liberal ideas" [9] and to appoint only bland professors with bland reputations. He warned Frankfurter that he had better be prepared to defend and justify his Bisbee and Mooney reports, which had identified him with radical causes.

Nevertheless, on Armistice Day, 1919, Frankfurter presided over a meeting in Faneuil Hall, Boston, and urged a policy of nonintervention in the Russian government and trade with the new regime. He had been reluctant to lead the gathering, urging the organizers, all of whom were distinguished Bostonians, to enlist "some leader with a good Back Bay name," telling them that "in the present ferment they should avoid having a Jew of alien origin preside at a meeting concerned with Russia." [10]

When none came forth, Frankfurter, believing both in what he called a "sensible policy as to Russia" [11] and in the duty of a teacher of the young to generate an atmosphere congenial to free inquiry by speaking his convictions, agreed to chair the meeting. He carefully talked along the lines that the respectable British statesman and South African general Jan Christiaan Smuts had advocated toward Russia: that Russia ought to be allowed to solve its own problems; that the rest of the world ought to stay out of the Revolution; that it was patience and help, not military and political interference, that would aid Russia in convalescence. If such a rational approach did in time become the policy of some governments, it was not a ripe time for Frankfurter to urge it in Boston, then painfully enduring the ominous presence of large numbers of "radical" laborers in its industrial suburbs. Frankfurter's speech only brought on himself sulfurous attacks of being "radical" and "Communist."

Frankfurter ignored the assaults. Before the 1919–20 academic term ended at Harvard Law School, Frankfurter had argued in court in behalf of the rights of a pair of Communist deportees, engaged in a controversy with the Attorney General of the United

States, and joined with a group of lawyers to chastise, in print, lawlessness on the part of the Justice Department.

The witch-hunter's witch-hunter of the 1920's was Woodrow Wilson's third Attorney General, A. Mitchell Palmer, a practicing Quaker who customarily used the Quaker "thee" and "thou" in speaking, but whose tactics were hardly Quaker-like. Palmer had Presidential aspirations; the "Red Menace," which had whipped the nation into a frenzy, was a convenient and, he hoped, effective peg on which to hang his high ambition.

A rash of mysterious bomb explosions in the spring of 1919, including one on the lawn of Palmer's Washington home, fed the national hysteria. Palmer seized on it as an excuse to send special detectives of the Department of Justice on what became known as the Red Raids to root out what he charged was an organized Communist conspiracy to overthrow the government of the United States. In confidential instructions to agents of the department, Palmer's assistant, W. J. Flynn, director of the Bureau of Investigation (which later became the FBI), ordered his men to conduct "a vigorous and comprehensive investigation of anarchistic and similar classes, Bolshevism, and kindred agitations advocating change in the present form of government by force or violence, the promotion of sedition and revolution, bomb-throwing, and similar activities. In the present state of the Federal law this investigation should be particularly directed to persons not citizens of the United States, with a view of obtaining deportation cases. . . ." [12]

In a trial run on the night of November 7, 1919, then in a full-dress performance on the night of January 2, 1920, special agents of the Department of Justice raided homes and labor headquarters coast to coast, rounding up that second night about 4,000 suspects in thirty-three cities. The agents had been instructed to search the residences and meeting places of all members of the Communist Party of America and the Communist Labor Party. Access was left entirely to their discretion; search warrants were to be obtained only if "absolutely necessary." [13] Persons taken into custody were not to be allowed to communicate with lawyers or families.

The raids were lawlessness at its crudest. Breaking into lawful meetings of the suspect Communist organizations, agents of the Department of Justice hustled into custody, without warrants, citizens and aliens alike; subjected them to third degrees; then wrote their statements into prepared question blanks, to which the victims —many of whom did not understand English well—were made to swear regardless of accuracy. The agents in their thorough searches of the homes and meeting places found no bombs and no weapons, only tons of pamphlets and books, which they carried off with the victims.

Citizens who could prove their citizenship were released. Aliens were crowded into close quarters and held incommunicado. Gradually they were released on bail to await hearings, although a number were held in custody overlong because of the records jam in the Bureau of Immigration. Some were actually deported.

Such an outbreak of official lawlessness was not one Frankfurter could keep silent about. It had too much of the bitter flavor of traditional European lawlessness. He had seen such terrorism in Bisbee, Arizona, and San Francisco three years previous.

Although the arrests had been made by Justice Department agents, deportation proceedings were the responsibility of the Labor Department. Louis F. Post, an Assistant Secretary of Labor, was the man in charge. He handled his responsibility with integrity —and not the way Palmer liked. At Palmer's instigation, the House of Representatives threatened Post with impeachment because of Post's "efforts to enforce the deportation laws with due regard to our constitutional proceedings" [14] and for his subsequent release of nearly half of those arrested within a few months.

When Frankfurter learned of the threatened impeachment, he telegraphed an offer of his professional services to Post. However, Post did not need Frankfurter's help; he acquitted himself creditably before the Congressional committee, and his accusers had to recant.

But Frankfurter found other outlets for his outrage at Palmer's lawlessness. In April, 1920, *Colyer v. Skeffington* came before Judge George W. Anderson of the United States Circuit Court in Boston. Mr. and Mrs. William T. Colyer, British subjects, had been arrested in the Attorney General's January 2, 1920, raid. With sixteen other similarly arrested aliens, the Colyers had petitioned for a writ of habeas corpus, alleging that their constitutional rights had been violated, in particular that they had been arrested and detained without due process of law, which was constitutionally guaranteed to aliens, as well as to citizens.

Judge Anderson invited Frankfurter and a colleague, Zechariah Chafee, Jr., to appear in *Colyer v. Skeffington* as *amici curiae*—friends of the court. Both Frankfurter and Chafee were known as forceful exponents of civil liberties. Chafee was so forceful, in fact, that only a few months later he was called before the Harvard Board of Overseers, one of the two governing boards of Harvard University, to explain his writings.

Frankfurter and Chafee were not counsel for the accused aliens but were charged with putting the facts of the raids and detention before the court. The issues, Frankfurter wrote a year later in phrases reminiscent of Henry Stimson's standards for government prosecutors, boiled down to "whether the Attorney General of the United States is to be allowed to act like an attorney general of the Stuart regime or whether upon the Attorney General of the United States and the official head of the bar of the country there rests an especial duty to be obedient to law." [15]

Judge Anderson decided for the prisoners, holding that there had been violation of regular procedure. One of the points of law on which the decision turned was a Frankfurter contribution quoted in the decision. Just prior to the raids in 1920 one of the rules controlling the procedure in deportation hearings had been conveniently changed. The effect was to cut off the aliens from representation by counsel and leave them unprotected, in their inability to comprehend English or even interpreters, at the mercy of overzealous agents of the Justice Department who were trying to obtain wholesale confessions of membership in the Communist Party or its affiliates.

The rule was soon restored, but not in time to protect the rights of the men in court, and Frankfurter was quoted in Judge Anderson's opinion:

> ... if there is one thing that is established in the law of administration ... it is that a rule cannot be repealed specifically to affect a case under consideration by the administrative authorities; that is, if there is an existing rule which protects certain rights, it violates every sense of decency, which is the very heart of due process, to repeal that protection just for the purpose of accomplishing the ends of the case which come before the administrative authority ... there was a sudden, calculated, and surreptitious deprivation of that safeguard which was sought to protect

the rights of all, and particularly protect those who were innocent.[16]

Judge Anderson held that if indeed the Communist Party was organized for the explicit purpose of overthrowing the government by force or violence, "It is plainly a criminal conspiracy" and ought to be dealt with in criminal court, not in the immigration office. However, he went on, "even if the arrests had been lawful and the proceedings had been regular throughout, it cannot be the law that an alien shall be held beyond a reasonable time, for trial and determination of his right either to go free and earn his living in this country, or to be deported." The Colyers' detention was clearly illegal.

In his opinion Judge Anderson included a plea for sanity on the part of the public:

> ... Marxian Socialism has for more than two-thirds of a century evoked the support of a set of radical thinkers and propagandists in most of the countries of Western Europe. Of recent years it has had some followers in this country. But these theories have never commanded the general assent or support of the believers in a sound and progressive democracy. Never, until this raid, were they treated seriously.... Whether our Anglo-Saxon institutions are or are not properly described as "capitalistic," hitherto we have had sufficient confidence in them and in their endurance, so as not to be frightened into intolerance and hysterical lawlessness by the specter of a dominating Marxian Socialism. Bismarck in Germany sought to suppress Marxian Socialism by legislation, with the usual result of promoting it....[17]

Frankfurter always interpreted the government's failure to appeal Anderson's decision as A. Mitchell Palmer's confession of guilt.

Based on the facts they unearthed for the court in the Colyer case, Frankfurter, Chafee, Dean Pound, and nine other prominent American lawyers published in May, 1920, under National Popular Government League auspices, a *Report upon the Illegal Practices of the United States Department of Justice*. In the report they condemned Palmer's cavalier attitude toward law and accused the department of infringement of civil liberties: of cruel and unusual punishments, arrests without warrants; unreasonable searches and seizures; use of provocative agents reminiscent of old Russia and Spain; compelling persons to be witnesses against themselves; and misuses of the office of Attorney General by the squandering of public funds and invading the field of propaganda.

"It has always been the proud boast of America that this is a government of laws and not of men," the report concluded. "Our Constitution and laws have been based on the simple elements of human nature. Free men cannot be driven and repressed; they must be led. Free men respect justice and follow truth, but arbitrary power they will oppose until the end of time. There is no danger of revolution so great as that created by suppression, by ruthlessness, and by deliberate violation of the simple rules of American law and American decency. . . ." [18]

Attorney General Palmer retorted with accusations that "several" of the signers of the report had appeared as counsel for Communists at deportation hearings. "I have difficulty in reconciling their attitude with that of men who have sworn to uphold the Constitution of the United States." [19] There followed an exchange of telegrams between Palmer and the two Harvard professors, Chafee and Frankfurter, in which Palmer denied the truth of the report's charges and Chafee and Frankfurter offered to defend their report publicly.

In the early months of 1921 the lawyers' report came before a subcommittee of the Senate Judiciary Committee, and its charges were investigated in hearings. But party politics pigeonholed the committee reports, which were eventually buried in the back of the *Congressional Record* of February 5, 1923.

In the meantime, Palmer overreached himself by overreacting to May Day, 1920, when he called out the National Guard to put down a nonexistent revolutionary plot to overthrow the government. May Day passed quietly, and the country stopped believing in him, although the Red Menace hysteria continued for a good many years. At the 1920 Democratic convention, Palmer reached for the brass ring, but it went to Governor James A. Cox of Ohio, with Franklin Roosevelt as his running mate.

Frankfurter's espousal of unpopular causes did not have the support of two of his closest friends. Holmes wrote to Harold Laski that Frankfurter "is so good in his chosen business that I think he helps the world more in that way than he does by becoming a knight errant or a martyr. . . ." [20] Frankfurter's activities became such a popular subject for drawing-room discussion that Henry Stimson felt called upon to ask for an explanation.

"Some weeks ago," he wrote to Frankfurter in fatherly, sober tones, "a number of my Yale classmates were dining with me . . . and during the evening the question of the situation of the country with regard to anti-American activities came up, as it quite often does in modern conversation, and your name was brought into it as one who is aiding such activities. I defended you, as I have several times had occasion to do during the past year or two; and then one of my classmates, who is a professor at New Haven, said that he had received from you through the mail some Bolshevist propaganda. I expressed my surprise at it and he said he would send me a sample. Since then he has sent me the Russian Press Review dated November 5, 1920, with a letter telling me he received a bundle of ten copies of this document 'addressed to me "Care Felix Frankfurter, U.S. America."' . . ." [21]

Frankfurter confessed ignorance about the document in point, but admitted that for about two months he had been receiving from Estonia some Russian language papers and the *Russian Press Review,* which went into the wastebasket except on three specific occasions when "there were specific accounts of the activities or the plans of the Soviet Government that I thought would interest friends of mine, not because they were Communists, or I am a Communist, but merely as a revelation of the Soviet state of mind. . . ." [22] But, he said, the origins of the packets remained a mystery. He had met Soviets both in Washington and abroad and had discussed with them events in Russia. However, he wrote, "I hardly need to say to you that I would not take as gospel truth what these Russians told me, and I think you will agree that an effort to probe their minds was decidedly relevant to a conscientious effort to make myself acquainted with conditions and forces in Europe. . . ."

Stimson had raised also larger questions involved in Frankfurter's outspokenness: its effect on his students, on the reputation of Harvard Law School, and on America's confidence in him.

In a confession of pedagogical faith, Frankfurter answered that in his classes he sought "painstakingly to convey the exact state of the law, to interpret even decisions and views with which I disagree in a fair and scientific attitude, and to be critical only in that spirit of truth-seeking. . . . Further, I must be judged by my legal writings, by my briefs, and by arguments in court,—all of them in cases of a public nature without retainer, using the courts as a laboratory for my ideas as a teacher.... This is the material ... upon which I am ready to be judged...."

Frankfurter declared that in all his activities he had been solicitous of the good name of Harvard, that, in fact, it was the good name of Harvard that was of major concern: "... I know that for the passing moment these were not popular causes, but I also know that law is something deeper than passing popular passion, and if a professor at the Harvard Law School should refuse to associate himself with causes that seek the vindication of the law, simply because for the moment such vindication runs counter to popular opinion, how much respect would you really have for the character of such a teacher?"

If public confidence demanded pandering, he would do without it. "Of course I can secure ... confidence by being wholly without convictions, or failing to express them on matters of vital concern to this country. Even then I would have a hard time of it, because my field of the law, the subjects in which I am most deeply interested, are not subjects as to which there is a fixed right or wrong, but involve conflicting considerations of policy on which men are bound to differ. ... It is as you say, fear—and care, and these unsettled times—which is at the root of so much unjust treatment of those who differ from the majority in opinion...." [23]

The Frankfurters spent the summer of 1920 in England, laboring in the vineyards of Zionism.

The question of Palestine had not been settled at the Paris Peace Conference. By 1920 it was apparent that uncertainty about its future was demoralizing the entire Middle East. Beginning on February 12, 1920, representatives of Great Britain, France, and Italy met in London to settle this and other related questions. After much Anglo-French wrangling, in London and at a full-dress San Remo Conference two months later, Great Britain was awarded the mandate for Palestine on April 26, 1920. Zionist goals were promised fulfillment, at least on the official level.

With a Jewish homeland in Palestine about to be realized, Brandeis, Frankfurter, and Jacob de Haas, another Brandeis lieutenant, sailed for London in the summer of 1920 to meet with English Zionists and try to settle the family quarrels that had split them. In these meetings began the break between Chaim Weizmann, leader of the English Zionists, and Brandeis that was to culminate the following year with Brandeis and his aides, including Frankfurter, severing their official relationship with the Zionist movement.

The deadlock among the Zionists had first shown itself at the Paris Peace Conference. Brandeis, who had never breathed anything but the free air of America, was far more intellectually than emotionally committed to the Jewish homeland in Palestine. He insisted that economic and social measures were the approach to building a strong, self-supporting nation. Weizmann, who had grown up in a small Russian town where humiliation of Jews had been refined to a science, believed the collective dream of a nation was the important factor. Brandeis wanted to make Palestine live through the leadership of expert businessmen and industrialists, whether they were Zionists or not. Weizmann believed the builders must be Zionists, ardent keepers of the faith, with the national dream uppermost in their consciousness. Brandeis gradually withdrew and, in view of what he considered his higher responsibility on the United States Supreme Court, refused to serve on a Palestine commission charged with the task of overseeing the early stages of development. In the end, he refused even an honorary position and left the responsibility for Palestine's immediate future to Weizmann and his English Zionists.

The final, irreparable breach between Brandeis and Weizmann came the following spring at the Cleveland convention of the Zionist Organization of America, to which Weizmann came.

Weizmann's idealism won the delegates over from Brandeis' pragmatism. Brandeis, Frankfurter, and some thirty others resigned from active high-level participation in the movement. For Brandeis, the pull of Zionism never lost its hold, and he remained an ardent believer in Israel for the rest of his life, channeling his interests through various economically oriented bodies to develop basic industries, housing, and finance.

For Frankfurter the choice had been difficult: He was able to understand and sympathize with both viewpoints, and he even believed both men were necessary to the movement. As the product of the Vienna ghetto he could understand Weizmann's impatience, his distrust of non-Zionists, his unquestioning, even naïve faith in Zionists. Frankfurter could admire Weizmann for the strength of his faith. But Frankfurter also believed that Brandeis' insistence on establishing Palestine on an economically sound basis would go furthest to build a nation of self-supporting Jews, although its premises were not so romantic and emotionally appealing as Weizmann's. Frankfurter could even understand why Brandeis could *not* understand Weizmann. But he chose to follow Brandeis and resign.

His interest in Zionism did not abate, however, although from 1921 on, it was unofficial. He remained Brandeis' Zionist confidant, on intimate terms with prominent Zionists, and assumed occasional Zionist assignments.

He had found expression for his Jewish pride in Zionism. Had events turned out differently at Cleveland with the Brandeis faction winning, possibly he would have sought out more opportunities for expressing himself in the excitement of building a nation out of the desert and in the later birth of Israel. On the other hand, he could find in the law a more effective expression of his deep-rooted Jewish heritage. As an alien Jew, Frankfurter had found a haven in American democracy, as millions of his fellows had. He could better articulate his belief in it by teaching the law, the strongest bulwark of that democracy. Zionism never became a consuming passion.

[2]

Soon after his return to Harvard, Frankfurter came to verbal blows with Abbott Lawrence Lowell, president of Harvard University—of which the law school is a part—from 1909 to 1933. Their feud, fed by later events, lasted throughout Lowell's presidency.

A. Lawrence Lowell was the product of two families of Massachusetts aristocrats: the Lawrences and the Lowells. He shared the biases of his class. There was a humanitarian streak in him, which allowed him to respect the respectable tradition of philanthropy, if in a condescending way.

As an educator of standing, the head of the country's leading university, he felt that the ivy mantle of academic freedom was sacred. Although in 1916 he publicly opposed the confirmation of Louis Brandeis as a Supreme Court Justice, it would have been beneath him to retaliate against the members of the Harvard faculty—including Frankfurter—who supported and agitated *for* Brandeis' confirmation; in fact, he appointed Roscoe Pound dean of the law school during this period, while Pound was publicly endorsing Brandeis. When the English Socialist Harold Laski, then teaching at Harvard, was criticized by Harvard alumni and called before a committee of the Board of Overseers for his support of the Boston police strike in 1919, Lowell stood up stoutly for Laski's right to speak his beliefs, although Lowell equally stoutly disagreed with them. Lowell did the same for Zechariah Chafee, whose views on civil liberties had been censured. Within a few years he would extend the same professional support to Frankfurter.

But Lowell was a snob, as even his closest friends admitted. In the spring of 1922, Lowell's snobbism was displayed to the country at large when he tried to impose a quota system for Jewish students at Harvard. He told a friend he was not anti-Semitic and had nothing against Jews as such. But the Jews who were getting into Harvard at the time were not the type that Harvard wanted. They lived at home, instead of in the dormitories. They studied; they did not engage in athletics and clubs. He wanted gentlemen at Harvard. Industrious students, of course, but students who also contributed to the nonacademic, clublike atmosphere of the university and who would take their places in the world as gentlemen.

His conception was anathema to Frankfurter. It was true that in 1922 the sons of Jewish, Polish, and Russian immigrants were getting into Harvard in large numbers—that was what the immigrants had come to America for. And they were diggers—most of them did not have much money, nor had they the time and the resources, not to mention the social acumen, that would draw them into the nonacademic activities of the university.

Lowell sought, that spring of 1922, to persuade the faculty to restrict the admission of Jewish students and to impose "racial" tests on candidates for admission, citing lack of space as the precipitating factor.

Judge Julian W. Mack, a Zionist colleague of Frankfurter's, a member of the Harvard Board of Overseers, a federal judge, and an opponent of Lowell's plan, tried to get Frankfurter appointed to the Committee on Admissions. A heated exchange of letters between Frankfurter and Lowell followed.

"I am told," Frankfurter wrote Lowell, "that you regard my views on a policy of limiting the proportion of Jewish students at Harvard as 'violent' and 'extreme.' . . ." [1]

Lowell replied: "I do not pretend to know anything about your ideas on the subject of Jewish students. I only know that the insistence with which Judge Mack has urged your appointment to the Committee gives the impression that he looks upon you as an advocate of his views. I have tried to select a committee that would not advocate anyone's views, but approach the question in a large and open-minded spirit." [2]

Frankfurter answered: ". . . I had not the slightest idea even of appearing to urge my appointment on your Committee. But you were quoted to me as regarding my views on the pending question as 'extreme' and 'violent' and I deemed it appropriate to bring this report directly to your attention.

". . . What gives me real concern about your letter," Frankfurter continued, "is its clear implication that you do not wish on your Committee anyone who shares the kind of views on this question which Judge Mack entertains. That, if I may say so, does not seem to me to be dealing with the matter 'in a large and open-minded spirit.' " [3]

Other letters were exchanged in this vein. In the end Frankfurter was not appointed to the Committee on Admissions. But neither was Lowell successful in imposing his quota system on the university.

Frankfurter and Lowell were never to make it up; personally, they were anathema to each other. Yet they had a certain respect, each for the other. Frankfurter respected Lowell's educational policies even if he abhorred his social prejudices. Lowell wrote Frankfurter when Frankfurter was appointed to the Supreme Court that while he did not expect to agree with his Court decisions from time to time, he (Lowell) was confident that these decisions would be made with integrity, uninfluenced by anything but the light of Frankfurter's conscience.[4]

Frankfurter's uninhibited participation in public controversies in the early 1920's won him a reputation beyond Boston and the law school. Among prospective students, there were two fundamental attitudes:

"He was one of the reasons I picked the Law School, in 1922," wrote one. "I had been reading pieces by him and Zechariah Chafee and Dean Pound in the *New Republic* and it was clear they were more than lawyers. . . . I thought that in the Law School one might obtain an education. . . ." [5]

On the other hand, parents warned their sons against him. W. Barton Leach, later a law school faculty member and friend of Frankfurter's, recalled his father's agitation when he decided to go to Harvard Law School: "When there you will find a professor with the ridiculous name of Felix Frankfurter," the elder Leach warned. "He is said to have a great influence with his students. You just watch out. He is a Communist, an anarchist or worse." [6]

Most students did not even meet Frankfurter until their third year. Gradually—and gratefully—he had begun to teach only advanced courses in which classes were small and the emphasis was on the individual.

In 1921 James Byrne, a leader of the New York bar and senior partner in the law firm in which Frankfurter had worked briefly following his graduation from Harvard in 1906, established the Byrne Professorship of Administrative Law; Frankfurter was appointed to the chair, which he held until his Supreme Court appointment in 1939. In 1922 his public utilities course was transferred to the third year. He also taught a seminar in federal jurisdiction—concerned with the complicated legal problems of the nation's two sets of courts, state and federal—and he worked with candidates for the Doctor of Juridical Science (SJD) graduate degree.

He did not teach constitutional law as a formal course; that was assigned to other professors. But the courses he did teach were necessarily and inextricably bound up with constitutional law and its history, so that in fact he did teach constitutional law south by southwest, and by the time he left the law school in 1939 he was recognized as one of the nation's most respected scholars of the Constitution and its interpreter, the Supreme Court.

His style of teaching had not changed since he had taught at Harvard before World War I—except that he had more personal experiences to contribute to make classes three-dimensional. He still believed, as he had in 1914—only undoubtedly more strongly—that students must be able to move freely not only among court precedents and decisions but also in history and economics and sociology. And his students read, in addition to their casebooks, the New York

Times, Congressional Record, American Political Science Review, Quarterly Journal of Economics, London *Times, Social Science Review, American Historical Review,* and *English Historical Review.*

Students who studied law under Frankfurter were of divided opinion about him. "There were no neutrals about Felix," said W. Barton Leach. "You either thought the sun rose and set down his neck; or you despised him. My guess is that the vote would have gone about two-to-one in his favor. . . ." [7]

A basic criticism was his sophistication and orientation toward the legal profession on the urbanized East Coast. "Frankfurter's always giving you Holmes. They don't make much of Holmes in Minnesota," [8] said one law school man.

Frankfurter would have denied it. He did teach Holmes, but he taught Holmes as a universal, with as much application to a small town in Minnesota as to the Supreme Court of the United States. And his favorite advice to students—and later his law clerks—was: "Go home; go back home, young man," where there was not only room but urgent demand for thoughtful, competent lawyers, however remote home was.

The major criticism of Frankfurter was his outspoken liberal stance in a silent and conservative generation. Both students and faculty frequently opposed his position on public issues.

Another criticism of Frankfurter was his reputation for showing favoritism to bright students while ignoring the more pedestrian. This was only partially valid. It was true he would not suffer fools or the questions they asked—which he ignored in class—and he was unique among the faculty for giving notice that his advanced courses were "open only to students of high standing with the consent of the instructor." But he did not automatically choose numbers one, two, three; he selected those who were most interesting to him, whatever their standings and who might even be the most difficult—those, for example, who argued with him heatedly, but showed they could think for themselves.

Frankfurter claimed he did not demand silent acquiescence, that he demanded only forthright, independent thinking solidly grounded. "For a teacher to inculcate in a student his own views is, on the whole, apt to be a disservice, for it usually means that he is a persuasive dogmatist," he wrote in 1930 to a former student. ". . . What I care about profoundly is that men should know what they think and why they think it; that they should know the forces behind their beliefs and the limitations of their knowledge, and should be capable of differentiation between first-hand views and second-hand views, between views derived from insight and views expressive of inertia. Nothing is more disheartening than the uncritical, parrot-like repetition of familiar formulas by so-called leaders of the bar; nothing . . . is more disheartening than the lack of leadership by the leaders. I do covet . . . the habit of critical inquiry and detached judgment. . . ." [9] There were many students, however, who believed Frankfurter ignored their brilliance because they disagreed with him.

Frankfurter's style of teaching, like the Frankfurterian style of friendship, was education by expectation. "Observation, generally, led me to conclude," he once wrote in a memorandum to himself, "that men will give themselves more effectively if more is expected of them. . . ." [10]

But it was not a lifeless, impersonal demand. If he expected more, he was willing to give more, and he did, unstintingly. He had a contagious effervescence—once asked if his spirits ever changed, Mrs. Frankfurter replied: "Yes. They go higher." [11]—that drew men to him. By teaching only small classes, he was able to know his students intimately, and he had a sincere interest in them. He shared their joys and their concerns, not only academic and legal, but family vicissitudes and the most trivial ailments. He was generous with understanding and compassion. He practically adopted his favorites into his own home; the very top ones were recommended for law clerkships with Justice Brandeis or Justice Holmes and later to lower court judges Augustus N. Hand, Learned Hand, and Calvert Magruder. He kept in touch long after graduation.

Frankfurter seemed to take for granted his students' capabilities. He seemed to assume they were intellectually gifted, hardworking, enthusiastic, and seized with as noble a vision of the law as he was. To hear him talk about his students, one could believe they were composites of Einstein and Moses; Frankfurter feigned shock when he discovered they were not.

Actually, he knew they were not; Frankfurter knew to the last fiber of what human cloth they were made—just as he knew intimately his own limitations. And he was quick to criticize where he or a student failed. But he wasted little time or energy worrying about either his own or his students' failures. He recognized each one's potential, demanded that he recognize it, and expected him to live up to it. He spent most of his energy on going ahead; he had no time for regrets, only time for a future teeming with possibilities.

This education by expectation worked. Students responded; they could not bear to disappoint him, who gave and asked so much. He showed them what they could be and they must be. It was intellectual midwifery at its most refined.

His influence was deep and far-reaching. Archibald MacLeish estimated he taught 4,500 men in his years at Harvard. They went into small law offices in small towns, into high-powered Wall Street firms, into town halls, state legislatures and Congress; into teaching, journalism, industry, trade unions, business, government, social work, and the judiciary. Justice Brandeis wrote in 1925: "... Given another twenty years ... [Frankfurter] will have profoundly affected American life...." [12]

Joseph Alsop is reported to have once said: "Arthur Krock is a frustrated jurist, and Justice Frankfurter is a frustrated journalist." [13] While Frankfurter was still at Harvard, however, he undoubtedly took the law more often into journalism than Krock took the New York *Times* into jurisprudence.

It is an honored academic custom for professors to write articles and books as part of professorial chores. The best of these become classics in the field. Usually they are scholarly, esoteric, and of use primarily to other members of the academic world.

Frankfurter, in contrast, seldom wrote for scholars. His writings in the 1920's and 1930's were unprofessorial and lacked any touch of the ivory tower. His writing, like his teaching, reflected the "world's business," as it explored the public issues of the day, usually controversial and immediate issues. If the style lacked gloss, it was precise, clear, and comprehensible to the laity. Passion was evident, but not so overdone as to invite doubt about his theses; his appeal was through reason to passionate conviction.

He wrote for the law journals both at Harvard and at other institutions. He lectured at other universities, and some of these lectures were published—most notably *The Commerce Clause Under Marshall, Taney and Waite* and *The Public and Its Government*. Although Frankfurter's scholarship is evident, one need not be a lawyer but only a concerned human being to grasp his essential meanings.

He also wrote articles for newspapers, frequent letters to the editor, which were in effect articles, and articles for popular magazines such as the *Nation, Fortune,* and especially the *New Republic,* of which he was for some years a trustee. Sir Norman Angell, a writer for the *New Republic* in its early days, recalled how the editorial staff—Angell, Frankfurter, editor Herbert Croly, Walter Weyl, Walter Lippmann, Alvin Johnson, Frances Hackett—would go out to the home of Willard Straight (financial backer of the magazine) on Long Island and have a weekend of "thrashing out things," talking "far into the night about the problems which were then confronting America." [14]

Then there were the annual "Frankfurter and so-and-so." Students who returned to law school after graduation to work for a doctorate (and the Brandeis clerkship which sometimes accompanied the degree) were frequently assigned to explore a particular phase of the law, with the fruits of their research usually appearing as an article in the *Harvard Law Review* or a book.

Frankfurter explained the program in a letter to a Yale law professor in 1929: ". . . Perhaps the great stimulus [to original effort in legal science] comes from the joy of publication, particularly first publication. This has been one of the chief reasons why from time to time I have associated in co-authorship with myself under-graduates and recent graduates, although the accepted canons of literary ethics would have been satisfied with a prefatory acknowledgment. In this way and through the publication of independent articles in the law reviews and in some instances in books, I think it can be fairly said that a good deal of legal talent has been enlisted on behalf of legal scholarship. . . ." [15]

One of the "ands," Adrian Fisher, described his apprenticeship for the Brandeis law clerkship: ". . . the first three and a half months of it, I worked on an article called 'The Business of the Supreme Court.' This carried the joint byline of Frankfurter and Fisher. . . . Felix was the world's most generous person in giving credit lines. . . . There's an awful lot of joking about Frankfurter and 'another' and it is probably true that in terms of the time spent on this particular article, I spent probably about four times as much as he did. On the other hand, when the article got through, I was after all one year out of law school, and he was quite an experienced professor . . . there was a good deal more Frankfurter in there than there was Fisher. . . ." [16]

Shortly after Frankfurter returned to Harvard in 1919, he began work on a scholarly and comprehensive book on the Fourteenth Amendment to the United States Constitution. Twenty years later, the research and thought interrupted by one thing after another, the book was unfinished, and he confessed that "there is nothing to show for those twenty years except the poor things in my head and a mass of largely illegible notes. . . ." [17]

Frankfurter also shot off letters in enormous quantities, offsetting his inability to be in Cambridge, Washington, and Albany at once. In his early days at Harvard, he shared a secretary with a colleague, Austin W. Scott. But Frankfurter's voluminous output made the arrangement impossible. "Whenever I went and asked her to take a letter," Scott recalled later, "she said yes, she would do it as soon as she was through with these letters she was typing for Professor Frankfurter. There are many, many things that I have been glad to share with F. F., but not a secretary. I thereupon proceeded to get a secretary of my own. . . ." [18]

He was advising Senators on the drafting of legislation and public commissions on methods and solutions to their special problems. He was consulting with Justice Department officials and advising his old friends of the National Consumers' League. He was corresponding with officers of the National Association for the Advancement of Colored People (NAACP), for whom he was a legal counsel, and the American Civil Liberties Union (ACLU), of which he was an early member.

He was briefing leaders of the bar on public issues and carrying on discussions by mail with individual lawyers. He corresponded with Supreme Court Justices, most frequently Holmes and Brandeis, but also others, notably Harlan Fiske Stone, who was said to have waited petulantly for his weekly Wednesday letter from Frankfurter containing congratulations for Monday's opinions.

Much of this enormous correspondence was neatly typed and written with all the august formality of style Frankfurter could summon. Some of it was brief notes, scribbled urgently and almost illegibly with a pen on pads of paper Frankfurter carried around with him and signed with the increasingly familiar "F. F."

In the 1920's corruption oozed from all levels of American life, from the President's Cabinet to the local bootlegger. Albert B. Fall,

President Warren G. Harding's Secretary of the Interior, is remembered, when he is remembered at all, for his starring role in the Teapot Dome scandal, in which he connived to turn government oil reserves over to private oil companies for $400,000 entered in his private bank account. Moonshining was a popular sport, as public disregard of the Eighteenth Amendment to the Constitution and the Volstead Act of 1918 implementing it—Prohibition—became widespread. Organized crime was rampant. There was violence in every headline.

On the official level, outrage took the form of a Senate investigation in 1924, spearheaded by Senator Burton K. Wheeler of Montana, of Harding's Attorney General, Harry M. Daugherty, and his "Ohio Gang." In the face of Wheeler's charges of malpractice, Daugherty was forced to resign, but not before he took his revenge by getting Wheeler indicted for some dubious dealings with a Montana client after he had been elected Senator. Daugherty's successor as Attorney General, Harlan Fiske Stone, inherited the Wheeler case, and although he was aware Wheeler had been railroaded, he believed the evidence sufficient for Wheeler to be tried in court.

Wheeler's friends and supporters organized themselves into the Wheeler Defense Committee and pressured Stone to drop the prosecution. Frankfurter, a member of the committee, wrote Stone that in the Wheeler case "the instruments of justice were resorted to for personal and partisan reasons, to obstruct or break the efforts of one who was performing a great and needed public service. I am fully aware that personal and partisan motives frequently lead to the vindication of law. The motives of complainants do not disprove wrongdoing. All I do mean to suggest is that where the circumstances are as egregiously suspicious as they are in the Wheeler indictment the administration of the law ought to be cleared of suspicion as promptly and as authoritatively as possible. . . ." [19] Stone answered politely but decisively that he did not think he should interfere. Frankfurter persisted, urging Stone to quash the indictment; Stone courteously but equally persistently refused, believing Wheeler's guilt or innocence, in view of the public nature of the case and the widespread public interest, ought to be determined in a court of law. Wheeler did in fact go to trial and was acquitted.

The public expression of outrage at the widespread crime of the 1920's made itself felt in the establishment of crime surveys. The most famous of these were the Seabury investigation in New York City in 1931 and the National Commission on Law Observance and Law Enforcement, headed by former Attorney General George W. Wickersham and popularly known as the Wickersham Commission. To the latter Frankfurter unofficially contributed personnel and advice, although he believed what was in effect President Herbert Hoover's commission was too politically motivated to survey the national crime crisis in a disinterested and scientific manner. There were also other crime surveys, and in two of these Frankfurter was officially active.

Aroused by a local shooting in which the chief justice of the municipal court was implicated and backed by the local bar association and other civic organizations, the Cleveland Foundation asked Dean Roscoe Pound and Professor Felix Frankfurter to direct a scientific study of criminal justice in Cleveland, Ohio.

Pound and Frankfurter, believing that participation in such a survey would add significant dimension to the teaching of criminal law, accepted. They commuted weekly to Cleveland, Pound going Monday through Wednesday; Frankfurter, Thursday through Saturday (to the dismay of President Lowell, who had begun to wonder if Frankfurter, questions of academic freedom aside, might not be spreading himself too thin, particularly in his academic chores).

They recruited a staff of experts—lawyers, social workers, psychologists, psychiatrists, criminologists—and surveyed firsthand the police department, courts, prisons, district attorney's office, press, medicine, and the politics interwoven through all. The survey resulted in the publication, in 1922, of *Criminal Justice in Cleveland,* a 729-page documented report of facts about law enforcement. It showed graphically the laxness of the way the law had been enforced and the politics that too often determined the enforcement. It did not, except indirectly, touch on the causes of crime. Nor did it solve the constant problem of the conflict between the necessity of power and vigilance on the part of law-enforcement agencies to control criminals and the necessity for restraints on those agencies for the protection of guaranteed liberties—a major problem Frankfurter would face later as a Justice of the Supreme Court.

In 1926, Frankfurter and a similar staff, drawn partly from the law school and partly from outside, undertook another crime survey, using Boston as its laboratory. Called the Survey of Crime and Criminal Justice, its purpose was to "trace the effect of legal control on the restraining of crime and the efficacy of the law's treatment of criminals." [20] It was undertaken "not as an agency for reform," Frankfurter wrote in one of its reports, "but as a contribution to knowledge, more particularly for the development of scientific standards and methods regarding concerns of society that heretofore had been left largely to improvisation, crude empiricism, and propaganda." Above all, he concluded, "the undertaking registered the responsibility of universities for research into these problems of human conduct and social policy." [21]

The staff intended to survey, based on guidelines laid by the Cleveland survey, the police department, district attorney's office, courts, prisons, press, juvenile delinquency, bar, the law itself—and their interlocking relationships. The study never reached fruition. Three volumes of reports—on juvenile delinquents, for which Frankfurter wrote the introduction; on criminal statistics; and on the police department—appeared in 1934. But other interests—including Frankfurter's New Deal involvement—diverted some of the staff, and the project lost its momentum. A great deal of material was left unpublished at Harvard Law School.

Nevertheless, from the data compiled in these surveys—from the sordid statistics, the arrests, deplorable prison conditions, the brutality of police, the case histories of juveniles and hardened criminals, the shameless political maneuverings of elected officials, the sensationalist motivations of the press—Frankfurter was able to enunciate and reinforce theorems he had long believed in regard to the administration of criminal justice.

The thing that stood out in all the data was the lack of adequate professionalism and the far-reaching consequences of this lack. No one knows the causes of crime, he wrote, because there is too little scientific and disinterested research into them. "We must understand," he said, "before we can remedy." [22] And before we can understand, we must discover the facts.

Understanding could not be left, as it had been, to untrained politicians, press, and the man in the street. Frankfurter prescribed a liberal dose of trained experts—schooled in the interrelated social disciplines and cooperating professionally—as one major step in solving the problems of crime and the criminal.

"The problems of crime are at least as difficult as problems of public health and hydraulic engineering," he told students at Yale in 1930. "But public health and hydraulic engineering are now a matter of course made the concern of specialists who give to their problems the devotion of a lifetime. That is the essence of professionalism—men adapted by nature for inquiries for which they are elaborately trained and which they pursue as a permanent career. . . ." Frankfurter deplored the fact that in the United States "there is no body of highly trained, capable men who are drawn to the enigmas of crime as problems to be solved, who are adequately disciplined for their exploration and who give the preoccupation of a lifetime to their solution. Broadly speaking, the directing officials are not technically trained for their work before they attain office, and the want of permanent careers through office deprives the community of capitalizing office itself as a school of training. . . ." [23] As there was no professionalism in the administration of criminal justice, there was also no professionalism in criminal research; both were requirements for dealing with problems of crime.

Frankfurter's prescription for solving the problems of crime was one he would prescribe frequently for curing ills of government. In New Deal days his actual injections of large doses of professionally trained men—the so-called happy hot dogs—was watched with humor, wonder, and not always friendly eyes.

Between 1917 and 1923 four state supreme courts upheld their minimum wage laws, and Congress passed such a law for women in the District of Columbia, a federal city administered by the Congress of the United States.

The District of Columbia minimum wage law was quickly challenged by Children's Hospital in the case which became famous as *Adkins v. Children's Hospital.* The law was upheld in the lower District of Columbia Court and then, in November, 1922, was held unconstitutional in the District of Columbia Court of Appeals. Frankfurter had compiled, in collaboration with the National Consumers' League, the traditional Brandeis brief—the impressive array of facts and experience on which the arguments were based—but the court decided against him.

The case went to the Supreme Court. Since the four to four decision on minimum wage laws in 1917, four of the Justices had been replaced by rigid conservatives. The Chief Justice was former President William Howard Taft, who was to lead the Court in the 1920's in protecting property rights by overturning a record number of social and economic statutes. In 1923 only Holmes and Brandeis remained of those who urged judicial restraint in such legislation.

In the Supreme Court, Frankfurter argued that Congress, "charged with the responsibility of safeguarding the welfare of the women and children of the District of Columbia, [had] found that alarming public evils had resulted, and threatened in increasing measure, from the widespread existence of a deficit between the essential needs for decent life and the actual earnings of large numbers of women workers of the District." In the judgment of Congress—and there had been no opposition to passage of the bill expressed in Senate and House hearings—"these conditions impaired the health of this generation of women and thereby threatened the coming generation through undernourishment, demoralizing shelter and insufficient medical care. In its immediate effects, also, financial burdens were imposed upon the District for support of charitable institutions engaged in impotent amelioration rather than prevention. . . ." Since passage of the minimum wage legislation, however, Frankfurter pointed out, "unfair depression in the wages of many women workers has been significantly reduced, without adversely affecting industry or diminishing appreciably employment for employees. . . ." [24] This legislation being in the interests of both the District of Columbia and industry, it was, concluded Frankfurter, a valid exercise of the police power.

His adversary in the courtroom argued, along the traditional lines of "liberty of contract," that no exercise of the police power justified the fixing of prices either of property or of services in a private business. "Requirement of a minimum wage, without corresponding requirement of amount of efficiency of service in return, is taking of property without just compensation, and not even for a public purpose, but for private purpose, contrary to the Fifth Amendment and the Ninth Amendment." [25] Clearly, minimum wage legislation was unconstitutional.

This time Frankfurter's 1,000-page documentary evidence in behalf of a social cause did not sway the Court, which divided five to three (again Brandeis did not participate) and held the act unconstitutional. Justice George Sutherland, who spoke for the Court, passed on the constitutionality by saying the law was invalid because it exacted from the employer "an arbitrary payment for a purpose and upon a basis having no causal connection with his business, or the contract of the work the employee engages to do." He also gave the method of argument an unexpected swipe: "We have been furnished with a large number of printed opinions approving the policy of the minimum wage, and our own reading has disclosed a large number to the contrary. These are all proper enough for the consideration of law-making bodies . . . but they reflect no legitimate light upon the question of [the law's] validity."

Holmes, as expected, dissented: "I confess that I do not understand the principle on which the power to fix a minimum wage for the wages of women can be denied by those who admit the power to fix a maximum for their hours of work . . ." [26] he wrote, referring to the Court's decision in 1908 to allow Oregon to legislate maximum hours.

Chief Justice Taft, strangely enough, turned from his usual conservative stance to dissent with Holmes and Edward T. Sanford, but he dissented separately from Holmes, and Holmes wrote to Harold Laski: ". . . the C.J. and Sanford seemed to think I said something dangerous or too broad, so they dissented separately. . . . I think that what I said was plain common sense. It was intended . . . to dethrone Liberty of Contract from its ascendancy in the Liberty business. . . ." [27]

"Liberty of Contract" was hardly dethroned by Holmes' dissent. The Court's decision served only to inhibit further efforts to pass minimum wage legislation and other related social measures for the next decade.

While minimum wage efforts languished, Frankfurter advised the National Consumers' League on strategy for abolishing child labor, another area in which "labor" was without power. A law excluding the products of child labor from interstate commerce had been passed by Congress in 1916 but had been declared unconstitutional, as was a second child labor law passed in 1918 assessing factories employing children under fourteen with special taxes. A child-labor amendment to the Constitution in 1924 failed of ratification.

Frankfurter was suspicious of such national legislation. It created, he believed, more problems than it solved: unnecessary political controversy and almost unmanageable litigation. Although the existing situation with regard to child labor was "among the blackest spots in our national life," [28] legislation national in scope was not the way to deal with it.

Proposed constitutional amendments and possibilities for federal laws came to Frankfurter from those who were concerned with the problem. He vetoed them all. The solution belonged not to the national government, but to the local level of government.

"Of course," he had written in the *New Republic* in 1922, "child labor is of national concern, and some benefits will accrue from national action. But this is true of many other fields which we have not turned over to Washington, because such concentration would be self-defeating in its execution and make for a corresponding paralysis of local responsibility." [29]

The effective way to deal with the problem, he said, was by state law. Through a definite and determined program of enlightening the public, of informing people of the evils of child labor, the state legislatures could be pressured into passing laws prohibiting the exploitation of children, and in time, political power, at the lowest level but where it was most potent, could get child labor laws written into the statute books of every state in the union. It was no more and no less than as a Supreme Court Justice, Frankfurter was to urge the people and the states to do. Here was the essence of democracy. It was not in amendments to the Constitution, nor did it lie in the Supreme Court, the most undemocratic feature of American democracy. Political power lay ultimately with the people, and he trusted them in 1922, just as he trusted them in 1952 and 1962.

After the ill-fated New York gubernatorial campaign of 1910, in which he had worked with Henry Stimson, Frankfurter never again involved himself so intimately in election contests. He did not, however, renounce all political activity. He held passionate convictions and, he believed, a responsibility to speak them, which he did, with force, when a candidate or an issue provoked him.

Such a time was 1924; such an issue was Robert M. La Follette; such an issue, as Frankfurter saw it, was progress or the status quo.

La Follette, nominally a Republican, had beaten Wisconsin's regular Republican machine in 1900 to become governor. With such achievements in the statehouse as the first modern income tax law and the first modern labor legislation, including an effective workmen's compensation law, he had turned his home state into a model of progressivism, then had gone to the United States Senate, where he championed the public welfare. At the Progressive convention in July, 1924, La Follette had won by acclamation the Progressives' nomination for President of the United States.

He ran against Democrat John W. Davis, prominent lawyer and former president of the American Bar Association, and Republican Calvin Coolidge, who had succeeded the late President Harding in 1923. Senator Burton K. Wheeler had nicknamed the pair of conservative candidates the Gold Dust Twins.

Frankfurter freely admitted he did not support all the planks in the La Follette platform. What he did believe in was La Follette's integrity and his general political direction toward government correction of social and economic evils—very much the same direction he had observed and liked in Theodore Roosevelt.

At stake, Frankfurter was convinced, was the future of the nation. "... The immediate results of the 1924 election do not appear very important," he wrote to a friend. "The directions which we further or retard for 1944 are tremendously important. Coolidge and Davis have nothing to offer for 1944; they have no dreams, no 'pictures in their heads' ... except things substantially as is. The forces that are struggling and groping behind La Follette are, at least, struggling and groping for a dream, for a different look of things in 1944. ..." [30]

And so he went on the stump for his candidate, debating and making speeches publicly, issuing statements to newspapers, and writing letters to their editors. He found forums in such unrelated publications as the *New Republic* and the *Harvard Crimson*. Privately he carried on a correspondence with friends, trenchantly expounding his reasons for supporting La Follette.

La Follette lost—running a poor third. America in 1924 was not ready to consider "a different look of things in 1944." The nation seemed prosperous so long as one did not search out the poverty behind the sleek veneer, and prosperous it wanted to remain—which it did, at least on the surface, under President Calvin Coolidge.

[3]

Henry Stimson's earlier fears of criticism of Frankfurter over after-dinner brandy were dwarfed by the national attention Frankfurter drew, in 1927, for his espousal of the most unpopular cause of them all: that of the convicted murderers Nicola Sacco and Bartolomeo Vanzetti. The inevitability of his involvement was set in motion at his birth in Vienna and nurtured by industry's reign of terror during World War I; his findings concerning the lawless vigilantes of Bisbee, Arizona, and his despair at the case of Tom Mooney; the lawless Red Raids of 1920 instigated by the nation's highest law-enforcement officer; and above all, his professional indignation as an educator of youth.

The case began simply. On the afternoon of April 15, 1920, the paymaster of a shoe factory in South Braintree, Massachusetts, and his guard were robbed of their payroll, then killed by two gunmen, who escaped in a car. The following day the police discovered what they believed was the getaway car in a garage for repairs. Assuming that whoever called for the vehicle were the murderers, they arrested, on May 5, 1920, Nicola Sacco, a shoe factory employee, and Bartolomeo Vanzetti, a fish peddler from Plymouth, after they appeared at the garage to reclaim the car. Neither man could substantiate his whereabouts on the afternoon of April 15, and the pair were charged with the shoe factory murders.

Both defendants were notorious Reds, associates of leading radicals, and draft dodgers. For some time they had been under surveillance by Department of Justice agents.

The time was that immediately following the Red Raids of late 1919 and early 1920. Public opinion in Boston and surrounding towns largely supported the raids because of a high percentage of foreign labor employed by local industries which had long been plagued by labor troubles.

On September 14, 1920, Sacco and Vanzetti were indicted. On May 31, 1921, they were put on trial in the county courthouse at Dedham, Norfolk County, Massachusetts. The judge was Webster

Thayer of Worcester, who had solicited the case with the intention of convicting two known anarchists.[1] The jury was made up of native New Englanders. The district attorney was Fred Katzmann, who, Frankfurter later wrote, "systematically played on the feelings of the jury by exploiting the unpatriotic and despised beliefs of Sacco and Vanzetti. . . ." The chief defense counsel was Fred H. Moore, a Westerner, a professional defender of radicals, and, as such, anathema to Judge Thayer. Frankfurter later wrote that "outside the courtroom the Red hysteria was rampant; it was allowed to dominate within." [2]

After a seven-week trial, in which the testimony was "a mass of conflicting evidence," Sacco and Vanzetti were found guilty of murder in the first degree. Applications for a new trial were made and denied. The case went before the Supreme Judicial Court of Massachusetts, whose scope in reviewing convictions was limited to reviewing, in effect, the conduct of the trial judge. The issue before the high court was not the guilt or innocence of the defendants, but this question: Had Judge Thayer observed "the standards of Anglo-American justice." [3] In a sixty-page opinion, the Supreme Judicial Court decided, on May 12, 1926, that Judge Thayer had so observed them; it found "no error" in his rulings and so could not, "as a matter of law," [4] reverse the convictions. In the meantime, the defense had gathered new evidence that it believed pointed to a notorious Morelli gang as the perpetrators of the Braintree crime. On the basis of the new evidence, a new trial for Sacco and Vanzetti was sought. Again Judge Thayer denied the application, and again the case went before the Supreme Judicial Court.

While the case was before the Supreme Judicial Court for the second time, an article called "The Case of Sacco and Vanzetti" appeared in the then-conservative *Atlantic Monthly* magazine. It charged Judge Thayer with irregularities and summarized the entire trial proceedings as legal lynchings. The article was written by Professor Felix Frankfurter of the Harvard Law School, and it stirred up passions at Harvard, in Boston, and throughout the nation. Frankfurter expanded the controversial article into a book, *The Case of Sacco and Vanzetti,* and in some circles Frankfurter became as much a *cause célèbre* as the case itself.

Frankfurter was in London at a Zionist meeting when the crime took place. He did not follow the case as reported in the Boston papers when he returned, although he later said his wife pestered him for his opinion. Not until 1923, when a prominent member of the Boston Bar with impeccable New England credentials, William G. Thompson, who in time was to experience a good deal of animosity from his friends for his part in the case, entered the case for the defense, was Frankfurter brought up sharp. He knew and respected Thompson, and in addition, the basis of Thompson's motion for a new trial was even more startling. He had filed an affidavit sworn by one of the prosecution's ballistics experts, on whose testimony a major point of the convictions hung, that the district attorney had deliberately formulated his questions to this ballistics expert in order to mislead the jury, and the ballistics expert, with foreknowledge, had cooperated.

Frankfurter began to study the thousands of pages already in the case record. In the spring of 1926 he was asked by Herbert Croly, editor of the *New Republic,* either to write something about the case for the journal or to find someone who would. Frankfurter asked a young Commonwealth Fellow from London, Sylvester G. Gates, to whom he was adviser, to write the piece. Gates studied the record and wrote an article which appeared anonymously in the *New Republic* of June 9, 1926. Sometime later the *Atlantic Monthly,* whose editor, Ellery Sedgwick, was a friend of Frankfurter's, invited Frankfurter to do an article about the Sacco-Vanzetti case. Frankfurter accepted and asked Gates "to do the donkey work." [5] He chose Gates not only because of his confidence in Gates' ability, but also because as an Englishman, soon to return to England, Gates would not be "involved in the contemporaneous or future emotional conflicts and difficulties to which such a controversy inevitably gives rise. . . ." [6]

Gates wrote the first draft. Frankfurter edited it, changing it in places. It appeared in March, 1927, causing a national sensation.

In the article and his subsequent book, Frankfurter charged that "the case against Sacco and Vanzetti for murder was part of a collusive effort between the District Attorney and agents of the Department of Justice to rid the country of these two Italians because of their Red activities" [7]; that by "systematic exploitation of the defendants' alien blood, their imperfect knowledge of English, their unpopular social views, and their opposition to war, the District Attorney invoked against them a riot of political passion and patriotic sentiment; and the trial judge connived—one had almost written, cooperated—in the process" [8]; that Judge Thayer's charge to the jury gave a "distorted perspective" [9] of the case by giving more weight to the testimony of the prosecution than to that of the defense. In defense of the pair, Frankfurter declared that witnesses for Sacco and Vanzetti had been "slightly more numerous" and "at least as well circumstanced" [10]; that they had conclusively established that Sacco had been in Boston on April 15, the day of the murder, and that Vanzetti had been peddling fish in Plymouth the same day; and that the identification of the two as the murderers, which was the only issue in question, was never conclusively proved by the prosecution.

Frankfurter wrote of the applications for a new trial. The first had been based on exceptions to Thayer's rulings at the original trial; then requests for a new trial were built on new evidence discovered by the defense, including evidence that the crime had been committed by the Morelli gang from Providence, Rhode Island, and including the affidavit sworn to by the ballistics expert that he and the district attorney had cooperated in misleading the jury.

Frankfurter charged that Thayer had discharged the applications in a cavalier manner. "Certainly in modern times Judge Thayer's opinion stands unmatched, happily, for discrepancies between what the record discloses and what the opinion conveys. His 25,000-word document cannot accurately be described otherwise than a farrago of misquotations, misrepresentations, suppressions, and mutilations. The disinterested observer could not possibly derive from it a true knowledge of the new evidence that was submitted to him as the basis for a new trial. . . ." [11] Rarely had a judge been so criticized.

The article did not defend the men or the anarchistic causes they sympathized with any more than the President's Mediation Commission report had defended Tom Mooney. Frankfurter never publicly commented on the guilt or innocence of Sacco and Vanzetti, although privately he had said he believed they were innocent.[12] The article was a plea that the sacred instrument of the law be used not perversely, but only to the ends of justice. The article was a plea for this gross miscarriage of justice—this unclean thing, a stain on the good name of Massachusetts, above all a blot on the holy of holies, the law—to be corrected while there was still time.

When the article appeared, the wrath of Harvard, Boston, and an indignant legal profession descended on Frankfurter.

There were efforts at Harvard to undermine Frankfurter's position on the faculty. Outraged because the article had appeared while the case was before the Supreme Judicial Court, the Board of Overseers met. A. Lawrence Lowell, whose later report gave final approval to Sacco's and Vanzetti's executions, did in fact stand behind Frankfurter. Would you have wanted, Lowell demanded, Frankfurter to wait in expressing his views until the men were dead?

There were others on the faculty of the law school who stood behind Frankfurter. Joseph Henry Beale, whose student Frankfurter had been and who remained a longtime friend, wrote to Frankfurter at the height of the controversy: "... I know what a strain you have been under since doing your duty as you saw it, and while I saw otherwise, believe me I have appreciated your point of view and have rejoiced in your brave way of speaking out. I had occasion in Washington to call down some of the grouchers and I assure you I did it with some effect, because at least one man was inspired to repentance by what I said." [13]

Not the least of the causes for unrest among the powers at the school was the money Frankfurter was believed to be costing it in alumni contributions. Harvard Law School was in the midst of an endowment campaign, and prominent graduates were refusing to contribute as long as such a radical professor was a member of the faculty. Prominent Boston lawyers wrote him that he ought to keep himself—and Harvard—out of the limelight in such unfortunate situations and that his efforts on behalf of the two convicted anarchists were harmful to the school.

Frankfurter replied: "... This school does not exist for the collection of money. This school exists for the perpetuation of certain professional and ethical ideals and the work of each of us on the Faculty is to be judged by our devotion to these professional and ethical ideals and not in the slightest by the influence which we have either in attracting or discouraging money to the exchequer. I refuse to believe ... that the School of James Barr Ames has been turned over to the money changers." [14] To another critic he wrote that he had spoken out on the Sacco-Vanzetti case "with complete indifference to its bearing on the Endowment Fund," and if he had it to do over again, he would do exactly as he had "with equal indifference." [15] In point of fact, there were indications that Frankfurter's outspokenness had brought in money, but whether he helped or harmed the fund in terms of dollars and cents could never be computed accurately.

Championing the rights of two Italian laborers who espoused beliefs in ugly philosophies gave expression to hostilities long pent up in the city of Boston, where Frankfurter's position was at best tenuous.

Holmes had written to the English jurist Sir Frederick Pollock in April, 1919, even before Frankfurter had returned to Harvard: "... There is also a prejudice against Frankfurter; I think partly because he ... is a Jew. ... Boston is nothing if not critical. ..." [16] Harold Laski, when he was teaching at Harvard, had found an effort in Boston to make Frankfurter's position untenable.

On the other hand, some of Boston's leaders "lionized" Frankfurter. "... He had a terrific reputation when he came to the Harvard Law School," said Herbert B. Ehrmann, a former student of Frankfurter's and a colleague on previous crime surveys with Frankfurter, whom Frankfurter had recruited to help defend Sacco and Vanzetti during the final stages of the legal proceedings, "and he was a warm, winsome individual, far brighter than most people, and sensitive enough not to rub it in ... except in cases where he thought that people had enough of a background to know what is right and what is wrong." [17]

Frankfurter's involvement with the Sacco-Vanzetti case, however, gave those who wanted it a chance to vent their bluestocking fury. Not surprisingly, it was not the oldest Yankee population of Boston that was most vociferous. Secure in its position, this deep-rooted Yankee group felt no threat from either the two miserable laborers charged with the crime or the Harvard professor who fought for them. In fact, a number of the old Brahmins were courageous enough to differ publicly with the currents of Boston opinion in the case—most notably William G. Thompson and Arthur D. Hill, who also defended Sacco and Vanzetti in the later stages.

The most voluble high feelings against Frankfurter came from the upper-middle-class Yankees, those just a rung or two from the top of the social and economic ladder, those who aspired to the top rung and feared to counter outraged public opinion lest they fail to realize their aspirations. They lumped Frankfurter with Thompson and Hill in their ostracism, even though Frankfurter was never officially associated with the defense counsel or the Sacco-Vanzetti Defense Committee.

Although Frankfurter had turned over the royalties from his Sacco and Vanzetti book to the defense committee, slanderous rumors ran through the statehouse that he had been on the secret payroll of the Sacco-Vanzetti Defense Committee and had been paid a sum of money for stirring up the whole affair. Mrs. Frankfurter, whose doctor had advised some gentle exercise for her, was blackballed when she tried to join a golf club.

To all this Frankfurter had two answers: "... As to the 'present unfavorable feelings' about me, well, one can't worry about things like that or else one's life would become a polyp. ..." [18] And "... I don't count in the issues raised by the Sacco-Vanzetti case, and up here, though the foulest and meanest slanders have been uttered of me even by people from whom one might expect responsibility of speech, I have consistently refused to make defense or otherwise divert attention from the central issue." [19]

Vindictiveness was no surprise to Frankfurter, who had never felt comfortable in Boston. In 1931, he wrote Arthur M. Schlesinger, Sr.: "... you now know how uncongenial to me is the spiritual soil here. It is fundamentally an arid soil—hostile to variety and color, to richness and espirit. And so a Holmes is an exotic and a Coolidge its natural symbol and glory. ... The civilization here is thin and self-defensive. ..." [20]

Whatever Frankfurter's reaction to the "slings and arrows" of Yankee critics, there is no question he was hurt by the riot of criticism from the legal community that was leveled at him for his article and book. These had been the very intellects he had been trying to reach, the exemplars of the community into which his students would be graduated.

The legal men on the Board of Overseers had questioned Frankfurter's publishing while the case was *sub judice*. A book review by Andrew R. Sherriff in the December, 1927, *Illinois Law Review* leveled the same criticism: "... The publication was a vicious breach of judicial prerogative, and might deservedly have won for both the author and the publishers a term in jail for contempt, had the court been so disposed. ..." The law review article also pointed out other failings, saying that Frankfurter had weighted his case for the defense and that the general publication of the book was "dangerous in the hands of the public, and therefore, under the circumstances, offensive to the legal profession ..." and concluded that the book "establishes a memorable instance of indiscretion, of misapplied talent and misdirected zeal, of academic naivety [*sic*]. . . ."

Frankfurter rebutted the charges in the same issue of the *Illinois Law Review*. He wrote the article and the book, he said, "as a matter of history, and in order to educate public understanding of the issues of the case with a view to executive relief if appeal to the courts should fail." He had not written it to influence the Supreme Judicial Court.

It was certainly true that there was an appeal pending. But it was not true, Frankfurter explained, that he had spoken "out of turn," the crux of the criticism against the article and book. ". . . Since two lives were at stake, the truth of what I wrote was much more important than a professional convention."

Frankfurter was prepared to submit to "any test of professional propriety." Neither the book nor the article published in the *Atlantic Monthly* was timed "to reach the Supreme Judicial Court while the appeal was pending from Judge Thayer's denial of a new trial. The *Atlantic Monthly* article was purposely delayed for a month after the case had been submitted to that Court. There was no possible way of knowing when the Court would decide the case, except that there was every reason for believing that, under the circumstances, the appeal would be disposed of promptly. Thus, the *Atlantic Monthly* article might well have appeared after the Supreme Judicial Court's decision. The book in fact came out only a day or two before the decision. Not only was my writing, then, not timed to reach the Court while the case was pending; it was expected that the Court would have disposed of the case before its appearance."

Furthermore, Frankfurter argued, he knew of "no canon of legal etiquette or of common sense that counsels against a disinterested and scientific discussion of a case within limits of fair comment simply because it happens to be pending in an appellate case. The practice of our profession is all the other way." Legal journals as a matter of practice discuss the decisions of the lower courts while appeals are pending, he declared.

He added that he heard no such criticism of the Worcester County Bar Association, which, when the appeal was pending, issued a formal resolution endorsing Judge Thayer. "It cannot be right," Frankfurter wrote, "for an influential bar association to approve of a judge whose conduct is under criticism, but not right for a disinterested law teacher to analyze the work of such a judge in the light of the record."

In late March, 1927, shortly after Frankfurter's article had appeared in the *Atlantic Monthly,* Dean John Henry Wigmore, of the Northwestern University Law School and an internationally respected authority on the law of evidence, privately told colleagues at a dinner in Chicago that he would make a reply to Frankfurter's *Atlantic Monthly* article. "Sacco and Vanzetti are dangerous to society," he is reported to have said. He intended to write an article showing up the character of the men and the influences behind them and to try to arouse public opinion to an understanding of the radical and subversive ideas represented by the men.

A colleague replied: "If you do that, you will be playing directly into Frankfurter's hands and proving his case for that is what he is claiming—that these men are sought to be executed because they are 'Reds' and not because they are murderers."

Wigmore answered: "Well, I am sure the facts are not as Frankfurter says they are. I will write Judge Thayer and find out what the facts really are." [21]

On April 11, 1927, the New York *Times* published an interview with Judge Thayer, given the day after Thayer had pronounced the death sentence on Sacco and Vanzetti. The interview read, in part: "In reference to the articles published by Professor Frankenstein [*sic*] of Harvard in the Atlantic Monthly, I would say that these will be answered by one of the best authorities in the United States at the proper time."

Two weeks later, the Boston *Transcript* published Dean Wigmore's article, which charged Frankfurter with libel against the honor of Massachusetts courts and defended the jury, judge, and prosecution. "An agitation against the fairness of the trial and the justice of the verdict was started among various alien Communist circles," Wigmore wrote, "and this was extended to the general public by the publication in the March, 1927, *Atlantic Monthly* of a fourteen-page exposition of the case by a prominent pundit in a leading law school." [22]

Frankfurter summoned his young aide, Gates, and announced the only thing to do: "We must sit down because this must be answered immediately. We must do it tonight and we must get it in the paper tomorrow morning." [23] Frankfurter got in touch with Frank Buxton, a friend and the editor of the Boston *Herald,* and asked if he could answer Wigmore's charges in the next morning's edition. Frankfurter and Gates sat down with wet towels over their heads, went through each of Wigmore's allegations, and dictated answers to them.

In the April 26, 1927, edition of the Boston *Herald,* Frankfurter charged that Wigmore's article "consists of a series of allegations based presumably upon the official record of the court proceedings. I say without fear of contradiction that Dean Wigmore could not have read the record; could not have read with care the opinion of Judge Thayer, on which his own article is based; could not even have examined my little book, to which he refers as a longer pamphlet publication of my *Atlantic* article."

About two weeks later, on May 10, 1927, Wigmore published a new list of charges against Frankfurter in the Boston *Transcript.* Again Frankfurter refuted them the next day.

The case of Sacco and Vanzetti dragged on through the spring and summer of 1927. Only a few days after the publication of Frankfurter's *Atlantic Monthly* article, the Supreme Judicial Court denied the application of the defense for a new trial.

On April 9, 1927, in the Dedham Court House, Judge Thayer pronounced the death sentence on Sacco and Vanzetti. Vanzetti's final eloquent statement is remembered as a classic. For forty-six minutes the interest of every person in the crowded courtroom was directed to the convicted man, who, standing erect in the prisoner's cage beside Sacco, his eyes flashing as he focused them on the judge, declared himself and Sacco the victims of prejudice. His statement was ungrammatical, the words of an uneducated man. What he said articulated the highest aspirations of man. "If it had not been for these thing," he said, "I might have live out my life talking at street corners to scorning men. I might have die, unmarked, unknown, a failure. Now we are not a failure. This is our career and our triumph. Never in our full live could we hope to do such work for tolerance, for joostice, for man's onderstanding of man as now we do by accident. Our words—our lives—our pains—nothing! The taking of our lives—lives of a good shoemaker and a poor fish-peddler—all! That last moment belongs to us—that agony is our triumph."

Sometime later Marion Frankfurter, who later coedited *The Letters of Sacco and Vanzetti* with Gardner Jackson, wrote to Vanzetti: ". . . I did not go to Dedham that day. I did not think I could bear

Felix Frankfurter as Harvard Law School student, 1906–9.

Courtesy of Malcolm A. Hoffmann

United States Attorney's Office, April 3, 1909.

Courtesy of David M. Dorsen

Standing (left to right): Wolcott H. Pitkin, Jr.; Goldthwaite H. Dorr; Felix Frankfurter; Thomas D. Thacher; Harold S. Deming; Emory R. Buckner; Daniel D. Walton; Hugh Govern, Jr.; Robert P. Stephenson; Francis W. Bird.
Seated (left to right): Winfred T. Dennison; William S. Ball; Henry L. Stimson; Henry A. Wise; D. Frank Lloyd; J. Osgood Nichols; John W. H. Crim.

Library of Congress

Justice Oliver Wendell Holmes, Jr., 1930.

Library of Congress

Justice Louis Dembitz Brandeis.

Henry Lewis Stimson, 1944.

U. S. Army

Courtesy of Helen Denman

Felix and Marion Frankfurter in the garden of their home on Brattle Street, Cambridge. Photo taken on day of Frankfurter's nomination to the Supreme Court of the United States.

Wide World Photos

Trial of Tom Mooney. W. Bourke Cockran, New York attorney (standing), who at this time (1917) was acting as chief counsel for the defense, glances at a section of metal which Tom Mooney is holding. Three members of the jury at right.

Harvard Law School Faculty, May, 1927. 1. Roscoe Pound, dean 2. Eldon R. James 3. John H. Maguire 4. Edward H. Warren 5. Samuel Williston 6. Morton C. Campbell 7. Francis H. Bohlen 8. Guy H. Holliday 9. Francis B. Sayre 10. Edmund M. Morgan 11. Joseph H. Beale 12. A. Pearce Higgins 13. James A. MacLachlan 14. Austin Wakeman Scott 15. Theodore F. T. Plucknett 16. Thomas Reed Powell 17. Calvert Magruder 18. William E. McCurdy 19. James M. Landis 20. Felix Frankfurter 21. Sayre Macneil. On leave, Zechariah Chafee, Jr.

Wide World Photos

Sacco and Vanzetti, front center, handcuffed together, 1927.

to be there. But when my husband came home and told me what had happened, I knew I had missed a rare experience. He had been lifted up by what he saw and heard there, through you and through Mr. Sacco; and I was lifted up and sustained when he told me about it. Ever since then the pain and bitterness of spirit I felt that such things could be, have been relieved, because I said to myself: 'If these men can have such composure, such dignity and beauty of spirit, then I must strive for calm.'

"That is what you and Mr. Sacco do for us. That is what you give to us—a sense of beauty of spirit that abides above the bitterness and ignorance and confusion that give us so much pain. And for this you have our gratitude always." [24]

Following the death sentence on Sacco and Vanzetti, petitions and letters had poured into the Boston State House addressed to the governor, Alvan T. Fuller. To quell the uproar which had become national in scope, Fuller appointed a three-man Advisory Committee, headed by A. Lawrence Lowell, to review the case and determine the necessity for a new trial.

While the defense worked on last-minute appeals, the Advisory Committee held long hearings. Early in the proceedings, the defense attorneys, Thompson and Herbert Ehrmann, heard reports that members of the Advisory Committee had already decided against the two defendants. Thompson and Ehrmann decided to withdraw from the case "so as not to lend an air of fairness to a farce." [25]

Frankfurter kept them at their jobs, pleading with them not to give up, arguing that their withdrawal would look as if they had lost faith. In a letter to Ehrmann he wrote: "No matter how dark the outlook you must, of course, continue the effort with unabated energy. . . . You cannot possibly know either what is in Lowell's mind or what the Governor may finally decide upon. . . . I . . . know that Mr. Lowell has a habit of changing his mind and his interim decisions are not final decisions, and certainly the same thing, from all accounts, is true of the Governor. . . . I cannot believe that they are ruthlessly determined to have these men go to the chair. . . . If the Governor were determined on their execution, he wouldn't have to go through the elaborate process which he is now pursuing. So cudgel your brains for effective roads to his mind. . . ."

And then Frankfurter's final plea: "You are acting in the most appealing cause that can possibly ever enlist a lawyer's mind and soul. The kind of fight in which you are engaged is literally never lost, no matter what the immediate outcome, for you are vindicating the eternal interest of right and justice. . . ." [26]

At 11:30 P.M., on August 3, Governor Fuller announced the findings of the Advisory Committee: There was no reason to grant a new trial. Sacco and Vanzetti were scheduled to die on August 23, and the governor would grant no reprieve.

Legal scholars who later analyzed the report found that parts of it were illogical and that testimony favorable to the defendants had been suppressed. An explanation for Lowell's conclusions in the report came from one of his best friends, John F. Cabot. Lowell, whose educational policies were invariably above reproach and who was one of Harvard's great presidents, Cabot said, was "incapable of seeing that two wops could be right and the Yankee judiciary could be wrong." [27]

Frankfurter was shocked at the Lowell report. When he had heard Judge Thayer's death sentence, he had said only that one couldn't blame Thayer too much; he was only a poor miserable uneducated minor judge. Lowell, however, intellectually gifted and in a position of responsibility, Frankfurter believed ought to have known better.

From that point on, Frankfurter maintained a public silence. Urged by Thompson to make a statement on the report, he said: ". . . So far as I am concerned (and this includes my wife) I am utterly free and have nothing to fear from a public comment on the Advisory Committee's report, and I am most keen to make such an analysis. But the essential thing for all of us, of course, is to do everything that will further the cause of two men we believe to be innocent, and to do nothing that will hamper that cause. The simple fact is that for me publicly now to intervene in this matter would hurt the cause of the men and not help them. I have aroused intense personal hostility among those whose good will is now essential and the interjection of my personality would further harden the situation against Sacco and Vanzetti. To a considerable extent I was on trial and the Lowell report is in part a report against me, although not a single fact in my book is controverted by that report. Therefore . . . my role for the present is silence. . . ." [28]

Last-minute appeals of the defense failed. "About midnight on August 22, 1927, the hour set for the executions," as the incident was later described in the *New Yorker*, "Frankfurter and his wife—who had helped him on the case and waited with him in his office for news of Fuller's decision—were worn by overwork and suspense. Unable to sit still, they set to walking aimlessly around the dark streets of Beacon Hill, accompanied by a friend. Suddenly a radio blared: 'Sacco gone, Vanzetti going.' Mrs. Frankfurter collapsed and was caught by two men. Mr. Frankfurter said nothing." [29] His capacity for indignation was at last exhausted.

Five months later, when the numbness had worn off, Frankfurter wrote to a friend: ". . . I am saddened and distressed that such things can be, but not too surprised. I have read a little history and had some personal contact with the forces of fear and hate operating against outcast people and outcast opinion. I think I can honestly say that the sadness of it all is very impersonal because the issues of the whole affair transcend individuals. Not that specific individuals are not responsible for what I regard a terrible miscarriage of justice, but even those individuals are expressions of deep psychological and social forces. . . ." [30] Civilization had failed.

Herbert Ehrmann recalled a poignant moment in later years when one of the prosecutors of Sacco and Vanzetti had become a justice of the Supreme Judicial Court of Massachusetts. The former assistant district attorney, now judge, called the former defense counsel for Sacco and Vanzetti into his chambers following a session in court. He said, "I sent for you because I know that you were sincere in believing that Sacco and Vanzetti were innocent. I want you to give me credit for the same sincerity in believing that they were guilty." [31]

Frankfurter had always intended to write another book on Sacco and Vanzetti, although he was never able to set aside the time. It would have been a study of the "psychological forces whereby the most influential citizens of Boston, with rare exception, failed to see that the great way to vindicate the greatness of the Puritan tradition was to show that 'a good shoemaker and a poor fish-peddler' were not real threats to the security of the Commonwealth—and that it shows confidence in a system of criminal justice to acknowledge that it has its own means of correcting the inevitable fallibilities of every human system. . . ." [32]

Had Sacco and Vanzetti had a fair trial? Had their case come before another judge besides Webster Thayer, would it have been decided differently? The Massachusetts Supreme Judicial Court emphatically exonerated Thayer of any judicial indiscretions. Herbert

Ehrmann illustrated with a story about a trial lawyer expounding the law to a judge.

"That is not the law, sir," the judge thundered.

"Begging your honor's pardon, it was the law until your honor spoke," the lawyer replied.

"What Thayer did," said Ehrmann later, went "to the uttermost limits of what was called judicial discretion, and I would have said that it went beyond the limits of judicial discretion, until the Supreme Judicial Court spoke and said it hadn't." [33]

Vilification of Frankfurter did not end with the death of Sacco and Vanzetti. It continued for some years, as the specter of Communism continued to stimulate the fears of the comfortable. Once Sacco and Vanzetti were executed, their cause was ruthlessly diverted and exploited by Communist propaganda, and in the minds of many Americans, their cause receded into just one more Communist lie. Consequently, Frankfurter's name became associated with the propaganda, instead of with the crusade for justice he had led, and he became identified as at least a co-conspirator.

[4]

With the summer of 1928 came a Presidential campaign: Republican Herbert Hoover against the Democratic governor of New York, Alfred E. Smith. Once again, Frankfurter joined in, at least peripherally, making speeches for and informally advising the campaign organization of Al Smith. Frankfurter hoped Smith could oust the Republicans, who had run the national government for eight years and who, Frankfurter believed, were responsible for corruption on all levels and for backward-looking social and economic policies. But more than that, Frankfurter was *for* Smith, who, derby and all, Frankfurter believed, had demonstrated in Albany that he was a statesman personally and a progressive politically.

Smith lost; Hoover went to the White House to face in the following year the greatest depression the nation had ever experienced.

In New York State, however, Frankfurter found some compensation for the loss and a candidate on whom to fasten future hopes. Franklin Roosevelt, although he never again walked without assistance, had fought his way back to physical and political health after his bout with polio and won the governorship of New York, making good the third of his boasts to his fellow lawyers at Carter, Ledyard and Milburn in 1907 and becoming a leading contender for the Democratic Presidential nomination in 1932.

The casual acquaintance between Roosevelt and Frankfurter, which had ripened during World War I into a close working relationship, further developed during Roosevelt's governorship into warm friendship, both personal and public.

As governor of New York, Roosevelt ruled a microcosm of the nation. The basic issue of government was identical: Who would control the nation's resources—its utilities, its power, its money? Would private finance arrogantly continue its accumulation of wealth at the expense of the public? Or could the state's—and later the nation's—resources be used for the benefit of society as a whole? How could this public supremacy, which Roosevelt championed even more strongly than his cousin Theodore had, best be achieved?

Frankfurter, who had been concerned with this problem in the public positions he had held and as a teacher at Harvard Law School, laid his legal and technical expertise at Roosevelt's disposal during Roosevelt's two terms as governor of New York (1929–31; 1931–33). The two men were in frequent touch by phone and letter. Frankfurter made occasional trips to Albany and Hyde Park, Roosevelt's home on the Hudson.

Roosevelt urged Frankfurter to come into his administration officially, but Frankfurter declined, as he was to decline later during Roosevelt's Presidency. He would plead the burden of his duties at Harvard or previous commitments; more likely he wanted to maintain his own independence, believing then, as he later believed, that he could be more effective outside the administration. Then, from his storehouse of acquaintances in public, legal, and academic life, Frankfurter would recommend a substitute.

During Roosevelt's governorship, Frankfurter was helpful, but not to the exclusion of Roosevelt's other advisers, nor was his advice always acted on.

Frankfurter gave of his personal charm as unstintingly as he gave of his legal knowledge. Temperamentally demonstrative, Frankfurter, during these early years of flowering friendship with Roosevelt, heaped praise on Roosevelt, congratulating him for his courage here, applauding his legislative program there, inscribing copies of his books to Roosevelt in inordinately affectionate terms: all acts which Frankfurter later repeated during Roosevelt's Presidency.

If some of these letters have a contrived ring, still Frankfurter was sincere. He had found in Roosevelt a man who approached government in the old progressive style, a man who desperately wanted to preserve the American system but to regulate it for the good of the nation as a whole. Roosevelt had bitter fights on his hands, particularly in the field of regulating public power and utilities. Frankfurter was keenly cognizant of them and understood the kind of courage it required for a political leader to take on entrenched interests. He also understood Roosevelt the man and the isolation of the office he occupied. He was therefore extravagant in his encouragement and praise, and Roosevelt made it abundantly clear that he enjoyed—in fact, needed—Frankfurter's applause. It was government by expectation.

In 1890 the Congress of the United States had passed a law which became known as the Sherman Antitrust Act. Its intention was to curb trusts and the monopoly of capital which had characterized the post-Civil War period of rapid industrial expansion. This act announced: "Every contract, combination in the form of trust or otherwise, or conspiracy, in restraint of trade or commerce among the several States, or with foreign nations, is hereby declared to be illegal." Federal courts received jurisdiction to enforce it, the Attorney General was empowered to secure injunctive relief and initiate criminal prosecutions against violators, and injured persons were permitted to sue the lawbreakers for triple damages. The act had been a trusted weapon with which Henry Stimson, as United States Attorney for the Southern District of New York, and his staff were able to haul the "malefactors of great wealth" into court during the early days of the century.

Ironically, however, the Sherman Antitrust Act became a weapon not only against corporations, at which it had been directed, but also against labor unions. It was invoked most notoriously in the Pullman strike of 1894, when the Attorney General secured an injunction against Eugene V. Debs and others of the American Railway Union for conspiring to restrain trade and interfere with the mails. For the next thirty years, the act was seized on as efficient a strikebreaker as a policeman's billy club. All the while, organized labor was fighting to obtain relief from these injunctions.

In 1926 Senator George W. Norris of Nebraska was driven around a Pennsylvania coal town, what was then called a company town, by the debilitated survivor of a mine explosion. During the drive, the miner told Norris about life in this company town: hazardous conditions in the mines; company ownership of homes and stores; the general lot of the wage slave. On his return to Washington, Norris began his battle against abuse of labor, including the labor injunction.

At his side was Frankfurter, who had written in 1922 about the labor injunction: "... It does not work. It neither mines coal, nor moves trains, nor makes clothing. As an adjuster of industrial conflict, the injunction has been an utter failure. It has been used as a short-cut—but it has not cut anything, except to cut off labor from confidence in the rule of law and of the courts as its impartial organs. . . ." [1]

The use of the injunction had been perverted to aid business and industry in curbing trade unions, another example of the absence of democracy in industrial relations. Whenever labor controversies loomed, employers went to court and sought injunctions against laborers for conspiring to restrain trade. The courts generally acceded.

Frankfurter believed this was a patent abuse of judicial power. There was no jury to ascertain validity of disputed questions of fact—an ever-present consideration in cases of injunction. Instead, the judge alone had the arbitrary power to grant or deny the order, and as the trend of judicial decisions was going, the masses of people were losing confidence in the courts and, as a corollary, in law and order. In addition, far from quieting labor conflict, the discretionary use of the injunction was increasing bitterness.

There was, Frankfurter believed, no valid reason for use of the injunction. In fact, adequate legal remedies existed for redress, should industry sustain damages caused by labor strife.

Employed as it was in a partisan cause, therefore, the labor injunction ought to go. "... For the moment," he wrote in the *New Republic* in 1922, "we know of no more pressing need for the country's well-being than the restoration of confidence in our courts and respect for law through the abandonment of the abuses of the injunction. And the abuse of injunctions in labor cases can be discontinued only by the discontinuance of their use." [2]

Senator Norris' efforts against the labor injunction, which culminated in the Norris-LaGuardia Anti-Injunction Act of 1932, began with a separate bill put forth by Andrew Furuseth, president of the International Seaman's Union, and introduced in the Senate in late 1927 by Senator Henrik Shipstead of Minnesota. It was referred to the Senate Judiciary Committee, whose chairman was Senator Norris. The subcommittee that considered the bill reluctantly decided it was inadequate.

In May, 1928, Norris summoned to Washington a group of expert legal advisers to redraft the bill: Frankfurter, Francis B. Sayre of Harvard Law School, Joseph P. Chamberlain and Herman Oliphant of Columbia, and labor lawyer and former Frankfurter student Donald Richberg. Frankfurter had already labored some years on such a bill—in fact, in 1928, with Nathan Greene, he published *The Labor Injunction,* a comprehensive and classic study of the situation —and had drafts ready to send to the advisory group before it met in Washington. When they arrived in the capital, the lawyers were locked in the Judiciary Committee's rooms for an intensive forty-eight-hour session, in which they produced a first draft of a bill.

Although it did not completely outlaw the use of the injunction, it defined and limited the scope of this weapon. It defined the normal activities of unions, such as picketing and striking, against which the injunction could no longer be used. It outlined certain procedural limitations on the issuance of labor injunctions, declaring injunctions could not be issued until there had been open hearings of witnesses to support a complaint, and these were subject to cross-examination. Furthermore, the court had to determine formally that a labor dispute had threatened substantial damage before an injunction could be issued.

The act proceeded on the assumption that there could be no equality of liberty of contract between employer and employee unless labor, heretofore placed at a disadvantage in relation to capital, could organize and bargain collectively. There must be, reminiscent of Frankfurter's World War I premises, a partnership of power.

The act's Section 2 declared that under present conditions which allowed capital to organize "in the corporate and other forms of ownership association, the individual unorganized worker is commonly helpless to exercise actual liberty of contract and to protect his freedom of labor, and thereby to obtain acceptable terms and conditions of employment. . . ." The laborer, the act said, must have "full freedom of association, self-organization and designation of representatives of his own choosing, and that he shall be free from the interference, restraint, or coercion of employers . . . for the purpose of collective bargaining or other mutual aid or protection."

Senator Norris introduced the bill into Congress in May, 1928. It failed to pass that Congress or the next one. It finally passed the Seventy-Second Congress and was signed by President Hoover in March, 1932.

At the same time that Frankfurter was working on the anti-injunction bill and his book on the same subject, he was also advising the state of Massachusetts and William Green, president of the American Federation of Labor, on unemployment compensation bills. In addition, he was making speeches on labor relations, advising governors, industrial commissioners and state officials on the strategy of obtaining new social measures.

All these activities he undertook without fee. In fact, the matter of not accepting a retainer was a precondition of participation. He explained his position in a letter to the New York *Times* in 1926. The newspaper had printed a story about some striking New Jersey textile workers and named Frankfurter as paid counsel to the strikers. Frankfurter wrote: ". . . I do not think it consistent with the best function of a law teacher to be under financial retainer by either side to a controversy involving public issues of the kind raised by the Passaic strike. He should keep himself in a position of disinterestedness. . . ." [3]

Frankfurter has been called pro labor. He was not any more pro labor than he was pro business. But he had spent his youth and young manhood watching capitalism gone mad, with all the power on the side of the money and none of the power on the side of the masses. He was pro labor in the sense that he wanted to see the power shifted and redistributed.

In fact, he was frequently a restraining hand on labor. Labor leaders over the years called on him for legal advice, and their point of view tended to be nearsighted, because they were so engrossed in their own problems. An SOS from labor for legal advice often meant in essence "Write us a constitutional amendment, Felix." But Frankfurter, with a broader perspective from his not-so-ivory tower, was often the one who pulled them back, substituting the less wide-ranging measure, searching for solutions along narrower lines.

Furor over the Sacco-Vanzetti case was slow to die in Boston. The name Frankfurter, linked as it was with the two men, turned Boston faces purple long after the event.

By 1932, however, Massachusetts had a new governor, Joseph B. Ely, a Democrat, a former trial lawyer and district attorney, a supporter of Al Smith, and a believer in the innocence of Sacco and Vanzetti. Herbert Ehrmann and William Thompson, lawyers for Sacco and Vanzetti, decided the way to stop slander of Frankfurter was to get him on the bench of the Supreme Judicial Court of Massachusetts, and the man through whom to do it was Governor Ely.

Indications were that there was a great need on the Supreme Judicial Court for a breath of fresh progressive air to dissipate the smog of conservatism. The court was one of old men who reflected the views of a past generation. Their opinions were always unanimous—as lockstepped as their daily luncheon walk from their meeting place to the Union Club. Chief Justice Arthur Rugg had called on Governor Ely when one vacancy occurred on his court to say, "I hope you are not considering Frankfurter." [4]

Ehrmann and Thompson brought Ely and Frankfurter together socially, and although nothing was said about a judgeship on these occasions, Ely and Frankfurter established a personal relationship. Then, working out of Frankfurter's sight, Ehrmann and Thompson urged Ely to appoint Frankfurter to the high court.

Ehrmann wrote later that he believed Frankfurter knew what he was about but thought either that his efforts would not be successful or that if they were, the offer of a judgeship was important whether or not he accepted it.

A vacancy on the Supreme Judicial Court occurred early in 1932 upon the death of Justice James B. Carroll. Justice Holmes, only a few days retired from the United States Supreme Court, wrote—apparently spontaneously—to Governor Ely: ". . . I venture to recommend Professor Felix Frankfurter.

"I am quite confident that he is superior in learning and ability to any one else available and that his character is equal to his gifts.

He has been a dear friend of mine for many years, but I am confident that the judgment that I express is not the child but the parent of my affection." [5]

The Springfield *Republican* editorially supported Frankfurter's nomination: ". . . Professor Felix Frankfurter of the Harvard Law School is a type of liberal jurist with special claims upon the governor's attention because of his qualifications. . . ." [6]

Thompson urged Ely to appoint Frankfurter, but Ely decided against it—he believed Frankfurter would not accept.[7] But by late spring of 1932 there were indications that two and possibly three vacancies would occur on the court, and Thompson assured Ely that if the governor submitted Frankfurter's name to the Executive Council, Frankfurter would accept. Thompson also asked Frankfurter's advice on writing Holmes to seek endorsement of Frankfurter, should Ely be persuaded to appoint Frankfurter and should the expected uproar over Frankfurter's fight for Sacco and Vanzetti occur. No doubt Thompson was also trying to feel out Frankfurter on the question of acceptance. Frankfurter replied: ". . . you ought not to write to him on the subject. Holmes after all is ninety-one and he has withdrawn from the passions and conflicts of the world. Your letter would really disturb him. . . .

"By nothing that I have said or have failed to say," Frankfurter added, "do I mean to imply that were the opportunity to come to me, even on a silver platter, I would accept it. By temperament and by training, I have the incorrigible habits of the Anglo-American lawyer, and so debate only concrete and not hypothetical cases. . . . I do not trust my judgment until I am actively called upon to make a decision. . . ." [8]

Then the first vacancy occurred—Justice George A. Sanderson died. On June 22, 1932, Governor Ely nominated Frankfurter, without notifying him, to the Supreme Judicial Court of Massachusetts. Then Ely went off to the Democratic national convention, meeting in Chicago, to leave Frankfurter to tackle the press, the clamor that the nomination created, and, not the least of the difficulties, the question of acceptance.

Frankfurter heard the news in a phone call from his wife as he took luncheon at the Faculty Club at Harvard. He wrote Ely that day that his nomination had left him "tongue-tied." [9]

Typically, Frankfurter refused interviews, declined to answer whether he would accept the nomination, and went off to the summer home of Justice Brandeis at Chatham to seek solitude and advice.

Public reaction to the nomination was about as expected: loud and vigorous pro and con. Those who believed the Sacco-Vanzetti case had been a blot on the name of Massachusetts believed Ely had made a first step back to respectability and vindication of Frankfurter.

"It isn't really very long since the mere mention of your name for the Supreme Court in Massachusetts would have been a jail offense," [10] wrote a Yale law professor. There were letters of congratulation and approval from lawyers, educators, former students, judges, and the public at large.

And there was opposition. Former Governor Fuller, who had held the office during the Sacco and Vanzetti affair, said, "With Ely pardoning murderers and Frankfurter, an open sympathizer with murderers, on the Supreme Bench, I see no reason why murder should not flourish here in Massachusetts." Fuller would "cut off my right hand" [11] before he would confirm the appointment.

State Representative Horace T. Cahill of Braintree wrote to the Boston *Globe:* "It is my opinion that certain radical groups opposed to our government will receive unlimited encouragement if Mr. Frankfurter is made a member of our highest court. . . ." [12]

The Boston *Transcript* said much the same thing but dressed it up in loftier language. Although the present court, said the *Transcript,* might be invigorated by Frankfurter's dissents, and Frankfurter's success as a teacher was certainly verified, as was his vast knowledge of the law and judicial processes, "what must not be forgotten is the fact that the characteristic which makes a good judge is not alone mental competence but a capacity for decision that is wholly detached from emotions. Herein lies the basis for our belief that the appointment of Mr. Frankfurter is not an appropriate one." [13] The Springfield *Republican* continued to support Frankfurter.

The public clamor became so great that the Boston newspapers opened their columns to letters: sometimes pro, sometimes con, always vehement. Ely was accused of playing politics, smirching the name of Massachusetts; Frankfurter was called "a menace to this country and American institutions." [14] In the Executive Council, which was to meet on July 6 to act on Frankfurter's appointment, opinions were also divided. Men who had been involved in the Sacco and Vanzetti case or who came from the districts where the events of that case had taken place were strongly and definitely opposed.

In the middle of it all, Mrs. Frankfurter was frequently asked if she was not proud of her husband. "No. I am not," she would reply, then produce one of her best bon mots: "I would be if I were Mrs. Ely." [15]

Frankfurter himself was undergoing "anguish," confronted as he was "with the most poignant decision I have ever been called upon to make—a real tragedy, the choice between two goods. . . ." [16]

Brandeis had counseled against acceptance, believing Frankfurter would "render to the Nation, the Commonwealth and the law service more far reaching and enduring by continuing your activities in the humbler office of teacher at the Law School." [17] Arthur D. Hill had written much the same thing at the first flurry of excitement over Frankfurter's possible appointment the previous January, adding only that he thought Frankfurter would be happier at the law school.

There was also some thought that Frankfurter was angling for higher office and feared his inevitable dissents on the high court would be lost in the customary avalanche of conservative opinions, just as inevitable, and ruin his chances for later nomination to the United States Supreme Court.

Holmes thought he ought to accept and endorsed his name for the second time. Ellery Sedgwick, editor of the *Atlantic Monthly*, believed that as a citizen Frankfurter was also a soldier and that the governor's nomination was an order. William Thompson, instigator of the appointment, wrote Frankfurter: ". . . it would be a dreadful misake for you to decline it now. It would be a bitter disappointment to your liberal friends and to those who have been working for the cause of liberalism, not only in Massachusetts, but all over the country; it would set back the reform of our courts for a long time; and it would discourage your friends. . . . You can do more good on the Bench in the next year or two than you could ever do at the Harvard Law School. . . ." [18]

However, on June 29, seven days after his nomination, Frankfurter wrote Governor Ely his declination. But Ely was in Chicago, where he nominated Al Smith for the Presidency of the United States. Through his secretary, he asked Frankfurter to keep silent about declining the nomination until he, Ely, had a chance to talk with him about it. Frankfurter agreed.

So, although Frankfurter had made up his mind, the controversy raged for nearly two weeks more. Newspapers all over the country ran letters pro and con. In Boston there were demands by the opposition to the appointment for public hearings before the July 6 meeting of the Executive Council, which was scheduled to act that day on Frankfurter's nomination.

Pledged to silence, Frankfurter declined to tell even his friends he was not going to accept the judgeship. He talked noncommittally to Franklin Roosevelt, who had interrupted his victory trip to the Chicago Democratic convention to phone congratulations to Frankfurter. However, when Holmes suggested that Frankfurter, by his silence, might be prolonging the controversy and that he had better accept, Frankfurter confided that he had already withdrawn and explained the circumstances surrounding his silence.

On July 5 the Republican members of the Executive Council agreed to postpone its consideration of Frankfurter's appointment and to ask the governor that public hearings be held on July 8.

Governor Ely returned to Boston, and Frankfurter met him the morning of July 6 at his apartment in the Copley Plaza. Ely tried to persuade Frankfurter to reconsider; Frankfurter refused. The Executive Council met the same afternoon and formally agreed to the postponement of consideration of the Frankfurter appointment for one week, but set no date for hearings. Informal tallying among the members of the council had totaled four votes for Frankfurter, four votes against. But the opposition finally collapsed; its leader announced he was leaving for a Labrador vacation and would be unable to attend the meeting scheduled for July 13. Indications are that Frankfurter would have been confirmed had his name come before the council.

But on July 12, his powers of persuasion exhausted, Governor Ely announced that Frankfurter had, on June 29, turned down the appointment.

Frankfurter had written in his refusal: "... As against the opportunities for immediate achievement on the bench, the long-term effects of legal education make their claim. The grave problems already upon us and those looming on the horizon require as never before a courageous and learned bar. And from such a bar alone can come an enlightened judiciary."

He continued: "The future direction of bar and bench will be determined by the quality of our law schools. Moreover, the fabric of the law, particularly our public law, we have been told repeatedly by the most farsighted in the profession, must be designed chiefly by the law schools. This work must go forward, and I cannot bring myself to believe that I should prematurely abandon my share in it, however great and honorable the opportunity you offer me. . . ." [19]

Privately, in a letter to a friend, he had written: ". . . Why do you think that being a judge is to sit at the right-hand of God, and being a teacher of future judges and lawyers is something that doesn't count? . . ." [20]

And Holmes wrote to Harold Laski: ". . . Felix and his wife come here to luncheon from time to time. I can't help feeling as if his declining the Massachusetts Supreme Judicial Court was a mistake, but he and Brandeis know better than I do. . . ." [21]

PART III

The New Deal

[1]

WITH the stock market crash of October, 1929, the Babylonian twenties came to a halt, leaving numbness, bewilderment, disillusion, and depression where optimism and vitality had so recently reigned. The question on the public's lips was: Where do we go from here? For nearly four years the nation went nowhere.

President Herbert Hoover was his own ideological prisoner; in addition, he was surrounded by unimaginative and backward-looking advisers. Although he sincerely tried to end the Depression and rehabilitate the country, he was too tightly bound by old solutions to old problems and did not possess the boldness to try new solutions that might fit the new problems. He is, perhaps, owed a debt by his successor for having eliminated at least the old avenues of approach to the crises created by the Depression.

To the funeral, in 1932, of unfettered laissez-faire came Franklin Delano Roosevelt to put the final shovelfuls of earth on the coffin. The victim had strangled itself to death, and Roosevelt came not to offer condolences to the survivors in the family of capitalism, but to offer confidence and revitalization in the future.

The advocates of Communism and Socialism were charging that capitalism had collapsed; many Americans who never embraced either ism agreed and were joining the ranks of Communists and Socialists because they had nowhere else to go. Felix Frankfurter was neither Communist nor Socialist, had never been, although he had been so labeled. As he had written Henry Stimson in 1921: "... I am not a Communist, and not even a Socialist. All such dogma seems to me violative of experience and too naïve for the complexities of this world. I decidedly believe in our democratic form of government...." He did not believe that "we have reached the last word in government perfectability. I do believe passionately, however, that all the necessary changes can and should come progressively and through orderly non-violent processes. . . ." [1]

The Depression was putting the American system to its severest test. ". . . The great and buoyant faith in capitalism, in the competitive system," Frankfurter told a Smith College audience on Washington's Birthday in 1933, "is largely deflated, and . . . it is not only a question of whether the system is just, but whether it works. When you have a system which is questioned by the masses, that system cannot last unless it wins back the loyalty and allegiance of the doubters. . . ." [2]

In 1932 Frankfurter would originally have preferred Al Smith to run against Hoover for the Presidency. But he was afraid that Smith, having been defeated in 1928, could not be nominated again and that the racial and religious intensities aroused because of Smith's Catholicism were "still more virulent than I should have supposed." [3] Newton Baker, Frankfurter's old chief in the War Department, was also a prominent candidate for the Democratic nomination. But Baker, or so Frankfurter believed, had a deep-seated orientation to laissez-faire and distrust of government, in addition to an inordinate preoccupation with international affairs.

Frankfurter therefore put his political faith in Franklin Roosevelt, whom he had observed closely in action during Roosevelt's tenancy of the statehouse in Albany.

As he had had about the other candidates he had supported, Frankfurter had reservations about Franklin Roosevelt. Roosevelt's dealings with the Tammany machine in New York City showed, Frankfurter believed, a lack of "both courage and political calculation." [4] Roosevelt also, according to Frankfurter, lacked a keenness of mind, and Frankfurter commented prior to the Democratic convention of 1932: "I am wondering what will come out of Chicago. If F.D.R. is nominated, it will certainly prove that there is no limit to the amount of fumbling one can do and still win a game." [5] In total, Frankfurter confessed, "Were I God, of course, I should want more of a fellow to guide our destinies during the next four years than is Roosevelt. . . ." [6]

However, Frankfurter could with a clear conscience vote for Roosevelt. Overall, "he is more likely to further the things I most care about than any other candidate for President," Frankfurter told a friend. As governor of New York, "he has been tested on the two major issues of our domestic concern—the social and economic problems behind the depression and [public] power." His direction had been "courageous and far-sighted," particularly in the areas of public utility regulation and future development of power. "If you are worrying, as I am worrying, about these matters," Frankfurter concluded, "and are concerned, as I am concerned, that these increasingly important forces of our national life be utilized for the public interest and not be centered in private hands, which are so powerful as soon to overawe public authority, then I think you will be bound to say that Roosevelt has shown both guts and understanding." [7]

Roosevelt had shown that he shared Frankfurter's public philosophy of progressivism inaugurated in Theodore Roosevelt's Square Deal and refined in Woodrow Wilson's New Freedom. Like these, Franklin Roosevelt's New Deal was an attempt to come to grips with the new industrialism that had overreached itself, not to bury it, but to control it, regulate it, so that it would continue to expand and produce at an increasing rate. But instead of enriching the rich, it would redistribute its wealth and raise the standard of living of all. These three Presidents believed that the sane application of legislation to business and industry and a reasonable approach to social measures could, in a country of such abundance as America, achieve true liberty.

Roosevelt carried on an old-fashioned stump-speaking campaign. He went into nearly every state in the Union, as if trying to prove to the voters that his physical stamina was equal to the demands of the Presidency.

With the Depression and its impoverishment and unemployment hanging over the nation, the issues were economic. Roosevelt announced bold plans for the New Deal—for the "forgotten man at the bottom of the economic pyramid." While Hoover ran on his record of four years in the Presidency, Roosevelt articulated specific new programs for recovery and reform of the system that had begotten the Depression. He talked about reemployment, repealing Prohibition, regulating business and industry, and saving the farmer.

He invited Frankfurter to work in the campaign, dangling before him the promise of high office in a Roosevelt administration. Frankfurter refused and chose to stay at Harvard. He did, however, continue in the role of informal adviser which had developed over the years of the Roosevelt governorship.

Frankfurter was in frequent contact with Roosevelt throughout that summer of strenuous vote gathering. Now, instead of proposing formulas for New York prison reform, he was mapping legal approaches to the problem of Prohibition. New York's program for developing waterpower was magnified to a national scale. Memorandums went out to Roosevelt's formal advisers on his record in all the facets of his governorship. When Al Smith sulked over his loss of the nomination, Frankfurter was instrumental in persuading Smith to submerge personal pique and campaign for Roosevelt. Only in the last days of the campaign did Frankfurter make formal his support of Roosevelt. On November 5, 1932, he delivered a radio speech, at Roosevelt's request, in which he chastised Hoover for doing nothing to alleviate the conditions of the Depression.

"Neither before the depression nor since has Mr. Hoover shown any awareness that we are living in a new economic world. Somehow or other, he thinks, this depression will pass, and then mass production will automatically make for well-being," Frankfurter said. Hammering on the old progressivism, he continued: "The task of modern statesmanship is to devise social inventions in order to deal with the maladjustments of our economic life in the spirit in which sanitary science has been dealing with epidemics. Such an attitude towards our economic ills is wholly alien to the President. . . ."

As for Roosevelt, Frankfurter outlined his accomplishments as governor and concluded that his "outlook and achievements and the courage and hope of which his life is a triumph, justify us in following his lead. Supported by the liberal and progressive sentiment of the country, he can help us out of our present moral and material morass and start new ways of thought into new deeds of action. And so his election on Tuesday next may well be the augur of happier days." [8]

"Tuesday next" saw the defeat of Hoover and the election of Roosevelt as President of the United States: 15,761,841 votes to 22,821,857 votes, with Roosevelt winning 472 electoral votes to Hoover's 59. The American people had, said Roosevelt in his first inaugural address, "registered a mandate that they want direct, vigorous action. . . ."

During the stagnant time between election and inauguration of a President, when the incumbent has little energy for constructive action he knows will be reversed shortly and the President-elect has no authority for action, the government comes almost to a standstill. All that can be done is preparation by the incoming administration.

During the interregnum between Roosevelt's election in November, 1932, and the inauguration on March 4, 1933, it was natural that he should further call on his informal adviser in Cambridge for help in setting up his administration. Frankfurter responded eagerly. At Roosevelt's invitation, Mr. and Mrs. Frankfurter arrived at the Roosevelts' Hyde Park home two days before Christmas, 1932, "to talk about things." [9] And talk about things they did—about what ought to be done after March 4 and about the men to do them—until two o'clock in the morning. Mrs. Frankfurter later said her husband treated Roosevelt like a student in one of his seminars. Frankfurter denied it, saying he was at all times friendly but "respectful."

"Oh, yes," retorted Mrs. Frankfurter, "but he was taking down notes almost as though he were in a seminar of yours." [10]

Frankfurter's major contribution to the incoming administration was in clearing the static in the communication lines between outgoing and incoming officials.

Roosevelt, about to assume control of a government without, of course, being familiar with the details of that government, hoped members of the Hoover administration would give him some orientation. Although such orientation became the practice in later years, in early 1933, President Hoover was still stirred by the animosities of the campaign and was reluctant to help the President-elect.

Particularly was this true in foreign relations, guided by Hoover's Secretary of State—Frankfurter's close friend Henry L. Stimson. Frankfurter became a self-appointed ambassador to bring Stimson and Roosevelt together.

The immediate dissension concerned a plan Hoover had outlined to Congress in December, 1932. In this plan he tried to tie together the problems of international war debts, for which there was an American payment nearly due, and disarmament with the Depression, which Hoover believed was international in origin and had international consequences.

During the interregnum Hoover wired Roosevelt asking him to support the proposal. It was a ploy by Hoover to get Roosevelt to repudiate his New Deal programs. Roosevelt refused. He had no authority to act at this time. More important, he believed the problems of the Depression—which had priority over international concerns—were strictly domestic and ought not be tied to the international exigencies. Above all, he did not want to become snarled in policies he had not himself framed with full knowledge of the facts.

On December 22, the day after Roosevelt replied to Hoover, Frankfurter and Herbert Feis, State Department adviser on international economic affairs, met in Cambridge. They decided Stimson and Roosevelt ought to meet. Frankfurter was on his way to confer with Roosevelt, and late that night he called Stimson in Washington to announce that "out of a clear sky" Roosevelt had said, "Why doesn't Harry Stimson come up here and talk with me and settle this damn thing that nobody else seems able to?" He added that Roosevelt "feels very badly that all cooperative efforts had been broken off." [11] Stimson said he would think it over and call Frankfurter in New York the following day.

Stimson thought he owed it to Hoover to take the proposed meeting up with him. On December 23, Stimson took Roosevelt's suggestion to Hoover, who heatedly denied permission. Hoover had already had one unhappy meeting with Roosevelt, on November 22. The misunderstandings that came out of that meeting only served further to aggravate past animosities. To Stimson's request, Hoover said, "You won't get anything, you won't get anything. You can't trust him." [12] Shortly afterward Hoover left for a Christmas holiday in California.

Stimson reported to Frankfurter that permission had been denied. Frankfurter said he hoped it would not prevent a later meeting, and Stimson agreed that he hoped that might be left open.

Stimson believed he ought to go. Whether or not he approved of Roosevelt, whom he knew only "second-hand," Roosevelt *was* the President-elect, and Stimson wrote in his diary for December 24, 1932: ". . . it is incomprehensible that we should take a position that would deprive the incoming President of the United States of important information about foreign affairs. . . ." [13]

Two days after Christmas, Stimson received a letter from Roosevelt on minor matters, but he took the occasion to tell Stimson that Roosevelt "would be glad to have me communicate with him either by telephone or in person underscoring the words in person. . . ." [14]

Three days after Christmas, Frankfurter came to Stimson to urge Stimson's meeting with Roosevelt, giving Stimson a character sketch of Roosevelt. Frankfurter told Stimson of his experiences with Roosevelt when they worked together on the War Labor Policies Board in World War I. Aware of Stimson's own courage and his admiration of courage in others, Frankfurter told Stimson of the courageous way in which Roosevelt handled his lameness, "how he had disregarded it instead of making any play upon it or any mention of it." Frankfurter went on to tell Stimson how he, Frankfurter, had watched Roosevelt go to bed or get up and "spoke of the elaborate harness the man had to wear and of his shrunken leg and yet the uncomplaining way in which he went through this elaborate process at least four times a day. . . ." In total, the portrait Frankfurter painted was "a much more attractive picture than we have been getting from the other side." [15]

Stimson had hoped Hoover's holiday might serve as a "cooling-down," and his hopes were realized. On January 3, 1933, Stimson again went to the White House. He told Hoover that he wanted to perpetuate Hoover's policies and that he was "sufficiently interested . . . in the welfare of the country to do my best to try and make the next Administration a success in recovery if possible." He said that he wanted to go and see Roosevelt, that when Roosevelt wanted information about his job and particularly about foreign affairs, "it was a very ticklish responsibility to refuse to give it to him. I said even supposing he was as bad as Hoover thought he was it was more dangerous to give him this grievance . . . than anything he could do in the way of treachery. . . ." [16] Hoover agreed to think it over. The next day he yielded; Stimson could meet Roosevelt, provided Roosevelt asked Hoover's permission.

Stimson quickly phoned the news to Frankfurter in Cambridge. Frankfurter phoned Roosevelt at nine o'clock in the evening and persuaded Roosevelt to write the required letter to Hoover. Roosevelt wrote it the same night. As Frankfurter had described his friend Roosevelt to Stimson, he now proceeded to describe his friend Stimson to Roosevelt. Stimson was different from Hoover, Frankfurter said, and Roosevelt should allow a great deal of time for his interview because Stimson's mind was slow and methodical, not quick and darting as Roosevelt's was. Forty-five minutes later, Frankfurter telephoned Stimson to report his conversation with Roosevelt and advise Stimson on alternative dates Roosevelt had given for the meeting. Again, Frankfurter found himself explaining to Stimson what sort of man Roosevelt was. In arranging a meeting between Stimson and Roosevelt, Frankfurter was bringing together two of his oldest and dearest friends. He hoped the two men, he told Stimson, would find in each other something of what Frankfurter had found in each separately; if so, Stimson might be influential in international relations throughout the Roosevelt Presidency.

On January 9, 1933, Stimson went to Hyde Park, half expecting to be eaten by the dragon that lived there. But Roosevelt's graciousness and willingness to listen pleasantly surprised him. They talked for six hours on all the current problems of international relations: the Far East, Philippine independence, Russian recognition, the upcoming economic conference, international debts, the problems of disarmament.

The conversation brought the two together on a basis of mutual respect and laid groundwork for future cooperation. In the last weeks of Hoover's administration, Roosevelt was able, by maintaining contact with Stimson, to keep abreast of the international scene.

Roosevelt tried to recruit Frankfurter to an official position in his administration. As soon as the election returns were in, there was speculation that Frankfurter would be appointed Attorney General. There were letters to the New York *Times* endorsing his appointment and opposition from the Daughters of the American Revolution.

Roosevelt appointed Senator Thomas J. Walsh of Montana as Attorney General (Walsh died before he took office; Homer S. Cummings was then appointed). He asked Frankfurter to become Solicitor General, the officer who argues the government's cases before the Supreme Court. Roosevelt explained that he wanted eventually to appoint Frankfurter to the Supreme Court but that he could hardly put a law professor on the highest court in the nation (although six years later he did exactly that), whereas the Supreme Court was the natural next step from the office of Solicitor General.

Typically, Frankfurter did not decide quickly or impulsively, but first consulted people close to him—although all his inclinations directed him to declining, as he had declined Governor Ely's appointment to the Supreme Judicial Court of Massachusetts. Brandeis still believed Frankfurter ought to remain at Harvard Law School. Holmes also advised him against becoming Solicitor General; he had already written to Harold Laski that he thought it would be "queer to turn down a seat on the Massachusetts Supreme Bench for a solicitor-generalship." [17]

Four days after Roosevelt's inauguration, Frankfurter met Roosevelt as President for the first time. They discussed the appointment in Roosevelt's Oval Office in the White House. Six days later, on March 14, Frankfurter wrote his formal refusal to Roosevelt, reiterating the arguments he had used in their recent conversation: Frankfurter was due to go to England in September for a year, and even if he canceled the trip, the duties of Solicitor General would absorb so much of his time and energy that he would no longer be free to continue his informal but valuable participation in the Roosevelt administration. He preferred to remain an unofficial part of the New Deal, and the matter of the Supreme Court would have to take care of itself.

What he did not say in the letter but what was undoubtedly a controlling factor was that he wanted to maintain his own independence—as he had when Roosevelt was governor of New York—yet still bring expertise and friendship to the President's problems. Had he joined the administration officially, he would have had to become, at least to some degree, a yes-man or risk being ousted—as many advisers were. Frankfurter could never be a yes-man; it was alien to his nature. It would also have destroyed his effectiveness. But by refusing to accept an official position while still proffering advice and suggestions, he was the one man who remained with the Roosevelt administration throughout its twelve years. The Moley-Tugwell-Berle group of the early Roosevelt days was in time replaced by the Cohen-Corcoran men, in turn replaced by Harry Hopkins. Frankfurter was able to avoid the palace intrigues and outlast the palace revolutions.

[2]

Frankfurter did remain a prominent, if unofficial, member of the Roosevelt entourage, and one of his first acts after Roosevelt's accession was supervision of the drafting of what became the Securities Act of 1933.

Business in general and the stock market in particular had long operated on the premise of *caveat emptor.* In the 1920's abuses of this buttress of capitalism reached disastrous heights as business investments were rigged against the ordinary stock purchaser. Financiers artificially hiked stock prices to attract new buyers, then dumped the stock on the market and pulled out with the profits. Wall Street operators spread rumors that a company was in trouble, sold their own stock short to drive down the price, then bought it back at a lower price. There were a number of shady practices, and a good many honest stock purchasers had their pockets picked.

The Democratic platform of 1932 reflected the public demand for reform: "We advocate protection of the investing public by requiring to be filed with the Government, and carried in advertisements, of all offerings of foreign and domestic stocks and bonds, true information as to bonuses, commissions, principal invested, and the interest of the sellers."

Shortly after his nomination as Democratic candidate, Roosevelt, on July 30, 1932, in Columbus, Ohio, promised that reform. Advocating federal regulation of several parts of the business of finance, Roosevelt promised that "government can prevent to a very great degree the fooling of sensible people through misstatements and through the withholding of information on the part of private organizations . . . which seek to sell investments to the people of the Nation. . . ."

He reinforced the promise in his inaugural address of March 4, 1933: ". . . there must be an end to a conduct in banking and in business which too often has given to a sacred trust the likeness of callous and selfish wrongdoing. . . ."

He made good the promise in a message to Congress twenty-five days later, when he asked for legislation "for Federal supervision of traffic in investment securities in interstate commerce." He did not ask that the federal government be a guarantor of a particular security. He asked that securities sold in interstate commerce "be accompanied by full publicity and information, and that no essentially important element attending the issue shall be concealed from the buying public. . . ." Such a proposal, he added, "puts the burden of telling the whole truth on the seller. It should give impetus to honest dealing in securities and thereby bring back public confidence." His purpose was, he assured business, as his purpose was in much New

Deal legislation, not to hamstring Wall Street, but "to protect the public with the least possible interference with honest business."

Immediately lawyers, bankers, and businessmen protested. Letters, telegrams, and telephone calls poured into administration offices.

Meanwhile, however, an investigation by the Senate Banking and Currency Committee, begun during the Hoover administration in 1932, was exposing a well of corruption on Wall Street. By early 1933 the committee, spearheaded by its counsel, Ferdinand Pecora, was revealing through interviews, questionnaires, and well-reported hearings that the financial wizards of Wall Street had used fraudulent tricks and circuslike wizardry to amass their enormous profits. Even J. P. Morgan, the grand master of Wall Street, had been successfully attacked in a committee question-and-answer session. The indignation of the bilked public soared; reform was in the air.

Roosevelt had laid out the guidelines. The specific bill was another matter. At least two were proposed, but Roosevelt and his advisers believed both contained serious defects.

Sam Rayburn, later Speaker of the House of Representatives for a record number of years but at that time chairman of the House Commerce Committee, went to Roosevelt's aide Raymond Moley and asked him to find someone to write a new bill.[1] On April 4, Moley called in Frankfurter, who typically and eagerly responded: "Three of us will arrive at the Carlton Friday morning. Please reserve rooms for us." [2]

It had not yet become fashionable for Presidents to call on leading academics for advice, and many people derided Roosevelt for listening to what they thought were the abstractions of a Harvard Law School professor remote from the scene. What the critics forgot was that Frankfurter had accumulated much of his knowledge not only from lawbooks but perhaps even more from active participation in government for years. After he left government service, he had made it his business to keep *au courant* with its inner workings. And when Roosevelt's New Deal programs needed engineers, Frankfurter was prepared, with both theory and practical experience on which to draw, to work out specifics.

Frankfurter was also well acquainted with what he called the "wickedness of Wall Street" [3] and the need for corrective legislation. "The greatest speculative carnival in the world's history" had followed World War I, he later wrote. "... Billions of new securities were floated, of which a large part had no relation to the country's need and which inevitably became worthless, worthless not merely for millions who had sought speculative gains, but for those other millions who sought to conserve the savings of a lifetime." [4]

The money which bought securities had been grossly misused, Frankfurter believed. Instead of being poured into the development and expansion of industry, the main purpose of capital investments, it had created more securities while still controlling the industries from which it was withheld.

Not only was the public misled, according to Frankfurter, by the fly-by-nights, but "stupendous savings of the American people were drained . . . by the most conservative houses and passed upon by leading law firms of the country," [5] which lent their respected names to reckless and scurrilous financial practices.

These were the conditions, Frankfurter believed, that created the need for legislation. He was eager to help the administration frame it.

As good as his word, Frankfurter with two aides arrived in Washington on Friday, April 7. One of the assistants was James McCauley Landis, former student of Frankfurter's, law clerk to Justice Brandeis, and, in the spring of 1933, professor of legislation at Harvard Law School. The other assistant was Benjamin V. Cohen, one of Harvard Law School's most brilliant graduates, an expert legal draftsman, a man who understood very well the vagaries of Wall Street, having made his own fortune there. Later he was one of Roosevelt's close advisers.

The trio breakfasted with Raymond Moley, then officially an Assistant Secretary of State but unofficially one of Roosevelt's intimate counselors. Frankfurter had known Moley in Cleveland, where Moley had been secretary of the Cleveland Foundation, which had hired Frankfurter to help conduct its crime survey in 1921. Moley's main point in this early briefing was to persuade the three men that it was essential to both fairness and success of the legislation that consultation with men from the street be undertaken, despite suspicions of the street's intransigence. Frankfurter agreed that such men would be consulted.

The trio then conferred with Roosevelt and later with Sam Rayburn. Frankfurter and Landis were scheduled to return to Cambridge Sunday night in time for Monday morning classes. Rayburn convinced Frankfurter that it was essential for them to stay on, that

Frankfurter himself must appear before the House Commerce Committee subcommittee taking up the Securities Bill on Monday morning to present general guidelines he thought should be followed in the drafting of a bill. Frankfurter wired Dean Pound at Harvard and asked him to make "appropriate arrangements in regard to my classes" [6] and Landis' also.

Landis and Cohen holed themselves up in the apartment of Thomas G. Corcoran, then officially on the staff of the Reconstruction Finance Corporation but unofficially a free lance for the administration. Corcoran kept them supplied with stenographers and contributed his own knowledge of Wall Street, where he had worked for five years. The three young men finished a draft bill by Sunday night and submitted it to Frankfurter.

On Monday morning Frankfurter, Landis, and Cohen went before the House subcommittee, and Frankfurter, in what Landis later called "an extraordinary job," [7] presented the results of the weekend's labors. Rayburn decided it was a bill worth working on, and Landis was temporarily detached from Harvard to work with Cohen and the legislative draftsman of the House of Representatives to produce the final bill. The three found a cubbyhole in the subbasement of a House office building where they worked all day, then at night took the bill back to the Carlton Hotel, where Corcoran joined them, for several weeks.

Frankfurter returned to Cambridge but continued as the general *in absentia,* keeping in close touch with Landis and Cohen and keeping Rayburn and Roosevelt informed of the bill's progress. Drafts went out to him; he sent them back with corrections and notes. When Landis and Cohen began to get on each other's nerves, Frankfurter sent Raymond Moley in to smooth things over.

Wall Street, sensing that its future might lie in the hands of a small group of New Deal lawyers, grew increasingly nervous and prevailed on Moley to persuade Sam Rayburn to listen to the other side of the story. Although this had been promised at the outset by Frankfurter, nothing had yet been done. Rayburn arranged a meeting between the members of his subcommittee, the legislation writers, and three New York lawyers—John Foster Dulles, Arthur H. Dean, and Alexander I. Henderson.

The lawyers came before the subcommittee either ill informed or ill prepared, and the House group was not impressed with the other side of the story. Rayburn was an admirer of the business world, but his admiration extended only to "clean" business; he wanted to renounce the "desperadoes." [8] After the meeting with the New York lawyers, Rayburn called Landis into his office and said, "I've been told by Chambers of Commerce and other outfits like this what I should do for years, and I've gone ahead and done whatever I thought was right to do." [9]

So, with a few finishing touches, Landis and Cohen submitted their bill to the subcommittee, which approved it and handed it on to the full Commerce Committee, which also approved. Shortly after, it was passed by the House of Representatives, with Cohen sitting alongside Rayburn to advise on amendments while the House debated.

In the meantime, another bill with the same purpose but different provisions was progressing through the Senate. Frankfurter believed it was unconstitutional and ineffective. He tried to get it stalled in the Senate committee until the Landis-Cohen bill was passed by the House but was unsuccessful. The Senate committee approved it. Frankfurter again tried to slow its progress, through Raymond Moley; again he failed, and the Senate passed its bill. As is the fate of such conflicts, the House and Senate bills were submitted to a conference committee to work out differences.

Frankfurter took his case for the Landis-Cohen measure to the highest authority: Roosevelt. In a night letter to the President on May 8, 1933, he urged, as the two bills went to conference, that Roosevelt support the House bill. It was, Frankfurter continued, "impossible to reconcile details of two bills because of great differences between two measures. To do so would involve interminable delay and jeopardize passage because powerful and increasing financial lobbies against all regulation will exploit differences to defeat enactment of your proposals. Great need is prompt enactment. This has nothing to do with pride of authorship but has everything to do with vindicating your desires effectively and constitutionally. . . ." [10]

Frankfurter continued to pressure Raymond Moley—who was also being pressured the other way by financial interests—to use his influence with Roosevelt to get the Landis-Cohen bill enacted into law.

Ultimately Roosevelt was persuaded. He did endorse the Landis-Cohen version of the Securities Act, as did Sam Rayburn, and it was substituted in conference for the Senate bill. Roosevelt signed it on May 27, 1933. Although the new law could not ensure against error of judgment, Roosevelt said, the measure had been designed to compel full and fair disclosure to investors of all material facts relating to new security issues publicly offered or sold through the mails or in interstate commerce. It assured that the federal government "will insist upon knowledge of the facts on which alone judgment can be based." Modeled on similar English legislation, the act provided that new securities be registered with the appropriate government agency (then the Federal Trade Commission; later the Securities and Exchange Commission), that every issue contain full information about the issuing company, and that any corporation officer who withheld pertinent information or misstated facts was criminally liable. Shortly after the bill was passed, James Landis was appointed to the Federal Trade Commission to administer it; Landis later succeeded Joseph P. Kennedy as chairman of the Securities and Exchange Commission.

Wall Street protested the new law vigorously. Raymond Moley himself believed it had been rushed through without adequate debate and without fair hearings of the "practical people who had to operate in the market and sell securities." [11] The bill undoubtedly was rushed through, as were so many bills that first Congressional session of Roosevelt's Presidency. Senator Henry Ashurst of Arizona wrote in his diary that year that Roosevelt's messages to Congress came so swiftly and the Congressmen "ground out laws so fast" that they had become "whirling dervishes." [12]

For his own part in it, Frankfurter received criticism from members of law firms and investment firms, strangers and friends.

He defended the act publicly in the August, 1933, *Fortune:*

> ... The Securities Act ... proceeds on the principle that when a corporation seeks funds from the public, it becomes in every true sense a public corporation. Its affairs cease to be the private perquisite of its bankers and managers; its bankers and managers themselves become public functionaries. This principle has been slow of acceptance, particularly with those profitably accustomed to the old and easy ways....

Frankfurter believed it was essentially a conservative act in that it assumed that "until less drastic remedies fail, the federal government should not embark on federal incorporation [or] exercise direct control over capital investments" or require the licensing of security issues. He believed it an act encouraging "self-discipline," rather than government intervention and control. By protecting the investor, it was designed also to encourage men to invest their capital and preserve this facet of the American system. It was legislation by expectation—designed in the assumption that financial interests had responsibilities, as well as rights, and that they would live up to them.

Frankfurter also defended the act privately. In the *Fortune* article he had written: "Legislation is not anticipation. It is a response . . . to serious need." [13] He told one critic privately that legislation may have to go very much beyond the elementary requirements of publicity and disclosure of the Securities Act if there were "unreasonable opposition to these minimum requirements" [14] on the part of Wall Street. The need would once again create new and more stringent legislation.

Frankfurter carried on a long and detailed correspondence with William O. Douglas, then a professor of law at Yale, later a member of the Securities and Exchange Commission, and an early Roosevelt appointment to the Supreme Court. Douglas had labeled the Securities Act of 1933 "a nineteenth century piece of legislation." [15] It did not go far enough, he argued, it was of secondary importance in a program of social control over finance, and that merely to tell the truth did not offer enough protection against skulduggery. Frankfurter agreed that the act was not a "world-shaker" and that it was essentially "an ordinary police measure." But, he added, "perfectionism in legislation . . . is hardly the goal of realists . . ." and "most of the complaints against the Act derive from hostility to its purposes." [16]

The Securities Act, he told one critic, would "only destroy those business practices which should never have been born. It will, on the other hand, fortify confidence in the proper activities of investment banking. For investment banking has, of course, a proper and important role. . . ." [17]

The act was, of course, typically Frankfurterian: designed to keep capital flowing into industry which required it, but designed also to restrain those who would exceed the speed limit. With only minimal restraints, it urged—expected—responsibility from financial interests.

The bill did not work. Wall Street was recalcitrant. The malpractices the act sought to eradicate were not eradicated. Another bill, more drastic and stringent, was put together by Cohen and Corcoran the following year while Frankfurter was in England. It removed securities from the Federal Trade Commission and created the Securities and Exchange Commission to deal with them. Enacted in June, 1934, just a year after the original legislation was signed, this second bill gave the SEC broad powers with which to cope with finance and to prohibit future malpractice. It accomplished what Frankfurter's more conservative bill had sought to do with publicity and "self-discipline." Frankfurter's fear that the need would again create sterner legislation had proved valid.

Public opinion, as expressed in the journals of the era, made Frankfurter seem almost sinister in his eagerness to man New Deal offices with young lawyers of his own philosophic, legal, or political persuasion. These young men were called variously the happy hot dogs or a plague of young lawyers or the stallions of Frankfurter's racing stable for lawyers, and they were charged with taking over the running of the government.

Frankfurter did indeed staff New Deal offices with young liberal lawyers. He sent Jerome Frank, later a federal judge, and Alger Hiss,* who on his recommendation had been a law clerk to Justice Holmes, to the Department of Agriculture.[19] He recommended Raymond B. Stevens to the Federal Trade Commission. He manipulated the appointment to the SEC of James Landis.

One of Frankfurter's suggestions was notable in that it initiated the tradition that the director of the Justice Department's Bureau of Investigation (later the Federal Bureau of Investigation) be a nonpartisan appointment.

Harlan Fiske Stone, who had been Attorney General under President Coolidge and who in 1933 was a Supreme Court Justice, wrote to Frankfurter in mid-April, knowing that Frankfurter was close to Roosevelt, that there were applicants for the post of director of the Bureau of Investigation of the old detective agency type who would be amenable to political influence. Stone explained that he, as Attorney General, had appointed a high-principled man to that post, J. Edgar Hoover, and urged that although Hoover was a Republican

* In 1949 Hiss was on trial for perjury in connection with charges that he had passed government secrets to Russian agents in the 1930's. Frankfurter, then a Supreme Court Justice, testified in court, with his colleague Justice Stanley F. Reed, as a character witness for Hiss. In his testimony Frankfurter described Hiss's character as "excellent" and explained he knew Hiss first as an editor of the *Harvard Law Review* and in 1929 chose him from the entire body of law graduates as "the man I could most confidently recommend"[18] to serve as law clerk to Justice Oliver Wendell Holmes.

appointee, he ought to be retained, that his administration of the office had removed it from political influence and activities that had characterized it in the past.[20]

Frankfurter replied to Stone: "Your letter of the 14th regarding the Bureau of Investigation seemed to me so important that I hope you will forgive me for having placed it directly in the President's hands. Knowing his desires and his attitude towards you, I thought direct action was the best action and that he ought to read what you had written as you had written it. I do hope you won't regard what I have done as a breach of confidence. . . ." [21]

Hoover was retained by Roosevelt—and Presidents Truman, Eisenhower, Kennedy, Johnson, and Nixon.

Frankfurter's triumphs in the Roosevelt administration were Thomas G. Corcoran—"Tommy the Cork"—and Benjamin V. Cohen. Corcoran, of the brash, high Irish spirits, had been law clerk to Holmes, was a close friend of Brandeis', and had for five years been a Wall Street lawyer. Yielding to a yearning for public service instilled by Frankfurter at Harvard Law School, he had gone to Washington in 1932, under President Hoover, to the legal staff of the Reconstruction Finance Corporation. When the administration passed to Roosevelt in 1933, Corcoran remained, to turn RFC into a funnel for Frankfurter men and a reservoir of talent for the rapidly expanding government agencies. His base of operations for a time remained the RFC, but he operated in every agency in town. When Louis Howe, Roosevelt's right hand, fell ill in 1935, Frankfurter recommended Corcoran as a replacement, a suggestion followed by Roosevelt. It has been said that this gave Frankfurter a direct line to the White House. In fact, Frankfurter had long had a direct line to the White House in view of his long-standing friendship and close public association with Roosevelt. Although he used Corcoran as both informant and conduit, Frankfurter's access to Roosevelt did not need improvement.

Benjamin Cohen was Corcoran's complement: shy, sometimes moody, "a man of ideas and reflection." [22] He became a prominent member of Roosevelt's kitchen cabinet, specializing in the drafting of legislation, often under Frankfurter's tutelage. Like Corcoran, Cohen began with the RFC. Stanley Reed, then general counsel for the agency, later Solicitor General, and finally a Supreme Court Justice, described the pair during their early days in Washington together as "inquisitive, talkative, bright. . . . I finally had to put them in a group all to themselves because I couldn't run them with anybody else. They never got there until twelve o'clock in the morning . . . they were just going well about six in the afternoon, and they went home about six the next morning. . . ." [23]

During these Roosevelt years, Frankfurter recommended men, sometimes through Corcoran, for jobs in all levels of government, not just high positions. Corcoran himself had once defined government as "not just the top man. . . . A government is the top one hundred or two hundred men. What really makes the difference is what happens down the line before—and after—the big decisions are taken." [24]

Corcoran and Cohen and the men who followed them came with bravado in their hearts and intellectual excitement in their heads and transformed Washington, wrote Ray Tucker in *Collier's,* "from a placid, leisurely Southern town, with frozen faces and customs, into a gay, breezy, sophisticated and metropolitan center." [25] They were self-confident—or cocky, depending on the observer—and bright, and their appetite for reform was inexhaustible. But, wrote Raymond Moley, a prominent New Dealer, "they were quite unacquainted with the art of administration and unfamiliar with the practical workings of the economic system." [26]

The men Frankfurter recommended were not necessarily Democrats. When Jerome Frank was enlarging the staff of the Agricultural Adjustment Agency, he found that Frankfurter, "both with respect to me and elsewhere, pretty much recommended men without regard to their ideologies but primarily because of their competence as legal technicians." [27]

Most of Frankfurter's recommendations were solicited; rarely, and he took pride in it, did he offer a man's name unasked. Sometimes his suggestions were acted upon; at other times they were not. One of his failures was to get his longtime friend Dean G. Acheson, former Brandeis law clerk, later Undersecretary of the Treasury and still later Secretary of State, appointed Solicitor General of the United States. Another well-known failure was his inability to persuade Roosevelt to appoint Learned Hand to the Supreme Court.

Frankfurter's staffing of New Deal offices in quantity partly stemmed from the insatiable hunger for talent demanded by these offices, expanding under Roosevelt at enormous rates, plus the Depression's depletion of opportunities in private practice for young law school graduates. Partly, too, it stemmed from Roosevelt's confidence in Frankfurter's dependability. But it was nothing new for Frankfurter. He had been operating a one-man employment agency at Harvard Law School almost since he had first set foot in the place. He had long sent promising young men to law firms in large cities. He had sent men into the Republican administrations of the 1920's. When Henry Stimson, as Secretary of State under Hoover or as senior partner of his New York law firm, was looking for a man to do a job, he applied to Frankfurter. Frankfurter had sent aides to Gifford Pinchot, governor of Pennsylvania, and to Herbert Lehman, governor of New York. He had recommended men to the Wilson administration, to private industry, to the Zionists, and to the judiciary.

The men he sent into government, whatever the administration, were the practical application of his ideal of an educated, trained civil service which was consonant with, indeed an extension of, his philosophy of teaching. This lack of such a bank of talent, he said in 1936, "transcends all other problems of government." [28]

Frankfurter was fond of telling an illustrative story about Lincoln during the depressing days of the Civil War. A friend found him sitting in his study and ventured the hope that there was no bad news from the front. Lincoln answered that it was not the Union armies he was worried about; it was "that damned post-mastership in Podunk." [29]

Government had changed remarkably over the past quarter century. From a simple policeman it had evolved into "an expression and agent of society," a "promoter of society's welfare," [30] Frankfurter wrote in 1936. It was subsidizing railroads and business, building dams and airports. It was helping farmers out of their economic difficulties. It was administering economic aid to the aged and unemployed. Alphabetical agencies were proliferating and promised to proliferate more. Government had enlarged enormously and would enlarge more in the future, with the tasks it would be called on to perform becoming proportionately more complex.

Such vast and complicated enterprise had to be manned by people with ability, intelligence, skills, and broad education. Government by improvisation, however honest and eager, was no longer adequate. "... We can no longer afford to do without a highly trained, disinterested governmental personnel," [31] Frankfurter had told Stimson in 1934.

Frankfurter believed that only thoroughly trained experts could unravel the technicalities. Not decide policy. That ought to be decided by the politicians as the expression of the will of the people appropriate to democratic standards. But, he told students at Yale in 1930, "In this country we have been so anxious to avoid the dangers of having the expert on top that we suffer from a strong reluctance to have him on tap. . . ." [32]

Anglophile that he was, Frankfurter found the model to copy in the British civil service, where, for example, "The commissioners for the Internal Revenue are some of the most scientific minds in England," he told an audience at Smith College in 1933. "They stay, no matter who comes and who goes at the Treasury, and all along the lines." [33] The policymakers changed with each administration; the technicians—trained, employed in accordance with rigid standards—stayed on to administer the policies enunciated by elected officials and appointees.

What was demanded by the complexity of the American government was a vast reservoir of educated talent, equipped to analyze problems and explore remedies, "a permanent and professional public service." [34]

The universities ought diligently to prepare men for government service, although "not through utilitarian courses, but by the whole sweep of their culture and discipline," [35] as Oxford and Cambridge turned out competent candidates for the British civil service. British experience had established, Frankfurter wrote, "that the civil service fares best with men of a high standard of general education who receive their specialized instruction in a probationary year in the departments. . . ." [36]

And government ought to take advantage of this well of talent. Government ought to imitate the biggest and most successful law offices in the country and devise a system of recruiting for lower ranks the top men from the graduating classes of universities. "From such recruits," explained Frankfurter, "the government could hope to develop at least a portion into permanent public servants of higher grade." [37]

At the moment, the government as an employer was at a disadvantage in its competition with private industry for the best talent.

However, Frankfurter urged, government ought to make itself more attractive in terms of salary and prestige. "It is right that government should not even pretend to compete with the enormous salaries by which private enterprise tempts. The satisfactions of government service lie on a different level," he told students at Yale in 1930. "But it is wholly wrong to expect civilized standards of public service from officials whose salaries are too low to enable them to meet the minimum standards of cultivated life. . . . Economy in public service means a wise expenditure of money. It does not mean salaries so low that only the unfit and the transient are attracted." [38]

Frankfurter's reputation as the employment agency for the New Deal attracted mail sacks of letters which began variously:

"You and I were classmates. . . ."

"I was one of your students. . . ."

"Reading about you in the newspaper today as being 'the most influential person in the United States' I immediately thought you might be able to offer some suggestions on my predicament. . . ."

"I have been so often told by Harvard boys of your admirable readiness to help out puzzled, young lawyers. . . ."

"I am desirous of contributing towards the solution of the great problems faced by the administration in Washington, D.C. . . ."

An understanding friend sent Frankfurter the résumé of an applicant with this note attached: "Dear Felix: He ought to be added to your file of 4,841 swell people who want exciting work in life. There must be a job for him somewhere in Washington." [39]

For the first nine months of the Roosevelt administration, Frankfurter commuted between Cambridge and Washington, attending his Harvard classes and seminars during the week. He knew all the men in the higher echelons. He could meet and work with them on terms of easy affability, dropping in and out of administration offices, checking on the progress of legislation here, an appointment there, discussing a delicate political matter somewhere else, his rapid-fire questions and explanations continuing long past midnight, his speech never slowing from its customary allegro pace. Frankfurter had a facility to make himself at home with almost any type of personality. He could summon sophistication, intellectuality, or august formality when occasion required it. He could also with equanimity settle down to a convivial drinking bout with Vice President John

N. "Cactus Jack" Garner. In fact, Roosevelt liked to tell how one afternoon Garner, who had a reputation for holding his liquor, and Frankfurter did just that. Garner had to be helped home; Frankfurter's careful enunciation, when he arrived at the White House for cocktails, was the only clue that he had been drinking at all.

When Frankfurter was not in Washington, his voluminous letters and telegrams poured in, not only to Roosevelt but to others within the administration.

Some of these were newsletters, apprising Roosevelt or one of his aides of support or opposition to administration action.

Some of Frankfurter's letters were simply words of encouragement or congratulation to Roosevelt, and in a sense, Frankfurter was an official handholder of the administration. To Roosevelt, barraged by articulate critics outside and his own advisers inside, these flowery letters of praise, often comparing Roosevelt to Lincoln, were refreshing, welcome, and more frequently answered than those in which Frankfurter proffered sage advice.

Some of Frankfurter's letters, to both Roosevelt and others of his officialdom, were packed with technical advice about bills being drafted by administration lawyers—Section 304 of the banking bill needed clarification, and Frankfurter would proceed to clarify it in detail. Suggestions to Raymond Moley on how to administer the act went out in memos. There were new drafts of bills submitted to cover contingencies Frankfurter believed ought to be covered.

Some of these were worked out with Justice Brandeis, Frankfurter's longtime mentor, who remained a shadowy figure in the background of the New Deal, but whose influence was often there. Cabinet officials consulted him on departmental matters. Frankfurter consulted him. His former law clerks were working directly with the administration.

But Brandeis, like Frankfurter, Moley, Rexford G. Tugwell, Adolf Berle, and the rest who completed the inner circle around Roosevelt during these early years, was but one of a diverse and frequently divergent group whose ideas were culled, sorted, and digested, then acted on by Roosevelt. Brandeis' influence was pervasive, but not controlling.

It was usual for Roosevelt to ask several people to take on the same task, then invite them to fight out their multiplicity of ideas around a conference table. He enjoyed gathering such a profusion of ideas so that he could choose the best of each, reject the bad features of all, and work out his own approach. A typical story about Roosevelt has it that when two speech writers presented him with texts containing two opposing philosophic concepts, Roosevelt said, "Weave them together."

Frankfurter was a regular caller at the White House, where he sat in on some of the President's conferences and presented his ideas in long conversations alone with Roosevelt. Grace Tully, Roosevelt's secretary, reported that she more than once "found the Boss slumped exhausted in his chair after a deskside luncheon session of two or three hours with Frankfurter. . . ." Roosevelt would remark: "Felix left here looking as fresh as a daisy and I'm like a wet rag." [40]

In addition to his letters and conferences with the doers of the New Deal, Frankfurter rushed about the country like an evangelist trying to convert people to Roosevelt's cause. He believed the nation was at one of the important junctures of history and no ordinary measures could point it in the right direction. He enthusiastically sought support for Roosevelt's extraordinary measures. He feared that if effective remedial action did not save the system, destructive action very well might kill it.

He demanded responsible action from national leaders outside the administration. The central philosophy of the New Deal, he wrote, "derived from the conviction that money is not a matter merely of private rights; it involves responsibilities and its responsibilities may call for a distribution of other people's money to those who have a just claim upon it. . . ." [41]

Through these early Roosevelt months, Frankfurter began to accumulate a reputation as sitting at the right hand of the President, and he, too, became the recipient of advice and suggestions which the senders—both strangers and friends—hoped he would pass on to Roosevelt. To such appeals he had a standard refusal: He was not in office and had no responsibility for public policy, reports in the press notwithstanding.

[3]

When Frankfurter turned down Roosevelt's offer of the solicitor generalship in March, 1933, he offered as one of his reasons, although not the controlling one, that he had accepted an appointment at Oxford for the 1933–34 term. He had been chosen George Eastman Visiting Professor in the fall of 1932, for the following term. It was an annual professorship endowed by the late George Eastman in 1929 for a professorship-at-large at one of the several colleges of the English university. Frankfurter accepted it eagerly, quickly, and with "a feeling of awe" [1] which Oxford aroused in him. He took sabbatical leave from Harvard, and sailed, aboard HMS *Britannic,* on September 24, 1933, for England, where he was to be a temporary fellow of Balliol College.

Long before he sailed for his year in England, Frankfurter had been what one English friend called an "Anglo-maniac." [2] He had the typical cultured Central European Jew's reverence for English liberalism and democracy, and he had reinforced that reverence with saturation reading in English history, law, and government. He cultivated English friends and instinctively admired what he saw as their general democratic perspective.

Throughout his life Frankfurter translated his admiration of the British into the public issues and causes with which he became involved. He cited English criminal codes as models for American law-enforcement agencies and the English civil service as a model for an American civil service. He used English legislation as models for American laws. Even when he joined the Supreme Court, he cited English law and quoted English jurists freely and frequently—to the point where a friend later wrote: "I admire the English, but F. F.'s rhapsodies—a favorite subject—make me a little weary. There is something about it that troubles me; quite uncritical. . . ." [3]

In his year at Oxford, Frankfurter reveled in the opportunity to observe English institutions firsthand; he also perceived a chance to further Anglo-American amity. Like his academic career at Harvard, his academic career at Oxford had two related sides: academic and public.

As the Frankfurters arrived in England, the academic world of Oxford was less than anticipatory. Visiting professors came and went in this ancient and hallowed shrine of learning. Most of them were at least as eminent in their fields as Frankfurter.

Among the more politically oriented, however, both at Oxford and outside the university, Frankfurter was looked on at the least as an unofficial ambassador from Roosevelt. He was a man who ought to be cultivated for public rather than academic reasons.

At Oxford, Frankfurter's primary purpose was academic. But he could not help being identified with public issues. They were, after all, his whole life, his consuming interest, a major preoccupation of his conversation, and the practical manifestations of his academic life.

Before he sailed for England, Frankfurter spent, at his own request,[4] an overnight visit at the White House in which he reviewed with Roosevelt the goals and accomplishments of the New Deal to date, with the purpose of explaining these to the British. In turn, Frankfurter promised Roosevelt firsthand reports on situations international, particularly English. Roosevelt gave Frankfurter notes of introduction to American ambassadors abroad and carte blanche to use the diplomatic pouch for communications to the White House.[5]

Frankfurter spent a good deal of his English year with other than academic personalities. He renewed his acquaintance with the noted unorthodox and controversial English economist John Maynard Keynes, whom Frankfurter had known at the Paris Peace Conference of 1919. Keynes was an intellectual and theoretical economist who had developed his views through the experience of winning and losing fortunes as a speculator and insurance company executive. Keynes was sympathetic generally to Roosevelt's handling of the American economic crisis but differed in some details. Frankfurter believed Roosevelt could benefit from a talk with Keynes and gave Keynes, who was shortly to leave for the United States, an introduction to Roosevelt.

Frankfurter sent others he believed important in English affairs to see Roosevelt, including Sir Stafford Cripps, at that time a leader in the Labour Party and, Frankfurter predicted, a dominant member of any Labour government likely to come to power. Frankfurter also renewed acquaintances with old friends such as Lord Eustace Percy, with whom he had lived so many years ago at the House of Truth and who by 1933 was prominent in English government circles.

He also made a host of new friends, many of them prominent and influential. Not all were in government. There were among his friends scientists, philosophers, economists, journalists, classical scholars, art critics—the whole gamut.

Frankfurter spoke, too, on the British Broadcasting Corporation radio. He explained American views of the English; he discussed the policies of the English press, from an American point of view, with moguls of the British newspapers—the substance of which he passed on to Roosevelt.

Harold Laski reported to Holmes about midterm that Frankfurter was doing an excellent job in bringing home to the elite America's importance and the real meaning of Roosevelt's policies.

Frankfurter listened as eagerly as he talked. He wanted to know what Englishmen were thinking, what they were saying, what they were writing about themselves, America, and the world. There were some who thought Frankfurter was a conduit to Roosevelt, and they spoke the things they wanted passed on.

On occasion, Roosevelt requested Frankfurter's perspective on English political matters, and Frankfurter reported in detail all he had read, heard, or seen from all his diverse sources; at the end of the term he had a long interview with the British Prime Minister concerning Anglo-American relations.[6]

In the spring of 1934, Frankfurter made a short trip to Palestine, his first visit to the Holy Land, although he had worked on its problems and been dedicated to its success for many years. On the return trip he bubbled to Henry Stimson: "... The land is of magical beauty and man's efforts here, at present, are not unworthy of nature. ... I explored almost the whole small country intensively and tapped all shifts of opinion, British, Arab, and Jewish. The Jewish renascence is really incredible, and it is lifting to decent levels the terrible squalid condition of the fellaheen. ..." [7] Frankfurter's faith in Jewish nationhood never wavered through all the dark days of the 1940's, when both Arab and Jew threatened to ruin their desert country by washing it with each other's blood. He did not support the United Nations' solution of creating two independent states out of Palestine—a separation that saw the birth of Israel. He had always hoped Arab and Jew would be able to reason together, in a civilized manner, and contribute to each other in the land they shared.

As for Frankfurter at Oxford, he was an overnight sensation. If his imminent arrival did not wrest the dons from their apathy, his presence did.

Frankfurter had an enormous quantity of personal charm. It was not always apparent in the seriousness and passion with which he embraced public causes. But people who knew him intimately pointed it out as his single most important gift of character. He had gaiety—what he called the Blue Danube side of his nature. He had wit—and he admired wit in others. He enjoyed frivolity and nonsense. He had an infectious exuberance for new ideas, adventures, and, most of all, people, which drew others to him—a rare genius for friendship.

He expended a vast amount of his charm on Oxford. He was enjoying an adventure with a relaxation he had seldom known before. While he was soaking up the atmosphere of English life and institutions, he was also relishing a life without deadlines—without statutes to devise or briefs to put together. He was relatively free to indulge his gaiety and wit and ebullience to the utmost, and he did.

He complimented his new colleagues with his almost childlike reverence for all things English, and most of them responded. He tore down the dons' traditional defenses of reserve and self-confidence with his uninhibited and unembarrassed joy and enthusiasm. He earned their respect for his intelligence. He gave lavishly of his affection; they returned it with theirs.

Frankfurter painted an idyllic picture of his English adventure in a letter to a friend. The letter is untypical Frankfurter in that its style, a departure from the usual crisp, urgent phrasing, is the rambling letter of a man simply enjoying himself: ". . . All goes well and interestingly with us. We are having a most glorious kind of fall weather; Cambridge could do no better, for roses would not bloom in Brattle Street as they bloom here, and the green on the various quads make history and peace in a much troubled world steal into one's soul. I am continuing to dine in one college after another, and Marion rightly says this is only a place for a feminist woman—not only one who needs no man but indeed has no use for him. But she is dining out on her own. . . . In order that Marion and I may see each other, she has asked me—to use her own words—'like other people, for an appointment.' And so from 2:30 till tea time—already a religious institution with us—we walk exploring moats and the town wall of the fourteenth century and Addison's Walk and all sorts of tucked-away ancient beauties and new delights. Oh, yes, don't worry, I am also lecturing twice a week and have a seminar attended by law dons. . . . The seminar is held in a lovely room at All Souls. . . . Besides, there are students and dons to see, and books to read, and delightful 'consilium' at Balliol—a sort of faculty meeting, once a week, and generally a good time is being had.

"But one knows," he added soberly, "one is in a strange land, with strange people who use our words but do not speak our language. . . ." [8]

For Frankfurter, the year at Oxford, with its firsthand contact with English life, vivified his interest in English people and institutions and reinforced his instinctive admiration for the British. The Frankfurters returned to England again and again for visits.

The experience also nurtured his professionalism. Seeing Parliament in action, having lunch with the members, talking with English men of affairs were in essence not much different from talking with Senators and Presidents and judges, economists, social workers, and laboring men back in America. It gave the added dimension he always craved to the academic side of his nature.

All that he had read about over such a long period of time came alive, like actors in a drama he had studied before he went to the theater.

Frankfurter made, too, a permanent impression on Oxford. In 1939 he was given the degree of honorary Doctor of Civil Laws. Then, after his death, for the first time in Oxford's 700-year history, a fellowship was named after a man not a British subject or citizen of a Commonwealth country. In 1966 the Felix Frankfurter Fellowship was endowed at Balliol College, Oxford, where Frankfurter had taught in 1933–34.

Frankfurter returned to the United States in the summer of 1934. In late August he reported to Roosevelt conditions in England and Europe generally as he saw them and caught up on administration affairs he had missed, although his reading of American daily newspapers and his numerous correspondents in the United States had kept him somewhat informed during his sabbatical. In the fall of 1934, he resumed his teaching duties at Harvard Law School.

At Harvard, Dean Roscoe Pound had passed the age of sixty. Not only had he carried the immense burdens of administering the law school for fifteen years, but he had also consumed his energies in works of legal scholarship. Dean Pound ran the law school, as a faculty member later wrote, "as if he had just bought fifty-one percent of the stock," [9] accepting differences with his opinions and policies somewhat ungraciously. Age seemed to emphasize this characteristic.

His irritation with Frankfurter, who had been at one time devoted to Pound, had begun with Frankfurter's espousal of the cause of Sacco and Vanzetti. Irritation had ripened into open feud with Frankfurter's becoming a prominent member of Roosevelt's retinue, whose policies Pound abhorred, and with Frankfurter's frequent postponement of classes so he could commute to Washington. The feud was further fed by Frankfurter's refusal, immediately after his return to the school from England, to attend, with the law school faculty, a ceremony in which Pound was given an honorary degree from the University of Berlin—and given it by the German ambassador. As Pound despised Roosevelt's programs, Frankfurter even more deeply despised the policies of Nazi Germany, and he refused, he said, to be a part of a "tail to a Nazi kite." [10] The rupture between Frankfurter and Pound divided the faculty into two camps and strained relations between them throughout Pound's deanship, which lasted until 1936.

There were also troubles developing within the Roosevelt administration. Business, which had begun to recover from the Depression, wanted no further disciplinary legislation and feared that recovery measures might lead to permanent reform. Business was ready to return to the old ways.

"We are back in the Harding-Coolidge days," Frankfurter was to write by spring, 1935. "In his little piece this morning, Will Rogers goes to the root of the phenomena. 'Everybody that is making money has it in for Roosevelt.' It is rather sickening the way they grouse and very sad for the outlook of things the way they have learned nothing." [11]

Dissident factions who attracted alarmingly large followings came from sources other than business. Senator Huey P. Long of Louisiana, piqued at Roosevelt's largess to Long's political enemies, began a campaign against the President. Father Charles Coughlin of Royal Oak, Michigan, a silver-tongued priest who took his sermons into politics, economics, and social causes, led his growing flock against Roosevelt, finally classifying Roosevelt with the "godless capitalists, the Jews, communists, international bankers, and plutocrats." [12] Dr. Francis E. Townsend agitated for a utopian tax plan to finance old age and drew an immense following. This trio of self-appointed messiahs, capitalizing on the discontent and confusion of the little man, for whom recovery was not coming fast enough—the small farmer, the lowly factory worker still chained to his machine—sought to unseat Roosevelt and wrest power for themselves.

Within the administration, quarrels over where to go next were dividing Roosevelt's advisers. One group was pulling Roosevelt to the left—believing he should cement temporary recovery measures with permanent and stringent reform. A second group was pulling Roosevelt to the right—with the Depression started on an upswing, government and business should be returned to their old distant relationship. Roosevelt himself was zigging and zagging, trying to steer a middle course. "I am fighting Communism, Huey Longism, Coughlinism, Townsendism. I want to save our system, the capitalistic system; to save it is to give some heed to world thought of today. I want to equalize the distribution of wealth." [13]

Frankfurter continued to send Roosevelt men and to reiterate the same theme: The system must be saved. He denounced pulls to the right and left and continued to project advice that he believed would alleviate economic and social problems without damaging the basic American system of free enterprise. Abuses must be curbed, but the government must exercise restraint—as later he urged the judiciary to exercise restraint—and business must be encouraged to assume responsibility.

Abuses, Frankfurter believed, were especially rampant in the field of public utilities, a preoccupation of his at Harvard Law School. As a young lawyer in the United States Attorney's office, he had believed the cases of railroad rebates and fraudulent financial manipulations that were prosecuted from that office were the aberrations of big business. In his study of the public utilities field at the law school and in his experiences as consultant to Roosevelt, during whose governorship of New York political and financial corruption in public utilities management was exposed, Frankfurter became more and more familiar with the devices of financiers to control utilities and reap enormous profits. More and more he came to believe that what he had thought were aberrations were in fact standard operating procedure.

Utilities were being run, he said, not in the public interest but, rather, only in the interest of the financial backers. There were two basic problems: Rates were set irrespective of service; regulation was ineffective.

Claiming economic efficiency, the trend in utility financing was toward monopoly—and manipulation. "In the consolidation of utilities extremely high prices are paid for the stock of the acquired companies, with consequent pressure for rates high enough to permit profit on the investment," Frankfurter had written in 1930. "Because of bankers' control of utilities, their policies are largely determined not by utility managers nor with reference to their public obligations. Bankers who finance utilities, naturally enough, look upon them like other investments." [14]

By complicated corporate arrangements—most prominent among them the holding company, in which several utilities affiliated under one financial unit—the public utilities had placed themselves outside the competence and legal jurisdiction of the existing regulatory system embodied in the Interstate Commerce Act of 1887 and the regulatory systems established by some of the states. To a utility lawyer Frankfurter had written in 1930: ". . . Utilities ought to be out of the stream of speculative money-making . . ." [15] where he believed the dominant influences then were. He feared that if they did not police themselves and if local controls were not improved, there was no alternative to policing by the federal government.

Roosevelt believed that at the root of the trouble was the holding company, whose manipulations had not been curbed. In an echo of Frankfurter's 1930 writings, Roosevelt said that the holding company was a financial unit, devised not to invest in utility development, but to make money. If the swollen profits to the holding companies, which did nothing except manipulate, were redistributed to the operating companies, which actually were concerned with service, then utility rates could be drastically reduced. That, at least, was the Roosevelt-Frankfurter thesis.

In the fall of 1934, Roosevelt began his attack on holding companies by summoning a group of advisers to his Warm Springs, Georgia, retreat and charging them with devising legislation to eliminate the culprits. Since these holding companies had eluded regulation, they had to be abolished.

Two months later, Frankfurter wrote Roosevelt that he had noticed Roosevelt's interest in holding companies and agreed that since these companies had no economic or social justification, they ought indeed to go. However, he warned, they could not be eliminated quickly, and perhaps, Frankfurter suggested, Roosevelt should try to discourage them with stringent regulation and taxation.[16]

The bill that emerged, known as the Wheeler-Rayburn bill, was written by Frankfurter's two Washington lieutenants, Cohen and Corcoran, and pronounced the death sentence on any holding company which could not show beyond any doubt that the public was better served by its financial control than without it. The business community came out in force to defend the holding company. One of the most articulate spokesmen for the financiers was Wendell L. Willkie, then president of the Commonwealth and Southern utilities system. Spearheading the lobbying activities of businessmen against the holding company bill, he admitted that there had been excesses within the companies but declared these were aberrations, and he even produced a regulatory plan of his own based on state regulation.

Early in the fight for the holding company bill, Willkie and Harvey Couch, also a utilities system executive, took their suggestions to the White House to discuss them with Roosevelt and federal power interests. The discussion turned soon to argument between Roosevelt and Willkie, with Willkie barking at Roosevelt and Roosevelt "jutting his chin out and becoming less and less conciliatory." The conference ended with Willkie's asking Roosevelt: "Do I understand then that any further efforts to avoid the breaking up of utility holding companies are futile?"

Roosevelt replied with finality: "It is futile."

A few weeks later Roosevelt asked David E. Lilienthal, then a director of the Tennessee Valley Authority (TVA), "Who was that fellow who was in here the other day with Harvey Couch and who leaned over and shook his glass at me?"

Lilienthal answered: "Wendell Willkie." [17] The two men—Roosevelt and Willkie—would meet again in 1940, when Roosevelt ran for a third term in the White House and Willkie was the Republican candidate opposing him.

Frankfurter estimated that the utilities companies spent $10,-000,000 to fight passage of the Wheeler-Rayburn bill. Knowing Frankfurter was an intimate of Roosevelt's, lawyers sent Frankfurter letters arguing that the financial backing provided by the holding companies was necessary to keep the public utilities operating.

In Congress, the fight for the holding company bill was uphill, as pressure not only from financiers but from local utilities managers was applied to Congressmen. The bill passed the Senate intact, but the House balked at the more drastic features and after a bitter debate passed a less stringent measure. The two bills went to a conference committee.

While the conferees tried to devise a bill acceptable to both houses of Congress, Senator Hugo La Fayette Black of Alabama led an investigation of the lobbying activities of utilities men. The Black investigation showed one of the rawest and most arrogant displays of immorality on the part of business. The Black Committee was able to report early in its investigation that the utilities had spent at least $1,500,000 on telegrams and letters as a spontaneous expression of sentiment against the bill, then charged the expense to the cost of delivering electricity to the public.

"I have no more sympathy in the attempt to regulate the holding companies," Senator Black had said, "than to regulate a rattlesnake." [18] The holding companies ought to go.

While the conferees worked on the Hill for a compromise bill, Frankfurter worked in the White House to devise a formula which both Senate and House would accept. The Senate bill would have abolished all holding companies which controlled more than one integrated utilities system. (Holding company-utilities arrangements had been piled one on top of the other, pyramid-style, until the super company at the top had very little relationship to the actual operating companies at the bottom. The Senate bill would have allowed holding companies to continue to finance utilities so long as they had not been pyramided and so long as there was no more than one holding company per utilities system.) The Frankfurter compromise allowed the utilities system to retain any or all holding companies whose financial backing was necessary to utilities operation and so long as the arrangement was not so scattered that effective public service was impaired. The Securities and Exchange Commission was to supervise and judge the adequacy of the arrangements.

The Senate and House accepted Frankfurter's compromise. On August 26, 1935, Roosevelt reluctantly signed the bill—he had wanted the holding companies eliminated. The bill was typically Frankfurterian—designed to save the system but curb the abuses. So long as utilities were not impaired by their parent companies and so long as the public interest was served, the parent companies could continue in operation. In short, so long as business lived up to its responsibilities, no action against it would be taken.

Throughout the 1930's, Frankfurter never abandoned his interest in minimum wage legislation. When the Depression descended on an economy that had appeared to be bursting at its seams, with its lowering of wages and further impoverishment of a large number of workers, once again the National Consumers' League made an attempt to reestablish wage legislation as a method of alleviating the poverty of these masses. The league enlisted Frankfurter, who had argued for the District of Columbia minimum wage law in 1923 and lost, and Benjamin Cohen.

Frankfurter warned the league it would be "foolish beyond words . . . to be hopeful that a changed Court or changing times will make for a very liberal outlook on the part of the Court" and a reversal of the 1923 decision. "I can assure you that there is no right to any such hope under the leadership of Hughes [Chief Justice Charles Evans Hughes, who had succeeded Taft in 1930], let alone the others."

The only way to establish minimum wage legislation, therefore, Frankfurter told the league, "is to get some kind of a law sustained which will start a new line of decision on which we can build. That kind of development, that mode of departing from a mischievous past, is . . . the mode by which effective modifications of past mischievous decisions and especially of a mischievous line of decisions, have been achieved. . . ." [19]

Frankfurter and Cohen collaborated in putting together a model bill which they hoped would be viewed by the Supreme Court differently from the District of Columbia statute and would initiate another line of decision. "Every word" of it was "written with the Supreme Court of the United States in mind." [20]

The Frankfurter-Cohen bill was introduced into the legislatures of eight states and passed in six, including New York. It was, of course, promptly challenged and went to the New York Court of Appeals, which declared it unconstitutional.

Six weeks after the New York Court of Appeals declared the law unconstitutional, Henry Epstein, solicitor general of New York, and Dean Acheson, for the Consumers' League, sought to show the Supreme Court of the United States that the new law was different from the one which the Court had declared unconstitutional in 1923. But the Court declared, in the decision which became famous as *Morehead v. New York ex rel. Tipaldo,* it found no such difference and upheld the decision of the New York State Court of Appeals.

"The right to make contracts," wrote Justice Pierce Butler for the majority in June, 1936, echoing previous decisions, "about one's affairs is a part of the liberty protected by the due process clause.... In making contracts of employment, generally speaking, the parties have equal rights to obtain from each other the best terms they can by private bargaining." [21]

The New York *Times* editorialized: "It is possible, of course, that a new law might be written in this State the constitutionality of which would be upheld by the present membership of the Court. But the outlook here is not promising, considering the care which went into the preparation of the invalidated law and the efforts made to accommodate it to the 1923 decision...." [22]

"The present membership of the Court" was the controlling factor in these minimum wage cases. One block within the Supreme Court was made up of archconservatives: James Clark McReynolds, George Sutherland, Pierce Butler, Willis Van Devanter—the "Four Horsemen" aligned in political conservatism, defense of wealth and property, and distrust of the people. Opposing these four was a tight block of three Justices: Louis Brandeis, Benjamin N. Cardozo, and Harlan Fiske Stone. The remaining two of the "nine old men," as columnists wryly named them, were swing men: Charles Evans Hughes, who had begun to move slightly to the left, and Owen J. Roberts. Prior to the Republican convention of 1936, there was talk of Roberts' being drafted as a Presidential candidate, and his Supreme Court opinions teetered from defense of property to defense of the masses. Then, as the search for a conservative candidate grew more serious, Roberts aligned himself more definitely with the Four Horsemen, making it Five Horsemen, a clearer majority for conservatism, and ruling that New York could not establish a minimum wage law for women.

It was to break this conservative group's hold on New Deal recovery measures—which it had been quick to overturn also—that Roosevelt sent to Congress in February, 1937, a bill to enlarge the Supreme Court—his famous Court-packing, or Court reform, plan, depending on one's viewpoint.

One of the most controversial events surrounding the relationship of Frankfurter and Roosevelt is this plan for reorganization of the Supreme Court and of Frankfurter's involvement in it.

Throughout the fight between Roosevelt and Congress, from February, 1937, until the plan was defeated in July, 1937, Frankfurter kept both public and private silence—in fact, he maintained his silence for the rest of his life. And since it was expected that one of Roosevelt's closest advisers and a leading constitutional scholar should have some public thoughts on this important public issue, Frankfurter's silence served to magnify the controversy that arose over his role in the conflict.

On the morning of Friday, February 5, 1937, Roosevelt announced to his Cabinet and Congressional leaders—and shortly afterward to the country—his bill to reorganize the Supreme Court of the United States.

For two years he had watched, helpless, while the Court destroyed the legislative program by which he had tried to cure the nation's ills. One New Deal measure after another—the Agricultural Adjustment Act, National Recovery Act, Railroad Retirement Act, and nine others—were declared unconstitutional. With a few exceptions —usually Justices Brandeis, Stone, and Cardozo—the Justices of the Supreme Court still conceived their duty, as they had in the earlier years of the century, when Frankfurter and Brandeis were vainly urging them to allow the states to pass minimum wage legislation, as the duty of passing on the desirability of a law. They had, said Brandeis in 1924, assumed the functions of a "super-legislature." And as conservatives still, they believed New Deal legislation undesirable.

With his plan for reorganizing the Supreme Court, Roosevelt intended to strike back.

He had been President for four years—more than a full term in office—and had not had an opportunity to appoint a single Justice to the Supreme Court. The reorganization plan was a device to allow Roosevelt to appoint men of his philosophic persuasion to the Court. It was a simple plan. The Supreme Court had nine members. Six were over seventy years of age. For each member of the Court who refused to retire at the age of seventy, Roosevelt proposed that a co-Justice be appointed to serve alongside the older Justice. If his bill became law, Roosevelt could immediately make six appointments of co-Justices, and the Court would jump in size from nine to fifteen members. If one of the six Justices over seventy chose to retire, Roosevelt would still be able to make an appointment to fill his vacant seat on the bench, as well as to name five co-Justices, but the Court would jump only to fourteen members. If all the Justices over seventy retired, Roosevelt could then fill the vacancies, and the Court would stay at nine members. Either way, through the appointment of co-Justices or through the retirement of Justices over seventy, Roosevelt would have authority to place on the Supreme Court men whose public philosophy squared with his own.

Probably because he knew Frankfurter would disapprove, Roosevelt did not solicit Frankfurter's advice while planning his attack on the Supreme Court. The scheme was the conception of his Attorney General, Homer Cummings.

In mid-January, 1937, some two weeks before he announced his plan, Roosevelt wrote to Frankfurter that he would give him a great shock shortly and asked Frankfurter not to make any judgment until he had heard all the facts.[23] Two days after Roosevelt's announcement of his plan, Frankfurter conceded that the President had indeed delivered a shock.[24]

Usually when Roosevelt announced a bold new plan, Frankfurter's praise was extravagant. He customarily heaped congratulations and praise on the President, compared Roosevelt to Lincoln, and offered his loyal and enthusiastic support. His response to Roosevelt's Court plan was straightforward, reserved, even cold. He only hoped this precipitate action would not harm the basic structure of government.

Frankfurter freely admitted the Court situation called for something bold. The long mischievous line of decisions had to be stopped. And since no perfect method existed, Roosevelt had to take risks. He hoped, Frankfurter concluded, that Roosevelt's action would accomplish present-day needs without permanent damage to the sacred safeguards of democracy.[25]

In the bitter public controversy that followed Roosevelt's announcement of his scheme, it was natural that enlightenment be sought from Frankfurter as an eminent scholar of the Constitution. However, Roosevelt exacted a pledge from Frankfurter to keep silent and maintain public neutrality.[26]

And utterly silent Frankfurter remained. Dean Acheson, perhaps his closest friend, wrote in his first book of memoirs, *Morning and Noon,* that even he did not know exactly where Frankfurter stood, that Frankfurter had never articulated his views. Frankfurter had a standard reply to all queries: "... I am compelled to adhere to an undeviating policy of mine not to comment on current issues...." [27] Nor did he comment to his students at the law school. Immediately after Roosevelt's announcement, students in his federal jurisdiction seminar waited expectantly for what they thought would be certain exposition. As soon as Frankfurter walked into class, a student asked: "What about it, Professor?"

"Well," answered Frankfurter, "I think you gentlemen have somewhat more to know about the Supreme Court than you know now before we can discuss the Court plan. And so we will defer consideration of it until the end of the course." [28] It never came up again.

There is little argument that Frankfurter opposed the plan. His writings before and after confirm this. As a constitutional scholar, he had written a great deal about the Court, and no one was more outspokenly critical than Frankfurter of the men who sat on the bench—they had consistently ruled against his own arguments and legislation in minimum wage cases. But he was always critical of the particular men, not of the Court as an institution. Like Roosevelt, he believed men who were writing their own predilections into the Constitution were hiding behind the sanctity of the Court.

In 1930, Frankfurter had written to an editorial writer of the *New Republic:* "... Never before in the history of the Court have the Justices been so ruthless in tearing down legislation as in the last decade. Thus in the six years following 1920, the Supreme Court has declared social and economic legislation unconstitutional under the due process clauses in more cases than in the entire fifty-two previous years during which the Fourteenth Amendment had been in effect...." He had accused the Court of setting "its own views on what is socially and economically desirable against the legislatures of the states and very frequently against the legislatures of many states in the case of tried social experiments, as was true of the Minimum Wage case. . . ."

Every nomination to the Court, he had written, "ought to be thoroughly scrutinized not with a view to packing the Court with partisans, but in order to prevent it from being packed with partisans—the kind of partisans that one knew Taft, Pierce Butler, Sutherland to have been. At best the Supreme Court's function requires the most delicate and sensitive powers of detachment and the capacity to be open to new facts and not to see facts through the dark glasses of abstract dogmas. . . . The success of our constitutional system, as questions of statesmanship increasingly become social-economic questions, depends on securing such men for the Court. . . ." [29]

Even though the men had defects, Frankfurter did not believe such a law as Roosevelt's could remedy this situation. And as for making permanent inroads on the Supreme Court, that was, to him, a serious threat.

He told a friend that were he a Senator charged with voting on the Roosevelt plan, he would conceive it his duty to explain—he thought it might require about three hours—all the implications of the plan. He said he would speak not in terms of the needs of the moment, but of the relationship of the institution of the Court to the democratic process, of the history of the Court and the course of events that had led to Roosevelt's action, of the relationship of outside factors and people to the Court, of the freedom of legislators and judges under the Constitution, and of alternatives to Roosevelt's scheme. He believed that this was the way in which the plan should be considered, not only by the Senators in whose hands the plan lay, but by journalists, lawyers, judges, housewives, streetcar conductors, copper miners, businessmen—all the people of the nation—and "in the perspective of the whole." [30] He did not, however, reveal a position on the specifics of Roosevelt's plan.

Looking at the question in such perspective, Frankfurter had noted in 1934 that whenever decisions of the Supreme Court ran against the tide of deep public sentiment, there were efforts to curb its powers. They had begun as early as the days of John Marshall, Chief Justice of the United States from 1801 to 1835. They had continued into the twentieth century down to the present day. There had even been several changes in the numbers of Justices sitting, and, as supporters of the Roosevelt plan were fond of quoting Frankfurter, "there is no magic in the number nine." However, Frankfurter believed, in 1934, that increase was "self-defeating," [31] and he continued to believe it.

In 1935, Frankfurter had written to Geoffrey Parsons of the New York *Herald Tribune:* ". . . the Supreme Court should continue its traditional function in our scheme of government. And this for me . . . precludes increase in the size of the court." [32] In 1923 there had been a movement to liberalize Supreme Court decisions by requiring a seven to two majority for declaring an act of Congress or a state law unconstitutional. This plan Frankfurter also rejected.

Mechanics, Frankfurter believed, was not the root of the problem. The essence was men. No "mechanical device fits the problem," he had written in 1930. "Such remedies create new difficulties and do not help in the slightest the ultimate requirement for the Court, namely, men adequately equipped for the peculiar tasks committed to it. Everything turns on men."

He had continued: "Unless the President, the Senate and the country are alert to the qualities that Justices of the Supreme Court ought to possess and insist upon suitable appointees, no mechanics will save us from the evils of narrow prepossessions by members of the Court. Contrariwise, if we are fully alive to the indispensable qualifications for the high work of the Court, and insistent upon measuring appointees accordingly, mechanical devices are superfluous and obstructive. . . ." The Supreme Court wielded an awesome power. "In good truth, the Supreme Court *is* the Constitution. Therefore, the most relevant things about an appointee are his breadth of vision, his imagination, his capacity for disinterested judgment, and his power to discover and to suppress his prejudices. . . ." [33]

Once again he had urged education as the cure for democratic evils: education of the public, of the bar, of politicians from the local alderman to the President, and education—broad as possible—especially for the judges. It was a long-range view, obviously not geared to solve Roosevelt's immediate problems, but geared to preserving the Court as an institution.

In this spirit he undertook to help Roosevelt in his 1937 difficulties. He was willing to, and did, outline and define the issues involved in Roosevelt's attack against the Court—not the issues of Roosevelt's plan. He was eager to present the case against the Court to the public and was willing to supply Roosevelt with this kind of ammunition. He shared Roosevelt's anger at the Court, and in the correspondence between Roosevelt and Frankfurter during this period, there were a good many letters and memorandums from Cambridge outlining background, the role of the Court, the circumstances which had led to Roosevelt's action, putting the question of the Supreme Court "in the whole perspective."

But previously Frankfurter had plunged headfirst into Roosevelt's causes in Congress, waving the President's banner at Senators and Representatives, working out compromises that would effectuate Roosevelt's fundamental goals. On this toughest and bitterest controversy of all, however, Frankfurter kept silent in Cambridge.

If he did not espouse Roosevelt's plan, he did not repudiate it publicly either. The bonds of friendship were too strong, the dictates of good taste too stringent. When Governor Herbert Lehman of New York, also an intimate of Roosevelt's, publicly repudiated the Court plan in July, 1937, Frankfurter wrote Roosevelt a sympathetic note accusing Lehman of hitting below the belt and undoubtedly letting Roosevelt know in this roundabout way that he, Frankfurter, would not be guilty of offending a friendship by letting the President down.[34]

An obvious question arises: Did Frankfurter put the obligations of friendship above the obligations to his country as an educator, constitutional scholar, and lawyer? This leads to a second question: Should an academic personality, charged with disinterest on public issues, become so involved in a political administration—both politically and personally—as Frankfurter did? They are moot questions.

When Roosevelt urged Frankfurter to join his administration officially, Frankfurter refused; by maintaining his independence, he could be more effective outside the administration. Nevertheless, he became as much identified with Roosevelt and his policies as if he had joined officially—perhaps more so because of his close personal relationship with Roosevelt. And so, in effect, his degree of independence was lessened, if not completely lost.

Had he publicly criticized Roosevelt's Court plan, he might, identified as he was with Roosevelt, have dealt the plan a serious blow. But he would also have destroyed his own effectiveness in the administration, which still had some years to run. So he kept silent.

No doubt his own conscience was clear. He had fulfilled his obligations of friendship by supplying Roosevelt with background material on the Court with which Roosevelt could present his case and, above all, by not publicly criticizing Roosevelt's plan. He had fulfilled his obligations to country by referring anyone who asked to his previous writings—which were there for everyone to see and which plainly opposed a mechanical solution such as Roosevelt's to the problem of the Supreme Court—and, above all, by not publicly supporting the plan.

Another question which arises is whether Frankfurter remained silent because he hoped for a Supreme Court appointment. Roosevelt's onetime adviser Raymond Moley believed that was the reason for Frankfurter's refusal to speak.[35]

This is patently false. Roosevelt had mentioned the Supreme Court to Frankfurter previously, when he offered Frankfurter the solicitor generalship, and Frankfurter told him the matter of a Supreme Court appointment would have to take care of itself. In asking Frankfurter's silence on the matter of the Court plan, Roosevelt had again mentioned the Supreme Court appointment, but he had said only that he hoped someday to put Frankfurter on the Court and did not want him embroiled in the politics of the Court plan, making confirmation difficult. It was not an either/or proposition—he knew better than to offer a bribe to Frankfurter.

The Supreme Court had ruled, in June, 1936, that the State of New York could not establish a minimum wage for women—had declared the legislation authored by Frankfurter and Cohen unconstitutional. The decision, Frankfurter said, left him "numb." The five conservative Justices who constituted the majority, he wrote to Justice Stone, "have demonstrated anew the versatility, or at least the resources, of unreason and folly." [36]

Less than ten months later, in March, 1937, with Roosevelt's proposal to reorganize the Court hanging over their heads, the Justices upheld the constitutionality of an essentially similar minimum wage law of the State of Washington. Justice Owen J. Roberts, who fairly regularly voted with the Four Horsemen, had changed his vote and given the liberal faction of the Court a majority, thus diverting administration pressure from the Court. A young lawyer named Abe Fortas called the move "the switch in time that serves nine." Robert H. Jackson, who sat at the government counsel table in the Court that day and heard Chief Justice Hughes read the decision upholding the Washington State law, called the legal maneuvering in the opinion "a bit of face-saving for the Court." [37] Frankfurter termed Roberts' "somersault" [38] "shocking behavior . . . no conceivably relevant, intellectual, legal reason can account for his flop. . . ." [39] (The same day the Court went on to hold constitutional the National Firearms Act, which in effect utilized the government's taxing power to regulate traffic in firearms; an amended Railway Labor Act, which promoted collective bargaining, mediation, and arbitration between railroad employers and employees; and a revised Frazier-Lemke act for farm relief.)

For the factions involved, the minimum wage decision was of mixed benefit. The administration had to approve because it was a decision on social legislation the administration had fought for. But it weakened administration arguments for passage of the Court reorganization plan while at the same time, Roosevelt people feared, it put legislative proposals at the mercy of Justice Roberts.

To the women of the National Consumers' League who had attempted for more than a quarter century to establish such legislation, it meant unqualified success and a step toward the 1938 federal Fair Labor Standards Act, which established a nationwide floor for wages. Similarly, for the workingmen and women of the nation, the ghetto dwellers, the arms that moved the machines that brought riches to the country, it meant decent rewards for their labors. Perhaps more important, a principle had been established. The road to social reform was no longer barricaded by the policemen of the Supreme Court.

For the Court itself, the decision contributed toward the defeat in the Senate of Roosevelt's Court-packing plan. If a liberal majority on the Court could be obtained to uphold social and economic legislation, there was no need to enlarge the Court.

That the Court would allow such a consideration to influence it, wrote Charles Evans Hughes, however, is "utterly baseless." The Washington State minimum wage case in which Justice Roberts was supposed to have switched, Hughes explained, was argued and discussed in the Court conference "before the President's attack upon the Court had been made or anyone had any notion that it was coming." At that conference, it appeared that four Justices—Brandeis, Roberts, Cardozo, and Chief Justice Hughes—were in favor of upholding the minimum wage law and of overruling the Court's 1923 decision which had struck down the District of Columbia statute. Justice Stone was absent on account of illness, but his view that a minimum wage statute was within the state's power was well known —he had dissented in the 1936 case in which the Court had struck down New York's minimum wage law. Therefore, explained Hughes, "it was manifest that there would be a majority of five Justices as soon as Justice Stone was able to attend conference. Accordingly we decided to hold the case. Justice Stone returned about February 1, 1937, and agreed to the affirmance of the Washington judgment. [Roosevelt's Court plan was announced on February 5.] The opinions, majority and minority, were prepared in due course and were announced on March 29th. The President's proposal had not the slightest effect on our decision. . . ." [40] The fact remains, however, that there was a switch, a decision which came in the nick of time and helped save the Court. Perhaps it was not a result of the rising clamor against the Court; more likely it was.

For Frankfurter, the decision was definitely a mixed blessing. It meant that much he had fought for had been won—that the social reformer in him could rejoice in better working conditions for the men and women of the machines; that the lawyer in him could rejoice in the victory of the state's right to establish such legislation.

But beneath these considerations lay his respect—in fact, his reverence—for the Court as an institution. The supreme authority on the side of law and order had abandoned integrity. In a sense, he believed the decisions were arbitrary, that they were decided not on the basis of law, but on the basis of political expediency—a procedure he hoped he had left behind in Vienna. He had long disagreed with Justices who fought for property and wealth against the rising tide of reform. But disagreement was one thing; turpitude was another.

The day after the decision was handed down, he wrote words of disillusionment to Justice Stone: ". . . as a teacher who owes his students the most fastidious obligation of intellectual integrity, and who also deeply believes in the Court as an institution, I am truly sad at heart about the Washington minimum wage case in connection with the Tipaldo [New York, 1936 case]. . . ." In addition to what Frankfurter believed were deliberate factual misrepresentations among the Justices, "there is Roberts' somersault incapable of being attributed to a single factor relevant to the professed judicial process. Everything that he now subscribes to he rejected not only on June first last, but as late as October twelfth when New York's petition for a rehearing was denied. . . . What kind of respect for the institution can be aroused in informed and able young minds when they come to consider in detail as they must . . . the intellectual process which underlies this minimum wage litigation? I wish either Roberts or the Chief had the responsibility of conducting the class when we shall reach this case shortly. It is very, very sad business. . . ." [41]

Justice Roberts later tried to exonerate his behavior in a memorandum he entrusted to Frankfurter on November 9, 1945, after Roberts' resignation from the Supreme Court. In it, he stated that neither the petition for certiorari nor the briefs and oral arguments by the lawyers in the 1936 New York State minimum wage case asked the Court to overrule the 1923 minimum wage case in which the Court had declared unconstitutional the District of Columbia minimum wage legislation. In fact, in devising the bill, Frankfurter and Cohen had attempted to make it different from the District of Columbia statute; carrying this through, counsel arguing for the New York State law had asked the Court, in the light of additional data and experience, to rule on separate grounds. Roberts said he found counsel's argument "disingenuous," but went along. He declared he was willing to reexamine the 1923 case, even overrule it if necessary, but was not willing to distinguish it, and so he joined the 1936 Butler opinion which struck down the minimum wage in New York on the basis of the 1923 decision. Roberts admitted in the memorandum he perhaps ought to have written a separate concurrence explaining his position, but he did not do so.

When the 1937 Washington State minimum wage case came to the Court, Roberts said, it did attack the authority of the 1923 case, and Roberts was then willing to reexamine the soundness of the 1923 decision and did, in fact, vote to overrule it, signaling the mighty switch in the Supreme Court.

There may be other motives more difficult to discover. A Philadelphia main liner whose background and inclinations dictated the rigid conservatism he had so often espoused, Roberts was nevertheless intellectually willing to weigh and consider reform; above all, in 1937, he later acknowledged, he was disturbed by the threat to the Court which Roosevelt's reorganization scheme posed.

In 1955, Frankfurter disclosed the contents of Roberts' memorandum—which paralleled the reasoning of the 1937 majority decision—and publicly apologized for his own intemperance at Roberts' "switch." Writing in the December, 1955, *Pennsylvania Law Review,* Frankfurter said: "No man ever served on the Supreme Court with more scrupulous regard for its moral demands than Mr. Justice Roberts."

The Court fight ended with Roosevelt losing the battle. His plan was defeated before it came to the Senate floor. But he won the war. Pressure on the Court from President and public forced the Court to reform itself. Justice Willis Van Devanter, one of the Four Horsemen of conservatism, resigned, making way for Roosevelt to name Senator Hugo Black, a liberal, as his first Supreme Court appointment. The Court itself had liberalized its decisions, upholding the Social Security Act and the Wagner Act granting certain privileges of striking to labor union members, and, of course, supporting the constitutionality of minimum wage laws. The threat of Executive-imposed judicial reform had been sufficient.

Frankfurter, while disapproving of Roosevelt's plan, believed it had at least some positive results. Just prior to the defeat of the plan in the Senate, Frankfurter wrote to Eugene Meyer, publisher of the Washington *Post:* "... Whatever else may be said for or against the Court proposal, I regard the public discussions which it has evoked, as one of the most valuable educational processes regarding our institutions, including the Supreme Court, in modern times. ..." [42]

And to Mr. Justice Stone, shortly after a reconstituted Supreme Court returned for the October term, 1937–38, Frankfurter wrote: "... After a while all the hubbub will abate, and perhaps you and I will agree ten years hence that it has not been bad for the Court, however passingly unpleasant, to realize and for the country to have realized the common human limitations of even the most august tribunal. ..." [43]

As for the specifics of Roosevelt's plan, Frankfurter's most significant comment may have been in a letter to a close friend: "... What awful ignorant advice he had on that subject from those who were in on the secret. ..." [44]

[4]

Assessing Frankfurter's impact on history in the years between 1933 and 1939 down to the last comma is difficult, partly because Roosevelt made it his business to solicit counsel from many people simultaneously, and who contributed exactly which words is difficult to deduce in many cases; partly because Roosevelt himself remains the more enigmatic figure. Frankfurter's side of their relationship is well documented by the voluminous quantity of letters and memorandums for speeches and appointments he left; Roosevelt's side is less well documented.

In the field of legislation, many New Deal statutes felt at least the touch of Frankfurter; some did not; some did more than others. Drafts of bills went out from Washington to Cambridge for Frankfurter's advisory opinions on constitutionality and effectiveness; some of these bills, if they were not actually written by Frankfurter, originated from one of his ideas. In addition, his protégés—Corcoran and Cohen—supervised a good deal of legislation writing, sometimes acting directly on Frankfurter's advice. Other protégés were installed in government agencies—David E. Lilienthal in the Tennessee Valley Authority, Donald Richberg in the National Recovery Administration, Charles E. Wyzanski in the Labor Department, to name only a few—and they in turn solicited advice from Frankfurter.

Although Frankfurter is usually said to have had nothing to do with the legislation establishing the National Recovery Administration in 1933, in fact, he was in frequent contact with the people working directly on the bill: Richberg, his former student who became counsel for the agency and later director; Senator Robert F. Wagner of New York; Charles Wyzanski; Grace Abbott of the Children's Bureau; and General Hugh S. Johnson, the NRA's first administrator. The final bill that emerged, however, contained certain provisions which Frankfurter believed were unconstitutional, and in any event the Supreme Court as constituted in 1934 and 1935 would never allow, he believed, such an enlargement of federal powers as the NRA dictated. Nevertheless, the NRA hierarchy was anxious to have the act tested in the Supreme Court, even if the ruling was adverse, in order to have a guide for new legislation. Frankfurter deemed that approach "suicidal" [1] and successfully urged the government to stave off a court test of the NRA as long as possible. For this, General Johnson denounced Frankfurter as "the most influential single individual in the United States" and dedicated to undermining the Constitution and the American government. When the Supreme Court finally did shoot down the NRA's blue eagle on what New Dealers called Black Monday—May 27, 1935—Frankfurter urged Roosevelt to shelve it. The NRA had largely accomplished its purpose of getting industry on the road to recovery. Frankfurter suggested Roosevelt attempt to obtain fair labor standards through legislation empowering the President to attach fair labor clauses to contracts for government purchases and to contracts made with the proceeds of government loans and grants. To facilitate the right of labor to bargain collectively, Frankfurter urged Roosevelt to support a bill written by Senator Wagner which embodied this right. Both these suggestions were followed by Roosevelt, although he was pressured by other advisers to try other means.[2]

As a kind of free-lance troubleshooter-about-Washington, Frankfurter was often able, in his informal calls on Senators and Representatives, Cabinet members, and lawyers, to effect compromises between opposing administration factions—of which there were many in the chaotic Roosevelt officialdom. When, in the spring of 1935, dissident Democrats and progressives were irate over Roosevelt's failure to push new progressive programs hard and fast enough, Frankfurter was instrumental in getting Roosevelt and the protesters together for a private and frank discussion that at least temporarily patched up relations.

Frankfurter sent people with ideas to Roosevelt, who used these men as a source of information in the way that most people use books. One of the men he sent was his close friend, Harold J. Laski, whose appointment to teach at Harvard in 1916 Frankfurter had been instrumental in securing. Laski had resigned from the Harvard faculty in 1920 and returned to England, but he returned periodically to the United States to lecture.

For Frankfurter, Laski was both an intellectual and a personal experience. Frankfurter always said he had loved Laski like a son. He had early introduced Laski to Holmes, between whom a friendship of mutual intellectual devotion sprang up. Frankfurter introduced Laski to a host of friends with whom he believed there might be a mutually exciting exchange of ideas. It was natural that on one of Laski's visits to America, Frankfurter should introduce him to Roosevelt, and he did in 1935.

Between Roosevelt and Laski there grew at least a casual friendship. And both Roosevelt for allowing it and Frankfurter for conceiving and sponsoring it were severely criticized. Roosevelt was denounced as without ideas, the tool of a Harvard professor who filled the vacuum in Roosevelt's head with Communist and Socialist doctrines. Harold Laski was their intellectual switchboard, plugging them in to all the alien philosophies.

Although both Roosevelt and Frankfurter recognized Laski's philosophical bias, both responded to the man's brilliance and the challenge and stimulation of talk with him. Laski in turn was devoted to both.

No doubt Laski was like many who entered the President's Oval Office; he hoped to convert Roosevelt with his gospel. Instead of engaging in a futile effort at reform, Laski would urge, Roosevelt should reconstitute the American government along the lines of a planned economy and strong State Socialism. No doubt Roosevelt listened eagerly, as Frankfurter also listened to Laski. Roosevelt may even have made use of some peripheral ideas. But neither Roosevelt nor Frankfurter ever really wavered from their fundamental belief that modification of the system, not destruction, was the key to building a better America.

Laski wrote Roosevelt frequently, at the same time outlining his ideas in detail to Frankfurter, on whom he relied to pass them on to Roosevelt.

But Frankfurter sent not just Socialists like Laski to Roosevelt. Possessed of an outsider's rare understanding of Roosevelt's operating procedure—no insider who had been a victim of Roosevelt's dual assignment procedure or who had been told to weave two opposing philosophies together could possess such perspective—Frankfurter recognized Roosevelt's hunger for new ideas and his reliance on culling them from people. With his numerous friends and acquaintances, Frankfurter was in a unique position to satisfy Roosevelt's avidity. He sent businessmen, scientists, statesmen, all of whom resided at various points of the political spectrum. He urged Roosevelt to interview anyone from whom he could profit. On occasion Frankfurter passed on his own correspondence with some luminary, or he would repeat in detail conversations possessed of ideas from which Roosevelt might benefit.

Throughout these six years Frankfurter's volume of advice and suggestions was sometimes acted on; sometimes it was not. But Roosevelt and Frankfurter were important to each other, both publicly and personally, with the areas overlapping.

Both men had immense personal charm which attracted the other. They could laugh and drink cocktails together as easily as they discussed the latest tax bill. If Roosevelt sometimes found Frankfurter's nagging persistence irritating—as it has been said he did in the case of his campaign to get Learned Hand appointed to the Supreme Court [3]—he also found Frankfurter intellectually fascinating and once remarked: "He has a brilliant mind but it clicks so fast it makes my head fairly spin. I find him tremendously interesting and stimulating." [4] Of course, he also found in Frankfurter a first-rate adviser whose reliability was multiplied by sincere devotion—which Roosevelt made clear he enjoyed, even required.

Frankfurter clearly worshiped Roosevelt. In Roosevelt he saw the man—and perhaps the only man at the time—with both the intellectual and the political acumen to translate his own ideals into action. Once again extravagantly spending affection and encouragement as he had during Roosevelt's governorship of New York, Frankfurter fed Roosevelt's ego—of which Roosevelt had an inordinate supply, but which no doubt even in him required comfort in difficult times—and prodded Roosevelt's own inner public desires. Frankfurter had no illusions about the failings of Roosevelt's New Deal programs. He knew legislation was often rushed through without adequate care; he could see the lack of coordination in the government, the *ad hoc* approach to some problems, and all the rest of the defects. But he also knew that overall, Roosevelt's New Deal held potential, and if praise and encouragement would help it fulfill its promise, Frankfurter had that to give, in abundance. It was a unique combination of friendship and government by expectation, not very different from Frankfurter's earlier, less mature, but equally devoted relationship with Henry Stimson.

Professor Alexander M. Bickel of Yale, a former Frankfurter law clerk, once wrote of Frankfurter that he was a "Michelangelo of friendship" and "Franklin D. Roosevelt is Frankfurter's best-known work." [5] Bickel added, however, that Roosevelt was "by no means his only one or his finest." Anyone who entered Frankfurter's orbit was a potential recipient of the same treatment, not only Presidents and politicians, but students and law clerks—especially students and law clerks—colleagues and children, liberals, conservatives, cabdrivers and tailors. At every display of political boldness, Frankfurter endowed Roosevelt with Lincolnesque stature. But his extravagance was proportionately no more than the praise he lavished on many others. John H. Mansfield, former law clerk to Frankfurter and later professor of law at Harvard, recalled how one day he and Frankfurter were discussing the word "serendipity"; afterward Frankfurter scribbled on a card: "Serendipity, an unexpected, unsought, happy discovery: e.g., Justice Frankfurter's happening on Professor Mansfield." [6]

Frankfurter was acutely sensitive to people; it was one of his outstanding personal characteristics. And his friends were legion. Mrs. Frankfurter once said, sighing wearily: "Felix has 200 intimate friends." [7] He discerned their moods, their problems, their prides, their needs, their virtues, their failings as precisely as he uncovered legal mysteries, and with utter lack of embarrassment at displaying his feelings. Their interests became his. He had warmth that easily turned to tenderness. He delighted in their joys, grieved in their grief, was unsparing of praise and encouragement.

There is a saying among Frankfurter's friends that all his geese were swans. He was supremely and incurably optimistic about people, at the same time acutely cognizant of their actual human worth. But by showing them what they could be, he begot pride which was transformed to self-achievement, in turn begetting pride and more self-achievement, until under his tutelage, all his geese *were* swans, geese though they might otherwise be.

As Professor Bickel wrote on another occasion:

> He was a hero worshipper who transformed all those he worshipped into real heroes. Friendship with Felix Frankfurter was a romance. It made everything worthier and handsomer, including the friend. But there were these differences. The private, hard judgment of Frankfurter himself was never finally beguiled. And the friend, drawn out, encouraged, beseeched, charmed, wheedled, needled, and finally driven by the canniest of teachers operating on the simple, unadorned premise that there is, after

> all, something in everybody—the friend actually became a little worthier and a little handsomer than he could ever otherwise have been. . . .[8]

Morris L. Ernst put it this way: "Felix was not particularly attracted . . . to the broken wings. . . . Felix [was] attracted to the people who've got both wings and are able to fly. And he's betting they will fly. He took an awful lot of people who never thought they could fly and he taught them how to fly. He put them in spots where they could fly. . . ." [9]

Throughout the Roosevelt years, the comings and goings of Frankfurter in Washington were watched with interest. There were those who saw him as an enigmatic figure, darting in and out of the White House on errands of mystery. Some saw him simply as a busybody. Wits labeled him "Jiminey Cricket to President Roosevelt's Pinocchio." The Hearst press attacked him as a sinister Bolshevist with Bolshevist friends through whom he was taking over the government. All his former associations with the Bisbee Deportations, the Mooney case, Sacco and Vanzetti, were dredged up and distorted. Some of the more conservative advisers within the administration had hoped Frankfurter would accept the solicitor generalship and exhaust his energies arguing cases before the Supreme Court, becoming impotent as far as advising the President was concerned.

Frankfurter brushed off such criticism with equanimity. Frankfurter was not so serene, however, but was deeply wounded by criticism from another quarter which followed him throughout the thirties. In a turnabout, this was criticism that he was *not* using his position and influence as a confidant of Roosevelt's, and it came from Jewish circles which attacked him for timidity and procrastination in protesting Nazi barbarism.

The fact is his protests were strong. They began early—earlier than most people's—and they were enduring. They were loud and addressed to influential circles. No one was prouder of his Jewish heritage than Frankfurter. He could not help being mindful of the fact that had he lived in Europe in the 1930's, he would have lived only a boxcar ride from a concentration camp. But he protested and labored in behalf of Jewish—and non-Jewish—refugees not as a Jew, but as a human being whose civilization was threatened by Hitlerism.

In an appeal in 1933 to Secretary of State Cordell Hull for this government to adopt a lenient policy in regard to granting asylum to victims of Hitler's brutalities, Frankfurter struck a poignant personal note: "... For once in my life I wish that for a brief period I were not a Jew. Then I would not have even the appearance of being sectarian in writing as I have written concerning interests that are not narrower than those of 'civilization.' ..." [10]

Frankfurter did not view Hitler as an aberration—as many people did—but as a long-nurtured expression of German nationalism and obsession with Germanic supremacy. Hitler's take-over of the German government the day after Roosevelt was inaugurated President of the United States for the first time was the victory, as Frankfurter saw it, of lawless force which had won power disguised as patriotism. Frankfurter believed that this lawless force "wanted Germany to be the sun and not to merely have a place in it," and that it "sought power to consign others to darkness." [11]

The terrorism had begun after World War I, and Frankfurter blamed its triumph on the many who by their silence approved the means because "the ends which were promoted were seemingly nationalistic." [12]

As Fascism thrived in Germany—and Italy—faith in democracy weakened, not only within Germany, but without, adding strength to the Nazi cause. From his listening post at Oxford, Frankfurter had written Stimson in June, 1934: "... for a time forces of decivilization seem to be in control over a considerable area of western Europe, and there is a strange kind of romantic glamor that invests the dictator both in the eyes of the timid and the adventurous. Moreover, fears are being sedulously and astutely cultivated—the fears of dangers from the left are being turned to excellent uses by the promoters of the right ... it is most interesting to see the germ of force and intolerance cultivated even in this, the most mature of all political societies. ..." [13]

Frankfurter believed the victory of Nazism in Germany was a "challenge to the whole blend of forces that constitute the process of modern civilization. In short, Hitler's challenge is against that vast stream of history of which the Greek and Hebrew influences have been the greatest tributaries." [14]

As such, Frankfurter was committed to the destruction of Nazism. One of the manifestations of this commitment, interestingly enough, was his urging a publisher to print Hitler's *Mein Kampf* unabridged. To an editor at Houghton Mifflin, which had brought out an abridged edition of the volume, he wrote: "I am ready to pay the price of my old-fashioned liberal belief in freedom of speech, and therefore will fight to have utterance permitted to views that I loathe." But even more important than his belief in freedom of speech, "I welcome the illumination that would come to uninformed American minds about Hitler's real meaning from his self-portraiture. But that required uncompromising completeness of disclosure; it precluded tampering with the picture that Hitler painted of himself before he came to power and began to resort to the familiar arts of speech for foreign consumption. . . ." [15]

Nowhere was he more insistent on protesting Hitlerism than in his own academic world. Throughout the thirties the Nazi regime ousted one professor after another either for Jewishness or for advocating "liberal" ideas. Frankfurter publicly urged American universities to open their doors to these exiles; he solicited funds—a task he customarily avoided—for the University in Exile, a graduate school established in New York City to employ professors exiled from German universities. He urged his own university to take in these men, many of whom were prominent scholars, and when many American universities were slow or recalcitrant, he publicly criticized them, Harvard included.

At Harvard he was especially vociferous. He urged the university and particularly the law school faculty to protest Nazi outrages on German professors and Nazi subversion of truth to propaganda. When Harvard was invited to attend university celebrations in Germany, at Göttingen and Heidelberg, Frankfurter urged Harvard to decline because, he said, these were no longer universities. They had become political propaganda agencies and, as such, could no longer pretend to the ideal of free scholarship, the common bond between universities. Furthermore, American universities had an obligation not to approve the Nazi regime by attendance. He urged Harvard also to register its protest of Nazism by absorbing as many exiled professors it practically could.

He even took his cause to Yale. When a wealthy New Yorker left a scholarship fund to Yale to be given to boys who were the sons of "white Christian parents of Anglo-Saxon, Scandinavian, or Teutonic descent, both of whom were citizens of the United States and were born in America," Frankfurter wrote to a member of the Yale Corporation that the bequest smacked of Nazism, and he criticized strongly Yale's acceptance of it.

As for his relationship to Roosevelt, Frankfurter never ceased in his efforts to remind Roosevelt of the threat to civilization Nazism and its manifestations posed. Roosevelt was very early cognizant of this threat. But as the leader of a diversified nation of people who had had their fill of European war in 1917–18 and who were also confused by events abroad, Roosevelt had to make haste slowly. Frankfurter realized the limitations imposed on Roosevelt; nevertheless, he kept the issues before the President.

Frankfurter's central concern during the thirties was refugees from Germany. He frequently urged Roosevelt to use the power of the Presidency in support of bringing these people out of Europe and also in support of persuading Great Britain, as mandatory for Palestine, to open Palestine to increased Jewish immigration. Great Britain was naturally reluctant, fearful as she was of incurring Arab wrath and dependent as she was on Arab oil. As Jewish leaders in London attempted to promote British leniency in Palestine, Frankfurter acted the intermediary, translating Jewish aims to Roosevelt, who, Jewish leaders hoped, would lend his influence with the British to their cause. Roosevelt was sympathetic but impotent, his hands tied by timid State Department advisers, a reluctant Congress, and adverse public opinion; he could admit only a relatively few refugees. Nor did Great Britain open Palestine. The great body of refugees remained in Europe.

One tragedy created by Nazism which Frankfurter did not take to Roosevelt was one which affected him personally. One day in 1938, Frankfurter received a radiogram from a friend who had been in Vienna saying that Nazi ruffians had pulled Frankfurter's eighty-two-year-old uncle, Solomon Frankfurter, a prominent Viennese scholar, out of bed at three o'clock in the morning and incarcerated him, with a group of other victims, in a stable. Frankfurter later confessed that his first thought had been to phone Roosevelt. He checked the impulse because he was fearful the American press would distort the incident out of proportion and find in it evidence that Roosevelt had all along been Frankfurter's puppet.[16] He did try inquiring about his uncle through the State Department. That department did, through its chargé d'affaires in Vienna, locate Frankfurter's uncle in a prison hospital. But direct action, the State Department said, was impossible.[17] When efforts to get his uncle released through the State Department failed, Frankfurter wired Lady Nancy Astor in London to use her good offices with the German ambassador. Although Lady Astor, whose home was a meeting place for Englishmen eager to appease Hitler, was identified as a German sympathizer, she did intervene and secured Solomon Frankfurter's release.

On July 9, 1938, Benjamin N. Cardozo, Associate Justice of the Supreme Court of the United States, died. Franklin Roosevelt had his third appointment to make to the high bench—he had appointed Hugo L. Black to succeed retiring Willis Van Devanter, and Stanley F. Reed, his Solicitor General, to succeed retiring George Sutherland. Two of the Four Horsemen of conservatism had been disposed of, and Roosevelt had a reliable liberal majority. Now Cardozo, one of that majority, had died at the age of sixty-eight, after only six years on the Court, and Roosevelt spent a suspenseful six months deciding on his successor.

Frankfurter was high on the list of possibilities, not only because of his friendship with Roosevelt, but because of his prominence as a constitutional scholar. Roosevelt had told Raymond Moley in early New Deal days that he expected to appoint Frankfurter, as well as Joseph T. Robinson, Senate Majority Leader, and Hiram Johnson, Senator from California, as vacancies appeared. When Van Devanter resigned in May, 1937, Roosevelt vacillated on whether to appoint Robinson. In talking then with his Secretary of the Treasury, Henry Morgenthau, Jr., he speculated on future appointments.

"If Brandeis resigns"—Roosevelt opened the question—"whom do you think I should appoint to succeed him—Landis [James M. Landis] or Frankfurter?"

Morgenthau replied that he thought Landis a better appointment.

"Frankfurter would rate a more popular opinion," Roosevelt argued.

Morgenthau agreed, but believed public confidence would be greater in Landis.

"Well," Roosevelt offered, "I think I would have a terrible time getting Frankfurter confirmed." Morgenthau agreed, adding that "one of the troubles with Frankfurter is that he is overbrilliant." [18] And the subject was closed.

A major consideration in filling the vacancy created by Cardozo's death was geography. The East was well represented on the Supreme Court with Hughes and Stone from New York, Roberts from Pennsylvania, and Brandeis from Massachusetts. The South also had good numerical representation with McReynolds from Tennessee, Reed from Kentucky, and Black from Alabama. Pierce Butler ostensibly came from the West, but he was from St. Paul, Minnesota, which placed him east of the Mississippi River.

Charles Evans Hughes had written in 1928: "It is manifest that geographical considerations should not control at the expense of exceptional fitness in determining appointments to the Supreme Court. Yet the confidence of the country should be maintained by selections which so far as practicable will represent all parts of the United States. . . ." [19]

There was a great deal of sentiment for an appointment from the Midwest or Far West expressed by governors and Senators of these states. Such sentiment is difficult for a politician to ignore.

There was also sectarian sentiment—Harold Ickes recorded in his diary that Catholics would like to see a Catholic appointed to the Court to represent the growing number of Catholics in the United States. Pierce Butler was Catholic, but at seventy-two he was nearing retirement.

As for a possible Frankfurter appointment, there was anti-Jewish sentiment. This came not only from anti-Semitic sources, but also from Jews, who feared Frankfurter's appointment would intensify already existing prejudices against Jews in this country. It would be wiser strategy, they believed, to wait until Brandeis resigned before appointing another Jew to the Court. A delegation of prominent Jews met with Roosevelt to urge him not to appoint Frankfurter.[20]

General Hugh Johnson was outspokenly opposed to Frankfurter's nomination to the Court. Within the administration, Roosevelt's Attorney General, Homer Cummings, fought Frankfurter's appointment up to the last moment, reminding Roosevelt that all the old charges of "radical" and "Red" would be resurrected and at the same time urging Roosevelt to consider Cummings' candidates for the nomination.

Frankfurter had his champions, too. Senator George Norris, of Nebraska, with whom Frankfurter had worked on legislative matters, most notably the bill regulating the use of labor injunctions, attempted to deemphasize the geographical factor by his urging of Frankfurter's appointment. Harold Ickes thought Frankfurter "would be in the fine liberal tradition of Holmes and Cardozo." [21]

Harold Laski had gone so far as to urge Brandeis to resign so that Frankfurter would be sure of a seat on the Supreme Court; Brandeis replied that he thought possibly Frankfurter could do more good teaching young lawyers at Harvard. Laski did abstain from writing or talking with Roosevelt about the appointment, however. He felt that interference from a foreigner might be resented, and that he might therefore do harm, he told Frankfurter.[22]

At a November meeting with Roosevelt, Laski reported, Roosevelt said at the end of their discussion: "You haven't mentioned Felix."

Laski answered it was not his place to mention Frankfurter.

Wasn't Laski worried about Frankfurter? Roosevelt asked.

"No," Laski answered.

"Well," said Roosevelt, "I don't think you need worry." [23]

Chief Justice Herbert V. Evatt of Australia wrote a confidential letter to Roosevelt pleading for Frankfurter's appointment. In his opinion, Evatt told Roosevelt, Frankfurter was the only man with the social outlook, the power of leadership, the knowledge of the Court's history and practice, and the confidence of the legal profession which were necessary to a nominee.[24]

Editors and politicians, Republican and Democrat, from all parts of the country and even from outside the country bombarded Roosevelt with reasons for naming Frankfurter until Roosevelt began to show irritation whenever Frankfurter's nomination was mentioned. In September, 1938, a Gallup Poll among 175,000 members of the American Bar Association showed Frankfurter mentioned five times as frequently for the vacancy as the two runners-up, Learned Hand and John W. Davis.

William Allen White, Kansas newspaper editor who was prominent in politics, wrote Roosevelt: ". . . President Hoover indicated that a seven dollar night letter that I sent him a day or two before Cardozo was named had weighed somewhat in the balance. If I could have one word to say to you now, it would be to urge the appointment of Felix Frankfurter to succeed Cardozo. . . ." [25]

Roosevelt replied that "on the fitness end of things again you are right."

However, Roosevelt added, referring to the Court fight of 1937 and recalling that White had opposed Roosevelt's reorganization plan, "Two years ago I took the position . . . that the Supreme Court should be broadly representative of the Nation—i.e., every section of it. I even went further and said I would support the establishment of a custom that no two Justices should come from the same judicial district. Furthermore, as a lawyer, I said I believed that there surely were several qualified people for the Supreme Court in every one of the nine districts. . . . I think it is pretty good American policy that will help the unity of the country.

"On top of that, eight sitting Justices of the Supreme Court come from east of the Mississippi. . . . That means two-thirds of the acreage of the United States has no representation—and one-third of the population has no representative."

Roosevelt concluded with a folksy statement of his own dilemma: "Sorta tough ain't it!" [26]

The Boston *Transcript* reported on October 22, 1938, that on the Court itself, Chief Justice Hughes and Justices Reed and Stone favored Frankfurter as successor to Cardozo.

Irving Brant, contributing editor to the St. Louis *Star-Times,* and Roosevelt confidant, urged Roosevelt to overlook the geographical factor this time, to name Frankfurter, then to consider Wiley B. Rutledge of Iowa for a subsequent vacancy.

Meanwhile, the object of this flurry of interest attempted to go about his work as calmly as possible under the circumstances. To Stimson he wrote: ". . . Please take all concern for me, in this strange publicity that has flared up about me, since Cardozo's death, off your mind—except one of sympathy for me for publicity that is exceedingly alien to my nature, and therefore, deeply distasteful. How silly all this popular talk is—and how puerile 'popularity' is, how meaningless. For, two or three short years ago I was a devil and now I'm almost the opposite. . . ." [27]

In early October, 1938, the Frankfurters went to Roosevelt's home at Hyde Park for their annual autumn visit, and Roosevelt, still apparently undecided on Cardozo's successor, warned his press entourage not to "go out on a limb" [28] by attaching any unusual significance to the visit. In fact, after lunch on the first day, Roosevelt ushered Frankfurter into his study and told him with regret that he could not appoint Frankfurter to the Supreme Court at that time, that he was committed to naming someone from west of the Mississippi. Roosevelt asked Frankfurter his opinion of some of the names that had been submitted to him for the appointment. Frankfurter agreed to assemble judicial dossiers on the men; this he did over the next few months.

By mid-November Washington was rife with rumors that Brandeis, seen at the White House twice within two weeks, was about to resign, leaving Roosevelt without resistance to the pressure that had built up for Frankfurter's nomination. The White House refused all comment.

In fact, two days before Christmas, Roosevelt, still vacillating, phoned Frankfurter to inquire about the qualifications of Wiley B. Rutledge, dean of the University of Iowa Law School. With help from colleagues who knew Rutledge, Frankfurter got together a memorandum which approved Rutledge's qualifications. (Roosevelt did appoint Rutledge—in 1943.)

By New Year's Day, 1939, with Congress about to reconvene, pressure was building within the administration for Frankfurter's appointment.

The previous day Roosevelt had invited Robert H. Jackson, then Solicitor General, and Harry Hopkins to lunch to discuss other appointments, but the conversation turned to the Supreme Court vacancy. Attorney General Cummings was "on his knees" [29] to get his candidate, Judge Harold Stephens of Utah, nominated. Roosevelt was also still considering Wiley Rutledge, Senator Lewis B. Schwellenbach of Washington, and Frankfurter.

Jackson implored Roosevelt to name Frankfurter. Roosevelt, then in the third year of his second term and so far not talking about a third term, ought to look at this appointment as if it were his last, Jackson advised. The Court needed a man able to interpret the Constitution with scholarship and with the self-confidence to argue with Chief Justice Hughes, who, said Jackson, "looks like God and talks like God" and who in fact had a reputation for trying to browbeat the other eight into unanimity. The Court also required a "bridge," [30] should the Republicans come to power in 1940, to the next liberal administration—as Brandeis and Holmes had been the bridge between the Wilson and Roosevelt administrations.

"My urgent request, Mr. President," Jackson concluded, "is that you . . . give me Felix as the new judge." [31]

Harry Hopkins joined in urging Frankfurter's nomination, and the luncheon conference ended a few minutes later, without a commitment from Roosevelt, but a feeling on the part of Jackson and Hopkins that they had scored. It was, however, a characteristic of Roosevelt to engender such a feeling in his advisers; it probably meant little, because Roosevelt soon indicated he had not yet made up his mind.

On January 1, Harold Ickes called on Roosevelt to ask that Frankfurter's name be sent to the Senate for confirmation. Roosevelt agreed that Frankfurter was certainly the most qualified, but he would not be appointed until Brandeis resigned.

"But will Brandeis resign?" Ickes asked.

Roosevelt assured Ickes that Brandeis would, and in time for Roosevelt to appoint Frankfurter his successor.

Ickes said he was not so sure, adding, "If you appoint Frankfurter, his ability and learning are such that he will dominate the Supreme Court for fifteen or twenty years to come. The result will be that, probably after you are dead, it will still be your Supreme Court." [32]

Senator Norris, at the urging of Tom Corcoran, Ben Cohen, and Robert Jackson, took the case for Frankfurter to Roosevelt. Roosevelt sent for Justice Stone for the Court-oriented and liberal Republican view and got the same advice: Name Frankfurter. It is interesting that he did not send for Chief Justice Hughes, from whom he might have got a negative.

"Of course, Mr. President," Stone said, "you could get a very good man from every judicial circuit in the country and thus constitute a Supreme Court of character and ability. But you could not get a distinguished Supreme Court that way because you cannot find a distinguished judge or lawyer in every circuit. . . ." [33]

Still Roosevelt said nothing. On January 3 he told the press that he had made no decision. The same day Roosevelt was told by advisers that if he failed to nominate Frankfurter, he would be charged with a retreat from the New Deal; that the rank and file of New Dealers would be discouraged and feel betrayed; that, on the other hand, the appointment of Frankfurter would be accepted as proof that he proposed to continue his policies, among them liberalization of the judiciary.

On January 4, Roosevelt delivered his annual message to Congress, the new Seventy-sixth. About 7 P.M. he phoned Frankfurter at his home in Cambridge, where Frankfurter was dressing for dinner.

Roosevelt told him he was sending Frankfurter's name to the Senate for confirmation of his nomination to the Supreme Court. Frankfurter's reaction is now legendary: "All I can say," he replied to Roosevelt, "is I wish my mother were alive." [34]

And indeed he must have longed to share this moment with her, who forty-four years earlier had led her children out of the bondage of Europe to the freedom of America, where a mother could, in truth, say of her children: "The doctor is four and the lawyer is two and a half."

It is certainly true that at that particular moment in history, Felix Frankfurter would not have received high office in most of the countries that constituted what was loosely termed the civilized world. As a Jew he would more likely have been in a concentration camp.

But in America his Jewishness really counted for nothing when high office was under consideration. It counted neither for nor against him. He was proof that the oft-told story of the boy from the humblest origins aspiring to and winning the highest offices was indeed real.

Frankfurter was proof that the factors which determined such realization were not ancestry or religion or any such irrelevancies, but that character and intelligence were what counted in America. Frankfurter was appointed to the Supreme Court because he was a brilliant lawyer, a constitutional scholar, an articulate man who could enunciate what he wished to say, and, most important, because he was a man of courage. He had never feared to take on the unpopular cause if he believed it right, whatever the consequences.

Reaction the next day was mixed. To William Allen White, who had pressed hard for Frankfurter's nomination, Roosevelt telegraphed: I HAVE DONE IT.[35] White applauded.

Frankfurter held an impromptu press conference at his house on Brattle Street, Cambridge, and observed the usual amenities for unconfirmed Supreme Court nominees: "I am, of course, sensible to the obligation and the honor involved," he said. "Otherwise I have nothing to say."

To a reporter who called him Judge, he protested: "Don't call me me Judge. I haven't been confirmed yet." He then broke up the session with: "I can't delay luncheon. The cook would be mad." [36]

In the classroom Frankfurter conducted business as usual. A burst of student applause greeted him when he entered for the first time after his nomination.

He smiled and said: "Thank you—but it won't make the course any easier. . . . At the end of the last hour we were discussing . . ." [37] and he perched himself comfortably on the back of a chair and continued a class discussion of government regulation of warehouses in Illinois and grain elevators about where it had left off at the end of the previous session.

Across the Charles River, in a fashionable Beacon Street drawing room, a latecomer to tea announced Roosevelt's nomination of Frankfurter. "What!" exclaimed the hostess in a reaction typical of the way much of America's wealthy responded. "*That* young radical?" [38]

In Washington, those who had urged Frankfurter's selection generally rejoiced. A few Senators declined to comment, and a member of the House Committee on Un-American Activities said that he could not "conceive of a worse appointment" and that Roosevelt "might as well have appointed Earl Browder." [39] (Browder was then leader of the American Communist Party.)

In most quarters, confirmation was accepted as a matter of course. At least one Washington observer was prescient enough to see that whoever the nominee was, he would be put under the Senate's microscope and thoroughly investigated and cross-examined by the Senate Judiciary Committee to elicit his views on all the important social, industrial, and labor questions then before the public.

As is customary, a subcommittee of the Senate Judiciary Committee, charged with recommending or withholding recommendation of Supreme Court appointments to the full Senate, was appointed to hold hearings on Frankfurter's nomination. Frankfurter resisted appearing personally as long as he could, content to be represented by his counsel, Dean Acheson. But as Homer Cummings had predicted, all the old charges that Frankfurter was a Red and a radical were revived. His role in unpopular causes, his foreign birth, his association with George Norris and Robert La Follette as sponsors of obvious radical legislation, his affiliation with Harvard, considered a hotbed of radicals, his Jewishness—all were attacked by witnesses in the subcommittee hearings. Frankfurter was asked to appear.

On Thursday morning, January 12, Frankfurter and Acheson made their way—preceded by a cordon of police to open a path—to the witness table in the crowded Caucus Room of the old Senate Office Building.

Frankfurter read a brief prepared statement in which he indicated that he would not express his personal views on controversial political issues affecting the Supreme Court. His viewpoint on "relevant matters" was available in his writings over a long period of time. It would be, he said, "not only bad taste but inconsistent with the duties of the office" [40] to speak now on such subjects.

Members of the subcommittee questioned him about his participation in the case of Tom Mooney, who, after twenty-two years in prison, had been pardoned only days before Frankfurter's appearance before the Senate committee. They questioned him on his membership in the American Civil Liberties Union; his answer is a classic:

The purpose of the ACLU, he explained, is to carry out its function of seeing that Communists get their constitutional rights along with Henry Ford, Nazis, and the Ku Klux Klan.

The climax came when Senator Patrick A. McCarran, who had been trying throughout the hearings to draw Frankfurter as a dangerous radical at best, held up a book called *Communism* by Frankfurter's friend Harold Laski and asked, "If it advocates the doctrine of Marxism, would you agree with it?"

Frankfurter answered: "Senator, I do not believe you have ever taken an oath to support the Constitution of the United States with fewer reservations than I have or would now, nor do I believe you are more attached to the theories and practices of Americanism than I am. I rest my answer on that statement."

A roar of applause and approval rose in the hearing room so that even the chairman banging his gavel could not be heard above it.

Frankfurter always savored as one of the more delicious moments of his life when, in 1945, the same Senator McCarran asked him to recommend two Nevada boys for study at Harvard Law School. Frankfurter obliged, but not without just a little teasing. Didn't the Senator, Frankfurter asked, want to save them from that "horrendous fate"? [41]

When the hearings on Frankfurter's nomination broke up at noon, the audience crowded in to shake his hand until police had to clear breathing space for him.

Frankfurter and Acheson left for a celebration luncheon with

Senator Henry Ashurst of Arizona, chairman of the full Judiciary Committee, who predicted speedy confirmation of Frankfurter. They then went on to the White House, where they regaled Roosevelt with noisy stories of the hearings and Frankfurter's triumph.

Frankfurter returned to his Harvard classes to await confirmation. On January 16 the Senate Judiciary Committee reported unanimously its approval of Frankfurter's appointment. The following day the full Senate confirmed it with a voice vote. No Nay was audible.

Frankfurter was in class when word came. A colleague, Thomas Reed Powell, slipped into the room and made his way to Frankfurter, who had been sitting in the third row to heckle while a student conducted the class. When the period ended, Frankfurter said, "This is the last time that I shall speak to you in this classroom. I should like you to know that it is not an easy thing for me to go to Washington. While there I shall think of you often. I wish you well in June and a very full life thereafter." [42]

The following night the Frankfurters took the train to Washington, where they were house guests of the Roosevelts and where they attended Roosevelt's annual dinner for the Supreme Court. Two days later the Frankfurters returned to Cambridge briefly to put their affairs in final order, then left for Washington permanently.

A friend stopped at the Frankfurters' Brattle Street home on the eve of their final departure. Resting from the rigors of packing, the new Justice, his usual aplomb gone, sat down on a trunk, hunched forward, and crossed his legs.

"Do you know," he said, "I'm scared." [43]

PART IV

The Supreme Court

[1]

ON January 30, 1939, one of the largest crowds that ever visited the chamber of the Supreme Court gathered to hear Professor Felix Frankfurter of Harvard Law School take the oath of office as Associate Justice of the Supreme Court.

Minutes before, Chief Justice Hughes had administered the constitutional oath in the privacy of the Court conference room.

For the first time Frankfurter met with the other Justices in the robing room behind the chamber's red draperies to put on the august symbols of their office. For the first time he participated in their conversation, which as a lawyer sitting below the bench he had many times heard as a low, incomprehensible hum.

As the Court crier banged his gavel, the spectators rose. The nine Justices filed in precisely at noon. Chief Justice Hughes announced that the President, "with the advice and consent of the Senate," had chosen the new Justice. Charles Elmore Cropley, clerk of the Court, administered the judicial oath to Frankfurter, who swore in firm, clear words to "administer justice without respect to person."

Then, as the most junior member, he took his tradition-prescribed seat at the extreme left of the Chief Justice, who sat in the center. The oldest Associate Justice in point of service sits at the immediate right of the Chief Justice, the next oldest at his immediate left, the next oldest in the next seat to the right, and so on. Frankfurter's position was next to that of Justice Black. As Frankfurter took his seat, Black, soon to be the leader of the opposing philosophic camp, welcomed him with a warm grasp of his hand. Frankfurter settled into the routine of the highest court in the land, the seventy-seventh Justice to be appointed. He was to stay twenty-three years and write a total of 725 opinions: 263 for the Court, 171 concurrences, 291 dissents.

Interestingly, on the day Frankfurter took his seat, the Supreme Court put the final stamp of approval on the controversial and experimental Tennessee Valley Authority. An advocate of public power since his days in the War Department of Theodore Roosevelt and Henry Stimson, Frankfurter had watched the development of the TVA with more than casual interest. Because he was known to have access to Franklin Roosevelt, Frankfurter was barraged with material by the advocates of both public and private power as they battled through the 1930's for supremacy in the Tennessee Valley. David E. Lilienthal, former student of Frankfurter's at Harvard and a member of the first TVA board, shot off memos and letters to keep Frankfurter apprised of TVA developments as the organization weathered lawsuit, Congressional investigation, and internal strife.[1] On the other side, George Roberts, attorney for Wendell Willkie's Commonwealth and Southern Corporation, which was one of the companies involved, a law partner of Stimson's, and a close friend of Frankfurter's, stated the case for private power companies in numerous letters to Frankfurter—in answer to which Frankfurter trenchantly cited the private power abuses which had invited public power.[2]

On this day a majority of the Supreme Court held that private companies were not immune from competition and could not stop the federal government from selling and distributing electric power. The practical result of the case was that the private utility interests sold many of their facilities and retired from the Tennessee Valley. It was a significant victory for the Roosevelt administration. It was a victory, too, for Frankfurter—although he had not, of course, participated in this decision—and he watched with intense interest as Justice Owen Roberts read the majority opinion.

In appearance, Frankfurter did not quite live up to his own idea of what a Supreme Court Justice ought to look like: "Supreme Court justices should be tall and broad and have a little bit of a bay window," [3] he once said. At fifty-six years of age, Frankfurter was short and rather slight, with an appearance of tenseness and physical energy. His carriage was inordinately erect and gave him an aura of dignity that lack of height had denied him. He had a finely rounded face, gray hair receding at the temples, and grayish eyes that could twinkle or grow somber. He wore pince-nez glasses, which he frequently took off to make gestures.

"His fires are inner," wrote one observer, "and they do not blaze out all the time." [4]

Frankfurter plunged into the work of the Court with all the intensity of an extraordinarily intense being. He worked far into the night and early in the morning. In his enthusiasm he sometimes forgot that others did not share his working hours. "You had to make it clear that you did not like telephone calls at five in the morning," [5] commented Justice John Marshall Harlan, who joined the Court in 1956.

It was a demanding job, even for a man who had taught law for a quarter of a century and could often give his law clerk the page number of a citation he wanted. He still had to read the lawbooks because, he once said, "I have colleagues who are from Missouri." [6] Shortly after he went on the Court, Mrs. Frankfurter asked him how he liked his work compared with that at the law school, and he replied it "was too enslaving to allow for much reflection upon it." [7]

It was exciting, of course, but it was also restraining. Accustomed to a certain amount of freedom, he had to settle into a routine: be there when the Court sat, read briefs and records on deadline, do research before cases were argued. Most Justices assign their law clerks to the task of writing summaries on the petitions for certiorari—the documents asking the Court to hear cases. Frankfurter did his own. Partly his judgment was better; partly it was a way of keeping on top of issues coming through the lower courts.

Working on "certs" also seemed a waste of a law clerk's time. It was more profitable, as Frankfurter ran his office, to assign a clerk some long-range exhaustive study, such as the history of the Fourteenth Amendment Alexander Bickel conducted when the desegregation cases appeared on the Court calendar; or a canvass of what Australia and England had done about a similar case; or research for a speech Frankfurter was scheduled to give. A law clerk might better spend his time putting together the first draft of an opinion—as Frankfurter's clerks did in later years, although when the opinion was finished, it was like the "Frankfurter and so-and-so's" which were co-authored at Harvard: much more Frankfurter than so-and-so. But a law clerk could best spend his time in a good "jaw" with the Justice—as Holmes, whose traditions Frankfurter unabashedly carried on, used to call his sessions with his clerks. A casual question more often than not led to an afternoon's seminar, a casual remark to intellectual banter, a casual statement to a long argument.

How Frankfurter loved talk! He was, for all his writings, basically a talking man. Court observers have often said that Frankfurter's impromptu explanations from the bench on opinion days of what his opinion said were much more persuasive than what he wrote. In his personal talk he spoke with exuberance and concentration and listened with equal exuberance and concentration, emphasizing his attention with a viselike grip on the arm of the other person. At the Court he bounced from office to office, arguing a point of law, gossiping, discussing opinions, politics, whatever happened to catch his attention that day, with or without reference to the Court. During the years Dean Acheson was in the State Department, Frankfurter and Acheson were a familiar pair walking from their Georgetown homes to Foggy Bottom, talking animatedly along the two-mile route. When they reached the State Department, Frankfurter was usually talking fifty to the minute—and he kept talking, insisting on closing a parenthesis or finishing a paragraph, although his car was waiting to take him to the Supreme Court and Acheson was impatient to get to work. Acheson would threaten to push him into traffic; Frankfurter would keep talking. Finally, Acheson said it had to stop. They agreed to cease all conversation at a certain point in the walk. It didn't work; Frankfurter simply stopped walking and went on talking at the boundary line.

When distance cut off face-to-face talk, Frankfurter would pick up the phone and continue a conversation, sometimes for hours. And when that course was impractical, he wrote letters by the gross—some of many pages, some of only a line or two or three. "Once you came into his orbit," said a former law clerk, "you were one of the possible recipients for this blizzard of letters that went out on anything from music to Greek history and sometimes even law." [8]

If the vast amount of work on the Court staggered Frankfurter, he did not show it. His ebullience remained intact. Except for an occasional ten-minute rest on a cot in his office in later years—after which "it was Vesuvius erupting all over again" [9]—the energetic mind and body never stopped.

Frankfurter brought a sense of informality and impish humor to the august tribunal. He would wave from the bench at friends among the spectators. He once escorted the child of a visiting Australian law school dean into the empty courtroom and let her sit on each of the Justices' chairs. When Mrs. Charles Fahy came to Court to hear her husband, the Solicitor General from 1941 to 1945, argue a case, Frankfurter once teased her with this note scribbled from the bench: "Anyhow—I'm for your hat!!" [10] He teased the law clerks of other Justices about those Justices' opinions. He teased his own law clerks incessantly. He whistled in the marble halls, anything from "The Stars and Stripes Forever" to the sextet from *Lucia.*

But underneath the gaiety and banter there was a seriousness of purpose equal to anything Frankfurter had undertaken in his life. He approached the Court with a kind of religious awe; he was indefatigable in guarding its traditions, and he felt, said Chief Justice Earl Warren, "the burden of carrying on the traditions of the Court more than any man." [11]

This intense caring about the Court was reflected in his view of his role on the Court. He saw himself, quite simply, as a teacher. He was one of nine professors whose duty it was to educate the entire legal world and the entire public.

To Justice Robert Jackson he wrote in 1942 that a case "should be decided in such a way as to afford a fair basis for judges to know how to decide the next case that may come before them involving the general doctrine. . . ." [12]

To Justice Stone he had once written: "You are writing . . . in the first place, for the law teachers, and if you think they don't need it, you are greatly mistaken. . . . Secondly, you educate students and the younger bar. Thirdly, it is more and more important to enlighten . . . the other departments of the social sciences and the influence that they exert upon the young and opinion generally. . . ." [13]

Frankfurter's peppery and piercing questions from the bench, which many lawyers learned to dread, were not asked just to harass counsel or to tear an argument apart—although it was certainly true he could indulge in legal fencing, the purpose of which no one, including the other eight, could fathom and which did on occasion serve only to obfuscate points of argument. Frankfurter claimed he asked these questions in order to elucidate points of law. He wanted to test counsels' ideas, not simply let them run on in rehearsed speeches—the rehearsed speeches were printed in briefs for the Justices to read in their offices. Oral argument, to Frankfurter, was the heart of the whole process. Questions—hopefully pointed, meaningful questions—served to bring out the essence of a case—for himself, for the other eight, for the bar as a whole.

Frankfurter also saw himself as professor with the entire nation as his class. "The evolution of our constitutional law is the work of the initiate," he had written in 1932. "But its ultimate sway depends upon its acceptance by the thought of the nation. The meaning of the Supreme Court decisions ought not therefore to be shrouded in esoteric mystery. It ought to be possible to make clear to lay understanding the exact scope of constitutional doctrines that underlie decisions. . . ." [14]

Frankfurter's concern for public understanding of the Supreme Court took him into a long running fight with the New York *Times.* The press, Frankfurter believed, had a semipublic function and a semipublic responsibility. The *Times,* as the one documentary paper in the nation, should, he thought, furnish its readers the kind of competence in its reporting of the Supreme Court that it furnished in other fields. It should, Frankfurter was fond of saying, cover the Supreme Court at least as well as the World Series. Beginning in 1933, Frankfurter barraged Arthur Hays Sulzberger, publisher of the *Times,* with letters in which he was outspokenly critical of its failings—and equally outspokenly congratulatory of its triumphs. Finally, in the mid-1950's, Frankfurter was instrumental in changing *Times* Supreme Court reportage. Sulzberger and Frankfurter lunched in Washington, and a young reporter and Pulitzer Prize winner named Anthony Lewis was sent to Harvard Law School for a year, then assigned to cover the Supreme Court. The *Times* expanded and deepened its Court coverage; a significant by-product of this development was the effect on other prominent newspapers which, encouraged by the *Times,* sought to improve their reporting of Court news and bring it up to World Series levels.[15]

Frankfurter's Court opinions often sound like professional lectures to a law school seminar. In fact, they were intended to. Their purpose was to educate the public, on whose confidence and trust the authority of the Supreme Court ultimately rested. If these opinions were stylistically somewhat gothic or if they frequently sent lawyers running for their dictionaries to look up unfamiliar or archaic words, Frankfurter nevertheless left no question on his ultimate meaning. This came across clearly and strongly even to the layman.

If Frankfurter had his interpretation of the role an opinion should play, he also understood that a Court opinion was not a Frankfurter opinion. He once said that opinions were not the "obvious map to the mind of the Justices" because opinions are the writings of the Court as a whole—"symphonies, not solos." [16] He always maintained he was eager for suggestions from his colleagues when he was writing for the Court: ". . . The day that I show the slightest signs of pride of authorship is a good day for me to take a vacation, at least a temporary one," [17] he once told Chief Justice Fred M. Vinson. However, Frankfurter could, in an occasional display of intellectual arrogance, send off a note to one of his brethren that clearly implied the recipient's intelligence was duller or his motives less worthy than Frankfurter's own.

Frankfurter was quick to write a concurrence when he agreed with the result of a majority decision but disagreed with the method of arriving at it. He would do so even when he disagreed with only a fine point of the majority opinion—precisely because he conceived the opinion-writing process as an educational one. An opinion was not merely an opinion; it was a "progenitor of future opinions," [18] he once told Justice Stanley Reed. Some cases, he told Reed, were "but the curtain raisers of future problems," and it was the duty of the Court to shed as much light as "we are capable of for the wisest unfolding of the subject in the future. This means not merely expressing a contrariety of views but even expressing the same views with different shades and nuances. . . ." [19] In fact, Frankfurter preferred the old custom, since abandoned because of the Court's increased workload, of all the Justices expressing individual views on constitutional issues, "even when one reaches a common result but would formulate it differently." [20] Conscientious opinions, whether for the Court, in concurrence, or in dissent, served to inform, to educate laity and bar.

However, he urged restraint, too: The opinion ought to stick to arguments on which a case turned and not take off on irrelevant issues; above all, a case should be decided on the narrowest grounds, and the opinion must adhere to these. He was fond of citing the example of Holmes who, when asked by his brethren to cut out some gem from an opinion, replied: "Very well, I'll put it in a letter to a friend."

Frankfurter was a perfectionist in his opinion writing. Men who had co-authored with him at Harvard remember his penchant for changing articles after they were in page proof—a penchant designed to make any publisher throw up his hands. In fact, a page proof seemed to stimulate him to revision and a second page proof, which begat more revision until six or seven sets were par for an article in the *Harvard Law Review*. It was said that on the Supreme Court he sometimes had thirty page proofs.

As Frankfurter saw himself as teacher to the bar and the public, he also saw himself as a teacher to his eight colleagues. There are Justices who look at a case, decide what they want to do, do it, and go on to the next case. "I always figured my job was done when I had made up my mind," commented Justice William O. Douglas. "For Felix that was just the beginning. He was like a Baptist preacher who had to get a convert." [21]

Frankfurter would have been complimented by the description. He cared about the results of a case, not only what the Court did, but how the Court did it; not only what the Court said, but how the Court said it. He barraged—not to say irritated—his brethren with long memorandums, brief notes, and frequent visits.

One law clerk remembers a day when Frankfurter was waiting for some citations to be added to a draft opinion. He was anxious to circulate it before opposing views had a chance to solidify. Impatient as he waited for the citations, he shouted at his clerk: "This is a war we're fighting! Don't you understand? A *War!*" [22]

Frankfurter would arrive at the Justices' weekly conferences with a pile of lawbooks and proceed to lecture his colleagues for an hour or so as though they were students in one of his law school seminars. Some of the Justices accepted this proselytizing with interest, even with humor. Frankfurter was fond of telling how in the conference room Chief Justice Hughes would mischievously call him Professor Frankfurter, then quickly correct himself to Justice Frankfurter. Other Justices resented the tedium of his long lectures and what they considered his intellectual arrogance, believing it a denigration of their own vast knowledge of the law.

A graphic description of Frankfurter in the conference room has been supplied by Hugo Black. Frankfurter, said Justice Black, "thrived on argument, and to say that his manner in our conferences was lively and animated can hardly convey the forceful, insistent, persuasive, eloquent, and at times explosive way in which he argued for views he deeply held. But he was never the kind of person to bear personal enmity toward others merely because they differed with him, and after a heated dispute when we passed on to the next case he was ready to ally himself cheerfully with his former adversaries."

And Justice Black caught, in these sessions with Frankfurter, other qualities. "Out of our discussion and our association," Black continued, "I learned that he loved his country with a passionate devotion and that long before I had even met him, he had dedicated his life to its service. I learned also that he had this same devotion to our judicial system. . . ." [23]

Frankfurter earned a reputation for courting every new appointee that came to the Supreme Court. During that period when a new Justice was adjusting to his new position, it was said that Frankfurter spent an inordinate amount of time in the new man's office and wrote an inordinate number of notes and memorandums. Partly, it was his interest in any new personality that crossed his line of vision; equally it was his hope to enlist the new Justice in his own philosophical camp. But this tutoring of the newcomer was one more manifestation of Frankfurter's intense caring about the Court, about what it did and how it did it. If he seemed to want to shape a new Justice in his own image, it was because he believed his methods were the best ones to assure the maintenance of the traditions and the authority of the Supreme Court as an institution.

The great bone-white and austere building on Capitol Hill to which Frankfurter came in 1939, which has been described as both a marble palace and a marble mausoleum, still had the smell of newness about it. The Court had met there for the first time October 7, 1935, having previously sat for seventy-five years, from 1860 to 1935, in the old Senate Chamber in the Capitol, across the street.

When the Supreme Court moved, with the rest of the federal government, to Washington in 1800, it was considered so unimportant that there had been no meeting place set aside for it. The Court was relegated to the basement of the old Senate Chamber. When John Marshall was appointed Chief Justice in 1801, the position was thought of as a sinecure. Only 10 cases came to the Court that term. Over the next five years only 120 cases were brought. From that time on, however, the number increased gradually until by the 1926 term the Court had 667 cases on its docket, and during Frankfurter's tenure, the number of cases customarily exceeded 1,000. In 1960–61, Frankfurter's last full term, there were more than 2,000 cases on the docket. The Court's influence on American life had grown even more significantly.

As an institution, the Supreme Court is the nation's umpire. It is the ultimate mediator of conflicts in American society—conflicts between individuals, between the states and the national government, between the executive and the legislative departments of the government. It is the final arbiter between the national interest and the parochial interest of the individual.

Through the technical device of ordinary lawsuits—*Doe v. Roe, Jones v. United States*—the Supreme Court decides which power will be recognized: individual, state, or federal. As Robert Jackson wrote when he was Attorney General: "Struggles over power that in Europe call out regiments of troops, in this country call out battalions of lawyers." [24]

When Frankfurter took his seat on the Supreme Court, editorial predictions of his judicial behavior ranged from comments that Roosevelt had appointed a dangerous radical to the bench to assertions that Roosevelt had assured his legislative program of a majority on the Court. Some editorials recommended a wait-and-see attitude.

The most interesting comments were those wise enough to transcend interpretations of Frankfurter's immediate positions and look more to his character and the meaning of his life. Two days after his appointment, the New York *Times* commented: "He will serve no narrow prejudice. . . . He will be free from partisanship. . . . He will reveal the organic conservatism through which the hard-won victories won for liberty in the past can yield a new birth of freedom. . . . He will vent no spites. . . . He will stand firmly for progress under law. . . . He will join the so-called liberal wing of the Court, but no more than Holmes or Brandeis, Stone or Cardozo, will he be stultified by dogma. . . ." [25]

And one prescient observer predicted: ". . . He may at times disappoint those liberal friends whose zeal for a 'cause' overruns their logic." [26]

Frankfurter did in fact frequently disappoint his "liberal friends" and was quickly disowned by them. He spelled out his explanation in a letter to a friend: "For twenty-five years," he said, "my preoccupation as a student of American law was protest against undue assumption of power by judges. I protested when judges declared law unconstitutional, not because they were laws I favored, but because it was a denial of the democratic process to have our society ruled by judges outside the democratic process.

"After I became a judge," he continued, "I could not change my convictions of what I conceive to be the proper function of a judge and nullify legislation simply because I may not like it. But I find that too many of my friends who protested against McReynolds and Company, acting as a super-legislature, now want me to be a McReynolds for the things they don't like—that is, to be indifferent to the limits that properly should confine a judge, leaving the remedy for foolish legislation where it mostly belongs, in the hands of an enlightened electorate. I had supposed that that was the best kind of 'liberal' doctrine, but as Holmes said long ago, people on the whole don't want justice, they want you to decide cases their way. . . ." [27]

Had Frankfurter's critics looked back at what he had been saying and writing on public issues throughout his public career, they would have found a certain consistency in the actions of the professor and the Justice. The times, the conditions, the causes had changed, not Frankfurter.

Frankfurter came to the Court with his bags packed. He was not an originator. He was not even so much a judge—although when it was required, he could be one. More than anything, he was a judicial philosopher, who, laboring under the same structural limitations of the American government but under changed circumstances, was carrying on the tradition of judicial restraint enunciated most recently and effectively by Oliver Wendell Holmes, Jr.

Frankfurter had learned, he always said, his philosophy of judicial restraint at the knee of a legal god of the late nineteenth century, James Bradley Thayer of Harvard, whose prophet was Oliver Wendell Holmes. Although Thayer had died shortly before Frankfurter enrolled as a student at Harvard, his teaching pervaded the Harvard Law School atmosphere, and Frankfurter had imbibed freely. In a twenty-six-page paper, which Thayer had read to the Congress on Jurisprudence and Law Reform in Chicago on August 9, 1893, and which was published in the *Harvard Law Review* of October, 1893, Frankfurter found the best single piece of writing on American constitutional law. It is a map to Frankfurter's judicial mind, defining as it did the role of both judge and citizen in the constitutional scheme.

On the part of the judge, there must be restraint. He "must not step into the shoes of the law-maker. . . ." For the legislator and the citizen whose spokesman the legislator is, there must be responsibility. There was, said Thayer, too much reliance on the courts to correct legislative error, too little reliance on the people for wise legislation. Through this dependence on the courts, Thayer warned, both the legislators and the people they represent, "not being thrown back on themselves, on the responsible exercise of their own prudence, moral sense, and honor, lose much of what is best in the political experience of any nation; and they are belittled as well as demoralized. . . .

"The safe and permanent road towards reform," Thayer advised, is not through the courts, but "is that of impressing upon our people a far stronger sense than they have of the great range of possible mischief that our system leaves open, and must leave open, to the legislatures, and of the clear limits of judicial power; so that responsibility may be brought sharply home where it belongs. . . . Under no system can the power of courts go far to save a people from ruin; our chief protection lies elsewhere. . . ."

These were the linchpins of a judicial philosophy—responsibility and restraint that gave Frankfurter the latitude as Professor Frankfurter to advocate "legislation that promotes the best interests of labor and thereby the social well-being of the country" [28] and as Justice Frankfurter to decide in 1949 that a state's right to work law was a constitutionally valid exercise of the state legislature's function.

It was, like friendship and education, judging by expectation: observing sharp limits on the Court and depending on the people and their elected officials for wise, effective, and honest lawmaking. He had no illusions about the character and ability of the electorate and its representatives. He knew—as he knew the limitations of his friends, his students, Franklin Roosevelt—he exaggerated the competence and disinterestedness of the people and their representatives. But by often enough and strongly enough endowing them with sagacity and honor and morality and by allowing them the latitude to realize their potential, they—and America—should, would, must realize their own ideals.

Frankfurter based his judicial opinions no less than he had his articles for the liberal *New Republic* on his concept of this nation's scheme of governmental structure, a rigid federalism. This federalism, conceived in 1787, has as its purpose providing a way of allowing the diverse people of a vast continent to live together in unity while permitting the greatest amount of freedom for the development of individual and local interests. Federalism is an attempt to reconcile the conflicting demands of unity and diversity, of cohesion and localism.

In 1777 the men who had declared their independence from Great Britain, embittered by long experience under London's control which had stultified individual and local enterprise, were reluctant to devise another strong central government which could conceivably hoard power to itself and once again sacrifice the interests of the individual, the region, the state, to the national interest. They devised a scheme of government, under the Articles of Confederation, which gave the states the widest latitude, the greatest power, and allocated very little power to central authority.

As a result, the nation nearly destroyed itself while parochial factions hoarded the power and sacrificed the national interests to those of individuals, regions, and states.

Clearly, a more centralized, more unified plan was required to knit the loosely federated states more closely. Yet those same parochial interests were just as clearly opposed to subordinate themselves to a strong central government.

The Founding Fathers, suspicious of concentrated power in either national or local governments, put their faith in the structure of federalism. They wrote the Constitution as the supreme law of the land, to distribute certain powers to the central government and certain powers to its constituent governments—the states. The states were given some latitude in developing their own governments, and each today has its own constitution, although the articles of these may not conflict with the Constitution of the United States.

Under this federal Constitution, each government—national and state—has its own officers, its own laws, its own courts and powers over the individuals. These powers are rigidly defined by the federal Constitution, and the authors wrote the document so that each block of power—state or national; executive, legislative, or judicial—serves as a check on and balance to the others. The Constitution cannot be changed by ordinary acts of Congress; change can come only through amendment which requires ratification by the states.

It is a relevant fact, wrote Professor Frankfurter in 1930, that the fundamental structure of the American government "has survived the rise and fall of the German Empire, has seen the pendulum in Russia swing from an extremist autocratic to an extremist proletarian regime, and in France has witnessed republic displace monarchy and monarchy supplant republic until, in 1875, the present durable republic was established. . . .

"The Constitution of the United States," he continued, "thus appears as a strange phenomenon of permanence. The formal changes have been very few in number and have not very seriously affected its structure. . . ." [29] The essential distribution of power between the states and the national government as formulated nearly a century and a half ago is substantially unchallenged. Although amendments have been added to the document over that time, most did not rebalance the powers.

This is not to say it all runs with well-oiled smoothness, that there is no conflict. There is a great deal of conflict between executive and legislative branches, between state and national governments, between legislatures and judiciaries, between individual and government. Frankfurter's own arguments before the Supreme Court in behalf of the state's right and responsibility to legislate minimum wages and the Supreme Court's decision to prohibit such legislation is an example of the conflict brought close to home.

The final arbiters of these conflicts must be the federal courts. Even though the state courts might be bound by federal laws, "final interpretation of such laws could not be left to a state tribunal," wrote Charles Evans Hughes in 1928, "much less to the tribunals of a number of states whose judgments might not agree." The Constitution was written for the federal government to act not through the states, pyramid-style, but directly on the citizen, so that the individual lived, so to speak in two territories—the state and the nation—with only the Constitution over both. Thus, there had to be some supreme tribunal to arbitrate the demands and limitations of the supreme law where it was thought to conflict with either state law or the individual citizen.

"Thus, in the most natural way," said Hughes, "as the result of the creation of Federal law under a written constitution conferring limited powers, the Supreme Court of the United States came into being with its unique function. That court maintains the balance between State and Nation through the maintenance of the rights and duties of individuals. . . ." [30]

Not only is controversy inherent in the structure of federalism, but it is also built into the deliberate vagueness of some of the language of the Constitution. Written in the late eighteenth century by men who realized they could not foresee the future, the authors of the Constitution abstained from straitjacketing future generations by writing into the document all the precise details of government for generations they did not know and conditions they could not predict. They purposely wrote in generalities which could in later years be interpreted in accordance with conditions at the time.

"The Constitution is not a code of rules," Frankfurter said at his fiftieth class reunion at Harvard Law School in 1956, "in which explicit answers can be found for specific questions." On the contrary, Frankfurter pointed out, "it designedly left room for inevitable changes and therefore ample scope, though not unbridled freedom, for judges in the application of large concepts to such changing conditions. . . ." [31]

Parts of the Constitution are, of course, explicit. There is no dispute that, for example, a President is elected for four years, that Senators are to serve six-year terms, and that members of the House of Representatives are to serve two-year terms.

But even the simplest language in the Constitution can be attended by controversy. Until recent years there was a great deal of dispute over what the Constitution meant when it commanded that the Vice President succeed the President upon the President's "Inability to discharge the Powers and Duties of the said office." The emphasis was on the word "inability" and how it should be defined. A constitutional amendment was needed to correct the situation.

The first ten amendments to the Constitution—the Bill of Rights—written in the same spirit as the body of the document and ratified in 1791, have occasioned a great deal of dispute. Cases involving the First Amendment—"Congress shall make no law respecting an establishment of religion, or prohibiting the free exercise thereof; or abridging the freedom of speech, or of the press; or the right of the people peaceably to assemble, and to petition the Government for a redress of grievances"—frequently come before the Court. What are the "unreasonable searches and seizures" prohibited by the Fourth Amendment? Are they simply searches without a warrant, or do they include such modern innovations as wiretapping? What is "due process of law," without which the Fifth Amendment to the Constitution prohibits deprivation of "life, liberty, or property"? Does this mean that a man whose confession of guilt has been forcibly, even brutally obtained by police officers can be convicted of a crime?

These questions leave themselves open to a wide range of interpretation for which the Justices of the Supreme Court are responsible. These are difficult questions. There is no legal calculus, no fixed mathematical formula to apply to decision making. The dispensing of justice cannot be relegated to a computer.

Frequently the Court is split, five to four, indicating that four men as knowledgeable and experienced as the majority disagree with those five men. Even within the majority there may be disagreements which require concurrent opinions; these may reach the same result as the Court opinion but for different reasons. As the membership of the Court shifts over periods of time, the principles involved in a dissent may win support to become the principles involved in a majority opinion.

As Frankfurter wrote in 1930: "In good truth, the Supreme Court *is* the Constitution." [32]

Men, as Frankfurter always said, are the controlling factors—men, with their divergent backgrounds, their prejudices, their ideals. "The history of the Supreme Court," Frankfurter wrote in 1938, "is not the history of an abstraction, but the analysis of individuals acting as a Court who make decisions and lay down doctrines, and of other individuals, their successors, who refine, modify, and sometimes overrule the decisions of their predecessors, reinterpreting and transmuting their doctrines. . . ." [33] It made all the difference in the economic and social history of the nation that James C. McReynolds, Pierce Butler, Willis Van Devanter, and George Sutherland were writing the majority opinions of the 1920's and early 1930's. One can only imagine how events would have turned out had a Holmes or a Brandeis or even a Stone been able to command a majority.

There are few more demanding jobs in the world than that of a Supreme Court Justice. He must decide questions of the gravest import to the country's political and social foundations. His is the onus of final responsibility; his is the temptation of ultimate power.

In Frankfurter's mind, there was one primary qualification for men who would do such a job well. It had nothing to do with their politics. ". . . It is of the very essence of the function of this Court that when a man comes on it, he leaves all party feelings as well as affiliations behind. I certainly do not and have not since January 30, 1939, for one split second felt like or deemed myself, or deemed it right for anyone else to think of me as a 'New Deal' Justice," [34] he wrote in 1943. Furthermore, although Presidents frequently use party ties as an index "to the behavior of future justices," [35] he wrote in 1957, "past party ties as such tell next to nothing about future justices. . . ."

Nor had this qualification anything to do with geography, which had delayed Frankfurter's own nomination to the Supreme Court. "The pride of a region," he has said, "in having one of its own on the Court does not outweigh the loss to the Court and the country in so narrowing the search for the most qualified." [36]

It does not even have anything to do with prior judicial experience. No other court faces the diversity of cases or the subtleties the Supreme Court faces daily.

The one qualification which overrides all others, Frankfurter believed, was "disinterestedness . . . disinterestedness . . . disinterestedness." It was the lack of this quality in the group of Justices Frankfurter called McReynolds and Company which had set the Court on a course of judicial overactivism and had brought it to the brink of self-destruction. Responsive to property rights and insensitive to the needs of the masses, the Supreme Court, with increasing frequency following the Civil War, had obdurately invalidated economic and social legislation passed by Congress and the states until Franklin Roosevelt threatened it with reform in 1937. Frankfurter strove not to be guilty of the same error himself.

No man, of course, can dissociate himself from the social, economic, intellectual, philosophic, and moral environment from which he comes. He cannot change his character. But he must cultivate the habit of self-discipline until it is "so inured that merely personal views or passions are effectively antisepticized and thereby bar a corrosion of judgment leading to arbitrary determination," [37] Frankfurter had written.

It was this exacting task which Frankfurter sought to accomplish during his tenure as an Associate Justice of the Supreme Court. His attempt at disinterestedness floods his personal writings and his opinions. "I do not conceive it is my function to decide cases on my notions of justice" is a constant theme in his writings. To one who telegraphed thanks for an opinion, he wrote: "I do not want to appear ungracious. But decisions are to be reached on the conscience of judges. Thanks for such judicial action are therefore irrelevant." [38]

He guarded the power of the legislature as jealously as he guarded the power of the judiciary. He once wrote to a colleague on the Court whom he believed had circulated a draft opinion that usurped a portion of legislative prerogative: "You told me yesterday that if you succeeded in making your draft the opinion of the Court you will 'have done something.' Indeed you will—you will have marched successfully on the Hill, taken your seat in the halls of Congress and written your own notions of policy into legislation." [39] He once said of his philosophic opposite, Hugo Black: "I greatly sympathize with the essential purpose of my Brother (former Senator) Black's dissent. His roundabout and turgid legal phraseology is a *cri de coeur*. 'Would I were back in the Senate,' he means to say, 'so that I could put on the statute books what really ought to be there. But here I am, cast by Fate into a den of judges devoid of the habits of legislators, simple fellows who feel that they must enforce the laws as Congress wrote them and not as they really should have been written.' . . ." [40]

In fact, it was Justice Black who represented a judicial philosophy diametrically opposed to that of Frankfurter. Sitting together on the Court for twenty-three years, these two became the polar forces of that body and the spokesmen for two opposing traditions of American jurisprudence. And generally, during the time the two sat together on the Supreme Court, the Court as a body teetered from one view to the other, with neither prevailing entirely.

Black and Frankfurter seldom disagreed about the ends to be achieved. Both were steeped in the progressivism of Woodrow Wilson and the two Roosevelts. Both were appointed to the Court by Franklin Roosevelt. And surprisingly frequently, they decided the same thing, although often for different reasons.

Their fundamental disagreement was in methods. Black believed in activism on the part of judges; Frankfurter urged restraint. When the Bill of Rights said "Congress shall make no law . . ." Justice Black believed it meant that Congress shall make *no* law. ". . . The history and language of the Constitution and the Bill of Rights," he wrote in 1960, "make it plain that one of the primary purposes of the Constitution with its amendments was to withdraw from the Government all power to act in certain areas—whatever the scope of those areas . . . there is, at least in those areas, no justification whatever for 'balancing' a particular right against some expressly granted power of Congress. If the Constitution withdraws from Government all power over subject matter in an area, such as religion, speech, press, assembly, and petition, there is nothing over which authority may be exerted. . . ." [41]

Such unqualified commands did, of course, contain risks for the government. "Strict procedures," Black once acknowledged, "may release guilty men; protecting speech and press may involve danger to a particular government." But he believed the authors of the Constitution took these risks into consideration when they wrote the document. "They decided," said Black, "that certain rights should be guaranteed regardless of these risks. Courts have neither the right nor the power to review this original decision of the Framers and to attempt to make a different evaluation of the importance of the rights granted in the Constitution. Where conflicting values exist in the field of individual liberties protected by the Constitution, that document settles the conflict, and its policy should not be changed without constitutional amendments by the people in the manner provided by the people." [42]

In effect, Black gave the judiciary a tremendous power to enforce the provisions of the Constitution as the judiciary viewed them. He never hesitated to use this power as an instrument for social justice. He would use the Court to right the wrongs imposed by society on the unprotected, the minority, far more important to him than legal abstractions.

Black and those who urged an active role of the Court believed Frankfurter and his followers not only abdicated responsibility, but deluded themselves into believing they could maintain objectivity. The very act of sustaining a law, Black would say, is in itself an exercise of power. Indeed, he believed, it was a dangerous exercise of power in that it might very well leave people without recourse—the victims of prejudice, the outnumbered, the nonconforming and those who are otherwise weaker than a majority, with no refuge. Restraint was judicial legislation, as patent as any indulged in by the so-called activists. And it was judicial legislation at its worst because it left the helpless still unprotected.

Frankfurter put his trust, on the other hand, not in the judiciary, but in the long run in the people; otherwise, he believed, the effect would be "government by judges," [43] which he emphatically declared undemocratic. Restraint, of course, contained risks, too—essentially, that the people and their representatives might not live up to their responsibilities. Nevertheless, judicial restraint, according to Frankfurter, put the responsibility where it belonged in a democracy. A democracy is hardly a democracy when its people compensate for their inadequacies by taking all their problems to the courts.

"My starting point is," he once wrote to Black, "of course the democratic faith in which this country is founded—the right of a democracy to make mistakes and correct its errors by the organs that reflect the popular will—which regards the Court as a qualification of the democratic principle and desires to restrict the play of this undemocratic feature to its narrowest limits." If the Court were to have the power to review legislation—"judicial review of political authority" [44] —then it must be under conditions of utmost scrupulousness on the part of the judges.

For all their philosophic disagreements, however, Black and Frankfurter maintained the friendliest relations. Shortly after Frankfurter's death, Black wrote a tribute in the *Harvard Law Review:*

> ... There is a widespread belief that men whose views about some things differ sharply must be enemies. During our long service together Felix and I did have disagreements about the law and the meaning of the Constitution, many of them, and we frequently expressed these differences with vigor and emphasis. Our differences in the main were far less about the ultimate aims of our Constitution than they were about the most appropriate way for our Court to aid in achieving those aims. . . .
>
> Felix many times gave me reason to know that he valued our friendship as much as I did, as when following one of my visits to him after he was stricken by his illness in 1962, he wrote me: "I cannot believe that any two Justices who sat next to each other on the bench had pleasanter times than we did during our all-too-short years together!". . .[45]

At the same time that Frankfurter guarded legislative power, he urged equal legislative responsibility. He trusted the democratic process; he trusted the people to elect sagacious representatives and these representatives to fashion policies for the states and the nation. If a special interest represented a great danger to the free life of the nation, he once said, "Congress can change it in five minutes this afternoon." [46] Whether Congress would or would not was, of course, another question, and he was under no illusions about what Congress would do. But this judging by expectation required that Congress be given the widest latitude for doing what was expected of it and, at the same time, be pressured—by encouragement, criticism, whatever weapons were at hand—into doing it.

In Frankfurter's concept of federalism, responsibility for policy-making lay with Congress, in some cases with state legislatures, in other cases with the executive branch. Redistribution of their respective powers would destroy the tenuous, yet at the same time constitutionally stringent, balance of the governmental structure.

Frankfurter was sometimes mistaken for a states' rights man. He was not. He was a states' responsibilities man, for he believed that true freedom lay in individuals assuming the burdens of their problems. In 1916 Oregon had assumed the responsibility for correcting the evils of unrestrained laissez-faire by establishing standards for minimum wages. Clearly, he believed and so argued in the Supreme Court, this was the province and the duty of that state.

The problem of child labor ought to have been dealt with similarly. Why was this problem a concern of the states? He had answered that question in 1925, when he wrote: "Of course, child labor is a 'national responsibility.' So is lynching, so is education. But that does not settle the very practical question as to the instruments and forces for realizing the national aim at any particular time or with reference to any particular subject. . . . I want to energize the people of the States. . . . I care for the gain through the educative process of having the people in each State secure social conditions which are within the compass . . . of the individual States. . . ." It was the nation's women who had been campaigning against the use of child labor. "If the women really cared," Frankfurter continued, "as much as businessmen cared *they* could get similar results from the States and the process of such an effort would give us a very different body of citizens than we now have. . . . These . . . views . . . may, in the long run, be fraught with more fruitful 'progressivism' than Constitutional amendments. . . ." [47]

Frankfurter also believed that, had there been appropriate state action or regional action to cope with the strangulation of utilities and bilking of the public by financial interests in the 1920's, national action would have been unnecessary and undesirable.

This was the essence of democracy: Self-regulation was the most desirable; when that was not forthcoming, regulation at the lowest level was indicated, and there must be a great deal of latitude for experimentation.

The hands of the Supreme Court are forever tied, Frankfurter believed. The Justices are bound by the constitutional limits on their power from writing legislation, from modifying it, qualifying it. That Court, Frankfurter believed, can only strike down or uphold what has been written. "The Court is the brake on other men's actions, the judge of other men's decisions," [48] Frankfurter wrote in 1938.

And the Court can strike down a law only when that law violates a fundamental principle of the Constitution. However foolish or detrimental a law seems from a Justice's experience, knowledge, or wisdom, unless it specifically infringes on constitutional demands, it must be upheld. Outside interference, he believed, is inherently bad; it encourages abdication of responsibility, the great developer of men and true bulwark of freedom for which all the laws and the Constitution were made.

[2]

Justices who assumed extrajudicial tasks are not unprecedented in American history. The first Chief Justice was John Jay. For six months he was Chief Justice as well as Secretary of State. While still on the Supreme Court, he ran for election as governor of New York. Then, for more than a year, he served both as Chief Justice and Ambassador to England. During Oliver Ellsworth's four-year tenure as Chief Justice, he also served as Minister to France for eighteen months. Bushrod Washington, Associate Justice from 1798 to 1829, openly supported the Presidential campaign of Charles Pinckney in 1800.

However, as a professor, Frankfurter believed Supreme Court Justices ought to take a vow of noninvolvement. "In suggesting that judges engage in public activities off the bench," he had written the Boston *Herald* in 1929, "we are in danger of forgetting that it is the business of judges to be judges. . . . It is necessary for judges to be less worldly than others in order to be more judicial. They must keep out of the rush and tumult of life in order to cultivate those habits of serenity and reflection indispensable to the adequate exercise of judicial function." Perhaps more significant, duties undertaken in a partisan cause leave a judge open to suspicion of partisanship in his judicial duties. "Judges need not be in the turmoil of the world," Frankfurter continued, "to be responsive to its needs and influences" [1] insofar as these are relevant to their judgments on the bench. Their worldly experiences should have been sufficient, when they came to the bench, to preclude necessity for further contact with the day-to-day affairs of men.

The issue has another side to it, however. Does a citizen abdicate other responsibilities when he takes his judicial oath? Frankfurter maintained that he need not. "Certainly one does not cease to be a citizen of the United States," he wrote in 1953, "or become unrelated to issues that make for the well-being of the world that may never come for adjudication before this Court, by becoming a member of it. . . ." [2]

Did Frankfurter stretch the responsibilities of citizenship while he was on the Supreme Court?

Some of his off-Court tasks were, of course, official. In 1941 he served, under the chairmanship of Justice Reed, on the President's Committee on Civil Service Improvement, an obvious channel for his long-studied ideas on placing qualified men in government positions and in building up a bank of talent for the government. Because of his reputation as a scholar of history and his vast knowledge of American history in particular, he served in later years as the Supreme Court's representative to the National Historical Publications Committee, a group formed in the early fifties for publishing original papers from the earliest days of the Republic.

When Frankfurter went to the Supreme Court, he believed it appropriate to resign from every formal association, such as the American Civil Liberties Union and the National Association for the Advancement of the Colored People. He even resigned from the

Harvard Club, and in 1959 he had to write for a special dispensation to get a room there in New York, where he was scheduled to speak to a reunion class.

These resignations, however, hardly stultified his unofficial off-Court interests, which continued to encompass the customary broad range. When he wasn't worrying about who would fill a vacancy in the State Department, he was worrying about who would be the next president of Harvard. He recommended men for the federal judiciary to the Attorney General. In 1941 his old friend Mayor Fiorello H. LaGuardia of New York brought his corporation counsel to the jurist's chambers for Frankfurter to referee unofficially a hassle between them over a provision of the New York State constitution. Nor was Frankfurter too busy to greet groups of high school students sent to him by friends or to talk with writers at work on books concerning historical judicial subjects.

People streamed through his office for luncheon, for tea, for brief visits. "Getting to see Felix," commented his colleague, Justice Douglas, "was like trying to get a barber's chair." [3]

None of these were, of course, so significant as his continued role as friend and confidant and adviser to Roosevelt. And his rationale was the duty of a citizen which transcended all others: patriotism. Frankfurter possessed an almost childlike patriotism. He could be aggressive about it, even arrogant, sometimes self-righteous. It was the patriotism of a man who had first seen America in the person of the Statue of Liberty at the impressionable age of twelve, had been welcomed regardless of how he spelled his name, had been given—as a right—unlimited opportunity. He reciprocated with a justifiably intense gratitude.

The first five years of Frankfurter's tenure on the Supreme Court coincided with the eve, outbreak, and fighting of World War II. Frankfurter was profoundly disturbed by the German threat to America—and civilization—and he spared no pains to involve himself in what he considered the best interest of the nation.

When Frankfurter took his seat on the Supreme Court in January, 1939, war, which had been brewing on the Continent for a decade, had nearly come to Europe; events were leading to American involvement. Frankfurter was frightened by what he called the "shortsightedness" [4] of people in Washington who thought it didn't make any difference who won the war in Europe. He was disturbed by the isolationism of factions within the Republican Party—an isolationism that was gathering support. He was worried about a prevalent attitude that the United States should be careful not to irritate or provoke Hitler—"if we only say nice pussy, the tiger will become a pussy," he wrote to Henry Stimson. "It is really not credible . . . that we should so completely shut our minds to the whole nature of Hitler's character, purposes and technique. . . ." [5]

President Roosevelt was caught between such isolationist and timid viewpoints among the American people and his own realization of the perils to the nation posed by Hitlerism. He did not want to go to war, but he realized the situation could easily get out of control, and he wanted to prepare for it—just in case. Frankfurter bombarded Roosevelt with notes and memorandums designed to support Roosevelt's view and to underline the necessity for the United States to stand by the democracies of Europe in every way short of an actual declaration of war. During the tense spring and summer of 1939, as events in Europe led to the German invasion of Poland on September 1, 1939, Frankfurter dispatched nearly 300 notes to Roosevelt pleading the urgency of the situation.[6]

It was an open secret in Washington that Frankfurter was continuing as an outside insider in the Roosevelt administration. Nevertheless, when Roosevelt publicized Frankfurter's role, the critics were quick to jump on it. In late September, 1939, Roosevelt invited the Frankfurters and the Harlan Fiske Stones on what was euphemistically called a social cruise aboard the Presidential yacht. A few days later, Roosevelt announced a plan for striking back at Congress, which had refused to appropriate money to house 100,000 new Army and Navy recruits. In his press conference, Roosevelt let it be known that after discussing it with Stone and Frankfurter, he intended to get the needed housing by incurring deficits. Immediately a storm of protest broke over the involvement of the Justices. Stone had a reputation for abstemiousness in public affairs. He never approved of Justices serving on committees or performing other services not directly related to the work of the Court. Stone had refused on that ground to head President Hoover's National Commission on Law Observance and Law Enforcement (Wickersham Commission). He complained in 1942 about Justice Roberts' absence from Court work when Roosevelt appointed Roberts to head the commission of inquiry into the Pearl Harbor disaster. In 1946 he unsuccessfully attempted to dissuade President Harry S. Truman from sending Justice Robert Jackson to Nuremberg to prosecute Nazi war criminals. After Roosevelt's unfortunate remarks to the press in the fall of 1939, Stone refused to go on any more "social cruises" on the Presidential yacht.

Frankfurter, however, never broke his pace. In the early forties, Grace Tully, Roosevelt's secretary, recorded: "Four Supreme Court Justices were frequent 'off the record' White House callers, these being Frankfurter, Douglas, Murphy, and Jackson. Their counsel was often of great help to the President but it was felt that exaggerated publicity on their visits would be out of keeping with their positions on the Court." [7] Samuel I. Rosenman, a chief writer of Roosevelt's speeches, frequently drove to Frankfurter's Georgetown home to discuss ideas of what a particular Presidential speech ought to contain.

The spring of 1940 saw Frankfurter cast in the familiar role of employment agency, this time on a high level.

In 1936, Harry Woodring had been appointed Secretary of War with the idea that he would in a few months be given another office. However, four years later, Roosevelt's advisers were still talking about what to do with Woodring, whose office had become increasingly important as war clouds drew nearer, but whose administration of the office had not proportionately improved. In addition to being a "nice fellow, but . . ." as Roosevelt frequently described Woodring, he was resisting Roosevelt's efforts to aid the European democracies in their struggle against Hitler. It was clear by February, 1940, that Woodring had to go.

In February, 1939, Frankfurter and Robert Jackson, then Solicitor General, had listened at the White House while Roosevelt hatched a plot with Francis Biddle, a Philadelphia lawyer then in private practice. Telephoning Biddle in his School House Lane home in Philadelphia, Roosevelt asked him to become a federal judge. Typically, Roosevelt was about to jump his men around the board like checkers. As he told Biddle, the judgeship would not be for long. "Frank Murphy wants to be Secretary of War, why God only knows," the President explained. "But it will take a little time to persuade Harry Woodring to resign, perhaps five or six months. When he does, I'll put Frank in his place, make Bob Jackson Attorney General, and you Solicitor General. What do you say? Bob Jackson and Felix Frankfurter are sitting here next to me and they are witnesses to the plot." [8]

Biddle did accept the judgeship and, in fact, later became Attorney General. But Frank Murphy did not become Secretary of War.

The original plan also included a provision that Alfred M. Landon of Kansas, who had run against Roosevelt in 1936, would go into the Cabinet as Secretary of Commerce and Frank Knox, Landon's 1936 running mate, would go in as Secretary of the Navy.

In the following months, the specifics of the plan were laid aside, partly because of Landon's opposition to Roosevelt's third term, but Roosevelt's determination to get rid of Woodring persisted into the spring of 1940.

Meanwhile, matching Roosevelt's determination to oust Woodring was the determination of Grenville Clark, a prominent New York lawyer, to secure the nomination of Henry Stimson as Secretary of War. Clark had turned his energies in the spring of 1940 to obtaining universal military training in this country. Both the Army and Congress were opposed. Clark decided, therefore, that the way to achieve universal military training was to install a Secretary of War who would advocate it strongly. He needed, he concluded, a man like Henry Stimson.

Clark had been a classmate of Frankfurter's at Harvard Law School, and the two had remained close friends. Knowing Frankfurter had the confidence of Roosevelt, Clark took his suggestion to Frankfurter. The pair had a long talk covering a wide range of suggestions for the post, but they kept returning to Stimson, although Stimson was seventy-two years old.

In spite of his age, however, he had had first-rate experience in government: Secretary of War under Taft, Secretary of State under Hoover, governor general of the Philippines, more important now with Japan's ascendancy in the Pacific. Stimson was clearly the best-qualified man.

In 1922, Elihu Root had suggested Stimson as successor to retiring Supreme Court Justice Mahlon Pitney. In a "Dear William" letter to Chief Justice Taft, hoping Taft would pass his suggestion on to the President, he had written: "What is the matter with Harry Stimson for the place? . . ." [9] Taft had replied: ". . . the only thing I know against Stimson is his good opinion of Frankfurter. I suppose it does not indicate an unsoundness of view as to the Constitution on Stimson's part. . . . But the influence of the Harvard Law School through

Frankfurter and Pound . . . is to break down that fundamental instrument and make it go for nothing. . . ." [10]

During the election of 1932, Stimson had made speeches for Hoover and against Roosevelt. Roosevelt and Stimson had met, however, in January, 1933, through the efforts of Frankfurter. They had formed a casually friendly relationship as they worked together on international problems facing the new administration. Since that time, Stimson, in private legal practice in New York, had kept a wary eye on developments overseas. As elder statesman, he had worked diligently to alert the country to the coming war. In 1937 he had urged England and the United States to stop supplying Japan, then at the beginning of its route of aggression through the Pacific, with vital oil, ore, cotton, and rubber. "A few years from now," Stimson had predicted, "if Japan is successful, we shall all of us very likely have to fight to the uttermost and then without any certainty of success." [11]

Frankfurter and Clark agreed that Stimson, as a man of experience in government and as a man aware of ominous developments overseas, was the man to be Secretary of War. To balance Stimson's age, they put together a "ticket" of Stimson as Secretary and forty-nine-year-old Robert P. Patterson as Assistant Secretary. Patterson was a former partner in Clark's law firm and, at the time of the Frankfurter-Clark conference, a United States Circuit Court judge. Frankfurter had scribbled to Patterson in 1932: "You will always remain my prize baby student—favorite editor-in-chief of the *Law Review*. . . ." [12]

On June 3, 1940, Frankfurter took the ticket to Roosevelt, who had been considering Fiorello LaGuardia or Herbert Lehman for the position. Frankfurter, convinced of the merits of the Stimson-Patterson combination, recommended against both of Roosevelt's suggestions. LaGuardia, Frankfurter believed, was too controversial a figure; Lehman, indecisive.

Then Frankfurter said, "Have you thought of Harry Stimson?" Roosevelt, Frankfurter later recalled, "didn't say anything in particular, but I could see the idea had hit home." [13]

In subsequent letters Frankfurter kept the names of Stimson and Patterson before Roosevelt, writing a long memorandum on the qualifications of Patterson, urging the dual appointment.

On June 17, Stimson spoke at Yale, stating the case for compulsory military training. The next day he spoke on the radio on "America's Interest in the British Fleet."

The following afternoon Roosevelt called him at his New York office and asked him to be Secretary of War. Stimson called Roosevelt back at 7 P.M. and accepted. They agreed that Patterson would be second man on the ticket. Patterson also accepted. Ironically, Patterson, as a member of a privately sponsored military group, was doing KP when he was told of his nomination to the second highest position in the military establishment. With these two, Frank Knox came into the Cabinet as Secretary of the Navy.

In Stimson, Roosevelt had not only a man of integrity and ability, but a Republican outspokenly alert to the dangers of Hitlerism at a time when more and more Republicans were embracing isolationism and Roosevelt wanted desperately to prepare for war. For Roosevelt, hiring Stimson was advantageous politically.

For Stimson, it was politically embarrassing. Roosevelt made the appointments of Stimson and Knox on the eve of the 1940 Republican convention to nominate a Presidential candidate. Protests of "dirty politics" rent the Republican air as prominent party leaders demanded that Stimson and Knox be read out of the organization.

Frankfurter saw the appointment of Stimson, who shared Frankfurter's international concerns, as an opportunity not only for bipartisanship in Roosevelt's Cabinet—an obvious advantage for a wartime leader—soon to be a war Cabinet, but also as a prod to the nation's preparing for war. To Stimson he wrote, prior to Stimson's confirmation by the Senate: ". . . I am confident that your appearance before the Senate Committee will be turned by you into a first rate opportunity for educating the American people to an understanding of what national defense really means, of the menace against which we must defend, and the relation of what is going on in Europe and more particularly in the impending battle of Britain, to our own immediate defense. . . ." [14]

Stimson was Secretary of War through World War II until 1945. During that time Frankfurter, according to Stimson (whose autobiography is written in the third person), "made himself a continual source of comfort and help. . . . Stimson found Frankfurter always the most devoted of friends and the most zealous of private helpers, and the Justice's long and intimate knowledge of the Roosevelt administration was placed entirely at his disposal. Time after time, when critical issues developed, Stimson turned to Frankfurter; sometimes he heard from Frankfurter even before he had turned. . . ." [15]

No doubt Frankfurter saw his role in this and other prewar and wartime government matters as apolitical. No doubt he believed that as a highly placed citizen, he was in a unique position to press his passionate conviction that the United States must ready itself for conflict with the Nazi war machine running unchecked over Europe.

The observer who commented at the time of Frankfurter's appointment to the Supreme Court that Frankfurter's liberal friends might soon be disenchanted with his judicial position did not have long to wait to see that prediction realized. On the day Frankfurter presented to Roosevelt the Stimson-Patterson ticket to head the War Department, June 3, 1940, to further the national defense effort, he handed down the Supreme Court's opinion in a controversial and emotional flag salute case. In writing the opinion, Frankfurter stuck to his guns of judicial restraint. However, there were many who believed that it was an exercise in circumlocution and that he had had to search far afield for its roots in law—although seven others, including activists Black and Douglas, joined in the opinion. Frankfurter, his critics said, had allowed his concern for the degenerating international situation—on which Harold Ickes said Frankfurter was "not rational" [16] by this time—to dictate his decision and turn it into a plea for national unity in tense times.

In November, 1935, Lillian Gobitis, aged twelve, and her brother, William, aged ten, of Minersville, Pennsylvania, were expelled from public school for refusing to salute the American flag on religious grounds. They were members of the Jehovah's Witnesses religious sect, which prohibits flag saluting, believing it to be idolatrous. Their father went to court asking that the school board be enjoined from punishing his children for adhering to their religious beliefs. He also sought $3,000 damages. The district court sided with him. Although it did not agree that idolatry or religious significance was attendant upon the flag ceremony, the lower court did say the children were justified in their objections if they conscientiously believed that freedom of religion was being abridged by saluting the flag. The Third Circuit Court of Appeals also upheld the Gobitis family. The Minersville School Board appealed to the Supreme Court of the United States.

Freedom of religion is implicit in the First Amendment to the Constitution: "Congress shall make no law respecting an establishment of religion, or prohibiting the free exercise thereof. . . ." The authors of the Constitution saw the First Amendment as a rejection of policies then practiced in some of the separate colonies and states. People had been taxed against their will for the support of religion, occasionally the support of a particular religion with whose tenets they did not agree. There were penalties for failure to attend public worship and sometimes for expression of heretical opinions. These were the very practices Americans had hoped to leave behind in Europe, the very practices the Founding Fathers had sought to guard against with their stern warning that the "free exercise" of religion must not be infringed.

However, society also has its claims. The Supreme Court interpreted the amendment to mean that "Congress was deprived of all legislative power over mere opinion, but was left free to reach actions which were in violation of social duties or subversive of good order." [17] In 1890 the Court applied it to decide that while the Constitution guaranteed freedom of religion, this guarantee did not extend, for example, to the practice of polygamy, which Congress had declared a criminal act by law.

Here is the Court's decision-making function: "to maintain," wrote Charles Evans Hughes in 1928, "this balance between the constitutional guarantees of liberty and legislative requirements in the interest of the social order." [18]

Here was the issue in the case of the expulsion from school of Lillian and William Gobitis for refusal to salute the flag. Was their action on the ground of "free exercise of religion," however conscientiously taken, disruptive of the social order? Had the local community the right to impose such a requirement in the face of the First Amendment to the Constitution?

Frankfurter's answer to both questions was Yes. The free exercise of their religion by those two children was disruptive of the social order, and the local community did have the right to prevent that disruption.

Frankfurter considered and reconsidered his stand, especially since Justice Stone, who was to be the lone dissenter in the case, strenuously doubted his arguments and voiced his objections to Frankfurter.

But Frankfurter held to his views that "constitutional power is on one side and my private notions of liberty and toleration and good sense are on the other . . ." as he explained to Stone a few days before the Court's decision was handed down. "... All my bias and predisposition are in favor of giving the fullest elbow room to every variety of religious, political, and economic view," he continued.

But, Frankfurter added, "we are not in the domain of absolutes ... we have an illustration of what the Greeks thousands of years ago recognized as a tragic issue, namely, the clash of rights, not the clash of wrongs. For resolving such clash we have no calculus. ..." Frankfurter feared, however, to "exercise our judicial power unduly, and as though we ourselves were legislators by holding with too tight a rein the organs of popular government. ... I wanted to avoid the mistake comparable to that made by those whom we criticized when dealing with the control of property," he emphasized to Stone, who was all too familiar with the judicial positions of McReynolds and Company, having been one of the few dissenters during the reign of conservatives.

"My intention," Frankfurter further explained to Stone, "was to use this opinion as a vehicle for preaching the true democratic faith of not relying on the Court for the impossible task of assuring a vigorous, mature, self-respecting and tolerant democracy by bringing the responsibility for a combination of firmness and toleration directly home where it belongs—to the people and their representatives themselves.

"I have tried in this opinion really to act on what will, as a matter of history, be a lodestar for due regard between legislative and judicial powers. ..." [19]

Frankfurter wrote the opinion for the Court, with the agreement of all Justices except Stone.

In this case, Frankfurter said for the Court, "judicial conscience is put to its severest test ... the conscience of the individual collides with the felt necessities of society. ..."

Certainly, the law could not infringe on a man's private religious convictions. Government may not interfere with expression of belief or disbelief, organized or unorganized, or propagation of that belief. However, "the manifold character of man's relations may bring his concept of religious duty into conflict with the secular interests of his fellow men. ...

"... Conscientious scruples have not, in the course of the long struggle for religious toleration, relieved the individual from obedience to a general law not aimed at the promotion or restriction of religious beliefs. . . ."

It was possible, Frankfurter maintained, to sustain political authority and fundamental religious freedom simultaneously.

Referring indirectly to the tragedy that was being played on the European stage in the spring of 1940, as Hitler's armies marched virtually unchecked across the continent, Frankfurter inserted a plea for patriotism. "National unity," he said, "is the basis of national security. . . . The flag is the symbol of our national unity, transcending all internal differences, however large, within the framework of the Constitution. . . ." The question asked by the Gobitis case—a question particularly relevant in a time of emergency—was: "whether the legislatures of the various states and the authorities in a thousand counties and school districts of this country are barred from determining the appropriateness of various means to evoke that unifying sentiment without which there can be no liberties, civil or religious." [20]

Frankfurter had answered the question in principle in 1917, arguing before the Supreme Court in behalf of the right of the State of Oregon to legislate a maximum ten-hour day for laborers. He had told the Court then: "You have no right to invalidate that which those who have the responsibility of legislation have done, because theirs is the final responsibility. The duty of this Court is merely to say that men charged with the responsibility have exceeded the speed limit. . . ." [21]

Had the Minersville School Board exceeded the speed limit? No, said Frankfurter—so long as the authorities were not specifically barred from making such a requirement, so long as "men's right to believe as they please, to win others to their way of belief, and their right to assemble in their chosen places of worship for the devotional ceremonies of their faith, are fully respected." [22]

There were times when the local authorities did exceed the speed limit. When they did, Frankfurter was prepared to be a traffic cop. In late 1947, a released-time case came to the Supreme Court. The public schools of Champaign, Illinois, regularly released schoolchildren during school hours to take advantage of a program of religious instruction. Private teachers used the physical facilities of the public school to give sectarian instruction.

A majority of the Court decided that this particular program was unconstitutional; Frankfurter, in a concurring opinion, agreed.

"Illinois," he wrote, "has here authorized the commingling of sectarian with secular instruction in the public schools. The Constitution of the United States forbids this." There might very well be released-time programs that were not forbidden by the Constitution, but in the particular program of Champaign, "Religious education so conducted on school time and school property is patently woven into the working scheme of the school" and "the basic Constitutional principle of absolute Separation was violated. . . ." [23]

This was not true, however, Frankfurter believed in the Gobitis case. The Minersville School Board had not exceeded the speed limit. If such a requirement, or law, as this school board had made, was deemed foolish or inadequate, or simply bad, the place to change it was in the legislatures, not in the courts. "To fight out the wise use of legislative authority in the forum of public opinion and before legislative assemblies rather than to transfer such a contest to the judicial arena serves to vindicate the self-confidence of a free people," [24] he wrote.

Justice Stone did not agree. Opinions of the Court are handed down on Mondays; the authors of the opinion generally give an oral summary of the decision in order to save time. On Monday, June 3, 1940, Stone was so agitated by the Court's opinion in the Gobitis case that he broke precedent and read his complete dissenting opinion in an emotion-filled voice.

The requirement of the Minersville School Board, he said, "does more than suppress freedom of speech and more than prohibit the free exercise of religion. . . . For by this law the state seeks to coerce these children to express a sentiment which, as they interpret it, they do not entertain and which violates their deepest religious convictions. . . ."

He conceded that the government "has a right to survive." It may even go so far as to suppress religious practices dangerous to morals, public safety, health, and good order. But it may not "as a supposed educational measure, and as a means of disciplining the young, compel public affirmations which violate their religious conscience." Where constitutional guarantees conflict with governmental functions, there must be "reasonable accommodation between them so as to preserve the essentials of both. . . ." It is the function of the courts to determine where such accommodation is possible.

"History teaches us," Justice Stone continued, "that there have been but few infringements of personal liberty by the state which have not been justified, as they are here, in the name of righteousness and the public good, and few which have not been directed, as they are now, at politically helpless minorities. . . ."

Stone was not persuaded of the advisability of restraint on the part of the Court. "This seems to me no less than the surrender of the constitutional protection of the liberty of small minorities to the popular will. . . .

"The Constitution," he continued, "expresses more than the conviction of the people that the democratic processes must be preserved at all costs. It is also an expression of faith and a command that freedom of mind and spirit must be preserved, which government must obey, if it is to adhere to that justice and moderation without which no free government can exist. . . ." [25]

The aftermath of the Gobitis decision did in fact bring the wrath of the majority down on the heads of the minority, who had nowhere else to go. Buttressed by law on their side, angry crowds attacked members of the Jehovah's Witnesses sect wherever the minority group gathered. Children who refused to salute the flag were suspended; adults were jailed or run out of town. The Supreme Court, their last resort, had failed.

The Frankfurters were childless—a fact they deeply regretted at least during their early years together; a fact also made more poignant by Frankfurter's well-known extraordinary rapport with and delight in the children of his friends. Then, for a brief period during the early days of World War II, they did have children in their home. And they reveled in it.[26]

Sylvester G. Gates of London had studied at Harvard Law School as a Commonwealth Fellow for the 1925 and 1926 terms. Through academic association and collaboration in writings on the Sacco-Vanzetti case, Frankfurter and Gates became intimate friends and kept in touch throughout the thirties. When the Frankfurters went to England, they spent part of their time with the Gates family, which came to include Gates' wife, whom he had married as a widow with two daughters, and their son. When most of the world feared Hitler was going to invade England after the debacle at Dunkirk in 1940, Frankfurter got in touch with Gates and urged him to send the three children to Washington. In a hurried transatlantic phone call, Gates agreed that the children would be packed up and sent with their nanny in three days. Mrs. Frankfurter, who had been in bed, is reported to have hung up the phone with the remark: "Well, if I'm going to have three children arriving in three days' time, I suppose I'd better get out of bed."

Get out of bed she did, and made over the top floor of the Frankfurter home, then at 1511 Thirtieth Street in the Georgetown section of Washington, for three children, ages eleven, eight, and three, and their nurse.

The advent of three young children in the relatively serene lives of a Supreme Court Justice and his wife should have created chaos. If there was chaos, it was not apparent to the children. The Frankfurters, who quickly became Aunt Marion and Uncle Felix, seemed to assume their roles as surrogate parents calmly, matter-of-factly, and eagerly.

The top floor of the house quickly began to smell of wet wool, with little sweaters drying on the radiators. The stairs became a sliding board for a three-year-old boy, and Frankfurter did remark to a friend: "You know, English children can be noisy, too." [27]

When in later years the youngsters reminisced about this period, they recalled that the Frankfurters had been able to create a natural atmosphere of family closeness and warmth. There was normal discipline and no nonsense about spoiling, but there was also love joyously given, comfort for tears, solace when every headline screamed that London had been razed to the ground, and eager interest in everything the youngsters did. Whatever the strong temptations for the childless Frankfurters to overdo their roles, however, they were always careful to remain surrogates, never trying to replace the children's parents.

In the summer of 1942 the children returned to England. It had been discovered that English children who had not been evacuated to America or Canada but spent the war years in England—in the country with relatives—were doing better. In addition, their mother wanted them back. But the incident that gave final impetus to the Frankfurters sending them back was a letter written by one of the girls and left on the stairpost for mailing. It was addressed to "Mrs.

Sylvester Gates . . . London, England Forever!" Frankfurter took them to New York and put them on a plane.

However, the Frankfurters remained "home" to all three. The children were driven back again and again in later years by memories of the two years they had spent in Washington, and they were welcomed with all the warmth they had known during their exile. When Oliver Gates, who had been three when he arrived at the Frankfurters' in 1940, returned to England from Frankfurter's funeral in 1965, he said only, "there doesn't seem much point in going to America anymore."

The authors of the Constitution commanded the Supreme Court to handle only "Cases" and "Controversies." As judges, its members were not authorized to play any role in government policy. George Washington had the issue settled for him very early in the nation's life. He suggested to his Chief Justice that he refer legal questions to the Justices of the Supreme Court for their advice. The Justices refused, stating that the executive, legislative, and judicial branches not only were separate but were "in certain respects checks upon each other" [28] and must keep their distance. The propriety of involvement in partisan causes militated against such judicial advice; so did practicality, since the judges could not render an authoritative decision without a specific case to study. The precedent became a hallowed tradition. Justices customarily refuse to give advisory opinions.

Nevertheless, when England needed weapons to continue its fight against Hitler, Frankfurter was able to set aside this unwritten judicial stricture and help England get them.

Roosevelt interpreted his election to a third term in November, 1940, as a mandate for him to turn the United States into a great "arsenal of democracy." At the end of that year, he devised a plan for what became known as Lend-Lease—a program under which Roosevelt as President would have the power to lend or lease equipment to those nations whose defense he believed necessary to the defense of the United States.

On the afternoon of January 3, 1941, Henry Morgenthau, Secretary of the Treasury, and Ben Cohen visited Frankfurter with a draft of the proposed Lend-Lease legislation, which was to be introduced in the form of an amendment to the Neutrality Act. Frankfurter examined it closely. There were possibly, he thought, a few alterations that would help. One was a change in the language of the section having to do with the powers of the President; it would not do to make these powers too discretionary. He also suggested that the bill contain a preamble, in easily quotable words, to show the bill's importance for national defense.[29] That, Frankfurter explained, would strengthen its constitutionality; it would also enlist support for Lend-Lease in the name of national defense from a people still reluctant to shoulder what it considered Europe's, not America's, burdens.

If Frankfurter seemed unduly willing to repudiate his vow of noninvolvement in an extrajudicial cause, once again the rationale was patriotism: the saving of England, America's first line of defense at that time, and perhaps all Western civilization from what he called "mad brute force." As he had written in a letter to Herbert Lehman: ". . . those who place any interest above that of freedom, place man's destiny below the level of moral dignity." [30]

At the beginning of 1941, the year that was to end with America going to war, communication lines between President Roosevelt and British Prime Minister Winston Churchill were temporarily down. Joseph P. Kennedy, Ambassador to the Court of St. James's, had been fired because of indiscreet remarks. John G. Winant had not yet replaced him. Still Roosevelt wanted to maintain a close relationship with Churchill. After some deliberation, he decided to send Harry L. Hopkins, his most intimate adviser and friend, to London to re-establish a personal relationship with Churchill.

However, Churchill and Hopkins had never met. When Churchill heard the name of Roosevelt's emissary, his immediate reaction was "*Who?*"—hardly a propitious beginning for a solid friendship between Roosevelt and Churchill, then the two most important men in what was left of the free world.

On his side, Hopkins, although he was eager to go, had reservations about, even distrust of, Churchill.

No one perhaps understood the significance of this mission better than Frankfurter, who had over the past two years expended a great deal of energy and persuasion on Roosevelt's prewar position; the fate of Anglo-American relations could very well hinge on the reports Hopkins sent back. Frankfurter understood Roosevelt as well as any man did; he knew Hopkins well; he understood the close relationship between the two.

Never one to shrink from action, Frankfurter approached one of his numerous friends in high places: Richard G. Casey, Australian Minister to the United States. He asked Casey to help pave the way for Hopkins in London. Frankfurter urged that Churchill be briefed on Hopkins and his mission before the latter arrived. Hopkins, Frankfurter told Casey, was Britain's firm ally in its attempt to fight Hitler. But having a regard for Roosevelt that bordered on reverence, Hopkins would be useless as an emissary unless Churchill showed that he viewed Roosevelt in a similar light. Emphasizing the significance of Hopkins' mission to effect a close relationship between Churchill and Roosevelt, Frankfurter told Casey that Churchill should go out of his way to express his own admiration for Roosevelt; should Churchill leave it to be taken for granted, Hopkins might mistake his attitude for one of indifference.

Casey telegraphed the Australian high commissioner in London the substance of Frankfurter's conversation. The high commissioner telegraphed back that the Prime Minister was grateful for Casey's message and would take appropriate action.[31]

At the same time, Frankfurter's close friend in London, Harold Laski, was writing a long memorandum to Hopkins to brief him on the powers and personalities of the men Hopkins was to see in London, from the influential men at the British ministries to Churchill himself. In conclusion, Laski apologized to Hopkins for his frankness but said he assumed he could be as frank with Hopkins as he could with Roosevelt or Frankfurter.[32]

The Hopkins mission was a success. Hopkins and Churchill established a rapport and spent several weekends together at Chequers. Hopkins was able to help put the Roosevelt-Churchill relationship on a more solid footing, as well as to bring back firsthand reports of the British war effort.

In 1960 Lord Casey was writing his memoirs. Telling the story of his and Frankfurter's involvement in the Hopkins mission, Casey used "X" instead of Frankfurter's name, then wrote Frankfurter for permission to substitute "Frankfurter" for "X." [33] Frankfurter replied that, of course, Casey could name him.[34] Although he customarily held himself aloof from political matters while a member of the Supreme Court, Frankfurter explained, the avoidance of misunderstanding between the two most powerful persons concerned with the war could not possibly be construed as remotely allied with politics.

On June 2, 1941, Chief Justice Charles Evans Hughes, aged seventy-nine, sent his resignation to Roosevelt, who was at his Hyde Park home. When Roosevelt returned to Washington, he immediately invited Hughes to luncheon to discuss a successor. Hughes recommended Stone, then the senior Justice in terms of service.

Roosevelt asked Hughes what he thought of Robert Jackson, then Attorney General. Hughes said he thought well of Jackson, but that Stone had earned the chief justiceship with his judicial record. Hughes then suggested Roosevelt consult with Frankfurter, a close friend of Jackson's and more knowledgeable about "the history of the Court and its needs than anyone else." [35]

Frankfurter was summoned to a luncheon meeting. Roosevelt quickly came to the point: the vacancy on the Supreme Court. Could he wait, he asked Frankfurter, until fall to appoint a successor, since the Court was adjourned through the summer?

No, answered Frankfurter. The new man ought to be appointed right away. If a new man was to be named, he needed the summer to break in. In addition, as senior Justice, Stone was the *de facto* head anyway; it would be unfair to allow him to continue as head through the summer, then not name him Chief Justice.

"As between Stone and Bob Jackson," Roosevelt asked, "whom would you make Chief Justice?"

"I wish you had not asked me that question," Frankfurter replied.

"Why?" asked Roosevelt.

"Because," answered Frankfurter, "on personal grounds I'd prefer Bob. While I've known Stone longer and our relations are excellent and happy, I feel closer friendship with Bob. But from the national interest I am bound to say there is no reason for preferring Bob to Stone—quite the contrary. Stone is senior and qualified professionally to be Chief Justice. But for me the decisive consideration, considering the fact that Stone is qualified, is that Bob is of your political and personal family, as it were, while Stone is a Republican."

Frankfurter continued: "Now it doesn't require prophetic powers to be sure that we shall, sooner or later, be in war—I think sooner. It is most important that when war does come, the country should feel that you are a national, the Nation's President, and not a partisan President. Few things would contribute as much to confidence in you as a national and not a partisan President than for you to name a Republican who has the profession's confidence, as Chief Justice."

Roosevelt listened carefully, but made no comment. Nevertheless, Frankfurter left the White House confident that Stone would be named.[36] On June 12, 1941, believing Stone would be better received by the nation on the eve of a national emergency and fearing that the appointment of an administration stalwart like Jackson would revive accusations of Court packing, Roosevelt sent Stone's name to the Senate for confirmation as the next Chief Justice of the United States.

The exigencies of war, transcending the importance of all other matters, dictated that Frankfurter assume many nonjudicial duties in 1941. He wrote memorandums on Atlantic islands defense—including recommendation of American occupation of Iceland—and, drawing on his own experience in an inefficient War Department on the eve of World War I, advised Roosevelt two days after war was declared to consolidate all the problems of war production under one head. Roosevelt did, in fact, in January, 1942, appoint Donald Nelson chairman of the War Production Board with wide powers. Frankfurter also did not stint of energy or time in offering Roosevelt, stranded on a lonely island of leadership in difficult times, advice, encouragement, and comfort.

In June, 1942, as Frankfurter completed his third full Supreme Court term, the "Washington Merry-Go-Round" by Drew Pearson and Robert S. Allen reported: ". . . it is a fact that second only to the President himself, Justice Felix Frankfurter has more to do with guiding our destinies of war than anyone in Washington. . . . Almost no move of major importance is made these days without Frankfurter having his finger in it." [37]

This was an exaggeration. Nevertheless, Frankfurter involved himself in a great many of Roosevelt's affairs.

[3]

If Frankfurter as a Justice seemed unduly circumscribed by his philosophy of judicial restraint, it is also true that there were areas in which he was not so restrained. He had no absolutes; perhaps the only absolute he adhered to was an absolute abhorrence of absolutes. But he had, as he once said about Holmes, a "hierarchy of values." [1]

Holmes and Frankfurter both deferred to legislative judgment in social and economic fields because they believed the legislature was the proper arena for the social and economic experimentation out of which the best measures would be fashioned. These fields were the responsibility of the legislature, not the business of the Court. Nor were the shifting arrangements in these fields fundamental to individual liberty.

However, Holmes and Frankfurter were not so constrained when it came to questions of what have come to be called civil liberties. "Those liberties of the individual," Frankfurter said, "which history has attested as the indispensable conditions of an open as against a closed society come to this court with a momentum for respect lacking when appeal is made to liberties which derive merely from shifting economic arrangements. . . ." These were "enduring liberties," outlined in the Bill of Rights and protected against state action "through a slow process of expansion of the liberties secured by the Fourteenth Amendment. . . ." [2]

Before Frankfurter joined the Supreme Court, he was famous—or notorious—for his eloquence and zeal in trying to protect these enduring liberties for the Bisbee deportees, Tom Mooney, the victims of the Red Raids of the 1920's, and, of course, Sacco and Vanzetti. After he joined the Supreme Court, he was equally zealous in guarding these liberties and is remembered as a champion of criminal justice. "He was devoted," said Charles Fahy, judge of the United States Court of Appeals for the District of Columbia and former Solicitor General, "to the importance of fair procedure and means to be used in obtaining results which civilized society seeks but which

Wide World Photos

Dean Acheson (left) and Felix Frankfurter during hearings of Senate Judiciary Committee subcommittee on the nomination of Frankfurter to the Supreme Court, January 12, 1939.

Pen-and-ink drawing by Clifford Berryman, March 9, 1937.

Library of Congress

OF COURSE WE MAY HAVE TO CHANGE REMEDIES IF WE DONT GET RESULTS
F.D.R.
NEW DEAL REMEDIES
CONGRESS
NRA
SAB
RFC
ICC
FESB
PWA
FERA
FEHC
FHLBB
FDIC
CWA
CCC
AAA
FACA
Berryman

1
2
3
4
GSC
RFC
CWA
IAB
DDC
AAA
CAB
DMC
NRA
PAB
TVA
CSB
FACA
NAC
ECNR
RTA
FDIC
EHFA
ECPC
SAB
CCC
ICC
PCT
SAP
NLB
PRA
CC
LAB
NEW DEAL
IT IS EVOLUTION, NOT REVOLUTION, GENTLEMEN!
Berryman

Franklin Delano Roosevelt, 1936.

New York *Times*

Marion Denman Frankfurter.

Courtesy of Helen Denman Hessler

Harris & Ewing

The Supreme Court, 1939.
Seated: Harlan Fiske Stone; James C. McReynolds; Charles Evans Hughes, Chief Justice; Pierce Butler; Owen J. Roberts.
Standing: Felix Frankfurter; Hugo L. Black; Stanley F. Reed; William O. Douglas.

The Supreme Court, 1962.

Seated (left to right): William O. Douglas; Hugo L. Black; Earl Warren, Chief Justice; Felix Frankfurter; Tom C. Clark.
Standing (left to right): Potter Stewart; John Marshall Harlan; William J. Brennan, Jr.; Byron R. White.

Harris & Ewing

With John F. Kennedy and Wilmarth S. Lewis on the occasion of a luncheon for editors and publishers of the papers of the American National Historical Publications Commission, June, 1963.

Reprinted with permission of Alfred A. Knopf and Wilmarth S. Lewis.

Wide World Photos

Justice Felix Frankfurter, 1957.

must be obtained by civilized means. It has in the long run the effect of lifting the level of decency and fairness in administering the criminal law." [3]

In the spring of 1943 Frankfurter, writing for a majority of the Court, made an eloquent statement in behalf of the fair administration of criminal justice; it serves as a map to his judicial mind in this area.

On a July night in 1940, four revenue agents surprised a band of Tennessee moonshiners loading cans of whiskey into a car. In the flight that followed, two of the federal officers were shot, one fatally, by unseen assailants. A few hours later, three brothers—Freeman, Raymond, and Emuil McNabb—were arrested at their home in McNabb settlement and taken to the Federal Building in Chattanooga, about twelve miles away. There they were detained in a barren cell, without access to lawyer, friends, or relatives, for about fourteen hours. They were not formally arraigned, as the law required, but subjected to intermittent questioning, during which incriminating statements were elicited and later used to convict them of second-degree murder in a federal court. On appeal, their convictions were upheld.

The Supreme Court, however, reversed the McNabbs' convictions. The evidence on which the convictions were based could not stand; it had been secured in a manner which was a "flagrant disregard of the procedure which Congress has commanded," [4] Frankfurter wrote in the Court's opinion.

The key word was "procedure"; Frankfurter used it frequently in his opinions; it was another linchpin of his judicial philosophy.

"A democratic society," Frankfurter wrote, "in which respect for the dignity of all men is central, naturally guards against the misuse of the law enforcement process. Zeal in tracking down crime is not in itself an assurance of soberness of judgment. Disinterestedness in law enforcement does not alone prevent disregard of cherished liberties. Experience has therefore counseled that safeguards must be provided against the dangers of the overzealous as well as the despotic. . . ."

The particular safeguard at issue—the legislation which required police promptly to take the accused before a judicial authority for arraignment—protected the innocent; it was also an aid to securing firm convictions for the guilty. It "checks resort to those reprehensible practices known as the 'third degree,'" Frankfurter wrote. "It also aims to avoid all the evil implications of secret interrogation of persons accused of crime. It reflects not a sentimental but a sturdy view of law enforcement. It outlaws easy but self-defeating ways in which brutality is substituted for brains as an instrument of detection. . . ."

Such procedure could not be ignored. "The history of liberty," Frankfurter concluded, "has largely been the history of observance of procedural safeguards. And the effective administration of criminal justice hardly requires disregard of fair procedure imposed by law." [5]

The McNabb decision was severely criticized by law-enforcement officers as undue curbing of police efficiency. The intent of the decision was precisely the opposite. In the field of criminal justice, Frankfurter had fixed ideas about the fairness of procedure and the responsibilities of law-enforcement agencies. He had developed them first as an Assistant United States Attorney, in the first decade of the century, under the tutelage of Henry Stimson. He further developed them in his work on the crime surveys of the 1920's.

He had summed these up in 1930: ". . . Because of our volume of crime, there are men, particularly those charged with the administration of criminal justice, who are impatient of the restraints imposed upon officers of the law by some features of the Bill of Rights.

"The Bill of Rights," he declared then and paraphrased it often in his judicial opinions, "was written into the Constitution to guard against the recurrence of well-defined historic grievances. Provisions for trial by jury in criminal cases and against self-incrimination and 'unreasonable searches and seizures,' requirements for freedom of speech and freedom of assembly, summarized the experience of early American statesmen as to abuses of arbitrary power. . . ."

There were, however, he continued in 1930, law-enforcement officers who, "with jaunty ignorance" of political history, "seek to transfer to government the efficient methods of a department store." To declare, as the police commissioner of New York City had declared, that "the Constitution is at the end of a police stick," said Frankfurter, "is to declare the community morally bankrupt." [6]

All was decidedly *not* fair in society's war against crime. ". . . Just because I believe in law and in our Constitution," he had written to Henry Stimson in 1922, "I believe a peculiar noblesse oblige rests upon our officials, particularly our law officers and the courts, to observe the Constitution, however strong the winds of passion may blow. . . ." [7]

Nearly thirty years later, after having sat on the Supreme Court for twelve years, he wrote to Justice Harold H. Burton: ". . . I am as sure as I am of anything that is not mathematically demonstrable, that crime is not to be reduced nor are criminals to be effectively brought to justice by being indulgent toward lawlessness on the part of law-enforcing authorities. The notion that since these have a tough time anyhow we would only obstruct the effective administration of justice in making them toe the mark is a false notion. The reverse, I am sure, is the truth." [8]

Savage conduct was as odious in the war against crime as the use of gas in conventional warfare. In the 1952 case of Antonio Rochin, suspected of selling narcotics, three Los Angeles deputy sheriffs had broken into Rochin's bedroom, and when the suspect gulped two capsules on his nightstand, the police handcuffed him, rushed him to a hospital, and directed a doctor to force an emetic into his stomach. The two capsules were found to contain morphine, and Rochin was convicted chiefly on the basis of this evidence.

The Supreme Court would not stand for it and reversed Rochin's conviction. Frankfurter, in the Court's opinion, lashed out at this display of brutality by police. ". . . The proceedings by which this conviction was obtained do more than offend some fastidious squeamishness or private sentimentalism about combatting crime too energetically. This is conduct that shocks the conscience. . . ." These were methods, he declared, "too close to the rack and screw." To "sanction the brutal conduct . . . would be to afford brutality the cloak of law. Nothing would be more calculated to discredit law and thereby to brutalize the temper of a society. . . ." [9]

Forced confessions, the third degree, wiretapping (which Frankfurter believed was outlawed by the Fourth Amendment), all forms of unreasonable search and seizure—these were beyond the pale of police. The framers of the Constitution had deliberately restrained police action in the Bill of Rights, "not in order to convenience the guilty but to protect the innocent," he said. "Nor did they provide that only the innocent may appeal to these safeguards. They knew too well that the successful prosecution of the guilty does not require jeopardy to the innocent. The knock at the door under the guise of a warrant of arrest for a venial or spurious offense was not unknown to them. . . . Arrest under a warrant for a minor or trumped up charge has been familiar practice in the past, is a commonplace in the police state of today, and too well known in this country. . . . The progress is too easy from police action unscrutinized by judicial authorization to the police state," [10] he said in 1950.

These restraints on police, Frankfurter believed, those embodied in the Constitution and those on the federal and state statute books, call for more alert enforcement by the courts not because they are more important than other laws, but because they are most likely to be encroached on in "a short-sighted desire to protect society against crime." The freedoms of the First Amendment, he wrote Justice Frank Murphy in 1947, "easily summon powerful support against encroachment. But the prohibition against unreasonable search and seizure is normally invoked by those accused of crime and criminals notoriously have few friends." [11]

It was a paradox that it was the miserable little crooks the Court was called on to protect in the context of the great themes of the Bill of Rights. "It is a fair summary of history to say," he wrote Justice Sherman Minton in 1950, "that the great safeguards of human liberty have most frequently been forged in controversies involving not very nice people." [12]

Perhaps, however, what Frankfurter was pointing out then is the essence of democracy: that the refuse of society, no less than the president of General Motors, can take a case to the Supreme Court and depend on the Justices to decide it conscientiously and with integrity.

Enforcing the lawful restraints on law officers does not, as many people charge, handcuff those law officers. On the contrary. The shortcuts indulged in by both lazy and overzealous police were unnecessary in the long-range purpose of bringing criminals to justice, and that they had, on occasion, wrongly convicted innocent people was Frankfurter's thesis. Frankfurter was, he said, "deeply wedded" to the Court's responsibility and sense of restraint in reviewing state convictions. "But," he told Justice Tom Clark in 1952, "there is the other responsibility: observance of the Fourteenth Amendment whereby State convictions must be had—and I know they can easily be had through competence and industry—without violating basic notions of Anglo-American decency in the prosecution of crime.

That principle must not be obscured by the fact that we are dealing with murderous gangsters. The whole point about procedural safeguards is that their disregard today to unworthy creatures establishes itself into rules of law and criteria for judgment which tomorrow may control decision in the cases of people who are not unworthy." And, he added, soberly, "it is vital to the quality of our civilization to observe what we profess." [13]

The prosecution of criminals, Frankfurter summed up in a 1952 dissent, ought not to be "deemed a dirty game in which 'the dirty business' of criminals is outwitted by 'the dirty business' of law officers. The contrast between morality professed by society and immorality practiced on its behalf makes for contempt of law." [14]

Prosecutors were, Frankfurter believed, as guilty of infringements of the law as policemen. Although district attorneys ought to try their cases with vigor and courage, their cause ought to be the proper administration of justice and not, as he believed too often true, the conviction of criminals for political ends. When Thomas E. Dewey was running for governor of New York on his record as a crime-busting district attorney, Frankfurter told a friend: ". . . Nothing is more important, from the long view, for the promotion of desirable standards of criminal justice in this country than to have Dewey so emphatically defeated that no prosecutor for the next generation will be tempted to use the prosecutor's office as a springboard to political preferment. One of the chief curses of American criminal prosecution has been precisely this intermingling of politics and prosecutions. . . ." [15]

One did not have to be a sentimentalist about criminals to observe, Frankfurter declared, that shortcuts to criminal prosecution put "premium on force and fraud, not on imagination and enterprise and professional training" and that they were as self-defeating as they were immoral. Of course, it was a loss to the community if a criminal was allowed to go free because the means by which his conviction was obtained were defective. However, Frankfurter quoted Holmes, it was patently "a less evil that some criminals should escape than that the government should play an ignoble part." [16]

This circumstance was not without remedy, however. Frankfurter put his hopes, his expectation, as always, in the democratic process, in the people to whom it mattered. No "sturdy, self-respecting democratic community" [17] should tolerate lawless police and prosecutors. If public opinion were mustered against these men as vehemently as it was mustered against a criminal, infringements of the law on the part of the law-enforcement officers would soon be dissipated.

Frankfurter frequently cited English experience as a guide to American administration of criminal justice. He believed enforcement of criminal law in England was more effective than on this side of the Atlantic, even though the English had no constitution into which safeguards were written. But, he said, these safeguards "are even more securely embedded in the texture of English feeling than they are enforced through the written words of our Constitution." [18] Law enforcement was more effective precisely for that reason —its officers were austerely responsible, and the reason for their abject responsibility was, as it should be in America, public opinion. English public opinion refused to tolerate such brutalities as the third degree, and at the mere suggestion of its use, all the parties of Parliament would be aroused to formulate careful rules against its further use. This same alert public opinion, Frankfurter believed, could be utilized in the United States.

Of course, criminal prosecutions in any case were treatment of the symptom and not the cause. The real difficulties lay outside the courtroom.

"Social phenomena like crime," he wrote in 1945 in echoes of his early crime survey writings, "are imbedded in the texture of our society. To be understood they cannot be severed from the total environment." [19]

". . . While we must continue the daily administration of existing law and steadily improve it," he had said in 1929, "we must devise new processes, we must train new personnel, we must secure a new public attitude. Society must protect itself from recurrences of anti-social conduct and at the same time must make possible the systematic pursuit of new knowledge for future action." It was not a problem that could be solved by courts; it could be solved only by the people of a democracy. "The emphasis must be society's protection on the basis of dependable experience, quietly, painstakingly, and systematically secured . . . only by painful, persistent, and scientific inquiry, with a professionalized service along the line— a professionalized police force, professionalized prosecutors, professionalized judges, professionalized psychiatrists, professionalized students of crime—will we achieve the necessary readjustments of attitude, of personnel, of institutions, and, above all, of a supporting public opinion. . . ." [20]

Frankfurter's judicial opinions by no means always sided with the criminal against the user of the third degree or the wiretapper. On the contrary. Within the framework of his restrained interpretation of due process of law, he was prone to allow the states a good deal of latitude in developing and enforcing their own laws.

The Bill of Rights, which protects the freedoms of the individual from invasion by the federal government, was not a part of the Constitution as originally written. The first Congress under the Constitution responded to popular sentiment and submitted twelve amendments to the document, ten of which were ratified. These covered freedom of religion, speech, the press, the right of petition, and the right of the people to bear arms; abuses through quartering of troops were controlled; unreasonable searches and seizures were prohibited; trial for a capital or otherwise infamous crime must be on presentment or indictment of a grand jury, except in military cases; double jeopardy was forbidden; witnesses were protected against compulsory self-incrimination; no person was to be deprived of life, liberty, or property "without due process of law"; private property could not be taken for public use without just compensation; protection to an accused in criminal prosecutions was provided by requiring speedy and public trial by an impartial jury in the place where the crime was committed; accused persons could compel witnesses to appear in their behalf and were afforded the assistance of counsel for defense; trial by jury was preserved in civil actions; excessive bail, excessive fines, and cruel and unusual punishments were prohibited.

These amendments applied only to the federal government. Originally they were not applicable to the states. Then, in 1868, the Fourteenth Amendment was ratified, declaring: ". . . No State shall make or enforce any law which shall abridge the privileges or immunities of citizens of the United States; nor shall any State deprive any person of life, liberty, or property, without due process of law; nor deny to any person within its jurisdiction the equal protection of the laws."

In the realm of deciding cases involving economic and social legislation during the early years of the century, Frankfurter believed the use of the two due process of law clauses—one in the Fifth and one in the Fourteenth Amendment—had been perverted. He had written to Henry Stimson in 1924: "... 'Due process' is the rock on which most social legislation founders. Both because the questions at issue are really social and economic, and therefore not the kind of things on which the Supreme Court should be involved, and because the Fourteenth Amendment is too powerful an instrument of undue centralization, I think the 'due process' clauses ought to go." [21]

Due process of law did not go, however. It is still a prominent part of the Constitution and, in fact, one of the most controversial phrases.

In Frankfurter's language, the due process "is the compendious expression for all those rights which the courts must enforce because they are basic to our free society." [22] Decency and fair play are the very heart of it. So is procedure.

Here is where the business of judging is at its most demanding and most strenuous. Here is where judges must decide what is fair dealing, and what is fair to one may be unfair to another.

Here is where a judge is forced into an interpretative role. "The Court reads not the Constitution but its own minds," Frankfurter wrote in 1930. "The Court is compelled to put meaning into the Constitution, not to take it out. . . . The scope for 'interpretation' of the Constitution is in this field relatively unrestricted, and the room for exercise of individual notions of policy by the justices correspondingly wide. . . ." [23]

Judgment, he wrote in 1957, "must not be an exercise of whim or will. It must be an overriding judgment founded on something much deeper and more justifiable than personal preference. As far as it lies within human limitations, it must be an impersonal judgment. . . ." [24] Judgment, in the application of so sweeping a phrase, must, said Frankfurter, "rest on fundamental presuppositions rooted in history." [25] It must rest on American experience—that of the authors of the Constitution and that of the nation since the Constitution was written, as expressed in decisions of the Court.

There is no tidy formula, however, for adjudication, even when a judge conscientiously searches the past. "Standards of justice," Frankfurter once wrote, "are not authoritatively formulated anywhere as though they were prescriptions in a pharmacopoeia." [26]

Of the two due process clauses, the one in the Fourteenth Amendment has perhaps caused the greatest controversy because of differences in interpretation. Although as early as 1884 the Supreme Court rejected what became his interpretation, and consistently held to it, Justice Black has militantly insisted that the due process clause of the Fourteenth Amendment is intended to enforce adherence of the states to the Bill of Rights. "My study of the historical events that culminated in the Fourteenth Amendment," Black wrote in 1947, "and the expressions of those who sponsored and favored, as well as those who opposed its submission and passage, persuades me that one of the chief objects that the provisions of the Amendment's first section, separately, and as a whole, were intended to accomplish was to make the Bill of Rights applicable to the States." In 1833 the Supreme Court had expressly stated that the first eight amendments did not apply to the states. However, said Black, "the framers and backers of the Fourteenth Amendment proclaimed its purpose to be to overturn the constitutional rule that case had announced." [27]

The Bill of Rights, he said, was designed to meet universal and timeless "human evils . . . wherever excessive power is sought by the few at the expense of the many." Black feared for the breadth of interpretation that could be imposed on a clause so vague and yet so sweeping as "due process of law" if it were not intended only to absorb the provisions of the Bill of Rights. "I would follow," he said, "what I believe was the original purpose of the Fourteenth Amendment—to extend to all the people of the Nation the complete protection of the Bill of Rights. To hold that this Court can determine what, if any, provisions of the Bill of Rights will be enforced, and if so to what degree, is to frustrate the great design of a written Constitution." [28]

Frankfurter disagreed. The due process clause had to stand alone. If it merely included specific provisions of the Constitution already outlined, it would only be redundant and meaningless. In addition, "A construction," he said, "which gives due process no independent function but makes of it a summary of the specific provisions of the Bill of Rights would tear up by the roots much of the fabric of law in the several States. . . ." [29] It would require, for example, the states to prosecute serious crimes through the grand jury system proscribed in the Fifth Amendment, although many states had abandoned the practice.

Due process of law, then, in Frankfurter's definition, embodies all the fundamental principles of the Anglo-American traditions of justice. In deciding whether a state conviction violates that Fourteenth Amendment guaranty, one cannot pick out a specific act and denounce it as depriving a man of due process of law. One must, instead, review the whole course of proceedings in a case in order to ascertain whether, as a whole, "they offend those canons of decency and fairness which express the notions of justice of English-speaking peoples . . ." [30] or, as Holmes pithily and earthily put it, whether state administration of its criminal law "makes you vomit."

How does this apply in specific cases?

These were the facts in one case before the Court: A surgeon was suspected of performing abortions. His office had been entered by police without a warrant. They picked up a notebook there and used it as evidence in the state court. The surgeon was convicted.

To Frankfurter the issue could be defined exactly. "The precise question for consideration," he wrote, "is this: Does a conviction by a State Court for a State offense deny the 'due process of law' required by the Fourteenth Amendment . . . ?" The notebook could not have been used as evidence in a federal court. Does this mean, Frankfurter asked, that it could not be used in a state court?

No, said Frankfurter, that is not the meaning of the Fourteenth Amendment. The Fourteenth Amendment, he believed, did not subject criminal justice in the states to specific limitations.

"The security of one's privacy against arbitrary intrusion by the police—which is at the core of the Fourth Amendment—is basic to a free society," he reasoned. "It is therefore implicit in 'the concept of ordered liberty' and as such enforceable against the States through the Due Process Clause . . . we have no hesitation in saying that were a State affirmatively to sanction such police incursions into privacy it would run counter to the guaranty of the Fourteenth Amendment. . . ."

But, he continued, the immediate question is whether protection against such arbitrary intrusion by police inherently prohibits the use of "logically relevant evidence obtained by an unreasonable search and seizure because, in a federal prosecution for a federal crime, it would be excluded."

Frankfurter declared that many people might, with complete integrity, disagree on whether illegally obtained evidence might be used in court. In fact, he said, "most of the English-speaking world does not regard as vital" to the protection of privacy the exclusion of evidence obtained in such a way. The separate states themselves, he said, were in disagreement on this issue, and some had established other methods for ensuring the right of privacy.

Frankfurter acknowledged that practically, the exclusion of illegally obtained evidence was an effective method for deterring unreasonable searches. However, he said, "it is not for this Court to condemn as falling below the minimal standards assured by the Due Process Clause a State's reliance upon other methods which, if consistently enforced, will be equally effective. . . ."

Therefore, the Court held, said Frankfurter, "in a prosecution in a State Court for a State crime the Fourteenth Amendment does not forbid the admission of evidence obtained by an unreasonable search and seizure. . . ." [31]

What, then, does fall within the power of the Fourteenth Amendment?

In 1930, seven white boys and two white girls were riding through Alabama in an open freight car. At Stevenson, Alabama, the train stopped, then slowly labored along an upgrade. Twenty or thirty Negroes climbed into the car; a fight ensued, and the white boys were thrown off the train. (A number of the Negroes also left the train until only nine were left.) One of the white boys who had been thrown off the train hurriedly phoned the sheriff at Paint Rock, the next scheduled stop for the freight train, and urged him to arrest the Negroes.

The sheriff and an armed posse met the train at Paint Rock, took the nine remaining Negro boys off, and hustled them off to jail at Scottsboro. The two girls who had remained on the train accused the Negroes of rape. Their story traveled swiftly through the Southern countryside, and by the time the captives had reached the Scottsboro jail a large and threatening mob was waiting. Its behavior became so ominous that the nine Negroes had to be taken to a stronger jail at Gadsden.

A week later they were returned to Scottsboro, indicted for rape, and put on trial—in an atmosphere so hostile that National Guardsmen with bayonets, tear-gas bombs, and machine guns were stationed around the courthouse to prevent lynchings.

The trial was a farce. Not being residents of Alabama, the accused had no friends or families on which to call for help. They had no counsel until the judge assigned to their defense the entire county bar—seven lawyers, six of whom quickly excused themselves. The seventh was powerless against the Southern white jury and the mob inside and outside the courtroom which dominated the proceedings. Although medical examiners had declared the two girls showed no evidence—either physical or mental—of rape, when one of the girls told her story to the court, the banging of the judge's gavel could not stop the roaring of the crowd.

The Negro boys were hastily convicted, and their conviction was upheld in the Supreme Court of Alabama, although over the vigorous dissent of that court's chief justice.

The case was appealed to the Supreme Court of the United States on the ground that the trial had been unfair. The Supreme Court decided that the "casual fashion" in which the matter of counsel in a capital case was disposed of "was a clear denial of due process.... The necessity of counsel was so vital and imperative that the failure of the trial court to make an effective appointment of counsel was likewise a denial of due process within the meaning of the Fourteenth Amendment." [32]

Not then a member of the Court, Frankfurter dispatched a letter to the New York *Times* congratulating the Court. "The Supreme Court last Monday wrote a notable chapter in the history of liberty," he said. Although the "stock offenses of American criminal law—murder, arson, rape, theft—are violations of State law and prosecuted solely through the State courts" and are outside the concern of the federal judiciary, nevertheless, "certain things are basic to the integrity of the judicial process. One of them is a proper tribunal, impartial and uncoerced...." The trial of the nine Negroes had not been a trial. It had been legal lynching.

"Not only must there be a court free from coercion," he continued, "but the accused must be furnished with means for presenting his defense. For this the assistance of counsel is essential. Time for investigation and for the production of evidence is imperative. Especially is this true in a capital case. The more heinous the charge," Frankfurter declared, "the more important the safeguards which the experience of centuries has shown to be essential to the ascertainment of even fallible truth. Never is it more so than in a case of rape, turning heavily upon the testimony of the alleged victim and requiring to be defended largely by evidence of circumstance and character.

"The Scottsboro case announces the doctrine that to every defendant must be assured the minimum conditions for an ordered and reasoned investigation of the charges against him. . . ." This did not mean, Frankfurter said, that the Supreme Court was to become a court for correcting criminal errors—this would be both an impossible chore and a debilitating one for it. It did not even mean the Supreme Court was passing on the guilt or innocence of the Negro boys—it was quite properly returning the case to be retried in the Alabama courts.*

But the Court was announcing that it would "not suffer in its own scathing phrase, 'judicial murder.'. . . The Supreme Court has declared only that the determination [of guilt or innocence] must be made with due observance of the decencies of civilized procedure." [33]

Frankfurter wrote this letter in November, 1932, nearly nine years before he sat on the Supreme Court. However, it was consistent with his views as a Justice on the power of the Fourteenth Amendment.

On the morning of October 23, 1942, a man named Malinski was arrested for the murder of a police officer. He was not arraigned but was taken to a hotel room in Brooklyn, stripped and kept naked for three hours, then given only a blanket, shoes, socks, and underwear. He was detained for seven more hours until about 6 P.M. he confessed to the crime. He was then allowed to dress but was kept at the hotel for three more days. He was questioned again, taken to the scene of the crime, then to a police garage, where he identified an automobile used in the robbery during which the police officer was killed, then taken to the police station and questioned again. On October 27, four days after his arrest, he confessed at the police station. That confession was used as evidence at his trial.

The Court reversed Malinski's conviction. "Considering the circumstances of Malinski's detention," Frankfurter wrote in a concurring opinion, "the long and continuous questioning, the willful and wrongful delay in his arraignment and the opportunity that that gives for securing, by extortion, confessions such as were here introduced in evidence, the flagrant justification by the prosecutor

* The Negroes were again convicted in the Alabama courts; the Supreme Court held the convictions unconstitutional on the ground that Negroes had been excluded from the jury. Again, some were convicted in the Alabama courts and served long term; others pleaded guilty to minor offenses and served shorter prison terms.

of this illegality as a necessary police procedure, inevitably calculated to excite the jury—all these in combination are so below the standards by which the criminal law, especially in a capital case, should be enforced as to fall short of due process of law. . . ." [34]

This was the kind of case, Frankfurter believed, which fell below the standards set by due process of law. This clearly violated the canons of decency and fairness of procedure "enshrined in the Constitution." [35] This was the sort of brutality that the Fourteenth Amendment was aimed at.

On January 4, 1943, the Supreme Court agreed to take on another flag salute case. The Court decided to review the decision of a federal circuit court at Charleston, West Virginia, that three members of Jehovah's Witnesses could not be compelled to salute the flag in violation of religious scruples.

Although it was less than three years since the Gobitis case had been decided, the Court was somewhat differently constituted. Justice Stone had acceded to the chief justiceship, replacing Hughes. Robert Jackson had been named to the Stone vacancy. Justice McReynolds had also resigned, replaced briefly by Senator James F. Byrnes, who was in turn replaced by Wiley B. Rutledge.

In addition, Justices Black, Douglas, and Murphy, who had voted with the majority in the Gobitis case, had publicly declared their displeasure with that opinion. They had, in the meantime, dissented from an opinion holding constitutional a municipal ordinance imposing license taxes on the sale of printed matter distributed by members of Jehovah's Witnesses. Confessing their judicial mistake, the three Justices wrote in this case that *Gobitis* was "wrongly decided. Certainly our democratic form of government functioning under the historic Bill of Rights has a high responsibility to accommodate itself to the religious views of minorities however unpopular and unorthodox those views may be. The First Amendment does not put the right freely to exercise religion in a subordinate position. . . ." [36] *Gobitis,* they feared, did "exactly that." This unique declaration gave weight to the belief that the Court would overrule itself in the second flag salute case.

The Court did exactly that. With Justice Jackson, who had not been on the Court when *Gobitis* was decided, writing now for the Court, it decided:

> If there is any fixed star in our constitutional constellation, it is that no official, high or petty, can prescribe what shall be orthodox in politics, nationalism, religion, or other matters of opinion or force citizens to confess by word or act their faith therein. If there are any circumstances which permit exception, they do not now occur to us.
>
> We think the action of the local authorities in compelling the flag salute and pledge transcends constitutional limitations of their power and invades the sphere of intellect and spirit which it is the purpose of the First Amendment to our Constitution to reserve from all official control.[37]

Frankfurter had to search his conscience thoroughly. These were sensitive questions, he had writen to Justice Reed, "in the realm which . . . touches the liberties of our people." [38] After Frankfurter had heard the arguments of counsel for Jehovah's Witnesses and the West Virginia State Board of Education, he wrote a long memorandum to himself on the role of the Court in overturning the laws of the states and Congress.

"Those who pass laws," he soliloquized, "are also under duty to observe the Constitution." That being so, the legislatures must be allowed considerable discretion to make and unmake laws. The Court, he concluded, must be "very self-restrained" since it can only "unmake laws." [39]

He apologized to Jackson for the inordinate amount of time he was taking with the flag salute case, not because it required a great deal of research, but because it was to be "the expression of my credo regarding the function of this Court in invalidating legislation" and "because it is credo . . . it is so recalcitrant." [40]

When his dissent came, it stuck to his judicial guns of restraint, which he had enunciated in the Gobitis case:

> . . . The legislature is charged solely with civil concerns of society. If the avowed or intrinsic legislative purpose is either to promote or to discourage some religious community or creed, it is clearly within the constitutional restrictions imposed on legislatures and cannot stand. But it by no means follows that legislative power is wanting whenever a general nondiscriminatory civil regulation in fact touches conscientious scruples or religious beliefs of an individual or group. . . .

see Bohr and asked Frankfurter to arrange a meeting. Roosevelt also authorized Frankfurter to carry a message to Bohr. Bohr, who understood the scientific considerations so well, could, when he presented his case to the British authorities, inform them that the American President was eager to "explore the proper safeguards in relation to X." [5]

Bohr returned from his visit to American atomic sites impressed with their efficiency but even more deeply impressed with their fearsome possibilities, still not completely comprehended. At Los Alamos he had found scientists already discussing the destructive potential not only of atomic bombs, but, even more terrifying, of hydrogen bombs. On his return from Los Alamos, he wrote to the British director of Tube Alloys, Sir John Anderson, that he was now even more convinced that customary measures of control would not be sufficient and that the world would live in real danger unless a "universal agreement based on mutual confidence" [6] could be worked out. But implicit in such an agreement were mutual exchange of information and openness of industrial and military projects. If such openness was unprecedented in international relations, Bohr believed it necessary to avoid an inevitable and probably disastrous arms race.

In late March, 1944, Bohr and Frankfurter met again. Frankfurter described to Bohr his meeting with Roosevelt. He reported that Roosevelt believed this was a matter for Prime Minister Churchill and himself to find the best ways of handling the project to the benefit of mankind and that he would heartily welcome any suggestion to this end from Churchill. Bohr, Frankfurter said, was authorized to convey this message to Churchill.[7]

Bohr returned to England in April. While in the United States, he had enlisted Lord Halifax, the British ambassador, in his cause. He had already convinced Sir John Anderson of the validity of his arguments. There remained only Churchill.

Anderson had written a memorandum for Churchill on the international effects of the bomb. In it he had declared that American-British efforts would certainly produce a workable bomb before the Germans did, but the Russians, Anderson warned, could easily make one the moment the war was over; furthermore, simplification of the production process would make a bomb available to a number of other countries. The result would be a vicious arms race. The only alternative was international control. Anderson recommended that

Frankfurter admitted that regard for such scruples may present a just claim for legislative accommodation. However, it is beyond the Court's power to rewrite the state's requirement by providing exemptions for those who do not wish to participate in the flag salute or by making some other accommodations to meet their principles. "A Court can only strike down," he reiterated. "It cannot modify or qualify, it cannot make exceptions to a general requirement."

Religious minorities, in the eyes of the early leaders of the Republic, were to be equal to the majorities. But they were not to be favored. "The constitutional protection of religious freedom terminated disabilities, it did not create new privileges. It gave religious equality, not civil immunity. Its essence," he wrote, "is freedom from conformity to religious dogma, not freedom from conformity to law because of religious dogma. Otherwise each individual could set up his own censor against obedience to laws conscientiously deemed for the public good by those whose business it is to make laws. . . ."

Of course, the flag salute may not enforce patriotism; it may even be a foolish requirement, Frankfurter conceded. But it is not the Court's duty, or even privilege, to decide the wisdom or unwisdom of a law. Its job is only to decide constitutionality.

If patriotism could not be enforced by the flag salute, "neither can the liberal spirit be enforced by judicial invalidation of illiberal legislation . . ." he concluded. "Reliance for the most precious interests of civilization . . . must be found outside of their vindication in courts of law. Only a persistent positive translation of the faith of a free society into the convictions and habits and actions of a community is the ultimate reliance against unabated temptations to fetter the human spirit." [41]

Frankfurter sent the opinions and his dissent, with which Justices Reed and Roberts joined, to Chief Justice Hughes in retirement. The former Chief Justice replied to Frankfurter that he thought the dissenters had the best of the argument.[42]

However, some of Frankfurter's "liberal" friends were disenchanted by his stand. "I recollect no decision of our former colleague Felix Frankfurter which dismayed us more than his labored defense of compulsory flag saluting," [43] said Roger Nash Baldwin of the American Civil Liberties Union, to which Frankfurter had belonged prior to his Supreme Court appointment.

[4]

Knowledge of the development of the atomic bomb—and concurrently, atomic energy, which was to be of international concern during World War II and after—in the United States was limited mainly to Roosevelt and the handful of scientists at work on it. Harry Truman was not even privy to the supersecret operation, either as a Senator investigating military expenditures or as Vice President.

Frankfurter, however, knew of it. He came upon the knowledge unofficially, and he never knew the technical details. He did, however, know of and understand the international ramifications involved in development of the atomic bomb and played an unprecedented—for a Supreme Court Justice—role in the making of decisions about its future use.

During Frankfurter's year at Oxford in 1933–34, he had made the acquaintance of Niels Bohr, renowned Danish physicist and 1922 Nobel Prize winner.[1] Bohr, with Lord Ernest Rutherford in England, had been responsible for elucidating the basic theory of atomic structure. English and American work on the atomic bomb stemmed directly from an article written by Bohr, with another physicist, in 1939 and published just after the outbreak of the European war.

Frankfurter and Bohr renewed their acquaintanceship in 1939, when Bohr visited Washington. Their mutual concern over the imminence of the European war and Hitler's brutalities turned acquaintanceship into warm friendship.[2]

Bohr returned to Copenhagen, where he remained through more than three years of German occupation of his native Denmark. His institute there was a haven for refugees from Fascist countries, while the British, who recognized what an asset to the war effort his scientific brain would be, devised plans to smuggle Bohr to England. At first Bohr declined British invitations to be spirited out. He believed he could be of greater use in protecting exiled scientists at his institute and in continuing the Danish fight against German outrages. But it was clear by the fall of 1943 that both he and his family were in danger of arrest. Through the Danish underground Bohr and his wife, followed a few days later by his four sons and a granddaughter, were smuggled to neutral Sweden in a fishing boat. On October 6, 1943, Bohr, with his twenty-one-year-old son Aage, also a physicist and his father's assistant, was taken to England in the bomb rack of a Mosquito bomber.

After consultation with the men in charge of the British atomic project—euphemistically coded Tube Alloys—Bohr and his son Aage went to the United States. His dual purpose in looking over the American atomic project was to assist the common British-American effort in any way he could and to cement the British-American partnership in atomic development agreed to at the First Quebec Conference of Roosevelt and Churchill.

Bohr, isolated at his institute in Copenhagen, had not realized to what an advanced stage development of atomic energy had progressed. When he learned about it on his arrival in England in the fall of 1943, his first reaction was that this revolution in science and warfare would both necessitate and provide the opportunity for establishing a new kind of relationship among nations. Like many other scientists involved in atomic projects, he feared for the possible devastation by the vast amounts of new energy unleashed; he foresaw and feared an international arms race of unimaginable proportions. Unquestionably, he believed, this new scientific achievement must be controlled.

But Bohr saw opportunity in this new development, too, for the postwar world. It appeared to him that the special circumstances of the time—the wartime alliance of Russia, England, and the United States; the Anglo-American lead in development of atomic energy; the great prestige of Roosevelt and Churchill—offered unique bargaining power to England and the United States in dealing with Russia. Bohr saw in an early approach to the Russians a rare chance for the wartime allies to transform wartime trust and confidence into postwar cooperation and friendship. Not only was such cooperation vital in the future arrangements for international control of atomic energy which were clearly necessary, Bohr believed, but it would go a long way in aiding settlement of many other issues which Bohr already foresaw as causes of East-West tension.[3]

When Bohr arrived in the United States, the Danish minister invited the Frankfurters to tea at the Danish Embassy to meet him. Frankfurter and Bohr quickly renewed their earlier friendship but had no chance at that public function for a private word. Frankfurter invited Bohr to lunch in his chambers at the Supreme Court.

Not long before Bohr's arrival in this country, Frankfurter had been approached by a group of scientists, because of past academic associations, for advice on nonscientific problems raised by the atomic energy project. They, as scientists, were unable to cope with these problems outside their technical competence. In such fashion Frankfurter had become aware of the Allied atomic energy project —of its existence and of its significance—but not of its technical details. He naturally surmised Bohr's mission to the United States.

Bohr turned up at Frankfurter's chambers at the appointed time, and they talked about recent events in Denmark, the war, England, the certainty of German defeat, the postwar world. Bohr did not remotely hint at the purpose of his visit to the United States.

In the course of the luncheon with Bohr, Frankfurter made a "very oblique" reference to the atomic project, which was referred to as X "so that if I was right in my assumption that Professor Bohr was sharing in it, he would know that I knew something about it, and, if not, I could easily turn my question into other channels," Frankfurter later wrote in a memorandum explaining his involvement.

Bohr replied in "an innocent remote way, but it soon became clear to both of us that two such persons, who had been so long and so deeply preoccupied with the menace of Hitlerism and who were so deeply engaged in the common cause, could talk about the implications of X without either making any disclosure to the other," Frankfurter wrote.

The conversation continued on this basis. Bohr expressed his concern that X could be either one of science's greatest gifts or one of its greatest disasters. The politicians who would control what was done with atomic energy, Bohr believed, must be alerted to all its international ramifications. Frankfurter described Bohr as "a man weighed down with a conscience and an almost overwhelming solicitude for the dangers to our people."

Touched by Bohr's solicitude, Frankfurter decided to communicate to Roosevelt what had come to him from Bohr and the other scientists who had approached him. Frankfurter knew relatively little about science. He understood, however, the impracticability of hoarding atomic secrets. Should Russia learn about X on her own, the result could easily be disastrous; on the other hand, the United

States and Britain might effectively utilize X as a lever to explore the possibility of an international arrangement with Russia for dealing with the problems raised by the bomb. Bohr impressed Frankfurter with his thesis that although specific details of the work on American and British projects might remain somewhat secret, the scientific principles were far from secret and that Russia, far from scientifically backward at that time, could easily obtain the necessary information if she had not already obtained it. Bohr knew personally many of Russia's scientific leaders, and he recognized their capabilities.[4]

Whatever the merits of Bohr's plan, put into the context of the time, it was daring in the extreme. Bohr was advocating that the Allies reveal their most precious military secret to a nation which had long been distrusted by both England and the United States. The Communist phobia that had followed World War I had never abated in the United States. There were even those in 1942 who believed that this country was fighting the wrong enemy, that the United States ought to be fighting Stalin instead of Hitler. Stalin's early friendship with England and France, just before the outbreak of World War II, then his about-face in August, 1939, when he signed a nonaggression pact with Hitler, only served to increase fears and doubts about Russian integrity. These uncertainties were even further enlarged when Russia annexed Finland and three other Baltic states the following spring.

When Hitler suddenly invaded Russia on June 24, 1941, Russia became a partner of the Allies, but it was considered at best a shotgun wedding. Few were going to allow themselves to be taken in by vows spoken at such an altar. Russia, displaying perfidy throughout World War II, remained for the duration a controversial and much distrusted partner.

Roosevelt's decision to extend Lend-Lease aid to Russia, two days after the German Army began its march toward Moscow, had been fraught with political difficulties. A decision to share atomic secrets with Russia would have been extremely dangerous politically indeed.

While Bohr sped off to Los Alamos to observe the American atomic installation, Frankfurter went to see Roosevelt. At first Roosevelt was surprised that Frankfurter knew about the bomb.

Then Roosevelt confessed that the whole postwar atomic problem "worried him to death and he was very eager for all the help he could have in dealing with the problem." Roosevelt said he would like to

Russia be informed that Allied efforts were about to produce this devastating weapon and then that Russia be invited to collaborate in devising a plan for international control. Should the Russians learn about the bomb independently, they would be far less inclined toward cooperation.

Churchill read the memorandum, added disapproving comments, then at the end wrote: "I do not agree." [8] He opposed any relaxation of secrecy, even to informing his own Cabinet.

Anderson, however, refused to give up hope. He attempted to persuade Churchill to see Bohr so that Bohr could relay Roosevelt's invitation to Churchill to explore crucial questions of atomic policy.

While Anderson was in the process of getting an appointment with Churchill for Bohr, however, Bohr received a letter from an old friend, a prominent Russian scientist named Peter Kapitza. The letter was an invitation to Bohr to come to Russia to live and work, and it was conveyed via the Soviet Embassy in London. Requesting to see Bohr personally to deliver the letter, a Soviet official pumped Bohr for information regarding American and British scientific operations. Bohr gave no information; he immediately wrote a report for Anderson and British Intelligence, to which he also showed the invitation from Kapitza, and he declined the invitation, graciously but firmly. However, the incident came to Churchill's attention and reinforced his penchant for extreme secrecy.

On May 16, 1944, Bohr was granted a half hour interview with Churchill. This served only to demolish what hopes were left. Churchill was preoccupied with the imminent invasion of Europe, Bohr's manner did not appeal to him, and he was no doubt distrustful of Bohr as a channel of communication between him and Roosevelt. Bohr was unable to reach Churchill's mind. As his half hour ended, Bohr asked if he might address a memorandum on the subject of his concern to Churchill. The Prime Minister replied that he would always be honored to receive a letter from Professor Bohr, but he hoped it would not be about politics.

Some months later, Churchill confessed to an aide that he and Roosevelt were worried about Bohr. "How did he come into the business?" Churchill asked. "He is a great advocate of publicity. He made an unauthorized disclosure to Justice Frankfurter. . . . He said he is in close correspondence with a Russian professor, an old friend to whom he has written about the matter and may be writing still.

The professor has urged him to go to Russia in order to discuss matters. What is this all about? It seems to me Bohr ought to be confined or at any rate made to see that he is very near the edge of mortal crime." [9]

Bohr then returned to Washington and reported to Frankfurter the disappointing encounter with Churchill, which in turn Frankfurter relayed to Roosevelt. Roosevelt said he wanted to see Bohr but would like to study his ideas in writing first. So all through June and early July Bohr worked on a memorandum for Roosevelt.

Stamped TOP SECRET and CONFIDENTIAL on receipt at the White House, the seven-page memorandum explained in simple terms the scientific principles of atomic energy, that prewar progress in the field was common knowledge to physicists throughout the world, that recent information had come to him (Bohr) that the Germans were working feverishly on nuclear problems, and that he believed Russian scientists had an interest in nuclear energy. Bohr explained his correspondence with the Russian Peter Kapitza and his conversations at the Russian Embassy in London.

The memorandum urged Roosevelt's attention to the problem of postwar control of the new energy, stressing the frightening prospect of an arms race. Only through open exchange of information could such an agreement be achieved. On the other hand, as Bohr had told Frankfurter, such openness could create a new pattern in international relationships. Postponement through the war could easily effect the forfeiture of the unique possibilities offered at the moment, riding, as they did, on the advantage of the British and American lead in atomic development.

Atomic energy had tremendous potential for peaceful use which would be aided by worldwide scientific collaboration. Should such scientific contact be made and should it be successful, it was possible that this collaboration might bring a turning point in history.[10]

Bohr asked Frankfurter's opinion of the memorandum before submitting it to Roosevelt. Frankfurter said it was "just right—precisely what it should be for its purpose.

"I cannot forgo saying that you are conducting matters of the deepest concern for mankind with a delicacy and wisdom worthy of the enterprise," [11] Frankfurter added.

Frankfurter sent the memorandum to Roosevelt, and on August 26, 1944, Roosevelt and Bohr met for an hour and a quarter, during which time Roosevelt declared he shared Bohr's hopes as expressed in the memorandum and asked him to enlarge on it. Bohr expanded on his reasons for urging an immediate approach to Russia. He said it must be assumed that the Russians knew about the existence of America's atomic bomb project and that with their current work, plus the secrets yielded by captured German scientists after the war, they would very soon equal Anglo-American progress. However, an approach now would inspire Russian confidence and allay suspicions, negating the possibilities of a future arms race.

Bohr suggested the West begin not by offering detailed information about the bomb, but by a general approach, and if the Russians responded in a cooperative spirit, the path would be open for more detailed discussions. If not, the West would know where it stood.

Roosevelt was friendly and frank in his discussion with Bohr and said an approach to Russia must be tried. He agreed about the urgency of the total situation and told Bohr he was scheduled to meet Churchill shortly and would discuss with him an early invitation to the Russians. He told Bohr to feel free to communicate with him at any time, and he hoped to see him again following the meeting with Churchill.

A few days later, Bohr and Frankfurter met again, and Frankfurter advised, that for Roosevelt's convenience and for clarity's sake, Bohr should write Roosevelt a thank-you note for the audience and include a restatement of the points discussed. A week later, accompanied by a covering letter from Frankfurter, Bohr's letter and statement were delivered to Roosevelt on the eve of his departure from Washington to meet Churchill in the Second Quebec Conference.

However, from that time, Bohr's hopes for swift international consultation went steadily downhill. In Quebec and at the continuation of the Quebec Conference at Hyde Park, Churchill gradually replaced Roosevelt's confidence in Bohr with his own suspicions. Churchill remained adamant on keeping the bomb secret, and the two leaders finally agreed to withhold atomic progress from Russia. Bohr was put off limits and placed under surveillance. Roosevelt did not see him, as he had said he would, when he returned from Quebec. Bohr remained in Washington, hoping for the invitation that never came. He continued to urge his views on Lord Halifax, who remained sympathetic to Bohr's arguments. Frankfurter himself maintained hope that Roosevelt would reconsider Bohr's case.

On April 12, 1945, Halifax and Frankfurter met in the privacy of Washington's peacefully wooded Rock Creek Park to discuss how they might once again put the questions raised by Bohr before Roosevelt in a new memorandum. Suddenly church bells began to toll. Roosevelt was dead. Later Frankfurter wrote to Halifax: ". . . Odd wasn't it that our dear friend should have died the very time you and I were pooling our forebodings?" [12]

Momentarily, the urgency of atomic control receded into insignificance beside national bereavement. For Frankfurter, as for many, Roosevelt's death was not only a public loss, but a personal one. The two men had cultivated a long and satisfying friendship over many years; it had overflowed with all the ingredients necessary to close human relationship. If what can only be termed Frankfurter's love for Roosevelt was more outspoken, it was perhaps because Frankfurter was a more open man; but there is no doubt that there was reciprocity to a large degree, even though, as a public man and a more reserved one, Roosevelt was necessarily not lavish with affection. When Roosevelt died, the loss was too great for Frankfurter, who could summon words as Roosevelt could summon armies, to write a letter of condolence to the bereaved family, and Frankfurter himself received some 500 letters of condolence from people who realized, as an old friend from Boston did, that something "vivid and vital" [13] had gone out of his life.

After Roosevelt's death, Bohr's latest memorandum was forwarded by sympathetic scientists in the government to Secretary of War Stimson, who was familiar with Bohr's views through Frankfurter and Lord Halifax. In May, 1944, Stimson had chaired an interim committee to consider the political questions of atomic energy and the possibilities of international control. But anxieties about Russian intransigence in Europe steered this committee into advocating that no information should be revealed to Russia until the first bomb had been dropped on Japan; then, the committee hoped, international control might be discussed fruitfully. Scientists advising the committee continued to urge an approach to Russia, France, and China, but the suggestion was whittled down to a recommendation that President Truman inform the Russians of the bomb at the Potsdam Conference scheduled for July and August, 1945. There Truman might add that he hoped for future discussions to ensure the peaceful use of atomic energy; this is what happened.

The missionary work of Bohr and Frankfurter had failed.

Bohr returned to England and then to Copenhagen, by then liberated from German occupation. Bohr continued to promote his case, but it was too late. The arms race, as he had predicted, had begun in earnest.

There is no evidence to suggest that Bohr's plan to take the Russians into early confidence would have prevented an arms race. There is, however, some evidence that the Russians had discovered the secrets of nuclear fission long before they were known to possess this information. But whether collaboration, with its implication of faith and trust in Russia, would have transformed the expectations of Bohr and Frankfurter into reality remains one of the great might-have-beens of history.

As a footnote to history, the security men of the American atomic operation learned of Frankfurter's involvement and of his correspondence with Bohr. Fearful of an information leakage, Lieutenant General Leslie R. Groves, director of the project, sent his security aide, who happened to be a former student of Frankfurter's, to see the Justice.

As a result of their conversation, Frankfurter agreed to "let us keep all of his papers on the subject for the duration of the War," [14] and they were placed in the government's safe until they were returned to Frankfurter after the war.

With Roosevelt's death months before the war ended, Frankfurter's influence gradually faded from the highest levels of the executive branch of the government. Not entirely, of course. Men with whom he had formed personal and public associations continued to work in government, and Frankfurter's door was always open to them. But the down-to-earth, pragmatic President who succeeded Roosevelt on April 12, 1945, and the intellectual Justice had little in common, and neither Frankfurter's counsel nor his friendship was so eagerly or frequently sought out.

The unemotional and austere voices in which black-robed Supreme Court Justices summarize their opinions in a courtroom singularly lacking in the human element belie the mental and emotional tortures to which a judge is subjected in reaching a decision. Judicial obligation can multiply its weight to that of an albatross.

When the weight of judicial obligation became intolerable, however, Frankfurter was not without recourse. He had one job; he conceived it with restraint—some would say undue restraint. But other men in a democracy had other jobs. What Frankfurter could not accomplish as a judge, he might accomplish as a man through other men not circumscribed by a judicial oath. It was, of course, judging by expectation.

In November, 1944, Willie Francis, a fifteen-year-old Negro of St. Martinville, Louisiana, killed a druggist in a holdup which netted the youth $4 and a watch. Some weeks later he was caught attempting another robbery at pistol point. Francis was indicted, tried, convicted, and sentenced to die in the electric chair.

On May 3, 1946, Francis was strapped into Louisiana's portable electric chair. But when the switch was thrown, the chair did not function properly, and Francis was not killed by the current. He walked away from the grim symbol of death, and his guards hustled him back to his prison cell. A new death warrant was issued, fixing the execution for May 9, but a stay was obtained while the case was argued in the courts.

On the ground that to send Francis for the second time to the electric chair would be an instance of the "cruel and unusual punishments" prohibited by the Eighth Amendment to the Constitution, Francis' counsel took his case through the state courts to the Supreme Court of Louisiana, which denied that the Eighth Amendment applied to the states and added that sending Francis again to the electric chair was not a violation of the due process of law clause of the Fourteenth Amendment. The case came to the Supreme Court of the United States in the fall of 1946.

The brief filed by Francis' attorneys with the Supreme Court said that the State of Louisiana had forfeited its right to execute Francis "by subjecting the petitioner to the torture, both mental and physical, of being prepared for death, of being placed in the electric chair, of having electricity applied to his body. . . ." [15]

On January 13, 1947, by the narrow division of five to four, the Supreme Court ruled that Louisiana could lawfully order another execution for Francis. Speaking through Justice Reed, the Court held that in again being sent to the electric chair, Francis would not be subjected to the double jeopardy prohibited by the Fifth Amendment to the Constitution or to the cruel and unusual punishments barred by the Eighth Amendment.

"When an accident, with no suggestion of malevolence," Reed added, "prevents the consummation of the sentence, the State's subsequent course in the administration of the criminal law is not affected on that account by any requirement of due process of law under the Fourteenth Amendment. . . ." [16]

Justice Burton dissented vigorously. "How many deliberate and intentional reapplications of electric current does it take to produce a cruel, unusual and unconstitutional punishment?" [17] he asked.

For Frankfurter, the decision was as torturing as any he ever made. He was revolted by capital punishment to begin with. He detested it not so much because of concern for the victim or for the risk of convicting an innocent man. He hated the sensationalism that accompanied any capital case, believing strongly that the uncivilized atmosphere of the gladiatorial arena had a debilitating effect on juries, bar, public, and judiciary. Nor did he consider the factor of deterrence worth much.

The case of Willie Francis deeply offended his personal sense of decency. "Something inside of me was very unhappy," [18] he later said. And he wrote to Justice Burton after he had seen Burton's dissent: "I have to hold on to myself not to reach your result." [19]

However, as a judicial philosopher more than as a judge, he found himself forced to agree with the majority. To Burton he wrote on New Year's Eve, 1946: ". . . When a case comes here from a State court, it comes as though that which the State court did had actually been written into a State statute. Whatever scope the State court gives to a State law is binding upon us even though the State court gave it a scope which we think it should not have given or failed to give it a scope which we think it should have given. All this is purely a State question beyond our purview. . . ." [20]

That is exactly what he wrote in a concurring opinion, stating that the Supreme Court, except in extreme circumstances, must refrain from interfering with state action.

". . . The Due Process Clause of the Fourteenth Amendment," Frankfurter wrote, "did not withdraw the freedom of a State to enforce its own notions of fairness in the administration of criminal justice unless, as it was put for the Court by Mr. Justice Cardozo, 'in so doing it offends some principle of justice so rooted in the traditions and conscience of our people' as to be ranked as fundamental.

"I cannot bring myself to believe," he continued, "that for Louisiana to leave to executive clemency, rather than to require, mitigation of a sentence of death duly pronounced upon conviction for murder because a first attempt to carry it out was an innocent misadventure, offends a principle of justice 'rooted in the traditions and conscience of our people.' . . . Short of the compulsion of such a principle, this Court must abstain from interference with State action no matter how strong one's personal feeling of revulsion against a State's insistence on its pound of flesh. . . ." The key words were "executive clemency." [21] Frankfurter's duty had been clear, but the governor of Louisiana, whose position in the structure of government was different, could easily commute the sentence of Willie Francis. No doubt Frankfurter knew Francis' chances for commutation by the governor of a Southern state were not very good; nevertheless, he was placing the responsibility where he believed the structure of democracy dictated.

Frankfurter confessed in his opinion that he was strongly drawn to Justice Burton's dissent. Yet he could not rid himself of the conviction—and it is very much the philosopher, not the judge writing—"that were I to hold that Louisiana would transgress the Due Process Clause if the State were allowed, in the precise circumstances before us, to carry out the death sentence, I would be enforcing my private view rather than that consensus of society's opinion which, for purposes of due process, is the standard enjoined by the Constitution. . . ." [22]

Frankfurter went through his own private hell in reaching such decisions; he chafed under all limitations to freedom. But he once wrote to a friend, "Why do I take part in sending men to their death although I feel about capital punishment as I do? . . . Let me remind you again that on becoming a justice, I did not take an oath to enforce the sense of right and justice of Felix Frankfurter. The oath I took was to perform my duties agreeble to the Constitution and laws of the United States. . . ." [23]

However, for Frankfurter, the case of Willie Francis did not end with the last flourish of his opinion. He had done his duty as a Justice; he had time left to do another job as a man. There were other blocks of power to whom appeal could be directed—the governor of Louisiana, the state Board of Pardons. And there was an avenue of approach through Frankfurter's close friend Monte Lemann, who had been a classmate at Harvard Law School and was in 1947 a prominent New Orleans lawyer.

On February 3, 1947, Frankfurter wrote to Lemann in behalf of Willie Francis: "A good many years ago I told a friend in California that if a half dozen of the leaders of their bar would take the responsibility of persuading their Governor to clean up the Mooney mess, they would be true to the best traditions of our profession and save their State much future misery." Although the Willie Francis case and the Tom Mooney case had different issues at stake, Frankfurter did not doubt "that if Louisiana allows Francis to go to his death, it will needlessly cast a cloud upon Louisiana for many years to come, and, what is more important, probably leave many of its citizens with disquietude.

"I do not know whether you know," he continued, "that in New York, when there is a real division in the Court of Appeals such as there was here, the death sentence is as a matter of course commuted to life imprisonment. There is no formal law about it, but it is settled tradition.

"Is there," Frankfurter asked, "any possible reason for saying that, if Francis is allowed to go to his death instead of imprisonment for life, the restraints against crimes of violence will be relaxed?

"This cause," he concluded, "has been so heavily on my conscience that I finally could not overcome the impulse to write you. It is difficult for me to believe that clemency would not be forthcoming, whatsoever may be the machinery of your State for its exercise, if leading members of the bar pressed upon the authorities that even to err on the side of humaneness in the Francis situation can do no possible harm and might strengthen the forces of good will, compassion, and wisdom in society." [24]

Lemann was not entirely convinced. He talked to colleagues who believed Francis ought to be executed. He called the governor of Louisiana, who was out of town, and learned from the governor's secretary that the governor was unable to act without a recommendation from the state Board of Pardons and that this board was unlikely to recommend any commutation of sentence to a man who had committed a cold-blooded murder in Louisiana, then attempted a second. He sounded out other lawyers about the likelihood of persuading leaders of the bar to bring pressure on the Pardons Board for commutation but was rebuked on the ground that they believed Francis should be executed.[25]

Frankfurter did not give up. Instead, he sent Lemann particulars of an English case with which circumstances could be compared.

Lemann was still hesitant, but he finally came around to thinking he would feel better in his own mind if he appeared before the Pardons Board and called attention to the English precedent and urged the board members to recommend the commutation of the sentence. He phoned Francis' lawyer and offered to appear at his side before the board. The attorney turned him down, believing it preferable that he appear alone.[26]

Then Lemann wrote to the judge who had tried Francis' case and whom Lemann had taught at Tulane Law School some years before—the trial judge was automatically a member of the Board of Pardons in a case which came before it. Lemann sent a copy of the letter to Frankfurter. Echoing Frankfurter's initial letter to him, Lemann wrote: "... I realize that the eyes of the world are in a sense upon us in this case, because I have myself had communication from lawyers of high standing, for whose opinion I have a great respect, one of whom wrote me recently that he felt it would be a serious blot upon our State if Francis was permitted to be executed.... Where at the very least there is so much room for doubt as to what is the proper course to adopt, the further punishment of Francis is not as important as adherence to the highest standards of decency and humaneness which a large and informed body of public opinion feels would be betrayed by Francis's execution...." [27]

Frankfurter was grateful. "You could not have made a better plea for saving Francis from execution than your letter to Judge [James D.] Simon," he wrote Lemann when he had received a copy of the note. "While, as I wrote you, I felt almost heartbroken that [Francis' lawyer] should have been so unimaginative as not to accept your offer of appearing before the Pardon Board, your letter may perhaps be more effective than a formal association as counsel for Francis.

"For more than forty years," Frankfurter continued, "if I can count straight, you have chided me for excessive enthusiasm about this, that or the other thing. If I tell you that Marion is as impressed as I am by your whole procedure in connection with the Willie Francis case, you cannot charge me with excessive appreciation." [28]

Frankfurter had written this hopeful and appreciative note to Lemann on April 22. The next morning the newspapers announced that on that same day the Louisiana Board of Pardons had denied the plea to save Willie Francis' life, in effect closing the last door on his hope for clemency.

Francis' lawyer continued to appeal through the state courts and even again to the United States Supreme Court until the last minute, but to no avail. On May 9, Willie Francis, a steel crucifix around his neck, was escorted to the same portable electric chair from which he had walked away a year before. He was electrocuted while the jailer's black pig grunted from its cage behind the jailhouse.

Louisiana's demand for its pound of flesh had been answered. Democracy had failed. Judicial obligation never weighed so heavily.

Before Frankfurter joined the Supreme Court, he had been a dedicated fighter for the civil rights of the workingman. He had held himself available with legal advice for those involved in devising legislation to secure these rights. He helped to discipline, where industry was reluctant to discipline itself. He also tried to educate by writing articles on the social and economic ills attributable to denial of these rights. He urged, using a theme of Brandeis', cooperation, a partnership of power between industry and labor.

When, in 1949, as a Supreme Court Justice, he upheld the controversial right to work laws, his basic tenets had not changed. Two other factors had changed, however. Labor conditions had altered; the pendulum had swung in a full arc and was beginning to swing back, with power beginning to be concentrated in the unions. As industry in the earlier part of the century had fought the laboring man's right to join a union, unions in the 1940's were fighting the laboring man's right not to join the union. The more important factor in Frankfurter's decision, however, was that he was sitting on the Supreme Court. He could no longer write laws; he could no longer choose between good drafts and bad drafts, wise statutes or unwise statutes. He could only uphold or strike down. And within the framework of his philosophy of judicial restraint, he must allow, so long as it was constitutional, the very kind of legislative experimentation in which he himself had been involved not so many years before.

In 1949 a suit of the American Federation of Labor complaining of an employer's invocation of an Arizona constitutional amendment came to the Supreme Court for adjudication. The amendment provided that no person shall be denied the opportunity to obtain or retain employment because of nonmembership in a labor organization. In shorthand, this was one of the right to work laws which had been passed not only by Arizona, but also by several other states.

An Arizona court dismissed the complaint on the grounds that the amendment did not violate the Constitution of the United States; the Supreme Court of Arizona upheld the lower court decision, and on appeal to the Supreme Court of the United States, this decision was again affirmed, with Justice Black writing for the Court.

In a concurring opinion, Frankfurter outlined the early history of the labor movement in the United States and the beneficial effects of the trade union "not only as an indispensable weapon of self-defense on the part of workers, but as an aid to the well-being of society in which work is an expression of life and not merely the means of earning subsistence" However, as the powers of industrial and financial aggregations are subject to control—and Frankfurter himself had helped control them in his participation in devising the anti-injunction bill in 1928 limiting the use of the injunction against labor—so the power of the union cannot "claim constitutional exemption."

Opponents of right to work legislation said it was "fatal to the survival of organized labor," Frankfurter wrote. "But can it be said that the legislators and the people of Arizona, Nebraska, and North Carolina could not in reason be skeptical of organized labor's insistence upon the necessity to its strength of power to compel rather than to persuade the allegiance of its reluctant members? . . . However necessitous may have been the circumstances of unionism in 1898 or even in 1923, its status in 1948 precludes constitutional condemnation of a legislative judgment, whatever we may think of it, that the needs of this type of regulation outweigh its detriments. It would be arbitrary for this Court to deny the states the right to experiment with such laws. . . ." Such experimentation is not forbidden by the Constitution in these matters—as it is in matters like press censorship or separation of church and state. On the contrary, it was Frankfurter's thesis, as articulated by Holmes, that such experimentation should be encouraged.

"Most laws dealing with economic and social problems," said

Frankfurter, "are matters of trial and error. That which before trial appears to be demonstrably bad may belie prophecy in actual operation. It may not prove good, but it may prove innocuous. But even if a law is found wanting on trial, it is better that its defects should be demonstrated and removed than that the law should be aborted by judicial fiat. . . ."

Aside from the value of social experimentation, and more important from Frankfurter's point of view, the structure of federalism and the Court's position in that structure militated against striking down the right to work law. "The function of legislating is for legislatures who have also taken oaths to support the Constitution while the function of courts, when legislation is challenged, is merely to make sure that the legislature has exercised an allowable [under the Constitution] judgment, and not to exercise their own judgment. . . ."

The Supreme Court, whose power was both broad and final—Frankfurter here reiterated a fundamental of his philosophy—must exercise its power with humility which "presupposes complete disinterestedness" and "with rigorous self-restraint." [29]

The decade of the 1950's was a time of severe stresses in America. The cold war between Russia and the United States had begun almost immediately after the hot war, in which Russia and the United States were allied against their common enemy, Germany, had ended in 1945. Russia's hunger for power in Eastern Europe, her violation of the Yalta and Potsdam agreements, disillusioned many who had thought Russia could be dealt with rationally. The temper of the country rose to high fever as postwar reaction to Russians and by extension to members of the Communist Party brought such demagogues as Senator Joseph R. McCarthy into national prominence. It was not unlike the postwar reaction of the 1920's, with McCarthy assuming the role of A. Mitchell Palmer. If the means used in the 1950's were not so physically vicious as those used in the 1920's, they were psychologically more brutal. They were designed to elicit simple answers to emotional and complicated questions and to offer outlets for the tensions and unrest generated by fear of Russia, the bomb, and the possibility of total destruction of civilization, either by revolution from within or nuclear attack from without. Many people jumped on the anti-Communist bandwagon.

Some of these tensions found their outlet in stringent restrictive measures passed by Congress to curb the activities of the Communist Party and bring back a sense of security—albeit perhaps a false one—to life. These measures in turn generated a heated debate over reconciling the demands of the Bill of Rights, especially those of the First Amendment, which guarantees free speech and free assembly, and the demands of national security which was threatened in the cold war. Or, as Lincoln so succinctly struck at the heart of the problem: "Must a government, of necessity, be too strong for the liberties of its own people, or too weak to maintain its own existence?"

In 1941 William Schneiderman, an avowed Communist and one-time Communist candidate for governor of Minnesota, petitioned the Supreme Court to review a decision of the lower courts revoking his citizenship because of his membership in the Communist Party. Politically, the case was a hot potato because Russia was at that time allied with the democracies against Germany, and no one wanted to antagonize her. Roosevelt was willing that the case be tried; the Secretary of State and the Justice Department were reluctant. There was a movement to postpone it. This failed, however, and the case was argued in November, 1942, and reargued in March, 1943. Wendell Willkie, who had been the Republican candidate for President in 1940, represented Schneiderman before the Supreme Court.

The point of argument revolved around whether Schneiderman, as a longtime member of the Communist Party, with all its well-known beliefs, doctrines, and methods, could or could not be attached to the principles of the Constitution; if he could not be, then, the lower courts said, he had obtained his citizenship illegally and it was revocable.

Frankfurter refused to consider the political implications of the case. When it became clear that the Supreme Court was going to reverse the decisions of the lower courts and allow Schneiderman to retain his citizenship, Frankfurter wrote to Chief Justice Stone, who was dissenting: ". . . I do not think there is the slightest doubt that if the same kind of a record had come up with reference to a Bundist, the opposite result would have been reached. Unfortunately, in the history of nations there is a too frequent change of political partners. What is plain as a pikestaff is that the present war considerations—political considerations—are the driving force behind the result of this case. . . .This case has nothing to do with the conduct of the war, with our relations with Russia, with one's past or present view regarding the Russian political or social system; . . . it has to do, on the other hand, with the conception of American nationhood and the relation of the principles of the Constitution to that nationhood. . . ." [30]

Only a few months before, Frankfurter had made to the Justices at conference on this case a long statement which is probably as eloquent a statement of his Americanism as he ever made and provides a significant clue to his later decisions in the cold war cases.

"I am saying what I am going to say," he told the Justices, "because perhaps this case arouses in me feelings that could not be entertained by anyone else around this table. It is well known that a convert is more zealous than one born to the faith. None of you has had the experience that I have had with reference to American citizenship. I was at college when my father became naturalized and I can assure you that for months preceding it was a matter of moment in our family life, and when the great day came it partook for me of great solemnity. . . ." Frankfurter recalled his days in the offices of the United States Attorney when he had represented the government in naturalization cases. "As one who has no ties with any formal religion," he said, "perhaps the feelings that underlie religious forms for me run into intensification of my feelings about American citizenship. I have known, as you hardly could have known, literally hundreds of men and women of the finest spirit who had to shed old loyalties and take on the loyalty of American citizenship. . . . American citizenship implies entering upon a fellowship which binds people together by devotion to certain feelings and ideas and ideals summarized as a requirement that they be attached to the principles of the Constitution."

That phrase—"the principles of the Constitution"—Frankfurter continued, was not an empty phrase. It was historic and pregnant with meaning. It could not mean, he believed, that one could want to overthrow the government, as was the Communist Party's avowed purpose, simply because "one of the principles of the Constitution is the right to amend it. . . ."

The question of Schneiderman's citizenship revolved around "whether we can say that the two lower courts were not, on this record, justified in finding that Schneiderman was not attached to the Constitution. . . .

"I have known the Schneidermans and a good many of them well since my college days," Frankfurter soliloquized, "and I have admired, and still do admire, their devotion to their ideals. They are the salt of the earth so far as character and selflessness goes [*sic*]. But they are devoted to a wholly different scheme of things from that to which this country, through its Constitution, is committed. . . ."

Frankfurter did not mean to suggest that mere membership in the Communist Party indicated a lack of attachment to the principles of the Constitution. Perhaps recalling the illiterate and downtrodden victims of A. Mitchell Palmer's Red Raids in 1919 and 1920, he told the conference: "Many a person is a member of the Communist Party merely as an expression of his deep feeling of injustice about the iniquities and hardships of our present society. . . ." However, in Schneiderman, the Court had before it a passionate, dedicated Communist who had belonged to the party since the age of sixteen, who had at that time "dedicated himself as an active organizer and important official of the orthodox creed of the Communist Party."

For Frankfurter, it was axiomatic that "no man can serve two masters when two masters represent not only different, but in this case, mutually exclusive ideas. . . ." [31]

Frankfurter's eloquence notwithstanding, a majority of the Court, speaking through Justice Murphy, found that evidence of active Communist Party membership did not convincingly prove a naturalized citizen's lack of attachment to the principles of the Constitution. "Under our traditions," Murphy wrote, "beliefs are personal and not a matter of association. . . ." Schneiderman, previous to his application for citizenship, had "behaved as a man . . . attached to the principles of the Constitution of the United States and well disposed to the good order and happiness of the same. . . ." [32]

When the majority opinion had been circulated among the Justices, Frankfurter had wryly written a note to Murphy: "Thorough and comprehensive as your opinion is in Schneiderman you omitted one thing that, on reflection, you might want to add. I think it is only fair to state, in view of your general argument, that Uncle Joe Stalin was at least a spiritual co-author with Jefferson of the Virginia Statute for Religious Freedom." [33]

Schneiderman was a prelude to the internal security cases which came to the Court in the 1950's. By that time the United States had indeed changed political partners and was engaged in the cold war with Russia—psychologically, if not physically, as tense as hot war. It was a period of strain for law, too. In a shooting war, one is far more likely to agree to the more drastic measures taken by the government in the name of national security. In a cold war, when the enemy is only a shadowy threat—real or unreal—there is a good deal of disagreement on the remedy required.

One of the most important steps toward national security had been taken by Congress prior to World War II in its passage of the Smith Act in 1940. The act declared, in its key sections, that it was unlawful "to knowingly or willfully advocate, abet, advise, or teach the duty, necessity, desirability, or propriety of overthrowing or destroying any government in the United States by force or violence, or by the assassination of any officer of any such government." It was unlawful, also, "with intent to cause the overthrow or destruction of any government in the United States, to print, publish, edit, issue, circulate, sell, distribute, or publicly display any written or printed matter advocating, advising, or teaching the duty, necessity, desirability, or propriety of overthrowing or destroying any government in the United States by force or violence." Nor could one "organize or help to organize" a group of persons who "teach, or encourage the overthrow or destruction of any government in the United States by force or violence." Nor may anyone belong to a group with these avowed purposes. Furthermore, "it shall be unlawful for any person to attempt to commit, or to conspire to commit, any of the acts prohibited by the provision of this title."

The constitutionality of the Smith Act came before the Supreme Court in 1950, in a case celebrated as the Dennis case. The defendants were ten of the principal leaders of the Communist Party in the United States, including Eugene Dennis. They had been convicted in a federal court of violating the Smith Act by willfully and knowingly conspiring: (1) to organize as the Communist Party of the United States a society to teach and advocate the overthrow and destruction of the government of the United States by force and violence and (2) to advocate and teach the duty and necessity of overthrowing the government of the United States by force and violence. The trial had lasted nine months and produced a record of 16,000 pages.

When the case came to the Supreme Court, the Justices were not asked to determine whether the defendants had committed the acts specified in the indictment. That had already been decided at their trial. The specific question before the Court, rather, was whether the sections of the Smith Act under which the ten Communists had been convicted violated the First Amendment and other provisions of the Bill of Rights.

A majority of the Supreme Court found that the Smith Act did not violate the Bill of Rights and the First Amendment in particular. Chief Justice Fred M. Vinson wrote for the Court: "... The obvious purpose of the statute is to protect existing Government, not from change by peaceable, lawful and constitutional means, but from change by violence, revolution and terrorism." There was no question that Congress had the power to protect the government from armed rebellion. The question here was not whether Congress possessed the power, but whether "the *means* which it has employed conflict with the First and Fifth Amendments to the Constitution." The Constitution did not allow untrammeled free speech; it did not allow, as Holmes had so neatly put it, a man to yell "Fire!" in a crowded theater. "The question in every case" of free expression, Holmes continued in his 1919 opinion upholding the Espionage Acts passed by Congress during World War I, "is whether the words used are used in such circumstances and are of such a nature as to create a clear and present danger that they will bring about the substantive evils that Congress has a right to prevent. It is a question of proximity and degree. When a nation is at war many things that might be said in time of peace are such a hindrance to its effort that their utterance will not be endured so long as men fight and that no Court could regard them as protected by any constitutional right."

Vinson saw the Court as confronted with the "clear and present danger" test in the Dennis case. He decided that that test could not mean that "before the Government may act, it must wait until the *putsch* is about to be executed, the plans have been laid and the signal is awaited. If Government is aware that a group aiming at its overthrow is attempting to indoctrinate its members and to commit them to a course whereby they will strike when the leaders feel the circumstances permit, action by the Government is required.... Certainly an attempt to overthrow the Government by force, even though doomed from the outset because of inadequate numbers or power of the revolutionists, is a sufficient evil for Congress to prevent...." [34] The defendants, the Court decided, had been "properly and constitutionally convicted." The sections of the Smith Act before the Court did not violate the Bill of Rights.

Frankfurter wrote a concurring opinion. It is another statement of his judicial restraint and an accurate charting of his course through the intricacies of many of the internal security cases that came before the Court in this period. Few questions, he believed, "of comparable import" had been before the Court in recent years. In conflict, he stated, were "the right to advocate a political theory, so long, at least, as . . . advocacy does not create an immediate danger of obvious magnitude to the very existence of our present scheme of society" and the government's "right to safeguard the security of the Nation by such a measure as the Smith Act."

There was no question that government has the right to protect itself. But even the "power and duty of self-preservation are not absolute" but are subject to constitutional limitation. "The First Amendment is such a restriction," he wrote. "It exacts obedience even during period of war; it is applicable when war clouds are not figments of the imagination no less than when they are. . . . The right of a man to think what he pleases, to write what he thinks and to have his thoughts made available for others to hear or read has an engaging ring of universality." Unquestionably, the Smith Act restricted that right.

That, however, did not dispose of the matter. "Free speech is subject to prohibition of those abuses of expression which a civilized society may forbid. . . ." The aims and methods of the Communist Party are not the aims and methods of the usual political party. The Communist Party "rejects the basic premise of our political system—that change is to be brought about by non-violent constitutional process . . . that there is a duty and necessity to overthrow the Government by force and violence."

How are these competing interests of national security and free speech to be reconciled? Who is to lay down the guidelines for accommodation between the two? Frankfurter threw the problem squarely back to the legislative branch, as he always did, as the direct manifestation of the will of the people.

"Full responsibility of the choice cannot be given to the courts," he wrote. "Courts are not representative bodies. They are not designed to be a good reflex of a democratic society. . . . History teaches that the independence of the judiciary is jeopardized when courts become embroiled in the passions of the day and assume primary responsibility in choosing between political, economic and social pressure.

"Primary responsibility for adjusting the interests which compete in the situation before us of necessity belongs to Congress. . . ." Unless the nation was to be once again governed by the judiciary, as Frankfurter believed it had been in the 1920's and early 1930's, when it had struck down a record number of economic and social measures and nearly brought about its own destruction in Roosevelt's Court-packing plan of 1937, it was not the Court's province to arbitrate this particular conflict. The Constitution had set up a procedure: Laws were made in the legislature; their constitutionality was decided in the judiciary. The Constitution did not say law had to be either wise or beneficial; it only said law could not abridge certain freedoms. If Congress, with its ear to the ground, had determined that the danger from advocacy of violent overthrow of the government justified restriction on freedom of speech, that was the right of Congress. The people had recourse in the ballot box.

"The wisdom of the assumptions underlying the legislation and prosecution is another matter," Frankfurter added. "In finding that Congress has acted within its power, a judge does not remotely imply that he favors the implications that lie beneath the legal issues. . . ."

Then he warned, in a paraphrase of James Bradley Thayer's 1893 article on constitutional law and in a paraphrase of his own writings before he sat on the Court, "Civil liberties draw at best only limited strength from legal guaranties. Preoccupation by our people with the constitutionality, instead of with the wisdom, of legislation or of executive action is preoccupation with a false value. . . . Focusing attention on constitutionality tends to make constitutionality synonymous with wisdom. When legislation touches freedom of thought and freedom of speech, such a tendency is a formidable enemy of the free spirit. Much that should be rejected as illiberal, because repressive and envenoming, may well be not unconstitutional. The ultimate reliance for the deepest needs of civilization must be found outside their vindication in courts of law. . . . A persistent, positive translation of the liberating faith into the feelings and thoughts and actions of men and women is the real protection against attempts to strait-jacket the human mind. . . ." [35]

One can compare this paragraph with another Frankfurter wrote in the *New Republic* in 1925: "... Our constant preoccupation with the constitutionality of legislation rather than its wisdom tends to preoccupation of the American mind with a false value ... the tendency of focusing attention on constitutionality is to make constitutionality synonymous with propriety; to regard a law as all right so long as it is 'constitutional.' Such an attitude is a great enemy of liberalism. Particularly in legislation affecting freedom of thought and freedom of speech much that is highly illiberal would be clearly constitutional.... Here is ample room for the patrioteers to roll in their Trojan horses. And here is ample warning to the liberal forces that the real battles of liberalism are not won in the Supreme Court. ... Only a persistent, positive translation of the liberal faith into the thoughts and acts of the community is the real reliance against the unabated temptation to strait-jacket the human mind." [36]

Frankfurter concluded in the Dennis case: "The mark of a truly civilized man is confidence in the strength and security derived from the inquiring mind. We may be grateful for such honest comforts as it supports, but we must be unafraid of its incertitudes. Without open minds there can be no open society. And if society be not open the spirit of man is mutilated and becomes enslaved." [37]

Justice Black dissented in the Dennis case and, in so doing, pointed up the issues that divided his activist philosophy from the restraint of Frankfurter. "So long as this Court exercises the power of judicial review of legislation," he wrote, "I cannot agree that the First Amendment permits us to sustain laws suppressing freedom of speech and press on the basis of Congress' or our own notion of mere 'reasonableness.' Such a doctrine waters down the First Amendment so that it amounts to little more than an admonition to Congress. The Amendment as so construed is not likely to protect any but those 'safe' or orthodox views which rarely need its protection...." [38]

It was exactly the people who espoused unpopular views in tense times that the Constitution was written to protect, in Black's judgment. Continuing his thesis in a 1960 lecture, he said: "We're well aware that the individual rights they sought to protect might be easily nullified if subordinated to the general powers granted to Congress. One of the reasons for adopting the Bill of Rights was to prevent just that....

"Misuse of government power," he continued, "particularly in times of stress, has brought suffering to humanity in all ages about which we have authentic history. Some of the world's noblest and finest men have suffered ignominy and death for no crime—unless unorthodoxy is a crime. Even enlightened Athens had its victims such as Socrates. Because of the same kind of bigotry, Jesus, the great Dissenter, was put to death on a wooden cross. The flames of inquisitions all over the world have warned that men endowed with unlimited government power, even earnest men, consecrated to a cause, are dangerous. . . .

"The First Amendment is truly the heart of the Bill of Rights," Black concluded. "The Framers balanced its freedoms of religion, speech, press, assembly, and petition against the needs of a powerful central government, and decided that in those freedoms lies this nation's only true security. They were not afraid for men to be free. . . ." [39]

Frankfurter was far from unmindful of the passions that were stirring people in those cold war days. The Court, however, had a responsibility "not to fan the flames." Indeed, he wrote to Justice Jackson in 1952, "we ought if possible to radiate examples of a self-contained, calm, and austere attitude toward the anxious situation confronting the country. Strong men do not have to indulge in rhetoric except when they want to whip up feeling. . . ." [40]

Frankfurter guarded the power of the legislature jealously; it was the will of the people in whom responsibility for democracy was ultimately lodged. During the 1950's he regularly acceded to Congress' power to deal with internal security. He did not give lawmaking bodies, either state or national, however, a blank check for repression.

In January, 1954, one Paul N. Sweezy had been summoned before the attorney general of New Hampshire for extensive questioning. By joint resolution, both houses of the New Hampshire legislature had authorized the attorney general to conduct an investigation of subversive activities in the state. Sweezy had willingly answered most of the questions put to him. He said he had never been a Communist, had never taught violent overthrow of the government, and had never knowingly associated with Communists in the state. He was a Socialist believer in peaceful change and had at one time belonged to certain organizations on the list of the United States Attorney General or cited by the House Un-American Activities Committee. However, he declined to answer as irrelevant or violative of free speech guarantees certain questions related to his knowledge of the Progressive Party of the State and its members. Six months later Sweezy was again summoned by the attorney general of New Hampshire and again interrogated. Sweezy answered all questions except those pertaining to a lecture given by him at the University of New Hampshire and those pertaining to activities of himself and others in the Progressive Party. He was found guilty of contempt in the New Hampshire courts.

The Supreme Court of the United States, speaking through the opinion of Chief Justice Warren, reversed Sweezy's conviction in 1957. The Court agreed that Sweezy's liberties had been invaded in the areas of academic freedom and political expression.

Frankfurter, in a concurring opinion, wrote an eloquent defense of both academic freedom and freedom of political expression. There was no question, he said, that a free society was dependent on free universities. "This means the exclusion of governmental intervention in the intellectual life of a university. It matters little whether such intervention occurs avowedly or through action that inevitably tends to check the ardor and fearlessness of scholars, qualities at once so fragile and so indispensable for fruitful academic labor. . . ."

Equally was there no question but that a free society was dependent on freedom of political expression. "For a citizen to be made to forgo even a part of so basic a liberty as his political autonomy, the subordinating interest of the state must be compelling," Frankfurter continued. ". . . In the political realm, as in the academic, thought and action are presumptively immune from inquisition by political authority. It cannot require argument that inquiry would be barred to ascertain whether a citizen had voted for one or the other of the two major parties either in a state or a national election. Until recently, no difference would have been entertained in regard to inquiries about a voter's affiliations with one of the various third parties that have had their day, or longer, in our political history. . . ." [41] New Hampshire had gone too far, had "exceeded the speed limit." Frankfurter was compelled to vote for reversal of Sweezy's conviction.

Remembering that Frankfurter had passionately criticized A. Mitchell Palmer's reign of terror which climaxed in the Red Raids of 1919 and 1920, liberals in the United States had nothing but contempt for most of Frankfurter's decisions in internal security cases of the 1950's. Where was this champion of liberalism of yesteryear?

In fact, the issues in 1920 and the issues in the 1950's were quite different. In 1920, Frankfurter was not questioning the government's power to deport alien members of the Communist Party under the Deportation Law of 1918. What he was questioning, and was passionately opposed to, was the *means*—searches without warrants; theft of property; forced confessions; beatings with blackjacks; the Justice Department agents employed to round up and imprison large numbers of suspects indiscriminately and brutally. Proper procedure was totally lacking—and in fact arbitrarily changed to suit the convenience of the Justice Department, as Judge Anderson had held in *Colyer v. Skeffington.* Had the Justice Department utilized similar means in rounding up deportees in the 1950's, no doubt Frankfurter would have found them equally reprehensible.

Frankfurter did not always embrace the wisdom of a law Congress passed in the name of national security. Perhaps if he had still been a professor at Harvard Law School, he would have fought vigorously against legislative repression, as he had fought vigorously while at Harvard for legislative expression and judicial repression.

However, in the 1950's he was not at Harvard. He sat on the Supreme Court. He had once written: "Respect for law cannot be turned off and on as though it were a hot-water faucet." [42] By the same token, neither could judicial philosophy. If one conceived the Court's role as a self-restrained one and opposed its activism in the 1920's and 1930's, one could hardly turn it off in the 1950's, with any integrity. Frankfurter once wrote to a friend: "Anybody can put law behind desire. But the test of the judicial function is when one is called upon to cross desire by law. . . . Apparently it was wrong for the Supreme Court to be a 'super-legislature' in the days of Brandeis only because the lads—Butler, McReynolds and Co.—legislated to the distaste of 'liberals.' It has become 'liberal' for this Court to legislate the 'right way.' . . ." [43]

In 1954 Mrs. Frankfurter became bedridden with arthritis.[44] For some years she had detected a weakness in her left leg, and after she had consulted a number of doctors and undergone several tests, it was found she had arthritis in her left hip. It was a painless variety of arthritis, but it disallowed the use of her hip, which one minute might give support, the next minute might suddenly collapse. A rather reserved and high-strung woman who was not particularly comfortable in Washington, she took to her bed.

Frankfurter's own motion was necessarily slowed. He rarely went out socially from this time on but declined most invitations with the excuse that his wife was an invalid and he did not go to formal and particularly mixed dinners alone. He did much of his visiting by phone, which became a large part of his contact with his former world. He would spend hours catching up on political gossip, legal gossip, and his numerous friends.

He brought the outside world in to Mrs. Frankfurter. Returning from the Supreme Court each day, he would recount in detail everything that had happened. They spent most of their evenings together and ate from trays in Mrs. Frankfurter's room.

The Frankfurters had never been partygoers or party givers in the Washington style. They had always, however, been active in giving small dinner parties where the talk was witty, stimulating, and intelligent and which could be achieved only in the intimacy of the small drawing room with a few well-chosen intimates. The dinner parties continued after Mrs. Frankfurter's illness, but she seldom attended.

There were no more trips to Frankfurter's beloved England, where they had spent several summers. Nor were there any more trips to the Massachusetts mountains, where they had also sojourned summers. Instead, they stayed in their Washington home, which by this time was on Dumbarton Avenue in the Georgetown section of the capital.

The Frankfurters were always hopeful that a new treatment, a new doctor, might cure her affliction. But their hopes were never realized; there never was any improvement.

[5]

The Fourteenth Amendment to the Constitution not only commands that no state may "deprive any person of life, liberty, or property, without due process of law," but also orders that no state may deny "to any person within its jurisdiction the equal protection of the laws." This was the basis on which one of the most far-reaching decisions of the "Warren Court" was arrived at: the 1954 public school desegregation decision.

Linda Brown of Topeka, Kansas, historically a free state, was nine years old in the spring of 1951. She was in the fourth grade of Monroe School, a public elementary school. All the children at Monroe were, like Linda Brown, Negroes. The Monroe School was a long walk through railroad yards and a bus trip from Linda's home, twenty-one blocks away. But she lived only five blocks from the Sumner School, a Topeka public elementary school. All the children at Sumner were white. Linda Brown often wondered why she could not attend the nearby school, which she passed on her way to Monroe. Finally, her father, the Reverend Oliver Brown, tried to enroll her in the Sumner School. The Browns were turned away because they were Negro. In 1951, Oliver Brown and twelve other parents sued the Topeka Board of Education in the local federal district court. A special three-judge court heard the case and decided that since Negro and white schools were substantially equal, there was no "willful, intentional or substantial discrimination." Linda Brown could not in fact attend Sumner School.

Oliver Brown and the twelve other Negro parents appealed to the Supreme Court of the United States. When the Court agreed to hear the case in the October term of 1952, it was the first time the issue of racial segregation in public schools had come squarely before that Court. It was to prove, as predicted at the time, the most explosive issue since the Dred Scott decision of 1857, which had touched off long-smoldering passions and contributed enormously to the causes of the Civil War.

The Supreme Court heard the first arguments in December, 1952. It required nearly eighteen months of agony before the august Justices of the United States Supreme Court could decide whether Linda Brown should be allowed to attend Sumner School. They were eighteen months of secretiveness, brisk discussion in the security of the conference room, of memorandums typed under conditions of strictest security. They were eighteen months of the most fastidious research on what the Justices' equally august predecessors had said in regard to segregation of the races and what the Constitution and the laws commanded the Supreme Court of the 1950's to decide. They were eighteen months of deepest concern for the future of the Court and of the nation, in whatever way the Justices decided. These men were, in a sense, fighting the last battle of the Civil War, and they were grimly aware of the fact that they could start another one.

And when in time the Justices came to a decision on what they would do, there was equally deep concern on how they would do it, when they would do it, and what they would say. It was, they believed, the most sensitive issue that had come before the Court in modern times. Its potential for revolutionizing a way of life, especially in the South but also in the North, was infinite.

A plethora of cases involving various aspects of segregation of the races had been crawling up the ladder of the judicial process to the Supreme Court throughout the two previous decades. Gradually legal sanction of segregation was being eroded by the Court's decisions.

In 1917 the Supreme Court said that residential segregation could not be required by state or local law, that such segregation, if enforced by the government, was a violation of the equal protection clause of the Fourteenth Amendment. After 1917, in both North and South, residential segregation was achieved by private discrimination in the restrictive covenants made by property owners forbidding transfer of property to persons of a particular race, color, or religion. In 1948 the Supreme Court in effect struck these down by saying that such covenants could not be enforced by law. Once again, said the Court, in a unanimous opinion written by Chief Justice Vinson, "in granting judicial enforcement of the restrictive agreements in these cases, the States have denied petitioners the equal protection of the laws, and that, therefore, the action of the state courts cannot stand." [1]

The Court had also moved into the area of voting rights. The Fifteenth Amendment to the Constitution, ratified in 1870 and one of the so-called Civil War Amendments, said: "The right of citizens of the United States to vote shall not be denied or abridged by the United States or by any State on account of race, color, or previous condition of servitude."

Nevertheless, because of evasive actions in the Southern states, this right was not wholly secured for Negroes until 1944, when the last legal bastion of white elections, the white primary, collapsed before the Supreme Court. The Court held that the states could not run the Democratic Party like a private club, as some had done, since elections are conducted under state authority. "Constitutional rights," said the Court, "would be of little value if they could be thus indirectly denied." [2] Although the decision could not deal with extralegal pressures of discrimination, it could remove legal approval of disenfranchisement on the basis of race.

Legal sanction of segregationist practices was based on an 1896 decision of the Supreme Court of the United States which had upheld the constitutionality of state statutes providing for separation of the races in public transportation. On June 7, 1892, Homer A. Plessy, a light-skinned Negro, boarded a train in New Orleans, Louisiana, bound for Covington, Louisiana, and sat down in the coach reserved for whites—"Caucasians." The conductor ordered him to move to the car reserved for Negroes, as an 1890 Louisiana law required—railroads, under this law, were ordered "to provide equal but separate accommodations for the white and colored races." Plessy refused; he was arrested and tried before Judge John H. Ferguson; the case became celebrated as *Plessy v. Ferguson.*

Plessy instituted an action to restrain enforcement of the Louisiana statute which forbade whites and Negroes to ride together in the same vehicle or the same portion of a vehicle—the Jim Crow laws prevalent throughout the South. He based his action on the ground that they violated the Thirteenth Amendment, which outlaws slavery, and the Fourteenth Amendment, which guarantees equal protection of the laws. The Louisiana courts denied Plessy's plea.

The Supreme Court of the United States affirmed the decision of the Louisiana courts in 1896. The Court held that mere separation of the races in transportation did not violate the equal protection clause of the Fourteenth Amendment. So long as facilities furnished to Negroes were equal to those furnished to whites, Plessy suffered no damages.

There was one lone dissenter to the Court's opinion: Justice John Marshall Harlan of Kentucky, grandfather of the Justice John Marshall Harlan who was appointed to the Supreme Court in 1955.

Harlan spoke out forcefully. "Our Constitution," he wrote, "is color-blind, and neither knows nor tolerates classes among citizens. In respect of civil rights, all citizens are equal before the law. The humblest is the peer of the most powerful. The law regards man as man, and takes no account of his surroundings or of his color when his civil rights as guaranteed by the supreme law of the land are involved. . . .

"The sure guarantee of peace and security of each race is the clear, distinct, unconditional recognition by our governments, National and State, of every right that inheres in civil freedom, and of the equality before the law of all citizens of the United States without regard to race. . . .

"If evils will result from the commingling of the two races upon public highways established for the benefit of all, they will be infinitely less than those that will surely come from state legislation regulating the enjoyment of civil rights upon the basis of race. . . .

"The judgment this day rendered will, in time, prove to be quite as pernicious as the decision made by this tribunal in the Dred Scott case. . . ." [3]

Nevertheless, the separate but equal formula articulated in *Plessy v. Ferguson* became the law of the land and remained so for more than fifty years. Although it covered only the field of transportation, it was used as the legal cornerstone for segregated public schools. Although cases indirectly related to the issue of segregation in the public schools had come before the Supreme Court between 1896 and 1952, the Court had avoided passing again on the validity of the 1896 decision in regard to public education.

Before the case of Oliver Brown and the other Negro parents reached the Supreme Court, other public education cases had got there. But these involved public education at the graduate level; the Justices were not forced to face the possibility of challenging the 1896-enunciated separate but equal formula, which had long since become an ingrained part of Southern public school systems.

In 1951, when Oliver Brown initiated his suit against the Topeka Board of Education, state constitutional provisions and laws or local ordinances required that the schools of seventeen Southern and border states and the District of Columbia maintain segregated schools. In four other states—Arizona, Kansas, New Mexico, and Wyoming—segregated schools were legally permitted on an optional basis. In Kansas, Linda Brown's home state, an 1867 statute permitted cities with a population exceeding 15,000 to maintain segregated elementary schools, and seven cities in the free state of Kansas maintained some form of segregation when Linda Brown attended Monroe School.

In the case which became celebrated as *Brown v. Board of Education* (Oliver Brown's was the first name which appeared alphabetically in the case of the Topeka Negroes, and so this landmark decision was given his name), the Supreme Court for the first time was squarely and unavoidably faced with a challenge to the separate but equal doctrine. The lower courts, upon investigation, had found that Negro and white schools involved in the case were either then equal or in the process of being equalized with respect to the "tangible" factors—physical plant, teachers, curricula, and such. But the Browns and the other parents, whose case had been taken by the National Association for the Advancement of Colored People (NAACP), contended that segregated schools were inherently unequal and could not be made equal.

Argument began in the Supreme Court on December 9, 1952. The courtroom was filled to its capacity of 300, nearly half the spectators Negro. Some 450 persons waited in line outside. There were five cases involved. In addition to Oliver Brown's suit, there was a case from a rural county in South Carolina, where school segregation was mandatory, one from Virginia, one from Delaware, and one from the District of Columbia. Neither side lacked legal talent.

John W. Davis, constitutional lawyer of note and the Democratic Party's nominee for President in 1924, argued the case for segregation in South Carolina. Thurgood Marshall, lawyer for the NAACP and later to be appointed to the Supreme Court, argued against segregation. J. Lindsay Almond, Jr., then attorney general of Virginia, later governor of Virginia, argued Virginia's case.

The first arguments lasted three days. Davis, Almond, and the others argued that segregation, in addition to its being a way of life, was a legislative matter with which the federal courts were powerless to interfere. The Fourteenth Amendment, they said, was never intended to apply to school segregation. Marshall declared that segregation statutes perpetuate slavery. He asserted that mandatory segregation denied to Negroes equal protection of the laws guaranteed under the Fourteenth Amendment. Briefs filed for the Negroes included, in the old Brandeis style, data from psychologists and sociologists pointing out why segregated education was harmful to Negroes.

Arguments ended on December 11, at 3:42 P.M., and a six-month silence followed. Other cases involving segregation laws in schools, transportation, and various public facilities—which had been instituted in the lower courts—stopped while the judges and litigants waited to see what the highest court in the nation would do about these five cases, lumped together as *Brown v. Board of Education.*

There was speculation that the Court might be sharply divided. A division was indicated not only by the questions the Justices directed at lawyers who argued the cases, but by the composition of the Court. It was headed by Chief Justice Fred M. Vinson of Kentucky. He was a Democrat who had been appointed by President Truman and considered judicially unpredictable. There was an outspoken liberal core, consisting of Justices Black and Douglas. And there was a relatively conservative wing, consisting of Justices Burton of Ohio and Minton of Indiana. Frankfurter and his frequent judicial ally Justice Jackson were not easily pigeonholed into conservative or liberal classification. On this issue the pair were considered unpredictable. So were Justice Reed, a Kentuckian and a Roosevelt appointee, and Justice Tom C. Clark, a Texan and a Truman appointee.

The nation got its first hint at the course of events inside the Supreme Court in June, 1953, six months after the first arguments had been heard. The Court ordered the cases brought back for reargument and posed five specific questions for counsel to answer in their reargument. The first three questions involved whether the framers of the Fourteenth Amendment had or had not intended that amendment to deal with segregation in public schools and, if so, how —through future Congresses or through judicial interpretation. The last two questions asked exactly how desegregation could be accomplished. Some Court watchers believed that the content and phraseology of the questions indicated that the Court may have made up its mind to abolish segregation in the public schools before June, 1953, although Frankfurter, in a note to Vinson, said the questions, as phrased, "by looking in opposite directions . . . would not tip the mitt." [4]

In addition, an invitation was extended to the Attorney General to appear for reargument. Justice Jackson had suggested, early in the deliberations, and the other eight agreed, "that the new Administration [Dwight D. Eisenhower had become President in January, 1953], unlike the old, may have the responsibility of carrying out a decision full of perplexities; it should therefore be asked to face that responsibility as part of our process of adjudication." [5]

Again the Justices retreated into silence to await reargument of the segregation cases, of major importance in their private discussions, if not in their public comments.

Reargument was originally scheduled for October 12, 1953, but on September 8, 1953, Chief Justice Vinson died of a heart attack, leaving the Court headless as it was about to consider one of the most significant cases of the century. Reargument was postponed to December, 1953.

What course of action would the Supreme Court have followed in the segregation cases had Vinson remained Chief Justice?

Those who believed the Court had made up its mind before it ordered the reargument necessarily believed Vinson, in presiding over the Court during the early deliberations, must share the praise or blame for the final decision. Moreover, it had been a unanimous Vinson Court which had decided several previous cases dealing with segregation and established the atmosphere for *Brown v. Board of Education*. J. Waties Waring, the dissenter on the three-judge federal court which had upheld segregation in South Carolina, believed Vinson would have decided the way the Supreme Court finally did. But Waring added that he did not think Vinson would have been very enthusiastic about it.[6]

Other observers believed that Vinson might have been inclined to hold public school segregation unconstitutional but that he was shaky at best and in his shakiness might have dissipated the momentum for unanimity.

On September 30, 1953, Earl Warren, Republican governor of California, was appointed to succeed Vinson as Chief Justice of the United States. Warren was sixty-two years old; he had been a county district attorney for fourteen years, attorney general of California for four years, Republican Vice Presidential candidate in 1948, and California's only three-term governor. Little more was expected of him than that he be quietly effective as a Justice, possibly a mitigating influence on such colorful and often contentious personalities as Justices Frankfurter and Black, Douglas and Jackson. "He had been hired," said a biographer of Warren later, "as the colorless manager of a team of all-stars." [7]

Frankfurter believed the appointment of Warren augured well. Although Warren's career had not had legal eminence, Warren had had a broad range of experience and broadness of viewpoint, which, combined with industriousness, open-mindedness, and concentration on his work, would make him a first-rate Chief Justice. In addition, Warren was an attractive individual who would be pleasant to work with.[8]

Frankfurter, in fact, courted Warren as he courted all new members of the Court. Undoubtedly he was fascinated by how such a political being would behave in his new judicial situation; in addition, he wanted Warren in his judicial camp. Warren himself undoubtedly looked to Frankfurter as the senior legal scholar on the Court. The pair enjoyed what is often referred to as a short honeymoon period.[9] Later Warren, as most men are after initial orientation, was ready for independence; he wanted to be his own man. Their relations deteriorated somewhat, although Warren contended their public tiffs were exaggerated by the press. He once said that Frankfurter was "not the easiest person in the world to work with," that Frankfurter was far from being a "calm person," that his long reports of cases in the courtroom were tedious, and that there had been "flare-ups" in the conference room. But on the whole, he said that "we got along very well" and that the differences between them "were so trivial you couldn't believe it." [10]

The segregation cases came well within the period of close relations between Warren and Frankfurter, and Court watchers have speculated that the final decision may have been a rare combination of Frankfurter's intellectual insight and Warren's political insight, as well as Warren's tremendous bargaining power in coming in as a new person whom everyone wanted to work with and who was generally respected.

In December, 1953, the cases were reargued in the Supreme Court, and once again the Justices played to a standing-room-only house, with people lined up in the corridor waiting to get in. On the second day of argument the weight of the Eisenhower administration was placed squarely behind abolishing segregation in public schools. J. Lee Rankin, Assistant Attorney General, spoke for the Department of Justice, which had been invited to appear. "The Fourteenth Amendment," he declared to the Court, "does not permit any discrimination based on race or color.

"The Court can find only one answer." When these defendants

stood before the Supreme Court and said "that the only reason for segregation is color, the Court must say that the Fourteenth Amendment does not permit this to happen," [11] Rankin asserted.

During the three days of reargument, counsel for the opposing sides of the segregation cases addressed themselves to the five specific questions asked by the Court the previous June. After exhaustive historical research, each side came to different conclusions on the meaning of the Fourteenth Amendment. The NAACP lawyers agreed that Congress had intended the Fourteenth Amendment to abolish segregation "as a last vestige of slavery." [12] They declared that the amendment had envisaged the establishment of complete equality for all persons regardless of race. Equality is denied to Negroes, they contended, as long as their children are barred from white schools. They argued that the states in ratifying the amendment clearly understood that the Fourteenth Amendment was designed to destroy public school segregation.

Opposing counsel said it had *not* been the intent of Congress in adopting the Fourteenth Amendment, or the understanding of the states in ratifying it, that this amendment would at that time or in the future be used to outlaw public school segregation. Segregation, declared John Davis, did not deprive Negroes of equal protection within the meaning of the amendment. The happiness, progress, and welfare of Negro children, he said, was "best promoted in segregated schools." [13]

On the question of remedy, should the Court decide to declare segregation in public schools unconstitutional, Assistant Attorney General Rankin said the government recommended sending the cases back to the lower courts for decision on how, in the light of local conditions, a Supreme Court decree should be enforced. The NAACP attorneys urged immediate admission of Negro children to the schools of their choice.

Reargument ended at 2:42 P.M. on December 9, 1953, two days and one hour short of a year from the time the original arguments ended. And once again the Justices retreated into public silence to unravel the constitutional puzzles these cases had presented to them.

In the first conference after reargument, the Court was led by its new Chief Justice, Warren, in a reconnoitering discussion with no thought of a vote. The Justices then took several weeks to reflect on the views expressed in that first conference. Two further conference discussions followed, weeks apart, before the Justices reached any decision.[14] They had determined only that the significance of the cases required the necessary time for a matured judgment and unhurried determination.

For Frankfurter, it was a time of searching from the moment the cases first came before the Court in 1952 until the final decision in May, 1954. During the 1952 term he had taken pains to assign one of his law clerks to "the reading of every word in the Congressional Globe relating to the history of what ultimately became the Fourteenth Amendment, including therefore also the history of related measures." [15]

There is no doubt about where Frankfurter stood on the practice of segregation—in any form. He had been counsel to the NAACP prior to his appointment to the Supreme Court. On the Court, he had hired the first Negro law clerk, in 1948–49.

He never forgot a poignant conversation concerning that appointment which took place in his chambers. When his Negro messenger heard about the appointment, he said, "Mr. Justice, that was a mighty fine thing you did, hiring one of our people to be your clerk."

Frankfurter chided him gently. "Tom," he said, "I have heard that kind of remark from others, but I am surprised to hear it from you. Don't you know that I selected William Coleman because, on the basis of character and ability, I felt he deserved the position?"

"Mr. Justice," replied the messenger, "do you think in this world our people get what they deserve?" [16]

Inequality determined by the color of one's skin offended Frankfurter's sense of decency as deeply as the brutal behavior of those policemen who trampled on individual rights in the name of the law. Both were expressions of the incivility of civilization, and Frankfurter, in his person and in his writings, was the very expression of the civility of civilization.

However, it was a question of *law* that was before the Court. Was public school segregation constitutional? Was it unconstitutional? If it was unconstitutional, could the Supreme Court call for its end? And if that Court did call for its end, what would be the impact on the Court, dependent for its strength and vitality on public confidence? Whatever the Court decided—whether segregation in public schools was constitutional or unconstitutional—the decision would be not the end, but the beginning of the problem.

Over the years, Frankfurter had laid a light restraining hand on the Court in this area, although he had confidently joined the Court's unanimous opinions against segregation up to this time. No doubt he believed racial problems would be solved in other ways, expecting that what Lincoln had called "the better angels of our nature" would in the end emerge, that civilization would overcome man's inhumanity to man. Consistent with his philosophy of judicial restraint, he hoped that the problems would be solved by the people involved, with democracy all the stronger for it, and that the Supreme Court would not have to impose its will on a large segment of the population.

With such hopes in mind, shortly after Frankfurter went on the Court, he gave a dinner for Walter White, head of the NAACP and then an influential Negro leader; William H. Hastie, then dean of Howard University Law School and later a federal judge; and a group of young Southerners, all lawyers, the sort of new Southern man that was beginning to be influential.[17] Certainly he hoped to initiate some dialogue between the Negroes and white Southerners; perhaps if they could find some basis for understanding, they might shed the prejudices of generations.

"By working together, by sharing in a common effort," he later wrote, "men of different minds and tempers, even if they do not reach agreement, acquire understanding and thereby tolerance of their differences. . . ." [18]

Unfortunately, however, such instances of meeting between white and Negro were too rare; the problems of race invariably and perhaps inevitably ended up in the courts. And Frankfurter, cognizant of the passions, the ingrained prejudices, that race just as inevitably aroused, urged a cautious approach when the issues of race came before the Supreme Court of the United States.

A number of people, while the various cases concerning racial discrimination were making their way through the courts, cited the dissent in *Plessy v. Ferguson* of the first Justice Harlan as scripture. Harlan had said, "The Constitution is color-blind," and the advocates of desegregation made a litany of it.

Frankfurter doubted their interpretation of Harlan's meaning and, in fact, carried on a lengthy correspondence with Harlan's grandson, his colleague Justice Harlan, about it. He thought that "Harlan I," as he always referred to the first Justice Harlan, had earned a bogus reputation as an opponent of segregation in public schools. Frankfurter believed that on the contrary, faced with the issue of segregation in public schools, Harlan I would have sustained it. In Harlan's 1896 dissent, he had been careful to limit his observations on civil rights to the public highways. Three years later, in 1899, in a case which did concern segregation in public education, he might, perhaps, in view of his *Plessy* dissent, have used the opportunity to speak out against public school segregation. Instead, with the Court, he avoided that issue and decided that the particular case turned on other points of law.[19]

Frankfurter also believed that if the Supreme Court were to support Negroes in their cause for desegregation of the races, the Court should do so with a minimum of inflammatory rhetoric. In a 1948 case concerning a state's right to forbid discrimination on an excursion boat, he had written to Justice Rutledge: "... Before coming down here, when I was counsel for the Association for the Advancement of the [*sic*] Colored People, considerable practical experience with problems of race relations led me to the conclusion that the ugly practices of racial discrimination should be dealt with by eloquence of action, but with austerity of speech."

This applied particularly to the Court. "Time has only deepened that conviction and it has compelling force, I believe, in regard to opinions by this Court within this field," Frankfurter continued. "By all means let us decide with fearless decency, but express our decisions with reserve and austerity. It does not help toward harmonious race relations to stir our colored fellow citizens to resentment by even pertinent rhetoric or by a needless recital of details of mistreatment which are irrelevant to a legal issue before us. Nor do we thereby wean whites, both North and South, from what so often is merely the momentum of the past in them." He added: "Forgive this little sermon." [20]

In 1944 the Supreme Court had abolished all legal sanction for the prevalent white primary of the South. Frankfurter was originally assigned to write the Court's opinion.[21] But Justice Jackson urged reassignment on the basis that in Frankfurter all the qualities that would excite the passions of the South converged: He was a Jew and recently from New England, where the abolition movement originated, and he had not always been sympathetic with the Democratic Party. Frankfurter agreed with this reasoning. Jackson asked Chief

Justice Stone to assign the writing of the sensitive opinion to one of the two Southern Democrats—Justices Black or Reed—from whom the South might be more amenable to accepting what was in effect a reprimand. In the interests of strengthening the opinion and of lowering the decibels of prejudice, Frankfurter agreed to withdraw, and Stone assigned Reed to the opinion.

In 1950 the case of Herman Sweatt came before the Court. Sweatt, a Negro, had been denied admission to the University of Texas Law School on racial grounds. Texas had established a separate law school for Negroes. The equality issue before the Supreme Court was whether that law school for Negroes was as good a school as the one available to whites. When the draft opinion of Chief Justice Vinson, which declared that the Negro school was *not* equal to the school for whites, was circulated among the Justices for approval or suggestions, Frankfurter once more urged restraint. The opinion, he believed, ought to accomplish "the desired result without needlessly stirring the kind of feelings that are felt even by truly liberal and high-minded Southerners. . . . One does not have to say everything that is so. . . . The shorter the opinion, the more there is an appearance of unexcitement and inevitability about it, the better. . . ." [22]

On a companion opinion, concerning a Negro who had been admitted to the Graduate School of the University of Oklahoma but who had been assigned a segregated seat in the classroom, a segregated seat in the library, and a table in a segregated section of the dining room, a colleague had suggested adding to Vinson's draft opinion: "These are handicaps to an effective education." Realizing the Pandora's box a statement like that would open, Frankfurter suggested changing it to "these are handicaps to graduate instruction." [23] (Vinson's final opinion stated that the Negro student was "handicapped in his pursuit of effective graduate instruction.")

In both cases, a unanimous Court decided for the Negroes and against the discriminatory practices. But neither opinion confronted squarely the separate but equal doctrine of *Plessy v. Ferguson.* Both opinions stated that the discriminatory practices involved were based on indisputable inequalities, and so *Plessy v. Ferguson* need not be discussed. "Broader issues have been urged for our consideration, but we adhere to the principle of deciding constitutional questions only in the context of the particular case before the Court," declared Vinson. "We have frequently reiterated that this Court will decide constitutional questions only when necessary to the disposition of the case at hand and that such decisions will be drawn as narrowly as possible."

Nevertheless, in the case of Herman Sweatt, who had been denied admission to the University of Texas Law School, the Court gave some hint of its future direction. Heretofore, equal facilities had meant equality in the tangible, physical factors. In this case the Court began to take a closer look at the intangibles that make up equal education. "... The law school," Vinson declared, "the proving ground for legal learning and practice, cannot be effective in isolation from the individuals and institutions with which the law interacts. Few students and no one who has practiced law would choose to study in an academic vacuum removed from the interplay of ideas and the exchange of views with which the law is concerned." The Negro law school in Texas "excluded from its student body members of the racial groups which number 85% of the population of the State and include most lawyers, witnesses, jurors, judges and other officials with whom petitioner will inevitably be dealing when he becomes a member of the Texas bar. With such a substantial and significant segment of society excluded, we cannot conclude that the education offered petitioner is substantially equal to that which he would receive if admitted to the University of Texas Law School. ..." [24]

Frankfurter was all for "aggressive candor," "eloquent action," "fearless decency." But he was not in favor of impatience of rhetoric. He believed race relations was the "most complicated and baffling of all our social problems," and there was required "more humility and gentleness and forbearance on the part of everyone who has concern for our national well-being." [25]

But in the case of Linda Brown, the validity of separate but equal could not be avoided as it had been in past decisions. The issue had to be met and decided.

The desegregation cases continued in limbo for five months after reargument in December, 1953. On March 30, 1954, Justice Jackson had a heart attack which hospitalized him for seven weeks.

Then, on May 17, with no prior warning the Supreme Court announced its unanimous decision in *Brown v. Board of Education*. On that day Justice Jackson went straight from the hospital to the Court to sit with his colleagues, the first clue that something important was about to happen.

The procedure that day was no different from that of any other Monday. A group of lawyers was admitted to practice before the Court—a traditional Monday ceremony. Justice Clark delivered an opinion concerning an antitrust case. Justice Douglas gave two labor decisions of the Court.

Then at 12:49 P.M., Chief Justice Warren began to read the opinion for the Court in *Brown v. Board of Education.* In a thirty-minute, unemotional recital, the lack of passion in his voice belying the passionate issue at stake, Warren retraced the facts of the cases which were lumped together in this one decision. "In each of the cases, minors of the Negro race," Warren said, "through their legal representatives, seek the aid of the courts in obtaining admission to the public schools of their community on a nonsegregated basis. In each instance, they had been denied admission to schools attended by white children under laws requiring or permitting segregation according to race. This segregation was alleged to deprive the plaintiffs of the equal protection of the laws under the Fourteenth Amendment." They had been denied relief in the lower federal courts on the basis of the separate but equal doctrine of *Plessy v. Ferguson.*

But, said Warren, the "plaintiffs contend that segregated public schools are not 'equal' and cannot be made 'equal,' and that hence they are deprived of the equal protection of the laws. . . ."

The Court had researched exhaustively the circumstances surrounding the adoption of the Fourteenth Amendment, from its consideration in Congress to ratification by the states. The Court had investigated the practices of racial segregation of the time and the views of proponents and opponents of the amendment. The Court found that all the evidence uncovered still shrouded the intent of the amendment in mystery, insofar as public school segregation was concerned.

Warren then traced the course of Supreme Court action over the years where the separate but equal doctrine in the field of public education was involved. In none of them had the separate but equal doctrine been challenged directly.

And so the Court found, Warren said, that it could not "turn back the clock to 1868 when the Amendment was adopted, or even to 1896 when Plessy versus Ferguson was written." He continued that the Justices "must consider public education in the light of its full development and its present place in American life throughout the Nation. . . .

"Today," Warren continued, "education is perhaps the most important function of state and local governments. . . . It is required in the performance of our most basic public responsibilities. . . . [It] is a principal instrument in awakening the child to cultural values, in preparing him for later professional training, and in helping him to adjust normally to his environment. In these days, it is doubtful that any child may reasonably be expected to succeed in life if he is denied the opportunity of an education. Such an opportunity, where the state has undertaken to provide it, is a right which must be made available to all on equal terms."

Then came the crucial question: "Does segregation of children in public schools solely on the basis of race, even though the physical facilities and other 'tangible' factors may be equal, deprive the children of the minority group of equal educational opportunities?" Warren asked.

"We believe that it does," he answered for the Court.

Even the Kansas court which had denied admittance of Negroes to Topeka's white schools, Warren reported, had conceded that segregation had a detrimental effect on colored children, however equal the tangible factors such as school plant and number of teachers were. Segregation generated a feeling of inferiority which retarded a Negro child's learning and so deprived the Negro of benefits he would receive in a racially mixed school.

"We conclude," Warren declared, "that in the field of public education the doctrine of 'separate but equal' has no place. Separate educational facilities are inherently unequal. Therefore, we hold that the plaintiffs and others similarly situated for whom the actions have been brought are, by reason of the segregation complained of, deprived of the equal protection of the laws guaranteed by the Fourteenth Amendment. . . ." [26]

The Court had, with fearless decency, abolished legal sanction for one of the strongest bastions of racial prejudice. With no division within the tribunal on which passions could play but, rather, holding unanimously, it had sternly and finally outlawed segregation in public schools. There was no needless rhetoric in the decision—the fact of the decision itself would stir up enough excitement—but it was a model of austere language and statement of fact—the more eloquent for its austerity.

It further allowed the South a long breathing spell in which to absorb the impact of the decision. The document ended with a statement of the complexity of the problems involved and ordered still another reargument of the cases with respect to how this transformation of the various school systems might be accomplished—questions four and five of the first reargument—early in the next term.

To Chief Justice Warren usually goes the credit for the unanimity of the decision. He marshaled all the talents of the political being he was to achieve it.

Warren is inclined to single out the three Southerners on the Court for plaudits—"not because they developed the legal philosophy for it, but because they had the courage to do what was done. . . . It was tough for them to go home" [27] for a time. After that 1954 decision, Hugo Black did not make an official visit to his home state of Alabama until May, 1968.

There are many who believe Frankfurter was reluctant to join the Court's decision. This is hardly the case. There is no question but that he had fears for the consequences of this decision—whichever way it went. It is true he hoped desegregation would be accomplished without coming to the Supreme Court; he was still a states' responsibilities man. But it was also true that he had no illusions about the passions that begat prejudice, and he knew his was a hopeless dream. If over the previous decade the anachronism of segregation as a way of life was slowly being eroded, it was only because the Supreme Court had forced it. It can be argued that in view of his philosophy of judicial restraint he had had to compromise his principles, that he was interfering in a matter that properly ought to have been fought out in the legislatures. It can also be argued that in the Supreme Court's role as reviewer of legislative action Frankfurter found the South's segregation laws "arbitrary," "wanton," and "spoiliative" [28] —in which case, and only in such case, as he had argued for the District of Columbia minimum wage law in 1923, the Supreme Court could strike them down. He could judge when it was required of him.

But it is doubtful that Frankfurter ever seriously contemplated deciding that segregation in public schools was constitutional, that he could find any legal sanction for it. He could not control what people did privately, and in fact, the state of Virginia evaded the

Court decision by making its public school system a private system. But he could unreservedly strip away legal support for segregated public education.

In such a far-reaching and potentially inflammatory decision, unanimity is of great importance. It is essential that the opposition find no "out." It is also important that the leading spokesman for judicial restraint lend his stature to it. There could be no dissent; it was advisable to have no separate concurrences. Recognizing this, and reluctant to sign an opinion which ordered immediate, wholesale desegregation of the schools, Frankfurter produced a formula that allowed those most worried about the decision, including himself, to join it.

From the first, the aspect of the decision which worried Frankfurter most was how the Court would implement its decision. Nearly five months before the Court handed down its decision, Frankfurter had circulated a memorandum to the Justices concerning the "how" of its decision—that is, how, in order to inflict the least amount of damage, the Court could most effectively transform the statewide school systems in nearly a score of states. Frankfurter doubted that declaring the method of operation of these school systems, frequently deeply rooted, unconstitutional was a wand by which the necessary transformations could be achieved. Even if the school boards and state officials were willing, he was certain there were still enormous considerations to be dealt with in areas of administration, teaching staffs, budgets, physical plants, and, of primary importance, the necessary time to accomplish the far-reaching changes, which would vary in depth with each local situation.

Time, Frankfurter believed, was a major factor. Desegregation could not be accomplished in a day, not even by judicial fiat. The Justices, he warned, must be extremely careful not to effect social deterioration where they sought social betterment. So long as the Court effectively got under way the righting of a constitutional wrong, the Court could consider its duty done. Perhaps, Frankfurter suggested, the Court might consider the language of Mr. Justice Holmes who had written in 1912 for a unanimous Court that West Virginia should repay a certain debt to neighboring Virginia not immediately and not within a certain time limit, but "with all deliberate speed." [29] Frankfurter had used this phrase in at least three opinions he had written; it was to become the keystone for public school desegregation.

The summer of 1954 Frankfurter spent in Charlemont, Massachusetts. But it was hardly an idle summer. He used a good deal of it pondering the problem of implementation of the May 17 decision, which had been postponed by the Court's call for rearguments on implementation.

One of the Court's first chores was to mold appropriate provisions against evasion, in particular, the tried and true American custom of gerrymandering, for which there would doubtlessly be a great temptation. The Court should, he wrote to Chief Justice Warren, in midsummer of 1954, gather as much relevant data in regard to school districting—districting done in a normal fashion without regard for the race issue—to understand legitimate geographical and population factors involved in drawing school district lines. While he hoped the Court would do no more than set general standards, leaving details to be worked out on the local level, Frankfurter felt the Court might benefit from understanding the genuine problems that confront healthy communities. He wanted the Court to understand how these healthy bodies solve their problems so that the Court would not, through ignorance, send the fever of the South higher or attribute normal controversy to inflamed Southern passion.[30]

Pursuant to Frankfurter's suggestion, Warren circulated among the Justices, in the late fall of 1954, a seventy-nine-page Segregation Research Report containing background information to be referred to by the Justices in their thinking about framing the segregation decrees. Section I of the report was a survey of normal practices of school administrators in determining school districts. It was to be used as a frame of reference for assessing the validity of desegregation programs and potential plans. Section II was a state-by-state summary of Southern reaction to the May 17 decision. Section III was a summary of the experiences of school districts which had sought to put into effect desegregation plans prior to the May 17 decision. Section IV considered some of the proposed plans to abolish public schools. Section V discussed the difficulties of court jurisdiction over school districting and pointed out the limited experience of the courts in this area. Section VI was a collection of maps of school districts showing distribution of white and Negro students and the magnitude of the problems which desegregation was to involve.[31]

For four spring days, April 11 to 14, 1955, the Supreme Court heard the question of remedy discussed, debated, argued, and reargued by lawyers for the original plaintiffs, by the attorneys general of states involved in the desegregation decision who had been invited to appear as *amici curiae*—and the office of Attorney General of the United States.

Six weeks later, the Supreme Court handed down its second historic—and again unanimous—decision. The reargument on the question of implementation had been "informative and helpful to the Court in its consideration of the complexities arising from the transition to a system of public education freed of racial discrimination," the opinion, written by Warren, declared.

The Court had decided to return the cases to the local communities and the local federal courts. "Full implementation of these constitutional principles may require solution of varied local school problems," Warren wrote. "School authorities have the primary responsibility for elucidating, assessing, and solving these problems; courts will have to consider whether the action of school authorities constitutes good faith implementation of the governing constitutional principles. Because of their proximity to local conditions and the possible need for further hearings, the courts which originally heard these cases can best perform this judicial appraisal. Accordingly, we believe it appropriate to remand the cases to those courts. . . ."

While the local courts were to give fair weight to local considerations, "the courts will require that the defendants make a prompt and reasonable start toward full compliance with our May 17, 1954 ruling. Once such a start has been made, the courts may find that additional time is necessary to carry out the ruling in an effective manner. The burden rests upon the defendants to establish that such time is necessary in the public interest and is consistent with good faith compliance at the earliest practicable date. . . ." The courts might consider the physical facilities of the schools, the transportation problems of desegregation, personnel, all the factors of districting and redistricting. They might consider any reasonable or legitimate plan proposed for desegregation. But they must act. And they must act, the Court said, incorporating Frankfurter's suggestion of more than a year previous, "with all deliberate speed." [32] The phrase set no time standard; it gave flexibility where it was needed, leeway where local conditions dictated, but it was intended to deny leeway for evasion.

"Looking back at it now," Justice Black said in 1968, "it seems to me that it's delayed the process of outlawing segregation. It seems to me, probably, with all due deference to the opinion and my brethren . . . that it would have been better—maybe—I don't say positively—not to have that sentence. To treat that case as an ordinary lawsuit and force that judgment on the counties it affected that minute. That's true, that it would have only been one school and each case would have been only one case. But that fitted into my ideas of the Court not making policies for the nation." [33]

The early fears of the Justices were quickly realized; they had virtually set off a second Civil War. The protest that arose following the brace of decisions outlawing public school segregation was unprecedented. Crosses were burned on the Justices' lawns. There was also legitimate concern among constitutional lawyers and in the lower judiciary that perhaps this time the Supreme Court had gone too far, that perhaps it had exceeded the speed limit. Warren's decisions were criticized as sociological decisions lacking basis in law.

Southern lawyers attempted to find loopholes by which the decisions could be evaded and at the same time kept out of the Supreme Court. Some Southern school districts sought to evade the decisions by basing segregation on such factors as "scholastic aptitude" or "psychological aptitude" or any such subterfuge aside from race. Others abolished their public schools and went so far as to reimburse students for attendance at private schools. Some developed methods to harass potential litigants who might take segregation cases to court. The passions of the public were stirred as high as the purveyors of hate and prejudice could stir them.

As for Linda Brown of Topeka, Kansas, she never did attend a desegregated elementary school. By the time the Supreme Court's decision to desegregate "with all deliberate speed" came down in 1955, Linda Brown had been graduated from Monroe School. In the fall of 1968 Linda Brown returned to the same school. Now she was Mrs. Charles A. Smith, and she was enrolling her young son in kindergarten there. Monroe School had been desegregated.

Frankfurter never abandoned his hope and faith that the racial passions would in time subside, giving way to a more reasoned approach to the Supreme Court decisions in particular and to the problem of race in general.

The same considerations that had led him to give the dinner in 1939 for Walter White and the group of young Southern lawyers dictated that he break the record of unanimity in civil rights cases that had ensued in the Court following the original desegregation decision and that he write a separate concurring opinion in 1958 in the case of the Little Rock, Arkansas, School Board. He hoped to reach those in the South, particularly those of the younger generation, who realized the inevitability of desegregation and who desired their communities to realize it and accept it. They might never agree to its merits, but they could agree to the supremacy of the law. It was his and the Court's duty to encourage these men. The Court must show that it understood the deep-seated problems, that it was willing to employ all the wisdom and magnanimity at its disposal to help solve them, that it was not simply coldly imposing its will.

Following the 1954 and 1955 desegregation decisions, Little Rock, Arkansas, had embarked on a reasonable plan for desegregating its schools. The Little Rock School Board had initiated an educational effort to obtain public acceptance of its plan. But the governor of the state, Orval Faubus, had his eye on another term as governor. He saw the heated issue of desegregation as the issue which would win it for him. When Little Rock's Central High School, formerly all white, was to begin the city's integration program in the fall of 1957, Faubus called out the Arkansas National Guard and ordered the men to take up positions outside Central High School. Ostensibly the Guardsmen were "to preserve peace and good order"; in fact, they were to keep Negroes from entering the school. The mere presence of the National Guard was enough to precipitate violence which was not quelled until federal troops were sent in.

As a consequence of the turmoil in the Little Rock schools, the district court, in June, 1958, suspended the desegregation plan of the school board and ordered that the Negroes be sent back to segregated schools. The Arkansas Court of Appeals reversed, and the case went to the Supreme Court of the United States.

The Court held, in a unanimous opinion which was signed, for emphasis, individually by each member of the Supreme Court, that the constitutional rights of the Negroes who had been sent to the white Central High School were not to be sacrificed or yielded to the violence and disorder which were initiated by the governor and legislature of the state. The Court adhered rigidly to its decision in *Brown v. Board of Education* as the supreme law of the land and refused to countenance any evasive action from any state executive, legislature, or judiciary.

Frankfurter duly signed the Court's opinion. But he also had views of his own which he wished to put forward, and he intended to write a concurrence. Chief Justice Warren, in the interests of unanimity and the weight which unanimity carried, urged him not to file a separate opinion.[34] Frankfurter insisted. He went with the Court opinion, but one week later, on October 6, 1958, he issued a plea to the young Southern lawyers whom he knew, and to the Harry Ashmores and the Hodding Carters and the Ralph McGills of the South, to persist so that one day civilization might somehow triumph over inhumanity. It was as eloquent a judgment by expectation as he ever wrote.

"While unreservedly participating with my brethren in our joint opinion," Frankfurter began, "I deem it appropriate also to deal individually with the great issue here at stake."

The legitimate program of the Little Rock School Board had been disrupted by the imposition of the state militia and "by other obstructive measures taken by the State.

"The use of force," he admonished, "to further obedience to law is in any event a last resort and one not congenial to the spirit of our Nation. But the tragic aspect of this disruptive tactic was that the power of the State was used not to sustain law but as an instrument for thwarting law." And now the Supreme Court had been asked to allow law to yield to force. "To yield to such a claim would be to enthrone official lawlessness, and lawlessness if not checked is the precursor of anarchy," Frankfurter said. "Violent resistance to law cannot be made a legal reason for its suspension without loosening the fabric of our society. . . ."

One need not agree with Supreme Court decisions, Frankfurter wrote. The Constitution does not require agreement. Dissent, criticism may be duly voiced. But "active obstruction or defiance is barred."

Unquestionably, "deep emotions have . . . been stirred" by the Supreme Court's May 17, 1954, decision. Frankfurter realized only too well it meant drastic changes in the mores of communities. But these emotions would never be calmed by violence, he believed.

In his conclusion, Frankfurter seemed to be summarizing his whole philosophy of government, his concept of man's relationship to man. Responsibility for the calming of these emotions, the adjustment to the decision, rested on the local authorities, the civic leaders, the leaders of the bar. "The responsibility of those who exercise power in a democratic government is not to reflect inflamed public feeling," Frankfurter said, "but to help form its understanding." And this, he continued, "is especially true when they are confronted with a problem like a racially discriminating public school system. . . . Compliance with decisions of this Court, as the constitutional organ of the supreme law of the land, has often, throughout our history, depended on active support by state and local authorities. It presupposes such support."

And when these officials do not live up to their responsibilities, the danger is the defeat of law and order and the end of government. "To withhold it," Frankfurter said, "and indeed to use political power to try to paralyze the Supreme Law, precludes the maintenance of our federal system as we have known and cherished it for one hundred and seventy years."

His last lines appealed to the goodness in man, man's heritage of decency. He showed us what we could be, what we must be. "Lincoln's appeal to 'the better angels of our nature,' " he wrote, "failed to avert a fratricidal war. But the compassionate wisdom of Lincoln's First and Second Inaugurals bequeathed to the Union, cemented with blood, a moral heritage which, when drawn upon in times of stress and strife, is sure to find specific ways and means to surmount difficulties that may appear to be unsurmountable." [35]

A corollary to Frankfurter's axiom that the Supreme Court stay out of the business of lawmaking was that it ought also to avoid the political arena—as rigorous and passionate an admonition as he ever fashioned, articulated in the major reapportionment cases of 1946 and 1962.

Beginning with the rapid and vast industrialism stimulated by the Civil War and post-Civil War period, the nation had undergone a shift in population concentration; farmers had left the land and moved into cities to man and profit from the new burgeoning industries. As a result, since election districts were not proportionately redrawn, the farm-to-factory movement concentrated the taxpaying population in metropolitan areas and, in effect, the political power on the farms.

In 1946 three Illinois voters had asked the Supreme Court to stop a Congressional election in Illinois because of inequities in the makeup of Congressional districts. They also asked the Justices to invalidate an Illinois law of 1901 which had defined these now inequitable districts. A federal district court in Illinois had dismissed the complaint as being outside its jurisdiction.

Frankfurter, writing for the Supreme Court, upheld the district court's decision. The three Illinois voters, he wrote, "ask of this Court what is beyond its competence to grant." In effect, they had appealed to the federal courts to reconstruct the electoral process of Illinois in order "that it may be adequately represented in the councils of the Nation." The Supreme Court was being asked to do for the state what the state legislature had failed to do.

As a practical matter, Frankfurter said, what they asked was impossible.

"Of course," he explained, "no court can affirmatively remap the Illinois districts so as to bring them more in conformity with the standards of fairness for a representative system. At best we could only declare the existing electoral system invalid. The result would be to leave Illinois undistricted and to bring into operation, if the Illinois legislature chose not to act, the choice of members for the House of Representatives on a state-wide ticket. The last stage may be worse than the first. . . . Assuming acquiescence on the part of the authorities of Illinois in the selection of its Representatives by a mode that defies the directions of Congress for selection by districts, the House of Representatives may not acquiesce. In the exercise of its power to judge the qualifications of its own members, the House may reject a delegation of Representatives-at-large. . . ."

However, the operative reason for the Court's refusal to do as the appellants asked was more important: ". . . this controversy," Frankfurter declared, "concerns matters that bring courts into immediate and active relations with party contests. From the determination of such issues this Court has traditionally held aloof. It is hostile to a democratic system to involve the judiciary in the politics of the people. . . ." The Constitution elsewhere provided remedies for disparities.

"Courts," Frankfurter insisted in a phrase which has often been quoted since, "ought not to enter this political thicket."

Remedy for unfair districting lay with state legislatures or with

Congress. If these were reluctant, there was recourse in the ballot box. "The Constitution has left the performance of many duties in our governmental scheme to depend on the fidelity of the executive and legislative action and, ultimately, on the vigilance of the people in exercising their political rights. . . ." [36] Compared to his dissent on the same question in 1962, Frankfurter's words seem restrained.

By 1962 the inequities of election districts had got more out of hand. In California, for example, Los Angeles County with more than 6,000,000 people had one state senator, while three small counties with a combined population of 150,000 were also represented by one state senator. This pattern multiplied itself throughout the nation, with city dwellers generally unequally represented.

In 1959, Charles W. Baker, with other Tennessee voters, filed suit in a federal district court against Tennessee Secretary of State Joe C. Carr, claiming that their right to "equal protection of the laws" had been violated by the malapportionment of the state legislature. Tennessee had not been reapportioned since 1901, and as a result, there were such disparities as Moore County, population 2,340, having the same representation in the state legislature as Decatur County, population 25,316. The Tennessee voters had sought to remedy the malapportionment. But to do so required the support of the state legislature, which benefited from the inequity and was not about to reapportion itself out of a job.

As in 1946, a federal court dismissed the case for want of jurisdiction, and it went to the Supreme Court. It was argued and then reargued.

On March 26, 1962, Justice William J. Brennan, Jr., who had been a student of Frankfurter's at Harvard Law School, spoke for the Court on what has since been judged to be the most far-reaching decision of the Supreme Court in recent years. In a lengthy opinion, Brennan denied that the case was a political one and held that federal courts do in fact have jurisdiction over the claim of the Tennessee voters, that these voters had been denied "equal protection of the laws." The case should not have been dismissed by the district court, he said, and these people were entitled to a trial and a decision.

Frankfurter was nearly eighty years old at the time of the decision, but his dissent displays no diminution of passion, even anger, at what he believed was misapplication of the Court's power.

"The Court today reverses a uniform course of decision by a dozen cases, including one by which the very claim now sustained was unanimously rejected only five years ago," Frankfurter began, referring to his own decision. This uniform course of decision—"a wholly different matter from denial of the franchise to individuals because of race, color, religion or sex"—was a reflection of the nation's political history from the beginning in matters of the relationship between population and legislative representation, and in casting aside this body of history, the Court, Frankfurter charged, was "asserting destructively novel judicial power."

Such an assertion of judicial power, which disregarded "inherent limits" on it, "may well impair the Court's position as the ultimate organ of 'the supreme Law of the Land.'.... The Court's authority —possessed of neither the purse nor the sword—ultimately rests on sustained public confidence in its moral sanction," Frankfurter wrote. "Such feeling must be nourished by the Court's complete detachment, in fact and appearance, from political entanglements and by abstention from injecting itself into the clash of political forces in political settlements."

Frankfurter did not doubt that inequities existed in districting. But he believed responsibility for proper redistricting belonged in the state legislatures rather than in the courts—and the Supreme Court decision in *Baker v. Carr* was placing that responsibility squarely on the federal courts.

There were two major objections, as Frankfurter saw it, to placing that onus on the courts.

The first was impracticability. This decision, he said, would give only "illusory relief" to a "hypothetical claim resting on abstract assumptions" and, in fact, foreshadowed "deeper and more pervasive difficulties in consequence...." Since the "umbrageous" decision gave no guidelines to the lower courts to which it was inevitably inviting litigation from every dissatisfied voter in the nation, Frankfurter warned, it was plunging these lower courts into a quagmire from which it offered no method of extricating themselves.

Frankfurter's second principal objection to the decision lay in his conception of the Court's role of self-imposed restraint. "There is not under our Constitution a judicial remedy for every political mischief," he wrote, as he had written hundreds of times, "for every undesirable exercise of legislative power. The Framers carefully and with deliberate forethought refused so to enthrone the judiciary ... appeal for relief does not belong here. Appeal must be to an informed, civically militant electorate. In a democratic society like ours, relief must come through an aroused popular conscience that sears the conscience of the people's representatives." This decision, he said, indulged "in empty rhetoric," sounded "promise to the ear, sure to be disappointing to the hope."

Throughout its history, the Court has been unwilling to "intervene in matters concerning the structure and organization of the political institutions of the States." When it intervened in cases involving Negro disenfranchisement, it was because "the controlling command of Supreme Law is plain and unequivocal. An end of discrimination against the Negro was the compelling motive of the Civil War Amendments." This, said Frankfurter, was an entirely different matter. But on what he considered basic political questions, "courts are not fit instruments of decision where what is essentially at stake is the composition of those large contests of policy traditionally fought out in non-judicial forums, by which governments and the actions of governments are made and unmade.... Apportionment battles are overwhelmingly party or intra-party contests. It will add a virulent source of friction and tension in federal-state relations to embroil the federal judiciary in them...." [37]

[6]

Baker v. Carr was one of Frankfurter's most passionate dissents; it was also one of his last. He had been in apparent good health for a man of his years since a mild heart attack in 1958 had hospitalized him briefly, then allowed him to return to the Supreme Court with only a slight curtailment in activity. On the morning of April 5, 1962, he spoke at the seventy-fifth anniversary celebration of the Interstate Commerce Commission. That afternoon his secretary found him lying on the floor of his office. She quickly summoned the first-aid attendant at the Supreme Court Building and then the

Justice's doctor. He was given emergency treatment and taken directly to George Washington University Hospital.

His case was diagnosed as a mild stroke; a few days later he suffered a second stroke, which left his speech slightly impaired and difficulty in using his left arm and leg.

He remained in the hospital until July 14, 1962, when he returned to his home in Georgetown. Initially, he had hoped that rest, therapy, and exercise might put him in condition to return to the Supreme Court for the October term, 1962; he worked doggedly to that end, continuing to have the petitions for certiorari sent up from the Court for him to read.

On July 26 he was well enough to get to his feet without assistance to greet President John F. Kennedy who paid a rare Presidential courtesy call on a Supreme Court Justice. It was also apparent that there was no diminution of Frankfurter's mental faculties as he discussed with Kennedy, for three-quarters of an hour over tea and toast in the downstairs drawing room, the complexities of modern Presidential leadership.[1] Frankfurter was greatly honored by the visit. He had sponsored such a visit nearly thirty years previous, when he persuaded Franklin Roosevelt, newly inaugurated and in the midst of the Depression crisis, to pay a similar call on retired Justice Oliver Wendell Holmes, Jr., then ninety-two years old. Nevertheless, he could not help wondering if the Kennedy visit was an inspection, and he was preoccupied during these summer days with the decision he had to make.

By late summer the decision had made itself; it became apparent that Frankfurter would not be able to resume full judicial duties. On August 28, 1962, he sent his resignation to President Kennedy. Since his return from the hospital, Frankfurter said in his letter to Kennedy, even though he had made "substantial improvement," his doctors now advised him that in order to return to the Court by October 1, he would have to undertake "stepped-up therapy" which involved "hazards which might jeopardize the useful years they anticipate still lie ahead of me." He could not, he said, return without taking on his full load of work, nor could he allow the Court to begin the new term uncertain about whether a member would be able to return to do a full share of work.

"I need hardly tell you, Mr. President, of the reluctance with which I leave the institution whose concerns have been the absorbing interest of my life. . . ." [2]

Kennedy accepted the resignation with reluctance and "disappointment." He had followed Frankfurter's recovery "with admiration" and shared the "general hope" that Frankfurter would be able to return to the Court.

"Still," he wrote to Frankfurter, "if you allow it, I will say there is also consolation in your decision. I believe it good for you as well as for the rest of us that you should now be free, in reflective leisure, for activities that are impossible in the demanding life of Justice of the Supreme Court. You have been part of American public life for well over half a century. What you have learned of the meaning of our country is reflected, of course, in many hundreds of opinions, in thousands of your students, and in dozens of books and articles. But you have a great deal still to tell us, and therefore I am glad to know that the doctors are telling you, in effect, not to retire, but only to turn to a new line of work, with new promise of service to the nation.

"Meanwhile," Kennedy concluded, "I should like to offer to Mrs. Frankfurter and to you, for myself and for all Americans, our respectful gratitude for the character, courage, learning and judicial dedication with which you have served your country over the last twenty-three years." [3]

Frankfurter, as he had promised, made the best of his enforced invalidism. He learned to walk short distances with the aid of a leg brace and crutch—an effort he said was fascinating, since the last time he had learned to walk he had been too young to be aware of what a remarkable feat it was. He got up and down the stairs of his Georgetown home with the aid of an electric chair. In October, 1962, however, the Frankfurters moved to a one-floor apartment on Massachusetts Avenue.

Frankfurter paid occasional visits to the Supreme Court. Frequently he attached dark glasses to his well-known pince-nez and went for drives about the city's parks, especially Hains Point, a spit of land dividing a channel from the Potomac River, where he had often walked in times past with Dean Acheson and Lord Halifax. He was not sensitive about his confinement in a wheelchair and attended occasional concerts and plays.

He closely followed events in government and the world at large by being read to—newspapers, books, letters from friends which poured in. He kept up on Supreme Court happenings and gossip through a frequent exchange of letters with his philosophically and personally close friend Justice John Harlan. He dictated a vast quantity of letters to friends, former associates, people in public life, newspapers, former students, and law clerks.

He welcomed visitors enthusiastically. Their stays were supposed to be limited. But a former Harvard Law School colleague later recalled that on a visit to Frankfurter, he had left a taxi waiting outside, assuming he would return in ten minutes. When the allotted time was up, the visitor rose to go, whereupon Frankfurter ordered his nurse to leave instead and kept his visitor engaged in conversation for an hour.

There were still the annual birthday parties with his beloved law clerks. Now they were held in his apartment, instead of his favorite restaurant, and they broke up in early evening instead of early morning. There was still laughter and gaiety and wit, but there was concern for the obvious failing of Frankfurter's energies, and the only thing that retained all its original effervescence was the champagne.

Frankfurter's effervescence had diminished considerably. No doubt he would have liked to grow old with the grace and dignity of Holmes, who had played out his last years holding court in his Washington home as elder statesman. Although Frankfurter's letters continue to display some of the old vigor and power, in person it was apparent that his stroke had been extremely debilitating, and the vast energy that had been almost a trademark had deteriorated. Confinement was unpleasant for a man who had set such a fast pace for himself for so many years. His speech was slowed and could not keep up with his still-rapid mind. Frustration sometimes turned ebullience to irascibility and power to misplaced passion, as his physical capacities further diminished over the years.

Tributes came. On July 4, 1963, President Kennedy named Frankfurter one of thirty-one persons to receive the new Presidential Medal of Freedom, the highest civilian honor a President can bestow in peacetime. The citation, which Frankfurter received in his wheelchair at a White House ceremony in early December, 1963, a few weeks after Kennedy had been assassinated, read: "Jurist, scholar, counselor, conversationalist, he has brought to all his roles a zest and a wisdom which has made him teacher to his time."

In August, 1963, the American Bar Association awarded its gold medal, its highest honor, to Frankfurter for his contribution as teacher, scholar, public servant, lawyer, and judge. This ceremony was held in Chicago, and Frankfurter was unable to attend. A former student, Dean Phil C. Neal of the University of Chicago Law School, accepted it for him.

Shortly after Frankfurter's formal retirement from the Court, Dean Edwin N. Griswold of Harvard Law School wrote to ask if there was a possibility he might return to Cambridge, where he would be installed as a resident scholar, but Frankfurter declined the honor.

On February 21, 1965, Frankfurter suffered a heart attack. He was taken to George Washington University Hospital, where he died the next day. He was eighty-two years old.

A simple and private memorial service was held in the Frankfurters' Massachusetts Avenue apartment. Agnostic although he was, Frankfurter had made arrangements some years before that a former law clerk, Louis Henkin, who was steeped in Jewish culture and religion, should recite the Kaddish at his funeral. Spoken by mourners for one who has died, the Kaddish has become an expression of a link between the generations of the dead and the generation of the living. It was Frankfurter's link with the heritage of his birth.

Paul Freund, professor of law at Harvard Law School and former student of Frankfurter's, read a passage from *The Pilgrim's Progress*—the same passage Frankfurter had read at the funeral in 1941 of Louis Brandeis:

> When he understood it, he called for his friends, and told them of it. Then said he, I am going to my Father's; and though with great difficulty I have got hither, yet now I do not regret me of all the trouble I have been at to arrive where I am. My sword I give to him that shall succeed me in my pilgrimage, and my courage and skill to him that can get it. My marks and scars I carry with me, to be a witness for me that I have fought His battles who will now be my rewarder. When the day that he must go hence was come, many accompanied him to the riverside, into which as he went, he said, "Death, where is thy sting?" And as he went down deeper, he said, "Grave, where is thy victory?" So he passed over, and all the trumpets sounded for him on the other side.

His ashes were taken to a crypt in the chapel of Mount Auburn Cemetery at the end of Brattle Street, Cambridge, where the Frankfurters had lived while he was a professor of law at Harvard.

For all of Frankfurter's apparent diffusion of interests over a half century of public service, nearly all could be narrowed into the law. He had dedicated most of a long lifetime to the law and the teaching of it. Men being what they are, endowed in various proportions with both humanity and inhumanity, Frankfurter believed that only law could keep their inhumanity submerged. Law was the very bulwark of civilization; only under a government of law could justice be sought—a law that was equally applicable to rich, poor, policeman, criminal, Negro, white man, the public, the government.

As a Supreme Court Justice, Frankfurter remained a teacher of law, and it was his purpose to inculcate in his now national student body a respect and devotion to the only instrument society had for defending itself against its own self-destruction. He was a judge who made day-to-day decisions, but more than this, he was a judicial philosopher, a direct judicial descendant of Oliver Wendell Holmes, Jr., and Holmes' link to a future generation.

As magnificent and beautifully woven a fabric as the law was, however, it was a last resort, and beyond Frankfurter's devotion to it is another quality which gives his life more meaning. Alexander Bickel had said: "He was a hero worshipper who transformed all those he worshipped into real heroes. . . ." Bickel wrote it in the context of Frankfurter's friendships. He could have written it in the context of education, legislation, or judging—any segment of Frankfurter's public life, as well as his personal relationships. Frankfurter *was* a hero worshiper. He worshiped mankind in all its heroic proportions, potentials, and aspirations. He acted on the assumptions that men were civilized, that "the better angels of our nature" were our ruling passions.

He knew they were not. He recognized human failing and the inevitability of it. He knew Sacco and Vanzetti were not going to get a new trial. He knew his students at Harvard were not all so diligent and nobly motivated as he constantly told them they were.

To hear Frankfurter speak of Harvard Law School, one would think it a veritable Valhalla of legal gods, from which all human error had been exorcised. Actually, he knew its failings as well as he knew its virtues; he did not fail to express his concern when the school he loved displayed less than godlike attributes. In 1957 a friend told Frankfurter he had been disturbed by Harvard's attitude of conformity as a consequence of the McCarthy era. Frankfurter quickly got up a memorandum, based on these comments and similar ones made by a Harvard professor, and dispatched it to faculty members whom he knew well and recent graduates whose judgment he respected. Was this true? he wanted to know, and he made it plain this was not the Harvard he remembered.

Frankfurter knew business in the 1930's was not going to discipline itself, and so laws had to be passed to impose discipline. And these laws in which Frankfurter had been involved still left some room for self-discipline, although they did not always work, as Frankfurter knew they would not.

Frankfurter knew the Minersville School Board was not voluntarily going to erase its ruling that compelled every public school student to salute the American flag; he knew that the governor of a Southern state was not going to commute the sentence of a Negro murderer and that Willie Francis was headed inevitably to the electric chair. But imposing his own will on either the school board or the State of Louisiana was not the answer for society. Only from self-achievement, he believed, came the self-respect and self-confidence vital to democracy.

Frankfurter was acutely aware that we all are made up of self-interest, greed, fears, irresponsibility, prejudice, and that "the better angels of our nature" counted for less in most of us than they should. He was often disappointed and deeply hurt when those who should have stood up against injustice did not.

But he was neither disillusioned nor disenchanted. He did not retreat into cynicism, which tempts the disappointed idealist. He never abandoned faith in the heroic stature of men and their ability to achieve it.

Instead, as Bickel said, Frankfurter "encouraged, beseeched, charmed, wheedled, needled" us. He showed us what we could do, what we could be, then cannily drove us until one day we must be. Archibald MacLeish once said of Frankfurter: ". . . no man ever left him smaller than he came. . . ."

It was, of course, civilization by expectation.

A Note on Sources

UNPUBLISHED

Interviews

The following persons were interviewed for this book: Dean G. Acheson, Sir Isaiah Berlin, Alexander M. Bickel, Francis Biddle, Mrs. Hattie Citroen, Jerome A. Cohen, Miss Helen Denman, Goldthwaite H. Dorr, Justice William O. Douglas, Herbert B. Ehrmann, Morris L. Ernst, Judge Charles Fahy, Adrian S. Fisher, Oliver Gates, Sylvester G. Gates, Justice John M. Harlan, Louis Henkin, Donald Hiss, Malcolm A. Hoffmann, Mrs. Venetia Kershaw, John Lord O'Brian, Ferdinand Pecora, E. Barrett Prettyman, Jr., George Roberts, Justice Stanley F. Reed, Albert Rosenthal, Frank E. A. Sander, Chief Justice Earl Warren, Harry Wellington, Henry A. Wise.

Letters

In response to requests for information, the author received letters from R. W. Baker, Aage Bohr, Robert F. Bradford, Earle W. Carr, Richard Gardiner Casey, Mrs. Jerome Frank, Archibald R. Graustein, Lieutenant General Leslie R. Groves, Albert L. Hoskins, Francis X. Hurley, Alfred M. Landon, Raymond Moley, Theodora G. O'Hare, C. F. Palmer, Bishop William Scarlett.

Papers

The principal sources of Frankfurter material were the collection of Felix Frankfurter's papers at the Library of Congress, Washington, D.C.; the Felix Frankfurter-Henry L. Stimson correspondence in the papers of Henry L. Stimson at the Sterling Memorial Library, Yale University, New Haven, Connecticut; the Felix Frankfurter-Franklin D. Roosevelt correspondence and other collections at the Franklin D. Roosevelt Library, Hyde Park, New York. Other papers consulted were those of Newton D. Baker, Harold Hitz Burton, Lloyd C. Griscom, Charles Evans Hughes, Cordell Hull, National Association for the Advancement of Colored People, National Consumers' League, George Norris, J. Robert Oppenheimer, Robert P. Patterson, Gifford Pinchot, Donald Richberg, Theodore Roosevelt, Elihu Root, William Allen White, all at the Library of Congress; the diaries of Colonel E. M. House, the diaries of Henry L. Stimson, and the E. M. House-Felix Frankfurter correspondence at the Sterling Memorial Library; the records of the War Labor Policies Board at the National Archives, Washington, D.C.; the papers of Charles Fahy at the Library of Congress and the Franklin D. Roosevelt Library.

Oral History Projects

The following oral history projects were consulted at Columbia University, New York City: Sir Norman Angell, Roger Nash Baldwin, Henry Breckinridge, C. C. Burlingham, Marquis Childs, Charles Fahy, Jerome Frank, Max Freedman,

Lloyd C. Griscom, Gardner Jackson, Arthur Krock, James M. Landis, Henry L. Stimson, Leonard Wallstein, J. Waties Waring.

Libraries

Libraries—other than those named above—which have been of great assistance are: American Jewish Archives, Cincinnati, Ohio; archives division of the City College of the City University of New York, New York City; Princeton University Library, Princeton, New Jersey; Sam Rayburn Library, Bonham, Texas; Smith College Archives, Northampton, Massachusetts; Zionist Archives, New York City.

Manuscripts

The following unpublished works were consulted: Mary W. Dewson's "An Aid to the End," Vols. 1 and 2, at the Franklin D. Roosevelt Library; Charles Evans Hughes' "Autobiographical Notes" at the Library of Congress; William Scarlett's "A Parson's Tale" from Bishop Scarlett's personal files.

PUBLISHED

ACHESON, DEAN G., *Morning and Noon*. Boston, Houghton Mifflin Co., 1965.

BAKER, LEONARD, *Back to Back*. New York, The Macmillan Co., 1967.

BEAVER, DANIEL R., *Newton D. Baker and the American War Effort 1917–1919*. Lincoln, University of Nebraska Press, 1966.

BIDDLE, FRANCIS, *In Brief Authority*. Garden City, New York, Doubleday and Co., 1962.

——, *Justice Holmes, Natural Law, and the Supreme Court*. New York, The Macmillan Co., 1961.

BLACK, HUGO L., *One Man's Stand for Freedom,* Irving Dilliard, ed. New York, Alfred A. Knopf, 1963.

BLAUSTEIN, ALBERT P., and FERGUSON, CLARENCE CLYDE, JR., *Desegregation and the Law*. New Brunswick, New Jersey, Rutgers University Press, 1957.

BLUM, JOHN MORTON, *Years of Urgency, 1938–1941,* Vol. 2, *From the Morgenthau Diaries*. Boston, Houghton Mifflin Co., 1965.

——, *Years of War, 1941–1945,* Vol. 3, *From the Morgenthau Diaries*. Boston, Houghton Mifflin Co., 1967.

Boston *Globe,* various issues as cited.

Boston *Herald,* various issues as cited.

Boston *Transcript,* various issues as cited.

BOWEN, CATHERINE DRINKER, *Yankee from Olympus*. Boston, Little, Brown and Co., 1945.

BURNS, JAMES MACGREGOR, *Roosevelt: The Lion and the Fox*. New York, Harcourt, Brace and Co., 1956.

CASEY, RICHARD GARDINER, *Personal Experiences 1939–1946*. New York, David McKay Co., Inc., 1962.

CRAMER, C. H., *Newton D. Baker*. Cleveland, World Publishing Co., 1961.

DOROUGH, C. DWIGHT, *Mr. Sam*. New York, Random House, Inc., 1962.

FRANKFURTER, FELIX, "Crime in the United States." *The Round Table* (March, 1930).

FRANKFURTER, FELIX, *Law and Politics,* E. F. Prichard, Jr., and Archibald MacLeish, eds. New York, Capricorn Books, 1962.

———, *Of Law and Life and Other Things That Matter,* Philip B. Kurland, ed. Cambridge, Belknap Press of Harvard University Press, 1965.

———, *Of Law and Men,* Philip Elman, ed. Hamden, Connecticut, Archon Books, 1956.

———, *Mr. Justice Holmes and the Supreme Court.* New York, Atheneum, 1965.

———, *The Case of Sacco and Vanzetti.* New York, Grosset and Dunlap (from a Little, Brown and Co. edition), 1962.

———, "The Federal Securities Act." *Fortune* (August, 1933).

———, "The Law and the Law Schools." *American Bar Association Journal* (October, 1915).

———, "The Palestine Situation Restated." *Foreign Affairs* (April, 1931).

———, *The Public and Its Government.* New Haven, Yale University Press, 1930.

———, "The Supreme Court Molding the Constitution." *Current History* (May, 1930).

"Felix Frankfurter: Talks in Tribute." *Occasional Pamphlet Number 8.* Cambridge, Harvard Law School, 1965. A record of a meeting at Harvard Law School in honor of Felix Frankfurter following his death in 1965.

FREEDMAN, MAX, *Roosevelt and Frankfurter, Their Correspondence 1928–1945.* Boston, Little, Brown and Co., 1967.

GERHART, EUGENE C., *America's Advocate: Robert H. Jackson.* Indianapolis-New York, Bobbs-Merrill Co., Inc., 1958.

GOLDMARK, JOSEPHINE, *Impatient Crusader: Florence Kelley's Life Story.* Urbana, Illinois, University of Illinois Press, 1953.

GLUECK, SHELDON and ELEANOR, *One Thousand Juvenile Delinquents.* Introduction by Felix Frankfurter. Cambridge, Harvard University Press, 1934.

GOWING, MARGARET, *Britain and Atomic Energy 1939–1945.* London, St. Martin's Press, 1964.

GRISCOM, LLOYD C., *Diplomatically Speaking.* Boston, Little, Brown and Co., 1940.

HALPERIN, SAMUEL, *The Political World of American Zionism.* Detroit, Wayne State University Press, 1961.

HAPGOOD, HUTCHINS, *The Spirit of the Ghetto.* New York, Schocken Books, 1966.

Harvard Law Review, various issues as cited.

Harvard Law School Alumni Bulletin, various issues as cited.

HOLMES, OLIVER WENDELL, JR., *The Common Law.* Boston, Little, Brown and Co., 1881.

The Holmes-Einstein Letters: The Correspondence of Mr. Justice Holmes and Lewis Einstein 1903–1935, James Bishop Peabody, ed. London, Macmillan and Co., Ltd.; New York, St. Martin's Press, 1964.

Holmes-Laski Letters: The Correspondence of Mr. Justice Holmes and Harold J. Laski 1916–1935, Mark DeWolfe Howe, ed. Vols. 1 and 2. Cambridge, Harvard University Press, 1953.

Holmes-Pollock Letters: The Correspondence of Mr. Justice Holmes and Sir Frederick Pollock, 1874–1932, Mark DeWolfe Howe, ed. Cambridge, Belknap Press of Harvard University Press, 1961.

HUGHES, CHARLES EVANS, *The Supreme Court of the United States.* New York, Columbia University Press, 1928.

ICKES, HAROLD L., *The Secret Diary of Harold L. Ickes: The First Thousand Days 1933–1936.* New York, Simon and Schuster, 1953.

ICKES, HAROLD L., *The Secret Diary of Harold L. Ickes: The Inside Struggle 1936–1939*. New York, Simon and Schuster, 1954.

JACKSON, ROBERT H., *The Struggle for Judicial Supremacy*. New York, Alfred A. Knopf, 1941.

KANIN, GARSON, "Trips to Felix." *The Atlantic* (March, 1964).

KATCHER, LEO, *Earl Warren: A Political Biography*. New York, McGraw-Hill Book Co., 1967.

KONEFSKY, SAMUEL J., *The Legacy of Holmes and Brandeis*. New York, The Macmillan Co., 1957.

LILIENTHAL, DAVID E., *The Journals of David E. Lilienthal: The TVA Years 1939–1945*. New York, Harper and Row, Publishers, 1964.

———, *The Journals of David E. Lilienthal: The Atomic Energy Years 1945–1950*. New York, Harper and Row, Publishers, 1964.

———, *The Journals of David E. Lilienthal: The Venturesome Years 1950–1955*. New York, Harper and Row, Publishers, 1964.

LOVE, ALBERT, and CHILDRES, JAMES SAXON, *Listen to Leaders in Law*. Introduction by Felix Frankfurter. Atlanta, Tupper and Love, 1963.

MARTIN, KINGSLEY, *Harold Laski*. New York, The Viking Press, 1953.

MASON, ALPHEUS THOMAS, *Brandeis: A Free Man's Life*. New York, The Viking Press, 1946.

———, *Harlan Fiske Stone: Pillar of the Law*. New York, The Viking Press, 1956.

———, *The Supreme Court from Taft to Warren*. Baton Rouge, Louisiana State University Press, 1958.

MAYER, MARTIN, *Emory Buckner*. New York, Harper and Row, 1968.

MENDELSON, WALLACE, *Felix Frankfurter: A Tribute*. New York, Reynal and Co., 1964.

———, *Felix Frankfurter: The Judge*. New York, Reynal and Co., 1964.

———, *Justices Black and Frankfurter: Conflict in the Court*. Chicago, University of Chicago Press, 1961.

MOLEY, RAYMOND, *The First New Deal*. New York, Harcourt, Brace and World, Inc., 1966.

MOORE, RUTH, *Niels Bohr*. New York, Alfred A. Knopf, 1966.

MORISON, ELTING E., *Turmoil and Tradition: A Study of the Life and Times of Henry L. Stimson*. Boston, Houghton Mifflin Co., 1960.

PHILLIPS, HARLAN B., *Felix Frankfurter Reminisces*. Garden City, New York, Doubleday and Co., Inc., Anchor Books, 1962.

PLIMPTON, FRANCIS T. P., *Reunion Runes*. Verses read at the 25th reunion of the Harvard Law School Class of 1925 on April 29, 1950. Privately printed.

POST, LOUIS F., *Deportations Delirium of 1920*. Chicago, Charles H. Kerr and Co. Co-operative, 1923.

ROSENFIELD, LEONORA COHEN, *Portrait of a Philosopher: Morris R. Cohen in Life and Letters*. New York, Harcourt, Brace and World, Inc., 1962.

SACHAR, HOWARD M., *The Course of Modern Jewish History*. Cleveland-New York, World Publishing Co., 1958.

SALOMAN, LEON I., *The Supreme Court*. New York, H. W. Wilson Co., 1961.

SCHLESINGER, ARTHUR M., *In Retrospect: The History of a Historian*. New York, Harcourt, Brace and World, Inc., 1963.

SCHLESINGER, ARTHUR M., JR., *The Coming of the New Deal*. Boston, Houghton Mifflin Co., 1959.

———, *The Crisis of the Old Order*. Boston, Houghton Mifflin Co., 1957.

———, *The Politics of Upheaval*. Boston, Houghton Mifflin Co., 1960.

SCHLESINGER, ARTHUR M., JR., "The Supreme Court: 1947." *Fortune* (January, 1947).

SCHWARTZ, BERNARD, *The Supreme Court.* New York, Ronald Press Co., 1957.

SHERWOOD, ROBERT E., *Roosevelt and Hopkins: An Intimate History.* New York, Harper and Brothers, 1948.

STEIN, LEONARD, *Balfour Declaration.* New York, Simon and Schuster, 1961.

STIMSON, HENRY L., and BUNDY, MCGEORGE, *On Active Service in Peace and War.* New York, Harper and Brothers, 1947–1948.

SUTHERLAND, ARTHUR E., *The Law at Harvard.* Cambridge, Belknap Press of Harvard University Press, 1967.

THOMAS, HELEN S., *Felix Frankfurter.* Baltimore, Johns Hopkins Press, 1960.

TODD, A. L., *Justice on Trial.* New York, McGraw-Hill Book Co., 1964.

TULLY, GRACE, *F.D.R.: My Boss.* New York, Charles Scribner's Sons, 1949.

United States Reports, various issues as cited.

WEAVER, JOHN D., *Warren: The Man, the Court, the Era.* Boston, Little, Brown and Co., 1967.

ZUCKER, NORMAN L., *George W. Norris.* Urbana, University of Illinois Press, 1966.

Notes

ABBREVIATIONS

COHP	Columbia Oral History Project
FFR	Phillips, Harlan B., *Felix Frankfurter Reminisces.*
FDRL	Franklin D. Roosevelt Library, Hyde Park, New York.
H-L Letters	*Holmes-Laski Letters: The Correspondence of Mr. Justice Holmes and Harold J. Laski 1916–1935,* Mark DeWolfe Howe, ed.
HLR	*Harvard Law Review.*
LP	Frankfurter, Felix, *Law and Politics,* E. F. Prichard, Jr., and Archibald MacLeish, eds.
LC	Library of Congress, Washington, D.C.
NA	National Archives, Washington, D.C.
NR	*New Republic.*
NYT	New York *Times.*
PMC	President's Mediation Commission.
STML	Sterling Memorial Library, Yale University, New Haven, Connecticut.
TCSV	Frankfurter, Felix, *The Case of Sacco and Vanzetti.*
WLPB	War Labor Policies Board.

Works listed in the bibliography are referred to by surname and key words of the title.

I. BEGINNINGS

Section 1

1. "Scared stiff": Frankfurter, in Love and Childres, *Listen,* p. 10.
2. "A kind of healthy . . .": *FFR,* p. 52.
3. "Float with the tide": *ibid.*
4. "Felix was born . . .": Boston *Globe,* January 8, 1939.
5. "Inner compulsion": Frankfurter, *Of Law and Life,* p. 70.
6. "I do take law . . .": *Time* (September 7, 1962), p. 15.
7. "And what are . . . the way": Elizabeth Glendower Evans, Springfield (Massachusetts) *Union* and *Republican,* undated clipping.
8. "The next generation . . .": Todd, *Justice on Trial,* p. 68.
9. "Believing unbeliever," "reverent agnostic": *FFR,* p. 338.
10. "Your God and . . .": Frankfurter to William Scarlett, January 11, 1965; files of William Scarlett.
11. "Some day . . .": author's interview with Mrs. Hattie Citroen, January 2, 1969.
12. "My ancestors go . . .": author's interview with Helen Denman, June 5, 1968.
13. "Frail health . . .": Matthew Josephson, "Jurist," *New Yorker* (December 7, 1940).
14. "A strong tendency . . .": Frankfurter to Stimson, March, 1916, undated; Stimson papers, STML.
15. " 'How old . . .' ": Hapgood, *The Spirit,* p. 7.

16. "I think Felix . . .": Goldthwaite H. Dorr to author, December 17, 1968.
17. "More important . . .": Morison, *Turmoil,* pp. 111–12.
18. "A remarkable bookworm . . .": author's interview with Henry A. Wise, October 10, 1967.
19. "It seems vitally important . . .": Stimson to Theodore Roosevelt, September 2, 1910; Theodore Roosevelt papers, LC.
20. "My only regret . . .": Stimson to Theodore Roosevelt, November 9, 1910; Theodore Roosevelt papers, LC.
21. "There never was . . .": Frankfurter to Stimson, November 9, 1910; Stimson papers, STML.
22. "Alliance for evil . . .": Theodore Roosevelt to William Allen White, November 11, 1910; Theodore Roosevelt papers, LC.
23. "The priceless privilege . . .": Frankfurter to Stimson, December 8, 1910; Stimson papers, STML.
24. "You take . . . proper place": confidential source.
25. "The right kind . . .": Frankfurter to Stimson, September 9, 1911; Stimson papers, STML.

Section 2

1. "Junior partner": *FFR,* p. 76.
2. "One of the prime . . .": Frankfurter to Philip Miller, October 31, 1911; Frankfurter papers, LC.
3. "No dominating impulse . . .": Frankfurter to Emory Buckner, March 4, 1912; Frankfurter papers, LC.
4. "Neither party has . . .": "Either party will . . .": Frankfurter memorandum, October 26, 1916; Stimson papers, STML.
5. "Politically homeless"; "tenant . . .": Frankfurter to Stimson, November 2, 1916; Stimson papers, STML.
6. "Genuinely stirred . . ."; "it's the business . . .": Frankfurter to Philip L. Miller, June 20, 1912; Frankfurter papers, LC.
7. "The call for active . . .": Frankfurter to Stimson, September 10, 1912; Stimson papers, STML.
8. "Reform should . . .": Stimson to T. Roosevelt, September 2, 1910; Roosevelt papers, LC.
9. "Thrill"; "alluring to . . ."; "the real work . . .": Stimson to Frankfurter, October 19, 1912; Stimson papers, STML.
10. "Freely expressed . . .": Frankfurter to Francis W. Bird, August 15, 1912; Frankfurter papers, LC.
11. "To his office . . .": Frankfurter to Emory Buckner, March 26, 1913; Frankfurter papers, LC.
12. "I am afraid . . .": Frankfurter to Emory Buckner, March 11, 1913; Frankfurter papers, LC.
13. "Every time Mac . . .": Henry Breckinridge, COHP, pp. 94–95.
14. "Felix is getting on . . .": Winfred Dennison to Emma Frankfurter, October 28, 1912; Frankfurter papers, LC.
15. "I love every brick . . .": Frankfurter, *Mr. Justice Holmes,* p. 2.
16. "He did not prefer . . .": Biddle, *Justice Holmes,* p. 7.
17. "Gave the most powerful . . .": Frankfurter, *Mr. Justice Holmes,* p. 12.
18. "The life of the law . . .": Holmes, *The Common Law,* p. 1.
19. "Felix erupted . . .": Schlesinger, *In Retrospect,* p. 83.

20. "But of course it was...": Frankfurter to Schlesinger, March 20, 1931; Frankfurter papers, LC.
21. "A very vivid...": author's interview with Francis Biddle, February 13, 1968.
22. "I have suspected...": Holmes to Laski, May 8, 1918; *H-L Letters,* Vol. 1, p. 153.
23. The account of Frankfurter's meeting with Marion Denman is drawn largely from author's interview with Miss Denman's sister, Helen Denman.
24. "Luina": Holmes to Laski, January 15, 1920; *ibid.,* Vol. 1, p. 234.

Section 3

1. "Dear Ned...": Winfred Dennison to E. H. Warren, June 12, 1913; Frankfurter papers, LC.
2. "To a man": Warren to Dennison, June 16, 1913; Frankfurter papers, LC.
3. "Academic life...": Holmes to Frankfurter, July, 1913; *cf.* Alexander M. Bickel, "Applied Politics and the Science of Law: Writings of the Harvard Period," in Mendelson, *Felix Frankfurter: A Tribute,* p. 165.
4. "The transition...": Stimson to Frankfurter, May 21, 1914; Stimson papers, STML.
5. "You are right...": Frankfurter to Stimson, July 8, 1914; Stimson papers, STML.
6. "It's full...": Frankfurter to Emory Buckner, undated letter of 1914; Frankfurter papers, LC.
7. "I'm not *enough*...": Frankfurter to Sofy Buckner, undated letter of 1914; Frankfurter papers, LC.
8. "Precedents, not...": Frankfurter to Morris R. Cohen, March 9, 1912; Frankfurter papers, LC.
9. "You learn no law...": Plimpton, *Reunion Runes,* p. 13.
10. "Slowly—innocents...": Ernest J. Brown, *HLR,* Vol. 78, p. 1524. (Copyright © by The Harvard Law Review Association.)
11. "Civilization at once...": Frankfurter to Manley O. Hudson, April 4, 1924; Frankfurter papers, LC.
12. "It is not enough...": Frankfurter, "The Law and the Law Schools," p. 539.
13. "Talk about 'courses'...": Frankfurter to Arthur T. Vanderbilt, October 27, 1941; Frankfurter papers, LC.
14. "Make as much money...": author's interview with Adrian S. Fisher, August 31, 1967.
15. Marion Denman... "to marry Marion": author's interview with Helen Denman, June 5, 1968.
16. "The statute necessarily..."; "We think...": Lochner v. New York, 198 U.S. 45 (1905).
17. "From the whole...": Goldmark, *Impatient Crusader,* p. 157.
18. "Woman's physical...": Muller v. Oregon, 208 U.S. 412 (1908).
19. "It was regular...": Frankfurter to Brown, January 27, 1917; Frankfurter papers, LC.
20. "You are talking..."; "You cannot dissociate..."; *ibid.*
21. "Ten hours"; "Your honor..."; "Good for you": *FFR,* p. 128.
22. "There is no doubt...": Frankfurter to Brown, January 27, 1917; Frankfurter papers, LC.

Section 4

1. "Washington is occupied . . .": Enoch Crowder to Frankfurter, February 24, 1917; Frankfurter papers, LC.
2. "It was remarkable . . .": author's interview with John Lord O'Brian, September 21, 1967.
3. "By law . . .": War Department, *A Report of the Activities of the War Department in the Field of Industrial Relations During the War* (Government Printing Office, 1919), p. 8.
4. "Be sent out . . ."; "can be counted on . . ."; "one of the leading . . ."; "The foregoing views . . .": memorandum, Frankfurter to N. D. Baker, September 4, 1917; Baker papers, LC.
5. "I am on this trip . . .": Frankfurter to Katherine Ludington, October 4, 1917; Frankfurter papers, LC.
6. "The breaking . . .": Scarlett, "A Parson's Tale," p. 70.
7. "With utmost . . .": telegram, Frankfurter to S. J. Rosensohn, October 16, 1917; WLPB papers, NA.
8. "Is the fundamental . . .": PMC *Proceedings,* Clifton, Arizona, October 25–29, 1917, p. 197.
9. "Mac": Scarlett, "A Parson's Tale," p. 71.
10. "We're ready . . .": Max Lowenthal, "Felix Long Ago," in Mendelson, *Felix Frankfurter: A Tribute,* p. 131.
11. Spent most of his life . . . : W. Barton Leach, "Felix," *Harvard Law School Bulletin* (March, 1968), p. 10.
12. An Arizona clergyman . . . : Scarlett, "A Parson's Tale," pp. 68–69.
13. "Wholly illegal . . .": PMC *Report,* November 6, 1917.
14. "No machinery . . ."; "establishing such . . .": *ibid.*
15. "It did not put . . ."; "stirring up a . . .": Frankfurter to Francis Hackett, January 6, 1921; Frankfurter papers, LC.
16. "There is one final . . ."; "Mr. Frankfurter . . ."; "Very well . . .": *Hearings on the Nomination of Felix Frankfurter* before a subcommittee of the Senate Judiciary Committee, January 11, 12, 1939 (Government Printing Office, 1939).
17. "An impregnating . . .": PMC *Report,* January 16, 1918.
18. "A solid basis . . ."; "the feeling . . ."; "if unchecked . . .": *ibid.*
19. "I never, directly . . .": *NYT,* July 27, 1918.
20. "Sit in judgment . . .": *NR,* October 19, 1921.
21. "Although, with . . . What makes the Mooney . . ."; "so long will . . .": *ibid.*
22. "You are engaged . . ."; "misleading"; "no human being . . .": T. Roosevelt to Frankfurter, December 19, 1917; Frankfurter papers, LC.
23. "I pursued . . ."; "I should like . . .": Frankfurter to T. Roosevelt, January 7, 1918; Frankfurter papers, LC.
24. "Only by a proper . . ."; "too many labor . . ."; "turn radical . . ."; "all practices which tend . . .": PMC *Report,* January 9, 1918.
25. "Not only is the country . . .": *ibid.*
26. With this influx . . . "to marry Felix": author's interview with Helen Denman, June 5, 1968.
27. "The creation . . .": Frankfurter to N. D. Baker, January 4, 1918; Baker papers, LC.
28. "Focus dramatic . . .": *ibid.*

29. "You know the general...": Frankfurter to Herbert Croly, May 9, 1918; Frankfurter papers, LC.
30. "Competition has been shown...": Schlesinger, *The Crisis,* p. 337.
31. "Our first step..."; "but the prime...": *NYT,* May 26, 1918, Section VII.
32. "Spending a good...": Frankfurter to William Scarlett, September 28, 1918; Scarlett's personal files.
33. "Formulation and...": Frankfurter to Elbert Gary, July 9, 1918; WLPB papers, NA.
34. "We have experienced...": Gary to Frankfurter, July 19, 1918; WLPB papers, NA.
35. "The best industrial standard...": Frankfurter to V. A. Olander, September 9, 1918; WLPB papers, NA.
36. "Humanitarian sentiment...": Frankfurter speech to National Boot and Shoe Manufacturers Association, January 14, 1919.
37. "What American business...": Frankfurter speech to Conference on Demobilization, November 29, 1918.
38. "Between the millstones...": Frankfurter to Brandeis, May 25, 1919; De Haas collection, Zionist Archives.
39. "Frankfurter came...": E. M. House, "Diaries," entry for April 29, 1919; STML.
40. "The task is to keep...": Frankfurter to Woodrow Wilson, May 14, 1919; Frankfurter papers, LC.

PART II: HARVARD LAW SCHOOL

Section 1

1. "Opportunity of..."; "being very active...": Frankfurter to Herbert Croly, undated; Frankfurter papers, LC.
2. "A small...": Paul A. Freund, in "Felix Frankfurter: Talks in Tribute," p. 10.
3. "Of course I want...": Frankfurter to Stimson, November 4, 1919; Stimson papers, STML.
4. "Two cooing doves...": Laski to Holmes, January 14, 1920; *H-L Letters,* Vol. 1, p. 233.
5. "I have learned...": Frankfurter to McGeorge Bundy, January 27, 1948; Frankfurter papers, LC.
6. "I think she...": Herman Adler to Frankfurter, October 17, 1921; Frankfurter papers, LC.
7. "Why don't you...": *NYT,* March 19, 1947.
8. "But there was really...": Elliot Richardson, "A Personal Appreciation," *Harvard Law School Bulletin* (March, 1965), p. 4.
9. "Everybody suspected...": Pound to Frankfurter, April 28, 1919; Frankfurter papers, LC.
10. "Some leader with..."; "in the present ferment": Frankfurter to Stimson, March 22, 1931; Stimson papers, STML.
11. "Sensible policy...": Frankfurter to Stimson, January 17, 1920; Stimson papers, STML.
12. "A vigorous and...": Exhibit 10, *Report upon the Illegal Practices of the United States Department of Justice* (Washington, National Popular Government League, 1920).

13. "Absolutely necessary": Frank Burke to George E. Kelleher, December 17, 1919; Frankfurter papers, LC.
14. "Efforts to enforce...": W. B. Wilson to Frankfurter, April 17, 1920; Frankfurter papers, LC.
15. "Whether the Attorney...": Frankfurter to Baltimore *Sun*, March 2, 1921.
16. "If there is one thing...": Colyer v. Skeffington, 265 Federal 17 (1920).
17. "It is plainly..."; "even if..."; "Marxian socialism...": *ibid.*
18. "It has always...": *Report upon the Illegal Practices of the United States Department of Justice* (Washington, National Popular Government League, 1920).
19. "Several"; "I have difficulty...": statement, A. M. Palmer before Rules Committee of House of Representatives; *cf.* Boston *Transcript*, June 2, 1920.
20. "Is so good...": Holmes to Laski, November 23, 1927; *H-L Letters*, Vol. 2, p. 999.
21. "Some weeks ago...": Stimson to Frankfurter, March 17, 1921; Stimson papers, STML.
22. "There were specific...": Frankfurter to Stimson, March 22, 1921; Stimson papers, STML.
23. "I hardly need..."; "painstakingly..."; "I know that for..."; "Of course I can secure...": Frankfurter to Stimson, March 22, 1921; Stimson papers, STML.

Section 2

1. "I am told...": Frankfurter to Lowell, June 19, 1922; Frankfurter papers, LC.
2. "I do not pretend...": Lowell to Frankfurter, June 20, 1922; Frankfurter papers, LC.
3. "I had not the slightest..."; "What gives...": Frankfurter to Lowell, June 21, 1922; Frankfurter papers, LC.
4. Respected Lowell's... conscience: Frankfurter to Joseph R. Hamlen, January 23, 1943; Frankfurter papers, LC.
5. "He was one...": Albert H. Hoskins to author, August 9, 1968.
6. "When there you will...": W. Barton Leach, "Felix," *Harvard Law School Bulletin* (March, 1968), p. 9.
7. "There were no neutrals...": *ibid.*, p. 10.
8. "Frankfurter's always giving...": Laski to Holmes, December 16, 1916; *H-L Letters*, Vol. 1, pp. 43–44.
9. "For a teacher...": Frankfurter to Charles E. Wyzanski, June 24, 1930; Frankfurter papers, LC.
10. "Observation, generally...": Frankfurter memorandum, March 28, 1932; Frankfurter papers, LC.
11. "Yes. They go higher": author's interview with Helen Denman, June 5, 1968.
12. "Given another twenty...": Alexander M. Bickel, "Justice Frankfurter at Seventy-Five"; *NR* (November 18, 1957).
13. "Arthur Krock...": *FFR*, p. 20.
14. "Thrashing..."; "far into...": Sir Norman Angell, COHP, pp. 132–33.
15. "Perhaps the great...": Frankfurter to Walter F. Dodd, August 16, 1929; Frankfurter papers, LC.
16. "The first three and a half...": author's interview with Adrian S. Fisher, August 31, 1967.

17. "There is nothing...": Frankfurter to Hugo L. Black, November 13, 1943; Frankfurter papers, LC.
18. "Whenever I went...": Austin Scott, "Felix Frankfurter: Talks in Tribute," p. 6.
19. "The instruments of justice...": Frankfurter to H. F. Stone, May 21, 1924; Frankfurter papers, LC.
20. "Trace the effect...": Sutherland, *The Law at Harvard,* p. 272.
21. "Not as an agency..."; "the undertaking...": Frankfurter, "Introduction," in Gluecks, *One Thousand Juvenile Delinquents,* p. xii.
22. "We must understand...": *ibid.,* p. ix.
23. "The problems of crime..."; "there is no body...": Frankfurter, *The Public,* pp. 155–56.
24. "Charged with..."; "these conditions..."; "unfair...": Adkins v. Children's Hospital, 261 U.S. 525 (1923).
25. "Requirement of...": *ibid.*
26. "An arbitrary..."; "We have been furnished..."; "I confess...": *ibid.*
27. "The C.J....": Holmes to Laski, April 14, 1924; *H-L Letters,* Vol. 1, p. 495.
28. "Among the blackest...": Frankfurter to William Draper Lewis, July 11, 1923; Frankfurter papers, LC.
29. "Of course, child labor...": Frankfurter, *LP,* p. 209.
30. "The immediate results...": Frankfurter to Walter Lippmann, July 18, 1924; Frankfurter papers, LC.

Section 3

1. Thayer... anarchists: author's interview with Herbert B. Ehrmann, June 3, 1968.
2. "Systematically..."; "outside the courtroom...": Frankfurter, *TCSV,* p. 46.
3. "The standards of...": *ibid.,* p. 90.
4. "No error"; "as a matter of law": *ibid.,* p. 89.
5. "To do the donkey work": interview with Sylvester G. Gates, July 10, 1968.
6. "Involved in the...": Frankfurter to Paul L. Sayre, March 5, 1948; Frankfurter papers, LC.
7. "The case against...": Frankfurter, *TCSV,* p. 68.
8. "Systematic exploitation...": *ibid.,* p. 59.
9. "Distorted perspective": *ibid.,* p. 65.
10. "Slightly more..."; "at least as well...": *ibid.,* p. 10.
11. "Certainly in modern...": *ibid.,* p. 104.
12. Privately he... innocent: Holmes to Laski, December 13, 1928; *H-L Letters,* Vol. 2, p. 1118.
13. "I know what a...": J. H. Beale to Frankfurter, June 27, 1927; Frankfurter papers, LC.
14. "This school does not...": Frankfurter to Stoughton Bell, April 9, 1927; Frankfurter papers, LC.
15. "With complete..."; "with equal...": Frankfurter to Thomas Nelson Perkins, April 28, 1927; Frankfurter papers, LC.
16. "There is also...": Holmes to Pollock, April 5, 1919; *Holmes-Pollock Letters,* Vol. 2, p. 8.
17. "Lionized"; "He had a terrific...": author's interview with Herbert B. Ehrmann, June 3, 1968.

18. "As to the 'present . . .' ": Frankfurter to Eustace Seligman, June 9, 1927; Frankfurter papers, LC.
19. "I don't count . . .": Frankfurter to Eustace Seligman, May 14, 1927; Frankfurter papers, LC.
20. "You now know . . .": Frankfurter to Arthur M. Schlesinger, March 20, 1931; Frankfurter papers, LC.
21. Dean John . . . "facts really are": Frankfurter memorandum, undated; Frankfurter papers, LC.
22. "An agitation . . .": Wigmore, Boston *Transcript,* April 25, 1927.
23. "We must sit . . .": interview with Sylvester G. Gates, July 10, 1968.
24. "I did not go to Dedham . . .": Marion Frankfurter to Vanzetti, undated letter; Frankfurter papers, LC.
25. "So as not to lend . . .": Herbert B. Ehrmann, "Felix," in Mendelson, *Felix Frankfurter: A Tribute,* p. 108.
26. "No matter how dark . . ."; "You are acting . . .": Frankfurter to Ehrmann, July 14, 1927; Frankfurter papers, LC.
27. "Incapable of seeing . . .": *FFR,* p. 239.
28. "So far as I . . .": Frankfurter to William G. Thompson, August 15, 1927; Frankfurter papers, LC.
29. "About midnight . . .": Matthew Josephson, "Jurist," *New Yorker* (December 7, 1940).
30. "I am saddened . . .": Frankfurter to Hans Zinzzer, December 17, 1927; Frankfurter papers, LC.
31. "I sent for you . . .": author's interview with Herbert B. Ehrmann, June 3, 1968.
32. "Psychological forces . . .": Frankfurter to Ferris Greenslet, January 2, 1946; Frankfurter papers, LC.
33. "That is not the law . . ."; "Begging your honor's . . ."; What Thayer . . .": author's interview with Herbert B. Ehrmann, June 3, 1968.

Section 4

1. "It does not work . . .": Frankfurter, *LP,* p. 220.
2. "For the moment . . .": *ibid.,* p. 221.
3. "I do not think . . .": *NYT,* April 30, 1926.
4. "I hope you are not . . .": C. A. Norton to Frankfurter, June 13, 1932; Frankfurter papers, LC.
5. "I venture to . . .": Holmes to Ely, January 15, 1932; *cf.* Boston *Globe,* June 23, 1932.
6. "Professor Felix . . .": Springfield *Republican,* January 21, 1932.
7. Believed Frankfurter would not accept: Robert F. Bradford to author, September 11, 1968.
8. "You ought not . . .": Frankfurter to Thompson, June 19, 1931; Frankfurter papers, LC.
9. "Tongue-tied": Frankfurter to Ely, June 22, 1932; Frankfurter papers, LC.
10. "It isn't really . . .": Thurman Arnold to Frankfurter, July 8, 1932; Frankfurter papers, LC.
11. "With Ely pardoning . . ."; "cut off . . .": *NYT,* June 23, 1932.
12. "It is my opinion . . .": Boston *Globe,* July 6, 1932.
13. "What must not be . . .": Boston *Transcript,* June 23, 1932.
14. "A menace . . .": letter to Boston *Transcript,* June 28, 1932.